The Good Women of the Parish

THE MIDDLE AGES SERIES

Ruth Mazo Karras, Series Editor
Edward Peters, Founding Editor

A complete list of books in the series is available from the publisher.

The Good Women
of the Parish

Gender and Religion After the Black Death

Katherine L. French

PENN

University of Pennsylvania Press
Philadelphia

Published by
University of Pennsylvania Press
Philadelphia, Pennsylvania 19104-4112

Printed in the United States of America on acid-free paper

10   9   8   7   6   5   4   3   2   1

A Cataloging-in-Publication Record is available from the Library of Congress
ISBN-13: 978-0-8122-4053-5
ISBN-10: 0-8122-4053-7

To Kate, Katelyn, Brennen, Michelle, and Sydney
With Love

Contents

Figures

Maps

Tables

Men talk in church, but they talk as if it is a market, about things like what they have seen in other countries . . . whereas women talking in church talk about other things to each other—one about her maidservant, how good the girl is at sleeping and bad at doing work, or about her husband, who is causing trouble, another about her baby not putting on weight. . . . You women, you go more readily to church than men do; speak your prayers more readily than men; go to sermons more readily then men.

—*Berthold of Regensburg*

Introduction

It is a truism, although maybe not true, that women are more religious than men. In modern South Korea, women make up three-quarters of the members of Christian Evangelical churches. Women are similarly drawn in larger numbers than men to Latin American Pentecostal churches.[1] In European churches, men stay away in droves, while old women listen to the liturgy, light the candles, and sweep out the dirt. Even in medieval society where church attendance was mandatory, preachers such as Thomas Bruton and Berthold of Regensburg complained that more women than men attended their sermons.[2] Although medievalists lack the measurement tools available to scholars of modern society, they have noted that medieval women practiced very different styles of piety then men.

For scholars looking at modern societies, one question of interest is what attracts women to religion, especially religions noted for their emphasis on women's subordination to men. Many argue that women's interest in so-called conservative or traditionalist religions grows out of attempts to negotiate the tensions and challenges of modern society, such as poverty, dissolving family relations, and changing gender roles. Religious involvement provides women with strategies and values to confront these problems. Through their religious participation, women could reassert the value of the traditional family and their own skills in maintaining it, while at the same time employing a powerful vocabulary with which to negotiate their own marriages and family standing.[3] For many women, religion provides a belief system and institutional structure that they can use to argue for the value of their contributions to the family. Even subordination to a husband could be qualified as a wife learns his physical needs and weaknesses and the influence she has in ameliorating them. She could also employ religious justifications to demand particular treatment and consideration.[4]

The insights of modern scholars of religion have much to offer medievalists who are also interested in why women were drawn to a religion and a religious institution that repeatedly accused them of a proclivity for sin and routinely denounced their connection to Eve. This book looks at what role Christianity played in medieval English laywomen's lives, and how women made their religious activities meaningful in the nearly two hundred years between the plague of 1348 and the Reformation, which started in 1534. This was a difficult time, with a tremendous amount of social and economic upheaval and I argue that women used Christianity and their religious participation to cope with the chaotic changes that followed the plague and to justify their own changing behavior. Through active participation in their parish church, women could promote their own interests and responsibilities, giving them social and religious significance. Although much current scholarship seeks to downplay the plague's impact, it is an obvious break point and accelerated and intensified social changes already present in the early fourteenth century. Certainly many contemporaries saw it as a bellwether.[5]

Scholarship on medieval women's religious experiences has focused predominantly on elite women, nuns, and mystics who were either literate enough to leave written records of their religious ideas and behavior or had access to literate men who did this for them.[6] These women were especially interested in affective piety, piety that focused on Christ's humanness—his birth, suffering, and death. In the human life cycle, these moments usually took place within the house and fell within the sphere of women's activities. This piety allowed women to draw on their own skills, knowledge, and family roles, and gave them value and influence.[7] Private confessors encouraged elite women to embrace the intense devotional practices of affective piety. Most women, however, were not literate, were not noble or nuns, and did not have private confessors. Most women practiced their religion in a parish church, where many scholars have assumed gendered religious practices did not exist or cannot be identified.[8]

The parish was the basic unit of public worship, and a source of moral instruction and correction. As a religious unit, the parish taught Christian behavior and integrated individuals into a Christian community by marking the passages of life with rituals and sacraments. The parish offered some employment to members with appropriate skills as church buildings needed maintenance and repair. It also served as a forum for self-promotion and social identity, making gender and social status critical for understanding lay involvement in the parish. Moreover, in our period, the parish came to permit women some leadership roles, which gave them new visibility and influence. As we will see in the course of this book, such opportunities did not go unnoticed or unchallenged. The clergy routinely complained that lust, ambition, and vanity, not piety, devotion, or spirituality motivated women's church attendance. As proof, the clergy offered up examples of women who gossiped with neighbors, flaunted new clothing, and flirted with men while in church, instead of attending to their prayers or the liturgy. These accusations were by no means new to the late Middle Ages, but I argue they take on new significance when considered in light of the fifteenth century's social and economic conditions. I suggest that we can reinterpret women's behavior in church as manifestations of their piety, although perhaps not a form of piety acknowledged or appreciated by the clergy.

Parish worship was collective and social. Although women did gossip, flirt, and preen while in church, they also socialized, commiserated, and prayed. All these actions, which might look quite similar to an observer, advanced women's own interests. While many women were no doubt impatient or dismissive of their local priest and church, many more still used it as a forum for acting on their social and familial concerns. As wives and daughters, women were not to diminish family and household reputations and no doubt hopes for family well-being were the stuff of prayers. Actions that promoted and protected one's family, especially if performed in a church setting, merged easily with piety. In this way, low-status women's religious practices were every bit as gendered as their better-documented elite counterparts.

The organization and activities of the late medieval parish have largely drawn the attention of scholars of the Reformation, interested in understanding the Reformation's causes and effects.[9] This has made the late medieval parish a creature of the Reformation, often creating a sense of timelessness about late medieval parish life that underplays any notion of change or the ability to respond to change. This book argues, however, that the late medieval parish culture was, in part, a product of the post-plague period, and the late medieval parish was an important institution for negotiating the social changes of that world. Parish life came to reflect parishioners' reactions to the possibilities of social mobility and economic growth, and their moral and spiritual anxieties during this period of upheaval.[10] Women were not only participants in these responses, but in many cases they were instigators of anxiety.

In the post-plague period, most commentators understood rapid economic and social change as a decline in morality.[11] Chroniclers and other observers recounted stories of men and women who demanded excessive wages and then used their newfound wealth to ape their betters and challenge those in authority, as examples of moral decline. Chroniclers accused women of giving into their lustful and vain natures, becoming willful and ungovernable. Parliament passed statutes that attempted to restore social order by regulating wages, clothing, and food consumption. Local courts increasingly prosecuted gossiping, eaves-dropping, sexual misbehavior, and disorderly ale houses, all in an attempt to clean up local society.[12] Communities and families worried about unsupervised women and purchased and recited didactic literature that emphasized modesty, passivity, and silence as the hallmarks of virtuous female behavior.[13]

The ideologies and practices that tried to keep women and lower-status people subordinate were not confined to the elites—the nobility, gentry, or royalty. Defining society in hierarchical terms aided patriarchs big and small.[14] Fathers, husbands, mistresses of households, wives, and social climbers of all stripes found meaning in a social ideology that defined their social position above someone else's. We cannot, therefore, look at late medieval society in terms of men versus women, townspeople versus rural inhabitants, or peasants versus elites. These groups intertwined, intermixed, and imitated each other, drawing meaning and identity from their place in the social hierarchy. To be sure, while the mistress of the household had authority over her servants, she did not have any more legal rights than her female servants, and in fact if her husband was alive, and her servant unmarried, she had fewer legal rights than her maid. Unless she had her husband's permission, a married woman could not control her property or enter into legal contracts. Unmarried women had no such limitations, although they were hardly equal to men in the eyes of the law or society. Married women may have had more respectability than their unmarried counterparts, but they still rarely held public office, nor did they serve on juries, as men did. Although women gained some new opportunities in the fourteenth century as a consequence of the demographic and economic situation, social commentators equated these new opportunities with sexual promiscuity. They understood it as a challenge to the patriarchal basis of family and society. As a result, society exerted a great deal of energy trying to make sure women's increased mobility did not lead to an elevation of status. Women in this period did not gain equality with men or raise their status vis-à-vis men.

Yet women were not merely passive victims or without resources when confronted by attempts to reinforce their secondary status. Religious practice was an important source of self-expression, creativity, and agency for women of every social status. The Church promoted submission, modesty, and motherhood as traditional Christian values for women, behaviors many felt women were abandoning in the fifteenth century. Yet the Church also provided religious significance to women's everyday lives and tasks. The parish, the local manifestation of the universal Church, offered women opportunities for leadership, visibility, and even on occasion authority, all in the name of religious devotion and in seeming contradiction to the goals of submission and silence. This paradox was one manifestation of the social dynamism of post-plague England. Some women seized these opportunities while ignoring the devotional underpinnings, others found these opportunities meaningful expressions of piety and a way of garnering status and acceptance in their villages or neighborhoods. However, women's parish involvement often reinforced the social tensions of the era, making women's religious behavior a subject of debate among contemporaries.

Women's involvement in their parishes grew throughout the fifteenth century, and communities tried to redirect this involvement toward traditional behavior. In order to understand the role that women played in the late medieval English parish and what it meant to women and to late medieval society, we must, therefore, understand something of this social world.

Post-Plague England

The fourteenth and fifteenth centuries were a time of demographic stagnation, economic recession, and political violence. Plague, which first arrived in Britain in 1348, revisited every decade or so shortening life expectancy. Labor shortages, due to high mortality, led to an increase in wages. Heretics espousing Lollardy moved throughout the kingdom, challenging Church authority and doctrine and even preaching political rebellion. The dynastic war between the Lancastrians and the Yorkists finally ended in 1485 with the accession of Henry VII. These changes affected women differently than men. The new demographic regime may have left more women than men, caused women to marry later if at all, and pushed more women into the job market than in previous eras. Under these conditions, it is not surprising that medieval people were anxious about women's position and activities.

Scholars estimate that England's population in 1300 was between five and six and a half million.[15] Such density made land expensive, labor cheap, and servile status among the peasantry common. Faced with limited opportunities at home, many peasants left their villages in search of work in England's rapidly expanding towns and cities. In the first quarter of the fourteenth century, the number of towns in England doubled.[16] Urban growth notwithstanding, there was not enough land to feed the population in times of crisis. Between 1310 and 1314, several poor harvests raised food prices, and between 1315 and 1324, England and much of northern Europe suffered through the Great Famine. There was a 50 percent drop in food production and prices increased 400 percent or more.[17] In some areas, death rates were three times their prefamine levels.[18] Scholars debate the Famine's long-term impact on the population. Although it did not affect the nobility and gentry as seriously as the peasantry, scholars now believe that the Great Famine began a population decline that the plague would accelerate.

Shortly before midsummer (24 June) of 1348, two ships carrying sailors from Gascony arrived in Melcombe, Dorset, on England's south coast. According to one chronicler, the sailors were infected with "an unheard of epidemic illness called pestilence. They infected the men of Melcombe, who were the first to be infected in England."[19] As an island, Britain had multiple points of entry.[20] In early August, infected ships arrived in Bristol, on the western coast, spreading plague to that major port city as well. By November plague had reached London, Britain's most populous city. And so England suffered a massive epidemic that moved throughout the kingdom for the next year or so.

The plague left tremendous upheaval in its wake. There were not enough priests to perform last rites and not enough laborers to work the fields. In some places the laity heard deathbed confessions, and in others, women performed men's agricultural work.[21] The *Eulogium*, a monastic chronicle from Wiltshire, complained that

By the time the plague ceased at the divine command, it had caused such a shortage of servants that men could not be found to work the land, and women and children had to be used to drive plows and carts, which was unheard of.[22]

A second epidemic in 1361, although not as devastating as the first, particularly affected men and children and contributed, so the chroniclers claimed, to further deterioration of the social order and increased immorality. Chroniclers particularly blamed women for the ensuing social problems. In the continuation of Ralph Higden's *Polychronicon*, the chronicler described how

In 1361, there was a great human mortality, particularly of men. Their widows as if degenerate and not restrained by any shame, took as their husbands foreigners and other imbeciles or madmen. For it is a failing of some women, forgetful of their own honor, to couple with their inferiors turning away from the more eminent and lowering themselves to baser men.[23]

John of Reading's chronicle elaborated further on women's scandalous behavior.

For this year the mortality was particularly of males, who were devoured in great numbers by the pestilence. However, the greatest cause of grief was provided by the behaviour of women. Widows forgetting the love they had borne towards their first husbands, rushed into the arms of foreigners or, in many cases of kinsmen, and shamelessly gave birth to bastards conceived in adultery.[24]

The plague revisited England about every decade thereafter.[25] Subsequent outbreaks were not as severe and were often localized, but they still killed thousands of people.[26] Other diseases, such as dysentery, tuberculosis, and malaria in the coastal regions, along with periodic famines also ravaged the population[27]

Chroniclers make the horror of the plague vivid to modern readers, but they are not helpful in assessing actual mortality rates. Local studies demonstrate the plague's tremendous impact on England. Westminster Abbey lost more than half of its monks.[28] Resident parish priests in the diocese of Coventry and Litchfield suffered a mortality rate of 46 percent, while residents of rural Essex suffered a mortality of 45 percent.[29] The port town of Grimsby, Lincolnshire, lost 30 percent of its pre-plague population by the spring or summer of 1349.[30] By 1377, when the first poll tax created documents that allow historians to estimate the total population, there was between two and three quarters and three million people, a loss of about a half of the population since 1300.[31]

England's population failed to rebound once the plague subsided.[32] Instead, the population stagnated for nearly two centuries, only beginning to recover by the 1520s. Why is a matter of some speculation. Mortality was certainly one of the causes. Life expectancy declined as a result of disease and famine.[33] There is also evidence that the mortality rate was not the same between the sexes or among age groups. Chroniclers of the second plague noted that it killed more men and children than women. Outbreaks in the 1370s and 80s seem to have particularly affected children.[34] If indeed plague mortality varied by sex and age, families would have grown smaller in the first few generations after the plague. As women who survived aged, they would not have been able to replace their deceased children. Fewer men would have also meant that fewer women married or remarried. Growing numbers of single women filled villages, towns, and cities.

Most demographers now argue that the primary factor in England's stagnating population was a low fertility rate brought on by late age of marriage for women.[35] If women marry late, they have fewer pregnancies and produce fewer children. According to Jeremy Goldberg, who analyzed the late fourteenth-century witness depositions for the city of York and the county of Yorkshire, men and women married in their mid to late twenties, perhaps a decade later than before the plague. As economic conditions changed again in the fifteenth century, the age of marriage increased again, but only somewhat.[36] Further evidence of reduced fertility in the post-plague population appears in the sex ratios Goldberg found for several towns. In his analysis of the 1377 poll tax returns, he calculated that one-third of women over fourteen were single, and many would never marry.[37]

The imbalanced sex ratios identified by Goldberg not only indicate reduced fertility among women, but also accelerated migration of women into towns in search of work. This trend, which probably started as towns grew in the twelfth century, became more pronounced after the plague. Goldberg argued that the demand for labor drew women into the workforce. "Women constituted a 'reserve army' of laborers and were drawn into a variety of occupations as men began to occupy niches higher up the work hierarchy."[38] By the end of the fourteenth century, the independent female worker was probably common in both the countryside and in towns. Scholars debate whether women moved to cities in search of work because they found it difficult to marry or they delayed marriage because the plague introduced new work opportunities that they saw as more beneficial than early marriage.[39] As the economy contracted after 1420, women were again cut out of the labor force in order to protect men's employment opportunities.[40]

Regardless of why women moved to towns, high mortality and stagnant population increased their wages.[41] Chroniclers and religious writers of the period complained bitterly that workers in general had become greedy and lazy. They wallowed in leisure, demanded high wages, and refused to work for yearlong contracts as they had in the pre-plague period. The Rochester chronicle reported that in 1350, "no workman or labourer was prepared to take orders from anyone, whether equal, inferior, or superior, but all those who served did so with ill will and a malicious spirit."[42] Wages would stay high until the end of the fifteenth century. Higher salaries gave workers heretofore unimaginable buying power. In contrast, landlords' income declined as the price of grain and rents dropped due to decreased demand. Rural land values continued to decline and by the 1470s some areas saw agricultural rents down by a third.[43] Some villages, most famously Wharram Percy (Yorks.), were abandoned as the surviving inhabitants searched out opportunities elsewhere. Many who continued to work the land turned to sheep farming and other less intensive forms of agriculture, which sent yet more workers away in search of work.

One of the most debated issues of the post-plague period was the impact of these demographic and economic changes on women's status. Often referred to as the "golden-age of women debate," Jeremy Goldberg and Caroline Barron argued that more economic opportunities for women increased their status, because they had more autonomy and choice, hence the post-plague period was a "golden age for women."[44] Judith Bennett has countered that women may have had more economic opportunities, but the plague did not abolish the patriarchy. Because laws still disadvantaged women and theorists continued to emphasize women's moral and intellectual inferiority, increased economic opportunities and later age of marriage did not raise women's status relative to men's.[45] Instead, women's increased economic opportunities seem to have inspired repeated assertions of women's secondary status.

Some historians have understood the consequences of dramatic population decline as a crisis of lordship.[46] Elites and patriarchs, whether large aristocratic landholders, town burgess, or peasant fathers in charge of a family that included a wife and daughters, found their authority challenged in different ways. Women were more mobile and the lower estates enjoyed an increased standard of living while their lords' incomes declined. Assessing the rise in the standard of living for survivors of the plague remains inexact, but overall, agricultural workers came to enjoy a more diverse diet that was higher in protein, while higher wages allowed them to spend more time in leisure, socializing at ale-houses, and to buy more goods, including better-quality clothing in the style of their betters.[47] The old distinctions between the free and unfree peasantry disappeared and new social divisions of yeoman, husbandmen, and smallholder emerged among the free peasantry. Among free peasants, social and economic boundaries were fluid. Even among the unfree, most commuted their labor dues to contractual tenures. Social climbing meant not only dressing and eating the part, but also arranging good marriages and proving one's worthiness. Office holding in manorial courts, parishes, and artisanal and merchant guilds provided men with administrative experience and served as a means for men to prove their reputations.[48]

Chroniclers and moralists repeatedly accused laborers of working less, wallowing in luxury, and engaging in behavior unacceptable for people of low status.[49] For some, their behavior constituted a crisis in immorality. In his poem *Mirour de l'omme* written sometime before 1378, John Gower wrote,

The labourers of olden times were not accustomed to eat wheat bread; their bread was made of beans and of other corn, and their drink was water. Then cheese and milk were as a feast to them; rarely had they any other feast than this. Their clothing was plain grey. Then was the world of such folk well-ordered in its estate.[50]

These changes in social behavior drew upon the visible markers of status and gender: food, clothing, and physical mobility. Although medieval people might not have understood how the "invisible hand of the market" worked, they could see on a daily basis the breaching of social boundaries, the undermining of old assumptions about social hierarchies, and the challenge to authority these behaviors represented. Some chroniclers singled out women's behavior for particular condemnation. An anonymous fourteenth-century poet summed up the moral challenges confronting England when he lamented that

plague is killing men and beasts. Why? Because vices rule unchallenged here. . . . the sloth of shepherds leaves the flocks straying . . . rulers are moved by favour not wisdom . . . [soldiers of Christ] dressed in rough garments, but few do so these days; instead they wear soft fabrics. They were distinguished by moral excellence, but the youth of today are learned only in squalid rites . . . women are no longer bound by the restraints of their sex.[51]

Although allowing for emotional hyperbole, this poet's complaints hit on the social problems that moral regulation, parliamentary legislation, and legal prosecution would try to rectify in the fourteenth and fifteenth centuries. Chroniclers and social commentators would continue to complain about worker laziness, corrupt rulers, and ungovernable women for the next two centuries and beyond. Whether women really were ignoring "the restraints of their sex," or not, many in society believed they were and judged their behavior accordingly.

There were repeated attempts on both the local and national levels to shore up these weakened social boundaries. Some attempts were in direct response to the plague, while others preceded the epidemic but became more insistent in its aftermath. Most attempts cast these efforts in moral, not economic, terms arguing that a weakened social hierarchy was the result of the erosion of morals. One of the most immediate attempts at such regulation was a royal ordinance of laborers, issued 18 July 1349, and recapitulated in a parliamentary statute, the Statute of Laborers, in 1351. The statute insisted that laborers accept pre-plague level wages, adhere to yearlong contracts, not perform day labor, nor move about seeking better positions while under contract. These measures did not reduce wages in any meaningful way and Parliament would continue to pass labor legislation for the rest of the Middle Ages to little effect.[52]

The royal government also tried to enforce its vision of the social hierarchy with sumptuary legislation that regulated the dress and diet of the population. The importation of new clothing styles and the ability of the lower orders to afford elite styles of clothing and food troubled many. Sumptuary statutes in 1363 and 1436 understood social climbing, as manifested by dressing and eating above one's station, as a threat to society. The legislation tried to restore society by legislating lifestyles for each estate. Only certain ranks of people would be entitled to wear luxury clothing and eat luxury food.

As with the Statute of Laborers, sumptuary legislation applied to women, although men were the drivers of changing fashions in the Middle Ages.[53] In specifying women's apparel, the statute connected women's status to the status of their husbands or fathers; it did not recognize women independent of men. For example, the statute of 1363 declared that the wives of yeoman and artisans, "shall wear no veil of silk, but only of yarn made in the realm, and shall wear no fur of budge (fine black lamb fleece from north Africa), but only lamb, rabbit, cat and fox."[54] Moreover, the wives and children of esquires who have land or rents valued at more than £200 a year "may wear fur facings of miniver (white winter fur from the stomach of the Baltic squirrel), but not ermine or lettice (fur of the snow-weasel); and may not wear any jeweled item of clothing other than a headdress."[55] Sumptuary legislation for women worked on the assumption that women were overly interested in nice clothes. When the clergy reiterated these accusations in the late fourteenth and early fifteenth centuries, they coordinated with governmental attempts to regulate clothing and minimize social advancement.

Society's concern with women's behavior was not new and indeed it is difficult to connect attempts to control women's behavior and movements directly to the plague. Goldberg has argued, however, that demographic tensions reinforced patriarchal attitudes, manifested in the "oppositional images" of women as either chaste and submissive wives or promiscuous whores or domineering shrews.[56] Such images appear repeatedly in the literature, plays, and sermons that were so popular in the late Middle Ages. An attendant development was the increased expectation that women belonged at home.[57]

A more subtle form of controlling women and reinforcing their secondary status vis-à-vis men was the increased regulation of women's speech in the late Middle Ages. In the late Middle Ages, the value of women's speech declined as evidenced by the rise in accusations of scolding.[58] Scolding, aggressive, loud, and opinionated speech first appeared as a crime in the early fourteenth century and became widely prosecuted in all jurisdictions by the second half of the century. Sandy Bardsley found that in a sample of manor, city, and ecclesiastical courts, from between 1353 and 1530, women made up between 65 and 93 percent of scolding prosecutions.[59] There was also a commensurate decline in women's ability to raise the hue and cry successfully. When villagers saw a crime committed they were duty bound to raise an alarm. Manorial courts, however, increasingly determined women's hues to be false in the late fourteenth century, another sign of the devaluing of their voices and opinions. Devaluing women's speech enforced their secondary status, potentially linking their economic independence with difficult behavior and promoting the idea that women did not belong in public.

Legal attempts to keep peasants at home on the farm eating brown bread, the urban bourgeoisie in homespun instead of furs and silk, and women from speaking their mind all reflect great unease with late medieval social changes and a feeling that the social order was under siege. Whether or not women or peasants were really enjoying greater status, their betters perceived that they were, and this perception threatened social stability and influenced the judgment of those in authority. The continuous repetition of these laws and continual prosecutions, however, also indicate their ineffectiveness. Social hierarchies in the fifteenth century were changing. Men took advantage of higher wages and used their newfound wealth to dress their wives in better clothing, hire female servants to work in their houses, and marry their daughters to men whose estates matched their own aspirations. For social climbers, the post-plague economy offered opportunities. Attempts to limit those opportunities met with resistance on both a large and small scale. Women were implicated in this mobility, which not only challenged status rules, but gender norms. Concerns with women's speech, movement, and sexuality were all bound together in a belief that all made women promiscuous. These concerns were by no means new in the post-plague period. However, they took on new significance in the context of this heightened anxiety surrounding late medieval social organization. Although women did enjoy some increased mobility and economic opportunities, there was a backlash of sorts that worked to prevent these changes from becoming new gender rolls or increased status for women.

Conclusion

Throughout the book, I have tried to juxtapose the experiences of real women as revealed in a variety of sources such as churchwardens' accounts, wills, visitations reports, ecclesiastical court records, and tax records with prescriptive literature such as sermons, didactic literature, saints' lives, and parish wall paintings and stained-glass windows. In so doing, I have been able to see how real women behaved and how didactic works interpreted this behavior. The repetition of negative stereotypes and the introduction of submissive and passive role models reveal a strong unease with women's mobility and public behavior.

Churchwardens' accounts are the sources most central to this book. Churchwarden's accounts were the financial records that the laity kept as they raised and spent money to maintain the nave of their parish church. Canon law made the laity responsible for maintaining and furnishing the nave, while the clergy took care of the chancel.[60] Churchwardens' accounts are highly idiosyncratic documents, varying considerably in style, quality, and detail.[61] They first began appearing in the fourteenth century, and there are about 250 sets dating from before the Reformation.[62] In order to understand the range of women's parish involvement, I have looked at nearly half of those churchwardens' accounts that survive, but have relied on the most detailed sets for the bulk of my study. The geographical survival of churchwardens' accounts means that my analysis is weighted toward market-town parishes and parishes in the West Country and East Anglia; there are few sets from the northern parts of England. This sort of survey means that regional variation in women's behavior is less visible than the impact of urban or rural differences. The often vague and inconsistent nature of churchwardens' accounts also means that many activities are missing or are only sporadically recorded and are, therefore, difficult to track over a long period.[63] While it is possible to see a broad chronology of the development of women's parish involvement, this chronology is not as nuanced as we might like. I have tried to compensate for these gaps by using other sources, but the poorest and most alienated women are still difficult to find. Taken together, however, these sources provide a great deal of evidence for women's collective and group activities and provide evidence for women's abilities to transform these activities into a coherent and meaningful vocabulary of piety.

Much of my analysis of women's parish involvement comes from detailed prosopographical analysis of several parishes. These parishes are not construed as typical in any way; I am unconvinced that we can fruitfully identify any place as typical. Rather, the parishes I have analyzed have fulsome records beyond churchwardens' accounts that allow for more detailed analysis. I have tracked individuals and their activities as they appear in churchwarden's accounts and guild accounts and, when possible, I have cross-referenced this information with wills, tax records, leases, and court records. This sort of parish reconstitution allows me to study systematically what it was that women contributed to parish life and how their contributions reflected their social and economic situations. In order to contextualize women's religious experiences, my study also addresses men's parish involvement. This approach shows that men and women were involved in the parish in different ways based not only on gender roles, but also on their economic and marital statuses. While women acted on their own interests as women, they also acted on their interests as wives, daughters, and mothers, seeking to promote their families' communal and spiritual well-being. In the chapters that follow, I look at various aspects of women's parochial involvement in light of the traumatic and dramatic social and economic changes of the late fourteenth and fifteenth centuries.

The first two chapters consider the ways in which women's household obligations, duties, and roles formed a vocabulary of piety for women. Household obligations did more than structure women's parish contributions. As women transferred their housekeeping activities to the parish, it gave them the ability to offer meaningful and visible good works to their parish communities. In so doing, women also transferred the familiarity and influence they had in their household onto their parishes, creating an environment that fostered their further involvement. The labor women did for the church and the objects they left to their parishes in their wills all reflect their household obligations and duties. In preparing for the life-cycle liturgies of baptism, churching, marriage, and burial, women again drew upon their household roles to modify the liturgical props, such as candles and clothing that families supplied to reflect family strategies for salvation and social advancement.

The next three chapters look at three different kinds of collective action undertaken by women within the context of the parish. All appear to be innovations of the fifteenth century. Both seating and all-women's groups or guilds actively promoted submissive and decorous behavior among women. Yet at the same time they inadvertently created opportunities for women's public visibility and action. For example, all-women's groups served as a means of socializing large numbers of unmarried women into proper gender roles during a time of women's increasing physical mobility. At the same time, however, these groups, like the better-documented and more permanent parish guilds for men, provided women with leadership roles and the opportunity to work together on behalf of religious concerns of interest to them. The final form of collective action that I address is a carnivalesque holiday called Hocktide. This holiday, I argue, tried to address and tame the tension surrounding women's increased prominence and economic activity in the parish and society at large. Yet even as holiday activities invoked concerns about women's power and authority, it created another opportunity for women to work together in all-women's groups and even gave some women an official role in the parish's administration.

The prominence of women in parish activities prompts the question of how parish communities responded to them. In the last chapter, I analyze clerical and lay definitions of women's piety and impiety to see the impact of women's wide-ranging parish activities on social expectations. Both the laity and the clergy shared concerns about women's sexuality and both desired women to connect their pious behavior to submissive, silent, and demure deportment. However, despite shared understandings of the gendered nature of piety and impiety, the laity and the clergy did not ultimately respond to women's parish behavior in the same way.

Finally, in a brief epilogue I consider how the imposition of religious reforms in the mid-sixteenth century changed women's behavior and opportunities in the parish. Although some women welcomed these changes, most women would have found their parish involvement significantly altered. To participate in this new religion, women had to draw upon different skills and practices.

The demographic and economic changes that followed the plague created turbulent social changes in late medieval England. These changes were particularly noticeable in the activities and opportunities for women.

Women moved into the workforce in larger numbers, delayed marriage if they married at all, and lived away from their natal families. Women's involvement in the late medieval parish also expanded at this time. Thus, some of the significance of women's involvement in the parish lies in the ways that it reflected and perhaps contributed to the social concerns of the post-plague period. Attempts to restore women to their pre-plague position are evident in the social legislation of the fourteenth and fifteenth centuries. Moreover, the misogyny of much clerical discourse, although by no means new to this period, constituted another attempt to try to control women's behavior. However, Christianity at the local level offered women the very opportunities that so worried the clergy and local leaders. These opportunities were a chance to construct meaning and value around their family and social lives. Understanding the dynamics and vibrancy of late medieval religious life requires addressing the important role women played in their own parishes. Placing them within the demographic and social world of the fifteenth century helps explain the tension surrounding their involvement and gives new significance to old clerical complaints about women's church behavior.

Chapter 1

"My Wedding Gown to Make a Vestment": Housekeeping and Churchkeeping

In the rural parish of Tintinhull, Somerset, as in many other places in medieval Europe, it was the custom of the women to dress the images of the saints in robes and kerchiefs. On saints' days and other holy days, the cloth decorated and beautified the images as a sign of love, respect, and supplication. Bequests from women's wills supplied some of the napery. When Alice Stacy died, she left a linen sheet to the statue of St. Mary, perhaps to be used as a veil.[1] With use and exposure to soot, wax, oil, and even droppings from the bats living in the church's eves, linens grew dirty; it was the laity's responsibility to clean them. In 1438 the churchwardens paid a group of women 6d. for washing the "alter cloths and for kerchiefs for the images."[2] Yet in 1449 and again in 1452, the laundresses refused their payment choosing instead to donate their labor to the church.[3] The actions of Alice Stacy and the laundresses reflect the ways women supported their parishes, the ways they connected their physical contributions to their piety, and the ways that their household obligations influenced their pious actions.

Canon law required that the clergy maintain the chancel of the parish church while the laity maintained the nave and furnished the liturgy with its candles, vestments, liturgical books, altar cloths, and vessels.[4] Books wore out, vestments tore, candles burned down, and altar cloths became soiled. Theft and repeated use forced parishioners to replace or repair lost, worn out, or broken items. Moreover, roofs leaked, windows broke, and masonry wore away, necessitating professional artisans to repair the building and its fittings. Meeting these obligations required lay organization and labor and by the fifteenth century, parishes had such organizations and administrations in place to oversee these tasks.[5] However, such work also had benefits; providing for the parish's upkeep and maintenance was a good work that benefited one's soul and the souls of the departed.[6] Work for the church honored God, and by maintaining the church and adorning it with objects, the laity provided a fitting home for the host.[7] Maintaining the parish, therefore, translated men's and women's financial and material obligations to their parishes into pious acts.

Medieval gender roles informed how individual parishioners supported their parish. The house was women's domain. The keys on a housewife's belt symbolized her position within the house. In their own households, rural women performed a multitude of different chores directed at keeping order.[8] They cleaned house, purchased and cooked food, tended to kitchen gardens and poultry, fetched water from the well, spun flax and wool, and mended clothes. If there were children, they cared for them as well.[9] Urban women did many of the same tasks, although the markets might have been closer, the wells further, and kitchen gardens smaller.[10] Most families had a servant or two and women would have also supervised their work as part of their housekeeping obligations. Felicity Riddy argues that the physical intimacy fostered by medieval urban houses and the housewife's tasks of feeding and cleaning the house and its inhabitants not only turned the housewife into a powerful image of a caregiver, but that the "embodiedness [of housekeeping] work[ed] against the hierarchical structures that were assumed by urban and natural law makers."[11] Women's care of their parishes mirrored that of their own households, and we find women cleaning, supplying, and interacting with God's house much as they would have their own. The familiarity and ease that developed out of such care fostered among women a proprietary attitude toward the parish church and its contents.

Housekeeping and domestic obligations not only translated easily to the parish, they allowed women to view their daily drudgery as meaningful pious activities. Although the parish was not the only venue of women's piety, non-elite women by and large practiced their piety in this context. This chapter will argue that women's domestic practices and household responsibilities informed much of their parish participation. Housekeeping chores provided women with a constellation of activities that when practiced in the parish gave a wide range of women the ability to perform meaningful, important, and visible good works within their community. Moreover, women's labor and material contributions to their parishes, although determined in large measure by the legal and economic constraints placed on them, allowed them to shape their pious practices in ways that reflected their concerns for family, community, self-promotion, and salvation. These activities were not new to the fourteenth century. In the sixth St. Radegund cleaned Frankish churches, "polish[ing] the Abbeys of the pavement with her dress and, collecting the drifting dust around the altar in a napkin, reverently placed it outside the door rather than sweep it away."[12] In Anglo-Saxon England, women left Bath and St. Alban's linens, curtains, bedclothes, and a woman's woolen gown.[13] What would have been new in the fourteenth century was the material culture that women left and cleaned.

In descriptions of women's parish work, which differed from the work of men, we can see that gendered religious behavior emerged among ordinary women. Scholars have long identified a tradition of affective piety among elite women.[14] Private confessors, private chapels, and religious texts promoted this form of piety. Non-elite women, peasants and urban laboring women, however, had little or no access to literacy or private confessors who could school them in the details of this style of worship. Nonetheless, non-elite women seem to have had an equally gendered set of pious practices centered on the parish and its identity as God's house. By interacting with their parish church as a house, non-elite women could share with elite women an interest in Eucharistic devotion and the saints.

Housekeeping and Churchkeeping

The Bible taught that the church was God's house. The gospels have many descriptions of a church as such. Jesus likens the kingdom of heaven to a house, with doors and gates to be opened to those who seek God (Matt 7:7–13). Later, when Jesus drives the merchants and money changers out of the Temple, he says "It is written, 'My house shall be called a house of prayer;' but you make it a den of robbers" (Matt 21: 13; see also Mark 11: 15–16; Luke 19: 45–46; John 2:13–16). This verse was central to the liturgies for both the dedication of a church and the anniversary of the dedication of the church in the *Sarum Missal*, the most common liturgy in late medieval England.[15] In a sermon for the occasion of the dedication of a church, the compiler of a fifteenth-century sermon collection, the *Speculum Sacerdotale*, explained that because the church is God's house, it is special. "In it [the church] is the habitation of God, concourse of angels, reconciliation of man, and the lowness of the earth is in fellowship with the height of heaven. And this place is the holy house of God and the gate of heaven."[16] John Mirk, a late fourteenth-century Augustinian canon, who wrote extensively for parish priests, found the comparison of a house and a church useful for instructing the clergy on how the laity were to behave in the church. In his *Instructions for Parish Priests* he explains that

Also within the church and chancel
Do right as I give you council
Songs and shouts and other bad behavior
You shall not tolerate in front of the savior;
Throwing of axes and throwing of stones
Are activities best left alone
Balls and bears and other such play
Out of the churchyard and put them away;
Court proceedings and other such fuss
Out of the sanctuary put them you must!
For Christ himself did teach us
That holy church is his house
That is made for nothing else
But to pray in, as the book tells.
There the people shall gather within,
To pray and weep for their sin.[17]

In maintaining the nave and its contents, therefore, the laity provided a worthy home for the host. The centrality of the association of the church with a house meant that medieval men and women would have been familiar with the concept.

In late medieval homes, people had their bodily needs cared for, found shelter from the cold, slept, and interacted with family members in close physical proximity. Homes were crowed, and one room held many functions. Homes and hominess denoted, then, familiarity, domestic living, and love.[18] Late medieval descriptions of homes and hominess typically assumed that women stayed in the house, while men returned to it. Once home, men received comfort and care. These assumptions would have influenced audiences hearing descriptions of the church as God's house.

The roles and obligations of household members provided models for involvement in the parish church. Men and women, mothers and fathers, boys and girls, and male and female servants all played different roles in a household, and either implicitly or explicitly these roles were incorporated into these groups' interactions with the parish. In this way, the association of the church with a house also created specific gendered expectations for women's parish involvement, which, in turn, influenced expectations for their religious behavior. It needed to fit into the context of domesticity and household obligations. Just as housewives dominated the household, women, especially married women in charge of their own households, moved about their parishes with equal comfort.

At the same time, the congruence between house and church was not total. Parish work opportunities offered women greater initiative and agency than they had in other institutions, and as a result women's parish participation periodically breached expected gender norms. The house-keeping women did for the church brought them into contact with other women and gave them opportunities for shared experiences, something lacking in much of their ordinary work. Such corporate and public work gave women a broader scope for their activities, and meant that "church-keeping" offered women opportunities for visibility and action that house-keeping did not.

There was a danger that women might start to presume upon their relationship with the parish and grow comfortable with the intimacy that such work afforded them. John Mirk, whose sermon collection, the *Festial*, was the most popular collection in late medieval England, addressed the problem of how to distinguish the value of work done for the church from work done for one's family or oneself in his sermon for Corpus Christi.[19] Many of Mirk's sermons came from the twelfth-century *Golden Legend*, but Mirk reworked them to address the concerns and activities of fourteenth-century English parishioners.[20] His collection continued to be popular up into the sixteenth century and the eve of the Reformation. In his Corpus Christi sermon, Mirk retells the story of the woman who made the bread used at a mass being said by Pope Gregory the Great.[21] She smiled when Gregory gave her a piece of the bread. When asked about her mirth she replied, "you call that God's body that which I made with my own hands?"[22] Gregory, saddened by her disbelief, prayed to God to convince her otherwise. Immediately the bread then turned to a piece of bleeding flesh, which Gregory showed to the woman. She cried out "Lord, now I believe that you are Christ, God's son of Heaven in the form of bread."[23] Gregory prayed again, and the flesh transformed back into bread. This story was a popular one for sermons writers in late medieval England, the same story also appears in the *Speculum Sacerdotale* sermon collection.[24]

Most obviously the story of the woman and the host explained the doctrine of transubstantiation and the importance of the priest's role in the daily miracle of the mass. This lesson was important for challenging the heretical Lollards, whose influence was growing in the late fourteenth-century. The story, however, also demonstrates that women's work prepared the church for mass. The doubting woman made an instrument of worship, but she made no distinction between her work for home or profit and her work for the church. The story explained that labor for the church was not everyday labor and should not be viewed as such. Work in a holy context was sacred work. Baking bread for the Eucharist might look like housework, but it did not mean the same thing. With the priest's blessings, the bread became God's body. In confusing housekeeping with churchkeeping, the woman misunderstood the meaning of her work. The women hearing Mirk's sermon learned that the kinds of quotidian activities associated with housekeeping, when performed for the church, were acts of piety.

Sermons writers frequently invoked housekeeping metaphors in their Easter and Lenten sermons. Cleaning house recalled the spiritual cleansing that Christians were to undertake in this season of repentance. This metaphor probably comes from Hugh of St. Cher's thirteenth-century *De doctrina cordis*, which appeared in Middle English by the fifteenth century. Hugh was a Dominican who guided beguine communities in the diocese of Liège, but the work itself may have had a broader readership. Its continued popularity across Europe, however, testifies to the importance of mendicant teaching and its ability to reach well beyond communities of religious. The *Doctrine of the Hert*, as it was called in English, focused on preparing the soul for receiving the Eucharist, and likened this internal spiritual space to a house, and spiritual cleansing to housekeeping.[25] These metaphors passed into the English vernacular sermon tradition, where they reached a far different kind of female audience, than the urban beguines. Homey analogies served preachers well; comparing confession and repentance to housecleaning taught women see religious significance in their work, and made good housekeeping skills a moral imperative. Mirk explains in his Easter sermon that, just as men and women

clean the house, taking out the fire and straw and flowers, just so they should clean the house of their soul, doing away with the fire of lechery and of deadly wrath and of envy, and add straw there, sweat herbs, and flowers.[26]

In a fifteenth-century sermon collection, known as the Ross Collection, the two sermons for the first Sunday in Lent focus on preparing for confession in this season of atonement. In the longer of the two sermons, the preacher explains the importance of repentance and the doctrine of contrition by comparing it to the work of washing clothes. The principle at issue is that the sinner must not only be sorrowful for the sin he or she has committed, but also be fervent in the desire to sin no more. Without this step, there will be no forgiveness. The meaning of contrition lies at the heart of this sermon and was central to the work of medieval pastoral care.[27] The sermon writer explains that

A laundress in washing clothes washes in this way: First she takes lye and casts [the] clothes in and suffers them to be there a long while. After she draws them out, turns, beats, and rinses them and hangs them up, the clothes are clean. This lye is made with ashes and water and it is very bitter, [the clothes] will not be clean if you omit this part. The ashes, that cause bitterness, signify the bitter consideration of the pains of hell. In this lye should man's soul lie eternally; how bitter the pains will be, our faith teaches us. And by this consideration I trust to God you must get fresh water to wash the lye out of the clothes. And this water shall be your own fresh tears.[28]

Washing clothes was almost invariably women's work, and the sermon writer assumes that the launderer is a woman. Such an extended description of a familiar task must have drawn the attention of women listening to this sermon, not only explaining to them the ways of true contrition, but giving them an alternative way of thinking about this backbreaking and difficult work. The sermon then moves on to explain why confession is necessary and likens it to housecleaning:

You must shrive yourself like a woman cleans her house. She takes a broom and drives together all the uncleanness of the household. And lest the dust descend and cover the place, she sprinkles it with water. And when she has gathered it all together, she casts it with great violence out of the door. So must you do likewise. You must cleanse the house of your soul and make it holy in the sight of God.[29]

The shorter sermon for that Sunday makes no reference to laundry and uses the metaphor of housecleaning in a slightly different fashion. "A man who comes to confession is like a man's house. For on Saturday in the afternoon, the servants shall sweep the house and cast all the dung and filth behind the door in a heap. But what then? There come the capons and the hens and scratch it all about and make it as dirty as it was before."[30] The preacher concludes that unless penitents tell all their sins, the unconfessed sins, like the dirt hidden behind the door, will attract the devil and make the penitent worse off. A clean house is like a clean soul; a dirty house will attract sin.

The use of metaphors so obviously associated with women and their work must have been directed at women and used to explain to them the need for proper confession, a central feature of medieval Christianity. The sermon also promotes a standard of work performance for women whether they were washing, sweeping, or supervising servants. Stained laundry was like half-hearted contrition, while dust bunnies in the corner would propagate like unconfessed sins. These examples not only taught basic theological concepts to women, but equated good housekeeping skills with piety and failure at housework with sin. By focusing on only some aspects of women's daily work, these sermons also reinforced a gendered division of labor. Beyond this, this sermon spoke directly to women's experiences, and validated their work both at home and in the church as potential religious expressions.

The connections between piety and housework were also understood in the cult of St. Zita, or Sitha as the English called her. Sitha came from Lucca, in Italy, where she had been an exceptionally pious servant until her death in 1272. She was not only obedient but also charitable, giving away food and money to those poorer than herself. Her cult came to England with the Lucchese merchants working in London, and London is the earliest known site of her English veneration.[31] From London, the cult moved west and north following the routes of the English wool trade.[32] Her cult became especially popular with the monks of St. Alban's. They made an English copy of her life around 1377, a fragment of which still survives.[33] They also dedicated an altar to her, and commissioned an elaborate series of wall paintings of her life.[34] In 1456, the Master of the Knights Hospitaller at Eagle, Lincolnshire, acquired some of her relics for his chapel dedicated to her. This chapel may have inspired a pilgrimage.[35]

By the early sixteenth century, images of Sitha appeared in wall paintings, rood screens, stained-glass windows, carvings, and even some brasses in parish churches throughout England.[36] Artists portrayed Sitha as an old woman simply dressed. Her emblem was a set of household keys (see Figure 1.1). Petitioners prayed to her for help finding lost items. A wall painting from the parish church of Horley, Oxfordshire, shows her surrounded by coins, pots and pans, and other items easily lost or else signifying domestic work.[37] Miriam Gill writes that the Horley image is one "which suggests both the sanctification of housework and her ability to recover lost items."[38] A Lollard treatise against the saints and pilgrimage condemns the housewife who loses her keys because she "will quickly seek St. Sitha and spend a noble or ten shillings in her journey."[39] With so many young women working as servants in the years prior to marriage, and wives having housekeeping responsibilities, Sitha would have had a potentially large following among late medieval women. Sebastian Sutcliffe found that proportionally more women than men remembered her in their wills.[40] She served as a

Figure 1.1. Sts. Apollonia and Sitha, Virgin Martyr rood screen, Barton Turf, Norfolk. Photograph courtesy of National Monuments Record.

model for turning housework into pious actions and an opportunity for charity.

This habit of seeing women's housework as a form of Christian behavior was a modification of a long-standing association of labor and piety. In monasticism, particularly as expressed in the Rule of St. Benedict, the work of God included not only prayer but manual labor. This idea had applications in the world beyond the monastic walls. In a late medieval courtesy text called *The Book of the Knight of the Tower*, the eponymous knight tells his daughters, for whom he has composed the text, that the matins they say upon waking "ought to be your first work and first labor."[41]

Work was not simply or unproblematically a form of piety. Theologians held contradictory opinions about the significance of work. Jacques Le Goff argues that, in the early Middle Ages, labor was a form of penance and personal discipline; it had little value in and of itself. These attitudes began to change in the ninth century as peasants cleared and colonized the forests of France and England; labor was now associated with conquest and gain in rural areas under the control of monasteries. George Ovitt argues for another shift in labor ideology in the twelfth century. Theologians abandoned the idea that labor, especially and particularly their own monastic labor, could return the earth to its original perfection. Theologians no longer participated in, or expected morally ordered, non-exploitative, cooperative labor to be the norm. Labor was now the purview of those living outside of monasteries. Labor and laborers had been in Ovitt's term "secularized" and given a new place in Christian culture. He wrote that in the twelfth century there was "an attempt to fashion a pluralistic view of society and of social obligations, one that insisted on the primacy of the solitary spiritual life but also acknowledged that more public forms of spirituality and a greater variety of professional occupations could be integrated into the church."[42] The different occupations and classes, however, still might be part of God's plan.

The time, place, and purpose of work were also crucial for understanding work as a form of piety, for example, medieval Christians were not supposed to work on Sundays. As far back as the fourth century and the Edict of Toleration, the clergy forbade some form of work on Sundays.[43] By the late Middle Ages, the clergy interpreted the third commandment as an injunction against work on Sundays and holy days.[44] Work was a necessary human condition because of the Fall, and it was a way of glorifying God if one did not work to accumulate wealth.[45] Work was both a sign and a means of sin, or if done in the right places, for the right reasons, at the right time, by the right people, it could be an avenue to salvation. Work could thus bring one to God or keep one from God.

If work equaled piety, then laziness or sloth equaled impiety. The sin of sloth initially referred to spiritual laziness, such as falling asleep at prayers or staying home from church. In the high Middle Ages, however, it also came to mean physical laziness or an unwillingness to work.[46] Taken together these ideas about labor formed a constellation of associations upon which the clergy could draw when teaching their parishioners about Christian behavior and upon which parishioners could ponder when thinking about the significance of their parish contributions.

In the late fourteenth and early fifteenth centuries, as a result of the labor shortage, the clergy and elites accused laborers and peasants of growing laziness because they refused to work unless they received high wages. Indeed, Parliament specifically justified the Statute of Laborers by accusing "the malice of servants, who were idle and unwilling to serve after the pestilence without taking outrageous wages."[47] Christopher Dyer, however, has argued that although these accusations were common, there is in fact little evidence that laborers had changed their work ethic following the plague. Those peasants with their own land would have had to work hard to support their families, and those who worked for wages could have improved their status in this period of great social mobility through work. Instead the accusations of laziness reflect the ability of the lower order to command higher wages, which they spent on better food, clothing, and drink, manifestations of increasing status. What laborers resisted in this period was working without any benefit to themselves.[48] Connecting piety and labor to the parish church, therefore, served a number of different agenda. For the clergy, it reconnected labor and prayer; for the parishioners it was another means of realizing the individual benefits of labor. Work on the church—God's house—brought hominess and furthered salvation.

The laundresses at Tintinhull, with whom we began this chapter, were aware of the connection between their work and piety when they donated their labor. Similarly, in Bassingbourne, Cambridgeshire, when the parish produced a St. Margaret play to raise money for a new statue of St. George, many women donated their brewing and baking labor to supply refreshments.[49] Even women who earned money for their work for the parish may have viewed their labor contributions as a manifestation of piety. Some may have reduced their wages, worked with extra care, or simply believed that all work for the parish was pious work, because it brought them in contact with the holy and because it provided a home for the host. The Corpus

Christi Guild in Cambridge treated working for them as a potentially charitable act. It expected member carpenters to work for the guild at 1d. less a week than their normal rate.[50] It may be the case that laundresses and other women employed by the parish were sometimes expected to do the same.

Women and Parish Work

To furnish and maintain the nave, parishioners contributed money and resources, they physically labored on the church and its contents, and they left items in their wills to enhance the church, the cult of the saints, and the liturgy after they died. Parish lay leaders, called churchwardens, kept records of their fundraising and expenditures on behalf of the nave and its contents.[51] Expenditures include both purchases of supplies and goods, such as wax for candles or cloth for hangings, and labor for maintenance and construction. As a result, churchwardens' accounts provide most of the information on women's labor for the parish.

Geography and gender determined work roles. While most women, whether urban or rural, were probably mothers, this was not their only social identity. In addition to or instead of mothering, women kept house and worked part-time at many different tasks to earn money for their households and to assist their husbands if they had one. Unmarried women in both the country and city worked as domestic servants prior to marriage, and both urban and rural women ran their own businesses.[52] Women's businesses tended to be small and temporary, such as brewing, laundering, and wax making. Rural women did not plow, but they harvested crops, tended kitchen gardens, and looked after livestock and poultry. Urban women worked in their husbands' shops if they were artisans or did piecework for workshops.

The surviving churchwarden's accounts record similar work patterns among the women employed by the parish. As part of their charge to supervise the maintenance of the parish church, churchwardens routinely hired men and women to work on the church or its furnishings. My analysis of women's parish work draws from a sample of twenty-nine sets of churchwardens' accounts from a range of different parishes. Although this sample is about 12 percent of what survives, it could not be a random sample, because many sets of accounts include little or no information on sources of fundraising or expenditures. Others do not name the individuals, male or female, hired to work for the parish. I did use accounts from a variety of parishes based on their wealth, size, and relationships with other local institutions. The accounts are also spread across the country to minimize the impact of any regional variation.[53] The professionalization of some occupations in cities and towns further influenced what work women performed for the church.[54] Although both urban and rural parishes required the skills of trained artisans, rural parishes had to hire them from outside the community more often than their urban counterparts. We find artisans' wives listed among the parish workers along with the local women who did the church's laundry and cleaned the church.[55] Working for the parish gave women opportunities to access the holy and to apply their care and skill to holy things. When they attended mass they could see their handiwork adorning the liturgy and close to the host. If they internalized the message of the *exempla* of the woman who made the bread for the Eucharist, they knew this labor mattered even if they received payment. They also knew that this intimate involvement offered them influence in God's house, much like they had influence in their own homes. Because parishes tended to hire women of the lower or artisanal classes, analyzing women's labor for the parish becomes an opportunity to see lower-class women's parish involvement.

All churches needed their altar cloths and vestments cleaned. Mirk valorized this work in his *Instructions for Parish Priests*, explaining that altar cloths and surplices must be clean for the mass.[56] Clean altar cloths and vestments were not simply an ideal, however; parishes that let their vestments and altar cloths remain soiled year after year courted trouble from ecclesiastical authorities. Episcopal visitors investigating the condition of the parish of St. Briavels, Hereford, found the vestments and altar cloths "dirty and unsightly" because there were no churchwardens to hire a laundress.[57] Laundry was most often women's work and it could be burdensome. Of the twenty-nine sets of accounts, twenty, or 69 percent, employed women to do this task. For example, from the churchwardens' accounts of St. Margaret's, Westminster, we know that in 1500 John Cross's wife laundered "36 pieces, that is to say albs, amices, towels, and altar cloths, and other things" for the parish. On another occasion, she laundered nine albs, nine amices, towels, and altar cloths.[58] Clearly the task of cleaning parish cloths and vestments could tax the resources of a parish. As a result, pious benefactions earmarked for parish laundresses were sometimes left by pious well-to-do women. When Dame Margaret Capell, the widow of a wealthy London knight draper, died, for example, she instructed her executors to turn her and her late husband's velvet and silk clothes into vestments for poor churches.[59] Recognizing the potential burden of caring for this bequest, she also left additional money for the churchwardens of these parishes to hire laundresses to care for her legacy.[60]

Parishes hired a variety of different kinds of women to perform this necessary and backbreaking labor. Some parishes employed clerks' or sextons' wives,[61] others hired the churchwarden's wife,[62] and still others contracted with outside washerwomen, unconnected to parochial administration.[63] In one case, a woman serving as churchwarden did the laundry herself.[64] These women all held different places in parish society, and these differences reflect the variety of motivations lying behind women's involvement in their parishes. No doubt, the concerns lying behind a churchwarden's wife's washing of the parish's linens differed from the same service done by a laundress or the clerk's wife.

Some churchwardens' wives were very involved in helping their husbands run the parish, even though they held no parish office. For example, Katherine Segraffe of All Saints, Tilney in Norfolk, kept the parish's money while her husband was churchwarden.[65] As the wife of the churchwarden, she occupied an important place within the parish's social hierarchy. Wardens and their wives had knowledge of parish business, and the ability of churchwardens' wives to influence their husbands—parish leaders—put them in a different position with respect to the parish's needs and their own livelihood than a lowly laundress. For churchwardens' wives, charge of the laundry extended their husbands' responsibilities for their church's fabric, and it reflected their own intimate connection with parish life. We can easily attribute their willingness to take in the parish laundry to a combination of pious concerns and local privilege. By taking in the church's laundry, the churchwardens' wives could touch things that had touched the host and influence the splendor of the mass. It was an intimacy similar to what a wife had with her husband and children's clothes. In the end, however, we do not know whether these women had servants to actually do the laundry or if they did this work themselves.

The clerk's or sexton's wife who did the church's laundry probably did it for a different reason; it was an extension of her husband's many janitorial obligations. Indeed, some parishes, such as Lambeth, paid the parish clerk or sexton himself for this work; although, one suspects, he still turned the job over to his wife.[66] Laundresses comprise yet another group of women involved in cleaning of parish vestments or cloths. The parish of Bridgwater (Som.) hired unnamed laundresses to care for their vestments and altar cloths.[67] These were low-status women who took in laundry to support themselves. In the minds of many civic authorities, laundresses were no better than prostitutes.[68] Whether doing the parish laundry was just more work or it had a redemptive quality is difficult to say, but it, too, put laundresses in contact with liturgical objects. Churchwardens' accounts do not identify the churchwardens' wives as laundresses, suggesting that their motivations for doing the laundry at least were not professional and economic, but rather religious or communal.

The churchwardens' accounts occasionally allow us to see little networks of women sharing work and handing down jobs. The employment history of the laundresses in two East Anglian parishes illustrates how women came to work for their parishes and how their parish involvement fostered relationships with other women of the parish. The Walberswick churchwardens employed Parnell Henby as a laundress for more than twenty years.[69] In 1482, her last appearance in the accounts, she worked with Isabel Pye, who mended the parish's vestments.[70] After 1482, Pye took over the laundry while continuing to do some of the parish's mending.[71] She in turn disappeared from the accounts after 1486, but her kinswoman Elizabeth Pye succeeded her.[72] The parish then hired a third woman, Isabel Passchelew in 1492.[73] Like Isabel Pye, she too did some sewing; she provided the image of St. John with clothes.[74] By 1497, the churchwardens turned to hiring the parish clerk to do the laundry, thus ending the need to search for an independent laundress.[75] Although we do not know how Parnell Henby gained her position initially, her working relationship with Isabel Pye allowed Pye to assume Henby's job after she died. Pye in turn passed on the job to her relative Elizabeth. The transition from sewing to laundry followed by both Isabel Pye and Isabel Passchelew points at the personal and economic relationships that brought these women into parish employment.

The laundresses in Walberswick appear to have been either single or widowed. Parnell Henby worked for the parish for twenty years, longer than most people, but no man with this last name appears in the accounts. During a fundraising campaign in 1475, it was she and not a husband who gave the parish 12d.[76] She also left the parish a nice set of beads when she died, which the churchwardens sold in 1498 for 3s. 10d.[77] The gift from such a humble woman suggests that Parnell Henby valued her connection with the parish. Whatever Isabel and Elizabeth Pye's relationship, no men in the churchwardens' accounts share their surname either. Only Isabel Passchelew comes from a prominent parish family. In 1451 and 1464, John and Thomas Passchelew served as churchwardens.[78] Both were masters of fishing boats, and Thomas eventually owned his own boat named *The Marga-*

ret.[79] Both contributed extensively to parish fundraising. In 1476, another Thomas Passchelew was a priest in the parish, and in 1486 Andrew Passchelew was the master of *The Margery* (possibly the same boat as *The Margaret*).[80] Whatever Isabel's position in this family, she was unusual within the context of Walberswick; unlike the other laundresses in this parish, she was part of a large family active in parish affairs, and what we might be seeing here is laundry in Walberswick being transformed from paid service to pious work.

Tilney, also in East Anglia, shows a different kind of social network leading to parish service. In 1526, Richard Taupe rented three acres of land named Bardolos Cross from the parish.[81] The same year, the parish paid his wife for boarding the glaziers working on the church.[82] In 1530, Gilbert and Alice Cotton took over Bardolos Cross, and Alice did the parish's laundry.[83] In 1533, Thomas King leased the property, and the next year his wife Margaret started doing the laundry.[84] Tilney's laundresses were all married, their husbands did small occasional jobs for the parish but never held parish office, and two of them lived in Bardolos Cross. Other renters of this property provided services for the parish as well. Richard Taupe transported tiles and lead to and from the parish in 1523.[85] In 1530 Thomas King mended a baldrick—the leather thong holding the bell clapper in the bell.[86] Renting this property might have come with obligations to serve the parish, or local knowledge of parish needs might have passed among the people renting parish land.

The experiences of the laundresses in Walberswick and Tilney show how different kinds of social networks brought women into parish employment. Working together for the parish provided women with an opportunity to talk about their parish work experiences, the objects they cared for, and to develop ideas about collective parish participation and piety. These experiences benefited their families and friends economically and socially and may have fostered a subculture among women around work, liturgical objects, and the value of shared action. The laundresses in Tintinhull, discussed in the opening vignette, acted on these connections when they donated their labor. Although we do not know their identities or how they made their decisions to donate their labor, they understood that their collective work could be transformed into pious work that benefited their parish.

Although menial, the laundresses' job was important, and it gave women access to the vestments and altar cloths, objects with proximity to the host and priest, a privilege that could be abused. Parishioners in Wanting, Wiltshire, leveled just this complaint about their parish clerk William Hardyng. According to the visitation report of 1405, when he took the vestments home, his children slept in them and he and his wife had sex while wearing them, "causing scandal to the church."[87] The concern does not seem to be with taking the vestments home—presumably he or his wife was supposed to wash them there—but rather with their misuse. The parishioners also added that Hardyng performed many of his other duties poorly or not at all, and he composed taunting songs about the former chaplain.

Church textiles not only needed cleaning, but repairing. Although most parishes employed women to sew and mend, men also performed this task. Of the twenty-nine parishes I surveyed, seventeen employed women for this kind of sewing. Typically, women made and repaired simple vestments and altar coverings such as surplices, amices, and towels.[88] Elaborate vestments, such as copes and chasubles, needed skilled workers. Parishes supplied the cloth and thread, and paid women, or men, for their labor. Rural parishes hired women for this task more often than market town or city parishes.[89] In the rural Somerset parish of Yatton, the clerk's wife "hem [med] the cloth for the Mary," while in Tilney, Agnes Nokke did the parish's sewing for thirty-five years. In the middle of this lengthy service, her husband served as churchwarden, suggesting she and her family had some measure of local status.[90]

In contrast, Anne Malte, who sewed for the Cambridge parish of Holy Trinity, does not seem to have had much parish status. According to the town's 1512 poll tax, Malte was a single woman, living in Market Ward, the most densely populated of the city's ten wards, with a servant named Alice Sympson.[91] Malte paid taxes on £1 of income, the lowest level taxed. In the 1524 lay subsidy, she paid her taxes on the same level of income, but apparently no longer employed a servant. In 1509, the churchwardens hired Malte to bleach two new surplices and mend four others.[92] Although she continued to sew for Holy Trinity until 1525, she moved from mending to sewing new vestments in 1517 when the wardens bought a new surplice with sleeves from her.[93] After 1525, she disappeared from the parish accounts.[94]

Both the large urban parishes of St. Margaret's, Westminster, and St. Mary at Hill, in London, occasionally hired women to do their mending, but more typically this task was in the hands of professional men or the parish sexton, a parish employee responsible for many other janitorial tasks such as digging graves, lighting lamps, and ringing bells.[95] Urban women, however, were more likely to be involved in the initial production of the elaborate copes, chasubles, altar cloths, and hangings that required embroidery and expensive and colored cloth. The churchwardens of Yatton hired a silk woman from outside the parish in 1504 to mend a cope.[96] She probably came from nearby Bristol, where a number of silk women lived and worked.[97] At St. Margaret's, Westminster, William Barnowey's wife embroidered an image of the crucifix with Mary and John for a church hanging.[98] For the most part, however, men did embroidery for hire, with women working in subordinate positions.[99] Some worked with their husbands as they traveled from parish to parish, such as the vestment-maker's wife, hired with her husband by the small market-town parish of Stogursey, Somerset.[100] Other women apparently worked in workshops, or did piecework at home, mass-producing items such as orphreys, the decorative panels adorning the edges of copes and chasubles. The London parish of St. Mary at Hill, for example, ordered new vestments from such a workshop in 1493. The wardens wanted a particular image on one of the orphreys and separately paid the woman who made it.[101]

Wax making was another activity crucial to the liturgy of the parishes. Candles adorned the high altar, side altars, burned before images of the saints, and stood by the font and at Easter; some Paschal tapers weighed tens of pounds. Candles were also integral to liturgical processions. Candles allowed for a series of associations of light and dark, which complemented Christian theology. Mirk's *Instructions for Parish Priests* explains that the priest should insist on wax candles that would burn cleanly, rather than ones with resin, which spluttered and smoked.[102] As with other activities, geography influenced the level of professionalization of this task. Wax chandler John Burton and his wife Joan supplied most of the wax for the London parish of St. Mary at Hill. When John died, in 1519 or 1520, Joan worked as the parish's wax chandler until she married Thomas Lawles, who moved into her house and took over her deceased husband's business.[103] Gentleman wax chandler John Attewell and his wife Ellen supplied their parish of St. Margaret's, Westminster.[104]

Lacking access to professional wax chandlers, rural churchwardens relied on many different people to make or supply wax. Rural women often kept bees and made wax; so not surprisingly, they had a greater role in candle production than their urban counterparts. When John Nokke served as churchwarden of Tilney, for example, his wife Agnes, the seamstress, also sold wax to the parish.[105] In the small Somerset parish of Tintinhull, Margaret Stacy and her husband William left the parish a beehive as a legacy, and another woman in the parish, Elizabeth Shues, took charge of the gift.[106]

The parish's interest in the bees and its maintenance of the gift precipitated the purchase of another hive the next year.[107]

In Prescot, Lancashire, meeting the parish's wax needs involved large numbers of people. In 1537–38, the parish bought wax from nine men and four women. Rafe Holland's wife supplied the wick yarn, and Margaret Dene tempered the wax.[108] The next year fewer individuals supplied wax, but a woman supplied the food and drink for those making the candles, Margaret Dene still worked in the process, and George Plumpton's wife supplied the grease and her maid tempered it.[109] As with the laundry, women from across the parish participated in the process. In meeting the needs of their parish, women also met each other, providing another opportunity for women to work together and to share in the religious life of the parish. Although there were certainly financial incentives for this work, there were also religious motivations. Certainly candles were crucial to the liturgy and helping to make them connected those involved to the liturgy.

A parish's location influenced how churchwardens met other needs besides wax making. Artisans generally lived in towns and cities, and when a rural parish hired them to work on the church, countrywomen tended to lodge and feed them.[110] Between 1489 and 1492, the wardens in the parish of Brundish, Suffolk, hired tilers, plumbers, and smiths.[111] The workmen all stayed with Alice Puttok, who paid off her deceased husband's debts to the parish by lodging the parish's workers. Alice Noress of Bassingborne (Cambs.) boarded the mason and his servant for twenty days while they worked on the parish.[112] It was also more common for rural women to brew ale for their parish and cook for their parishes' communal feasting than urban women. In Great Dunmow, Essex, the parish widows worked on the May Day and Corpus Christi feasts, supplying some of the ingredients, and doing some of the cooking, baking, and brewing.[113] They are not listed as the chief cooks or bakers, but as support staff for those running the feast. In a marriage dispute from London, two deponents testified that the plaintiff was in the kitchen helping other women to prepare a feast; she was not away getting married.[114] Provisioning the parish drew upon women's skills of provisioning a family. As collaborative work, it also drew women together toward a common goal. Brewing, cooking, and wax making had been professionalized earlier in towns and cities, so that, while women might have done this work, it was organized and supervised by their husbands who were the professionals.[115]

Female artisans working with metal or in the construction industry also occasionally worked for parishes, but this was less common than fe-

male involvement in parish laundry, sewing, or cooking.[116] As with embroiderers and silk women, they were more likely to work with their husbands
in towns and cities than in the country. A few though worked indepen-
dently. Margery Ingram, a goldsmith in the town of Salisbury, mended (but
apparently did not manufacture) several liturgical items for the parish of
St. Edmund's.[117] St. Laurence's in Reading hired John Painter's wife "for
gilding part of Saint Vincent's tabernacle."[118] She probably worked with her
husband, a painter responsible for the finishing of this tabernacle, which
would cover the saint's image. Similarly, Lambeth parish, across the river
from Westminster, hired the mason's wife to finish installing an altar,
started by her husband, who had moved on to another project.[119] This task
gave the mason's wife access to a space and object normally off-limits to
women. Two London women also worked as bell-founders. After their husbands' died, Johanna Hill and Johanna Sturdy provided bells for a number
of parishes throughout southeastern England.[120] The labor of these women
artisans appears more related to commercial and artisanal organization
than to the idea that household tasks could become acts of piety, but these
women were also helping their husbands or supporting a household with
their labor, and their work for a parish augmented the liturgy. Nonetheless,
many of these women were not members of the parishes that employed
them.

Although women did work in most industries, parishes typically hired
women to clean what the men had built. In addition to laundry, women
scoured the candlesticks clean of wax, grease, and soot.[121] The pattern of
women's labor for the parish matches women's work patterns in the larger
medieval English economy. Most women who labored for their parishes
were local and invested in the community and its success. Traveling artisans
may or may not have been less interested in the pious ramification of their
labor, but local women could see their labor enhancing their own religious
community. We might be tempted to assume that wages nullified pious motivations, but such an assumption ignores the care and attention women
could put into work for the parish that they might not give to other work.
They may also have donated part of their labor. It also ignores the contact
with sacred objects women gained from their work and the belief that participation in the parish was a form of piety.

"Churchkeeping" involved women in the maintenance of their parish
churches. Although women generally worked in secondary positions vis-à-
vis men, the skills women had were necessary for the proper performance
of the mass. Much of their work on behalf of the church brought them into

contact with other women. With encouragement from sermons, women learned to understand their labor as a form of piety and as such, their churchkeeping augmented the mass and involved these low-status women in the Eucharistic devotions so popular in the late Middle Ages.

Pious Bequests and "Domestic Piety"

Women not only gave of their labor, but also of their household goods. Their pious bequests reflect the same connection between piety and domestic obligations that we have seen in women's work for the parish. Women typically gave the very items they or other women cared for on an annual basis.[122] This pattern demonstrates how women could understand their work on behalf of the parish as piety, even when remunerated. Their bequests to their parish display particular interest in Eucharistic devotions and the cult of the saints. Their instructions in how the parish should adapt their bequests to meet their goals reveal a great deal of creativity and an easy familiarity with the church and its needs.

A significant part of a churchwarden's annual obligations revolved around raising money to maintain the nave. Churchwardens oversaw fundraising and managed testamentary bequests. Churchwardens' accounts often subsume women's financial contributions to a parish collection or church ale under the aegis of household contributions, thus we know less about women's individual monetary or material donations. Wills, however, preserve the wishes of individuals rather than households. Usually made when the testator was near death, they record the final disposition of goods and property to family, friends, and the Church. English law did not allow a married woman to make a will without her husband's permission, so the majority of medieval English wills are by men, and the majority of women's wills are by widows. Moreover, the economically better-off section of the population usually drafted them, skewing any study of testamentary bequests in favor of those members of society with more to give.[123] In spite of their limitations, wills can tell us much about female bequests, the ways that gender rolls influenced their piety, and the relationship women had with their parish.

Wills also provide a great deal of evidence for the material culture of piety. Goods were not as firmly controlled as property and cash and their disbursal signaled the testator's personal regard for the beneficiary and was a public pronouncement of the relationship between testator and beneficiary.[124] Men and women were equally determined to remember the Church in their wills. The testator's own parish and its images, side altars, guilds, and lights were the most common ecclesiastical beneficiaries in late medieval England, although monastic communities and individual clerics and nuns received bequests as well. Men gave more money than women, but this was related to their greater wealth and greater control of resources, rather than a sign of their greater religious devotion.[125] The Bible affirmed the extra spiritual value of the "widow's mite," making quantity less important than the sacrifice involved in the donation. A popular didactic text, *The Book of Vices and Virtues*, states explicitly that "God looks more into the heart than into the hand."[126] Although both men and women bequeathed personal items and both men and women remembered their families most often, women left personal or household items to their parishes twice as often as men. Moreover, men and women did not give the same kinds of material goods to their parish churches. An analysis of the types of goods, rather than the amount of money left to the church, shows a gendered vocabulary of giving that reflects men's and women's different feelings toward the parish and their different life-long relationships with that institution.[127] Martha Howell observed that testators in Douai were reluctant to give moveable objects to the church because the churchwardens would have to sell them. In choosing instead to give cash, Howell argues, Douaisiens connected themselves to the church in a more "abstract" way.[128] In England, however, this was not the case, and women appeared especially eager to connect themselves to their parish in personal and visible ways through their movable property.

The most commonly donated goods, given equally by men and women, were livestock, grain, and wax. They are as ubiquitous as cash, and in rural parishes they often stood in for monetary bequests.[129] For example, Isabel Alyn of Long Bennington, in the diocese of Lincoln, left a calf to the high altar and a cow for the repair of the church, but she also left 4d. to St. Mary's altar and another 4d. to St. Thomas's altar.[130] Bequests of personal items, such as clothing or jewelry, however, reflect more personal choices and express more than generic concerns for the financial well-being of the church. Testators divided personal items among beneficiaries according to an internal set of priorities and decisions related to the perceived appropriateness of the goods for the recipient.[131]

We can see the difference between men's and women's pious bequests clearly in the surviving wills from two dioceses: Bath and Wells and Lincoln.[132] I analyzed a total of 2,317 lay wills for these two dioceses dating from

Figure 1.2. Men's and women's wills, Bath and Wells and Lincoln (1327–1536).

between 1327–1536. As is typical of late medieval English wills elsewhere, only 10 percent (234) are those of women and 90 percent (2,083) those of men. Nonetheless, if we simply count which wills left material goods, such as household objects, clothing, jewelry, or knives, we find that a greater proportion of women—71 percent (167)—left material goods to their beneficiaries, compared to only 39 percent (820) of men (see Figure 1.2). Regardless of which court proved a women's will—local or archiepiscopal—women gave more goods than men. This is a pattern that scholars have identified across medieval and Early Modern Europe.[133] The survival of a spouse, survival of children, and the stage in the family's life cycle when the testator died all influenced the nature and size of religious bequests. The survival of a spouse and children, especially those underage, decreased a testator's willingness to leave goods to their parish, but widowhood alone does not account for women's greater willingness to bequeath household or personal items to their parishes.[134]

The majority of male wills in our two dioceses—84 percent (1,636)— were from married men, who left behind a widow in need of provision; 17 percent (355) of these men's wills, moreover, specifically mention underage children or pregnant wives. Of the 619 married male testators leaving material goods in their wills, 76 percent (466) left some to family members, 26 percent (160) left some to their friends, and only 14 percent (88) left some to their parish. Of the 355 male testators with underage children, 38 percent (135) left material goods in their wills, but only 8 percent (11) of them in-

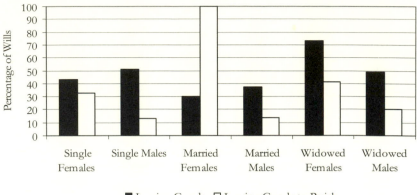

Figure 1.3a. Marital status of testators leaving goods, Bath and Wells and Lincoln (1327–1536).

cluded the parish as a beneficiary. Clearly, although married men were willing to leave goods in their wills, their parish was not a priority. Women appear to have behaved differently. Only ten women's wills (4 percent) from these dioceses are from married women and only twelve wills (5 percent) mention underage children. While a third of the married women left goods, and all left something to their parishes, the number of married women leaving wills is so small that these statistics may not be very meaningful.

Having of-age children or being childless increased the likelihood of bequests of goods, and in this situation, women again remembered their parish more often than men. Of those testators with of-age children who include goods in their wills, 26 percent of women (10) compared to only 18 percent of men (11) gave something to their parish (see Figure 1.3a, b).

Finally, widowhood for men and women increased their likelihood of leaving goods to their parishes. The majority of women's wills, 93 percent (198), are from widows, compared to only 12 percent (251) of male wills.[135] These wills typically reflect the end of a household; 49 percent of widowers (124) left material goods to a variety of benefactors, yet only 25 percent (25) of this group left goods to their parishes. On the other hand, 41 percent (60) of widowed female testators left goods in their wills to their parishes. Interestingly, the seven wills from single women imply that single women were more likely to leave goods to their parish than single men, although

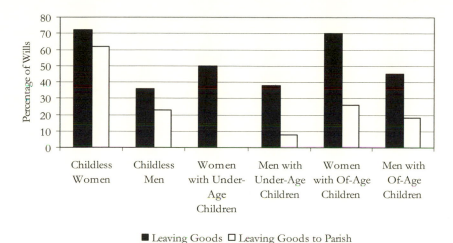

Figure 1.3b. Family age of testators leaving goods, Bath and Wells and Lincoln (1327–1536).

these numbers too are quite small and difficult to interpret. These differences reflect, in part, how men's and women's priorities changed over the course of their lives but they also echo men's and women's different priorities more generally.

Women's devotional interests become clearer when we examine what they gave and how they specified the parish should use their gifts (see Figure 1.4). Men were more likely to give books and liturgical items to their parishes than women. Men had greater literacy and greater economic resources. They were better able to afford chalices, paxes, and candlesticks than women, and they were more likely to own books.[136] Both men and women bequeathed household items, but women gave them more often. The most common items women gave were sheets and table cloths. Men, for their part, also gave dishes and the occasional piece of furniture. Clothing was the next most common item, and jewelry was the third most common item bequeathed by women; 23 percent (17) of women giving objects to their parishes gave jewelry, compared to only 4 percent of men (5). It is difficult to interpret what gifts of vestments, altar cloths, and liturgical dishes mean in the context of a will. The testator could have these items among his or her possessions and was, therefore, giving actual liturgical items. The testator could also expect the parish to purchase them, but did not specify the amount of money to be set aside. Finally, the testator might

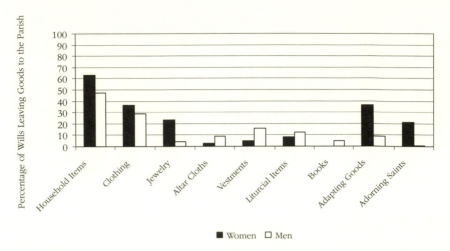

Figure 1.4. Priorities of men's and women's bequests, Bath and Wells and Lincoln (1327–1536).

have assumed that the parish would adapt some personal belongings to liturgical use, but did not leave specific directions. This vagueness, however, highlights the similarities between outfitting a house and a church.

One of the most striking differences between men's and women's gifts to their parishes was their different levels of instructions as to how their bequests were to be used. Men were more willing to let the churchwardens decide on the disposition of their bequests.[137] Men seem to have expected the churchwardens to adapt or sell the items they had given. Women, however, were less likely to leave decision making to churchwardens. Twice as often they left explicit instructions to the churchwardens for how they should adapt their gifts to make them useful. Only 9 percent of men (12) leaving goods to the parish, compared to 36 percent of women (26) specified how their gifts should be altered, adapted, or used by the parish.

Women's work often required them to piece together limited resources in what some have called an economy of makeshifts.[138] Their instructions reflect hard-learned frugality and the different meaning women gave material goods. According to Martha Howell's study of wills in Duoai, women "tended to treat property less as economic capital than as cultural and social capital."[139] In suggesting adaptations for household goods, women took into their own hands the kind of administrative details usually left to the churchwardens, probably because they had a lifetime of experience adapting things as they made do. Women may have had less to give, but their directions as to how the parish should use their gifts obliged churchwardens to address their specific concerns. By offering suggestions, women posthumously involved themselves in parish administrative decision making: they could express what they thought the parish needed and determine how their own property could be placed closer to God. Their instructions also reflect their relationship with the parish. A lifetime of cleaning up after clumsy priests and clerks and the residue of mass candles helped dissolve the boundaries between the sacred and the profane, potentially giving women the same presumption of control over the church's goods that they had over their own.[140] Their instructions underscore the ways in which women merged their notions of home economy and domesticity with their piety. Even in death, these women attended to the housekeeping of God's house, publicly asserting the importance of their relationship to the parish.

Most commonly women suggested that their bequests adorn a saint. Parish churches had numerous statues of saints. They could be in the chancel by the high altar, by side altars off the nave, or in the nave itself. Parishioners dressed up the saints for their feast day and carried images in processions as part of the annual cycle of liturgy and celebration. While fifteen women, or 21 percent, leaving goods to their parish wanted them to adorn a saint's image, only one man did. Women gave rings, kerchiefs, veils, girdles, and even clothing to the saints. Agnes Awmbler of Barroby in Lincoln, for example, gave a kerchief to "the image of Our Lady within the choir."[141] As we might expect, wealthier women gave more. When Sybil Pochon left St. Katherine "her best silk robe," in 1403, she expected the parish to clothe Katherine in it on special occasions, such as her saint's day.[142] After years of bequests, a saint could amass an elaborate wardrobe. In 1500, the image of St. Mary at Pilton, Somerset boasted a mantle adorned with fourteen rings, six pilgrim badges (three of St. James's shell and three of Henry VI), seven pairs of beads (two of amber and five of jet), two kerchiefs, and a cushion. A number of these items had been the gifts of women. Three years later, two more women had donated kerchiefs to Mary.[143] Kathleen Kamerick uncovered a similar pattern of giving in her analysis of Norfolk and Suffolk wills. There she found women were more likely than men to support parish images with bequests (32 percent of women compared to 23 percent of men).[144] Colin Richmond has argued that this pattern, seemingly widespread in England, reflected women's greater attachment to their parish churches and its contents.[145] This attachment, I would argue, grew out the greater care and attention they paid to their parishes in their life-time and the way that this care reflected and amplified their household obli-gations.

Women did more than simply dress the saints with their bequests, they also turned their clothing into vestments of liturgical significance, suggest-ing they wanted and valued involvement in the liturgy. When Elizabeth Tymprly of the parish of St. Michael's in East Hamsted, Buckinghamshire, died in 1518, she left "unto the church of Savret my wedding gown to make a vestment thereof."[146] Agnes Bruton, a wealthy widow in Taunton in the diocese of Bath and Wells, left her "red damask mantel and [her] mantel lined with silk . . . to the Mary Magdalene play" for costumes.[147] Such vivid and opulent clothing was appropriate for Mary Magdalene the prostitute-saint. Dame Margaret Chocke of Ashton in Bath and Wells left her parish her "gown of blue velvet, [her] kirtle of blue damask . . . and a coverlet of tapestry work with eagles," which were to "lie before the high altar in prin-cipal feasts and other times." When they were not in use, they were to "be occupied on a bed in the chantry house to keep [them] from moths."[148] In her final instructions, Dame Margaret shows that her household manage-ment skills were just as applicable to the parish, but perhaps not obvious to the male churchwardens entrusted with the care of her gift.

Women were inventive when it came to adapting everyday items for the mass. Most commonly they turned table cloths or sheets into altar cov-erings, suggesting their desire to see their own possessions next to the host. Recycling material and clothing into altar cloths and vestments also helped poor parishes supply the liturgy in accordance with canon law. Janet Yngyll left her kerchief to be a corporas, a cloth holder for the host.[149] Agnes Sy-grave left to "the high altar of Stowe (Lincs.) my best sheet to be an altar cloth, and my best kerchief to be a corporas."[150] Testators' suggestions show a lifetime of adapting what they had on hand to meet new needs. Avice de Crosseby of St. Cuthbert's parish in Lincoln left a wooden board to the par-ish clerk "suitable for making wax tapers," "1 carpet . . . to cover the bodies of the dead," and "1 very little leaden vessel to mend the eaves or gutter of the church."[151] Denise Marlere, a brewster in Bridgwater, Bath and Wells, gave vats from her brewing business to the vicar, the parish chaplain, the parish, the chapel of St. Katherine, the local hospital, and the Franciscan friary. She believed they would be useful to all for making wax.[152] Isabel Fitz James asked the prior of Bruton, whose monks shared their church with parishioners, to use some of her gilt dishes for mass.[153] Differences in a woman's wealth are marked by the quality and quantity of the goods they gave, but thinking about how to adapt household items for church use was not limited to only high status women.[154]

Women readily transferred to their parish churches the home economy with which they dealt every day of their adult lives. Like their houses, parish churches needed furnishing, and the saints, like their children, required clothes and care. To meet the material and physical needs of their families, women adapted what they had available to the immediate circumstances. Even in the wealthiest noble households, problems of supply could challenge the lady's household administration.[155] Such duties within the house made women flexible, because for much of their lives they could not count on being able to liquidate their material assets.

The different relationships men and women had with their parishes must have determined in important ways their choice of bequests of clothes and other property. In death, women reconceptualized their relationship with the parish. In the course of their yearly dealings with the parish, men were more readily involved with the parish's lay administration. Although some women did serve as churchwardens, as a group, they were generally excluded from parish offices.[156] Women must have expressed opinions about the running of their parishes, but they might have had to do so through their husbands. While women worked visibly and frequently for the parish, it was as an employee or volunteer who received instructions; as a benefactor, however, they gave instructions. Men did not use their wills in this fashion. Moreover, experiences with cleaning and mending church goods, or conversations with the women who did, gave women knowledge of the church's needs, which they could act on in their wills. By giving items from their households, women were shaping the religious experiences of the rest of the parish community and involving themselves directly in the adornment of the parish and its liturgy. The items they chose imposed their aesthetics and social identity onto the visual spectacle of the liturgy. In short, this form of gift giving served as a way for women to act on their knowledge of parish needs and on their desire to participate actively in the liturgy. Testamentary bequests of material goods allowed women to make an end run around their more restricted role in parish decision making, which might have otherwise ignored their input. Through their bequests, women extended the relationship they had created with their parishes through their labor, a relationship modeled on the relationship they had with their own households.

Some churchwardens' accounts record testamentary bequests from women whose wills are lost or were never written. These accounts reveal that women of humble status shared habits of parish benefaction with women wealthy enough to leave wills. In St. Margaret's, Westminster, in 1464, Robert Boteler's wife gave the parish some old curtains when she died.[157] In 1500 an unnamed old woman left a silver ring.[158] Women also donated towels or diaper cloth, plain white linen without any embroidery or other identifying marks, in the expectation the parish would use them close to the host. When Margaret White died in 1515 she left an old kerchief, and in 1529, Mother Clark gave a diaper towel.[159] Rural women gave similar bequests. In Yatton, Somerset, women were far more likely to leave the parish rings than were men. Between 1445 and 1519, fifty-eight different women left sixty-two rings compared to only eighteen men who left just twenty rings.[160] For example, husband and wife Joan and Robert Oyir died in 1470; Joan left the parish a kerchief and a ring, Robert left a bushel of barley.[161] Like the better-documented and better-off women who left wills, these women, and many others like them, donated their household goods and clothing to improve the liturgy and to have their personal possessions close to the body of Christ.[162] Even when the donor's name was lost or forgotten, this sort of gift still elevated or sacralized the mundane items of her everyday life. Women in the congregation would see this connection and the possibilities that their own goods could be put in touch with God. Adapting household items to the liturgy connected their own work to the worship of God.

Through their bequests, therefore, women were involved in adorning the liturgy. The inventory from 1500 for St. Dunstan's, Canterbury, shows that parish women gave banners, altar cloths, rood-loft hangings, and curtains to the church; men had donated the more expensive items such as books and liturgical vessels.[163] Decoration was not simply an expression of love and piety, canon law and tradition demanded it. The Easter sermon from the *Speculum Sacerdotale* explains that parishioners had to decorate their churches for Easter, and the sermon explains how they were to do it.

On the wall are curtains and hangings to be hung and raised. In the choir are to be set dosers (ornamental hangings), tapits (ornamental hangings) and bankers (tapestry chair coverings), and a veil that was before the crucifix shall be removed and a pall put behind him because that which was hidden before the passion of Christ is now opened and showed. The banners that symbolize the victory of Christ are raised up high. The altar is honored with his ornaments and with crosses set in order and in a row with the corporas case, the box with God's body, texts of the Gospels and the table of the commandments.[164]

Parishioners listening to this sermon were in a position to understand that it described contributions made by women and female listeners would be motivated to put their handiwork to such use. In attaching their household objects to the liturgy, for Easter or otherwise, women participated in the deepest message of Christianity, Christ's death and resurrection. Like elite women, these women were shaping their own Eucharistic devotions. What is more, this connection was through objects that defined their domestic and gendered lives.

Women's gifts reflected how they functioned in the world, the relationships they had to material goods and household possessions, and their identities as women. Just as women wore kerchiefs on their heads, decorative girdles around their waists, and necklaces around their necks, so, too, did the saints, who received these items as gifts from dying women. The gifts women gave to the saints in their parishes had physically marked them as women, and had often signaled the donors' marital and social statuses.[165] These gifts articulated women's concerns for marriage, family, and fertility. The wedding rings and kerchiefs left to images of the saints signaled marital status. Pots and pans showed skill at brewing or cooking or the ability to feed a family. Girdles in particular symbolized faith, as legend had it that Mary threw down her girdle to Thomas as proof of her assumption into heaven. The gift of a girdle to Mary reversed this exchange and symbolized the testator's faith.[166] Beads used in prayers showed piety, but medieval lapidaries tell us the gemstones strung on necklaces and set into rings were also apotropaic. These texts claimed that coral, which made up the set of beads a Westminster parishioner left "to be hung upon the image of St. Margaret everyday or else every single holy day as the wardens of the church shall see best,"[167] would stop bleeding and excessive menstruation, and promote fertility.[168] Beads of jet, such as those given by Sybil Pochon to the image of the Holy Trinity in her Bath parish of St. Mary de Stalle, provoked menstruation and discerned virginity in women.[169] And the set of amber beads allegedly stolen by Agnes Jorden from her parish of Netherbury, Wiltshire, helped pregnant women with childbirth.[170] Women would have valued these stones' special attributes. As such, testators often left to daughters and friends jewelry made from them. Rings and beads of coral, jet, and amber make up a significant portion of the jewelry finds in excavations of medieval London, suggesting they were indeed common possessions among the city's women.[171] Donated to the church, perhaps in thanksgiving for a successful pregnancy or recovery from an illness, they could be shared more widely by other parish women. Consequently, women's identification with objects

that signaled their domestic skills, their marital status, and their gender
seems stronger than men's and became a part of women's pious vocabulary.
Moreover, these gifts spoke to women's shared experiences as women and
their ability to forge connects between that experience and their piety.

The enthusiasm with which the wardens or the rest of the parish received these donations is difficult to gauge. Parish inventories are idiosyncratic. Some are brief appendages to the annual churchwardens' accounts;
others are more thorough. The churchwardens of Yatton, for example,
listed with reasonable regularity the parish goods in their care. These included the rings given to the parish by women.[172] Whereas in 1468 the parish had only two rings, the gifts of Christine Hycks and Joan Prewett, by
1480 the parish held twenty rings.[173] Although gifts might not meet with
everyone's approval, and indeed, some parishes undoubtedly became clut-
tered, the Yatton wardens took their duties seriously and held onto those
gifts donors did not want sold. Still, there seems to have been little, except
for pressure from the donor's family and friends, to prevent the wardens
from selling unwanted goods filling the nave.

Conclusion

The equation of the church as God's house provided a template for gendered pious behavior, making women's physical and material contributions
to their parishes different from men's. The tasks and obligations women
had in the church drew upon their responsibilities in their own houses. At
the same time, however, this template gendered pious behavior in ways that
privileged married women, rather than single women. Most single women
worked as servants, and while their daily tasks might be similar to those of
the housewife, servants did not have the same authority or level of responsibility. Yet as women cleaned and adorned God's house, they could still give
full expression to the belief that their domestic actions could express piety.
Caring for the church gave women proximity to the sacred, allowing them
to venerate the saints, express devotion to the Eucharist, and work for their
own and their families' spiritual and physical health. Men shared these concerns, but they expressed them differently. These differences not only reflected women's economic circumstances vis-à-vis men, but also their
different pious concerns and actions and household roles. The process by
which women turned their labor into piety was often creative and reflective
of a lifetime of negotiating the legal and economic limits placed on them

because of their sex. Caring for and adorning the church integrated women into the parish community, even as their sex kept them out of much of its official decision making and most parish offices. Ultimately the overlap between house and church gave women a great deal of license to involve themselves in their parish and connected them to other women, laying the groundwork for shared experiences and collective action on behalf of the parish. The shared experiences and skills of managing a household, whether opulent or impecunious, gave women resources they could use in God's house, their parish church.

Women's work for the parish fit with the gendered work expectations of the late Middle Ages, but it also fostered the behavior late medieval society feared in women. Housewives might be allowed some license with their husbands, because as wives, they provided comfort and care and knew their husbands' physical needs and weaknesses. However, the confidence and ease women felt in their own houses could also be brought to play in the parish. Through their work with the church's goods, women gained similar insight into the priest and his limitations. Such license within the church, however, was more problematic. When housewives transferred the emotional and behavioral assumptions they had in their house onto the parish, they transformed the parish into a similar kind of homey space, where they could also establish intimacy and familiarity. We see evidence of how women understood their relationship to the parish in the ways they framed their pious bequests to the church. In instructing the churchwardens on how to use their gifts, women assumed the prerogatives of the housewife, with charge of the house's provisioning and organization. Such presumption did not always sit well with the clergy. In the context of the parish, women's housekeeping could look like independence and lack of governance, especially when that familiarity led to confrontations with the priest or the churchwardens. As we will see in subsequent chapters, the clergy repeatedly condemned women's church behavior as inappropriate. In acting on the idea that the church was God's house, women created a new kind of space for themselves that challenged social expectations for women even as women acted according to these expectations. This challenge added to the belief that the fifteenth century was a time of social turmoil, and that women were assuming more influence than was warranted.

Chapter 2

Hatched, Matched, and Dispatched: Life Cycles and the Liturgy

On 6 April 1423, twelve men assembled at Stoke Gifford in Gloucestershire to testify as to the age of Maurice, son and heir of Maurice de Berkeley, knight, and his wife Joan.[1] The jurors all agreed that Maurice was at least twenty-one years old, born in Stoke Gifford, and baptized in Stoke Gifford parish church on 2 February 1401, the Feast of the Purification. As proof, the jurors offered their own memories of the rituals surrounding his birth. Henry Dagger remembered Maurice's baptism because he "carried a basin and ewer from the manor of Stoke Gifford to the church to provide water for the godfathers and godmother to wash their hands after Maurice was raised from the font." John Averay remembered he had "carried a torch from the manor to the church before Maurice the son and held it while he was baptised." John Dymmok had ridden to Bristol that day to collect Margaret Berkeley who was to be godmother. For William Perys, the day was memorable because his own daughter Joan had been baptized in the church on the same day. John Haynes had witnessed his daughter Katherine's wedding in the church that same day, while Thomas Lynde attended his sister's wedding in the church. Finally, Thomas Risby buried his brother in the churchyard on that day. With two baptisms, two weddings, and a funeral all on 2 February, the church of Stoke Gifford had been an exceedingly busy place.

These men remembered pivotal moments in the human life cycle in terms of the sacraments that marked them. By the thirteenth century, the church had delineated the seven sacraments of the Christian Church. Sacraments conferred grace on an individual and were crucial for salvation. Five of them integrated the passage of the human life cycle into the larger Christian community. Baptism marked birth; confirmation, although rarely documented in the Middle Ages, ideally marked the coming of age; marriage and ordination to the priesthood signaled a transition to adulthood, and extreme unction death. The other two, confession and communion, were annual. A Christian confessed and received communion once a year, usually around Easter.

Over the course of the late Middle Ages, the celebration of the sacraments became more elaborate as the laity added pararituals, extra adornment, furnishings, or complementary actions to the liturgies such as when John Averay held the torch at Maurice's baptism.[2] Pararituals augmented the official and required rituals of the sacrament. In the Christian liturgy, pararituals typically took the form of processions, optional adornments, such as candles, and feasts and rewards for attendants and the poor afterward. The composition of the processions and the range of adornment were highly variable. By escalating or minimizing their involvement in these sacraments, the laity incorporated their own concerns with family, status, ambition, and identity into them. These additions make the sacraments more than spiritual obligations, sacraments also became an expression of social identity and were subject to historical forces and social expectations and pressures.

In the performance of the sacraments of baptism, marriage, and extreme unction there was a tension surrounding the roles of the laity and the priest and the use of the church. Neither baptism nor marriage required a priest, nor did they need to take place in a church. Midwives fearful of a newborn's imminent death could baptize an infant moments after birth in the birthing chamber. If the baby survived, the parish priest was to bless it in the church. Couples could exchange marriage vows at home, in a tavern, or in a garden, in the presence of family, friends, employers, and even strangers. Although receiving the priest's blessing at the church was expected, it was not necessary to create a binding marriage. During the plague in 1348, the Bishop of Bath and Wells permitted laymen and laywomen to hear confessions of the dying because of the dearth of priests.[3] Generally, however, priests heard last confessions and gave the last rights, but usually to the dying in their beds, not in the church. When these liturgies did happen in a church, pararituals gave the laity different roles to play from those at their weekly masses. There they sat or stood behind the rood screen; while some listened and watched the priest in the chancel, perhaps saying prayers along with or in competition with him. Others ignored the liturgy and the priest and talked with friends, feuded with neighbors, or conducted business. But in baptism, wedding, and funeral liturgies, the laity were not just observers of the liturgy, but participants, and they were often physically much closer to the high altar, the center of liturgical attention and action.

The ability to mark or create social identity in the liturgy took on further significance in the post-plague period. Like clothing and food, pararituals were a means of expressing new or improved social position, a way of trying to fix status, or part of the attempt to forge a new identity in a changing and increasingly stratified world.

Because of women's connection to Eve and original sin, medieval liturgies officially relegated women to supporting and submissive roles. Yet women's obvious role in childbearing, their position as caregivers and nurturers of the young and sick, and their traditional responsibilities for preparing a body for burial intimately involved them in these stages of the life cycle. An additional liturgy further acknowledged women's role in childbirth. About a month after childbirth, women went through a liturgy called churching, which marked the end of their period of confinement. Churching had ancient roots. The Hebrew Bible insisted that Jewish women were impure during and after childbirth and remained so until they made a special offering and the priest said special prayers for them (Leviticus 12). Bede also mentions it, stating that it was a beneficial and pious act for a woman to be churched, but not strictly necessary. No actual English evidence for such a liturgical ceremony appears until the twelfth century.[4] Churching was connected to baptism as part of the childbirth rituals, and like the life-cycle sacraments, involved the laity in a number of possible pararituals that accompanied the service. Women's family roles as mothers, wives, and widows made them more prominent in the planning and enactment of life-cycle rituals than the liturgies actually dictated. As wives, widows, daughters, and servants, women shared concerns for lineage, social status, and survival. This chapter argues that women negotiated the conflicting roles placed on them by family and Church through their manipulation of the pararituals. Their own concerns about status, lineage, and family were a central feature of the pararituals, running parallel to or counter to the message that women were inherently sinful. To understand women's roles within these liturgies, we must consider their family position, comparing it to their husbands'.

Information on medieval baptisms, churchings, weddings, and funerals is by no means consistent. The quantity of data on funerals and death allows for detailed comparisons that are not possible for the other life-cycle liturgies. Wills and parish financial records allow for statistical comparisons of funerals according to sex and social status, while the other liturgies were not as fully documented. Historians are left to rely on much more occasional records for baptisms, churchings, and weddings, usually from court proceedings, such as proofs of age, episcopal visitations, and witness depositions. These records are more impressionistic, variable, and often recorded information about these liturgies because something went wrong. While these records allow for a general discussion of how baptisms, churchings, and weddings could differ and the range of pararituals that the laity could incorporate into liturgies, they do not permit the same quantitative analysis of the ways that pararituals varied according to status or sex of the participant that is possible for funerals. Yet a comparison of how pararituals varied in these liturgies shows that the range of variations was quite similar in all life-cycle ceremonies. The laity typically modified the list of participants, their clothing, and the numbers of candles used in the liturgy. For the funerals in some parishes, we can correlate these variations with stage of life, family status, community aspirations, and sex of the deceased. The similarities in pararitual variations in baptisms, churchings, weddings, and funerals make it likely that laity used these variations to reflect the same issues. The process of representing familial and gender roles in these liturgies was not unproblematic or simple, however. Families had to negotiate liturgical priorities, which subordinated women with their own family strategies for salvation, economic survival, and the realities of each family's dynamics. A family headed by a widow with mounting debts staged her child's baptism, her own churching, the wedding of a child, or the funeral of her husband differently from a proud and up-and-coming father. Although both might have wanted the liturgy performed correctly in order to promote the salvation of those concerned, the poor widow might defer some pararituals while the well-to-do father might add some. Moreover, the well-to-do father was likely more susceptible to social pressure and local expectations that his liturgies meet some standard of opulence and generosity than the poor widow, because his celebrations promoted his own ambitions and augmented his reputation, which depended on the opinions of observers.[5] Understanding women's roles in these liturgies requires considering a broad array of family and economic relationships. As a result, these liturgies held in tension family concerns, gender roles, social identity, and the desire for salvation.

The Clergy and the Liturgy

Proper performance of the liturgy required prayers said in particular ways, proper ritual actions, and appropriate props, such as candles, vestments, and church plate. Sermons and didactic works were adamant that the liturgy be performed in a church whenever possible, and that the sex of the person undergoing the life-cycle liturgy should be identified and appropriate gender roles emphasized. Late medieval clerical authors discussing these matters insisted that women's association with both Eve and sexuality be highlighted in the life-cycle rituals and that Lollardy should be attacked. Lollards denounced sacraments not found in the Bible, and some even argued that because women could baptize infants, they could administer other sacraments.[6] This, then, was one reason for orthodox commentators' insistence that priests perform the sacraments in church. Identifying the sex of the individual undergoing a sacrament also warned lay participants and observers that women must behave and that men must both control them and not to be led astray by them. By embedding the sexual identity of the sacrament's recipient into the life-cycle rituals, the clergy was reinforcing the patriarchal order of lay households—with husbands or fathers in charge of subordinate women.[7] This order was perhaps difficult to maintain in the actual moments of birth, marriage, and sickness and death, when women's roles were so prominent, and during a period of stagnating population, when women married later and lived away from their families. Having a priest perform the sacraments accompanying these life stages and removing them from the house as frequently as possible can be seen as a move to limit women's influence at these important moments.

The liturgies surrounding birth, marriage, and death identified the sex of the individual through actions and prayers. The *Sarum Manual*, the most common liturgical book in post-plague England, stipulated in its baptism liturgy that an infant be exorcized before it could enter the church for baptism. This exorcism took place at the church door or porch. Male babies were placed on the right side of the priest and female babies on his left. The prayers said during the exorcism also differed somewhat for male and female babies.[8]

Some days following the baby's baptism, the mother was churched, a ceremony that ended her confinement. Ideally the length of time between the birth and churching depended on the sex of the child. John Mirk explained in his sermon for the feast of the Purification (2 February) that although Mary did not need purifying, she adhered to Jewish law, which held a woman to be unclean for seven days after the birth of a boy and forty days after the birth of a girl. Mirk admonished the women listening to his sermon to "double the days of coming to church" and resuming marital relations for a girl.[9] Mirk goes on to explain that the reason for this difference is because a male fetus forms quicker in the womb than a female fetus, because "Eve vexed God more than man, therefore, she is takes longer to form than man."[10]

Sarum's wedding liturgy also treated men and women differently. When the priest inquired as to the couple's consent to the union, he asked of the man "N., will you have this woman to your wedded wife, and love her and honor her, hold her and keep her, in health and in sickness, as a husband ought his wife, forsaking all others for her, so long as you both shall live." Yet in addition to these questions, the priest asked the woman if she would "obey him and serve him, honor and keep him."[11] The bride and groom also took different vows. The groom took the woman "to my wedded wife, to have and to hold from this day forward, for better for worse, for richer, for poorer, in sickness and in health, till death do us depart, if holy church will it ordain; and thereto I plight thee my troth." The bride promised these things, but additionally promised to be "bonour (be good and obliging) and buxom in bed and at board."[12] Her vows emphasized her role as food provider and willing sexual partner. Both the inquiry into intent and the marital vows reflected an idealized household order. The liturgy also provided for different actions. As with baptism, men stood on the right and women on the left of the priest because, so the *Sarum Manual* explains "Eve was fashioned from the rib on Adam's left side." During the man's vows, the groom held the bride's right hand uncovered if this was her first marriage, covered if she had been widowed.[13] In words and actions, the liturgy identified and reinforced women's secondary status, vis-à-vis her husband and her previous marital status.

The funeral liturgy identified the sex of the individual being buried with funeral bells. The fifteenth-century funeral sermon from the *Speculum Sacerdotale* declares that, "when a person dies, bells should be rung, so that the hearers will pray for the departed, specifically, for a woman twice, . . . and for a man it is rung thrice," because, the sermons states, woman "made alienation and parting between God and man."[14] Extra funeral bells made a man's funeral more elaborate than a woman's. The sermon goes on to add "the dead ought to be borne to the earth by those who are most like them in order, craft, or degree.[15] By repeatedly asserting women's connection to Eve, the liturgies tried to countermand the otherwise prominent role women played in these moments of the human life cycle and reaffirmed their subordinate position to men.

Although many life-cycle liturgies did not have to be celebrated in a church, the clergy were wary of those that were not. In his *Instructions for*

Parish Priests, Mirk recognized the dangers of childbirth and that it might not be possible for the priest "to baptize the child with all speed." His manual instructed priests on how to teach midwives to administer baptism, even making allowances for her squeamishness if the mother had died and the baby needed to be cut out of the womb.

And teach the midwife never the less,
To have ready clean water with no mess,
Then bid her spare without shame,
To baptize the child there at home,
For 'though the child be almost born,
Head and neck and no more,
Bid her continue and wait no later
To christen it by casting on water;
And if she might see just the head,
Insist she baptize it unless it is dead;
And if the woman then dies,
Teach the midwife that she must hurry
For to undo her with a knife,
And therefore save the child's life
And hurry that it christened be,
For that is a deed of charity.
And if her heart holds great anguish,
Rather that the child should languish,
Teach her then to call a man
That in her need, he will do what he can.
For if the child be so lost,
She will weep at the high cost.
But if the child is to be born,
And in peril as you see its form,
It is right as you must bid her to do,
Cast on water and follow it through.[16]

Infants who died without baptism faced eternity in limbo. Over the course of the late Middle Ages, the laity became increasingly anxious that such occurrences not happen. Across Europe, there were shrines that many grieving parents believed temporarily resurrected deceased infants. The infants revived long enough to receive baptism before expiring again. The tomb of Philippe de Chantemilan in Vienne was one such place. Philippe died in 1451 and between 1453 and 1480, of the fifty-six miracles that happened at her tomb, a third were temporary resurrections.[17] Yet anxiety over the fate of infants should not give midwives undo power. Mirk attempts to minimize the power of midwives at this crucial spiritual moment by admonishing priests to

Teach them all to be cautious and quick
That they say the words to do the trick,
And say the words all in a row
As now I will you show;
Just this and no more,
For anything else is women's lore.[18]

The last line hints at the variety of other words and practices women added in emergency baptisms. Mirk further instructs that any household vessels used in the baptism be burned or turned over to the church, in order to prevent misuse of objects that had been used in a sacrament.[19] Underlying these instructions was an attempt to restore the division between house and church that the emergency baptism had erased and to curtail the superstitious practices of the laity.

Mirk calls a home baptism a "mischance" and insists priests interrogate parents and midwives on the propriety of the baptism,

If a child by mischance at home,
Is baptized and has his name,
If it to church is brought to you
As parents ought to do,
Then must you skillfully
Ask of them just how carefully,
Did they then compromise
When the child was baptized,
And whether the words were said correctly.
And not said wrong or imperfectly;
If the words were said in a row
As I here now do show.[20]

Robert Mannyng's didactic text *Handlyng Synne* includes the story of a midwife who erroneously christened a child with the verse "God and Saint John / Christen the child, both flesh and bone."[21] The child died and its soul was lost. Even though priests and a church were not strictly necessary, Mirk questioned women's ability to learn the simple phasing necessary for a correct baptism.

We have little evidence for midwives actually baptizing newborns. In one rare exception the midwife, Elizabeth Gaynsforde, seeing Thomas Everey's child in imminent danger of death, baptized it correctly before it was completely born, "Afterwhich the child was born and was had to the church, where the priest gave it that Christendom (blessing) that [it] lacked, and the child is yet alive."[22] Thus, even children baptized by midwives needed a further blessing from the priest. Moreover, it seems that lay people did what they could to ensure that priests perform the baptism. In the episcopal visitation for the diocese of Hereford, in 1397, the parishioners of Clunbury complained that "certain parishioners came with an infant of William Corvyger's for baptism as it was dying and could not find the said chaplain, and so it was necessary for them to go to the church of Clungonford for the baptism.[23] Even in this moment of crisis, the parishioners apparently preferred a priest to a midwife.

Mirk expressed similar anxieties about marriages performed outside of a church, although he recognized their legitimacy. Mirk warns that without the Church's involvement, the bride and groom might stray into sin because they could already be married or might be too closely related to wed. Thus he admonishes priests,

Look also they make no irregular wedding,
Lest all will be cursed in so doing.
Priest and clerk and others besides,
That this service may hold and abide,
But do right according to the legal ways
And give the banns for three holy days.
Then let them come and witnesses bring
To stand by them at their wedding;
So openly at the church door
Let them wed one another.[24]

The implication is that nonchurch weddings were secretive affairs, susceptible to error, even sin.

The clergy's concerns with the liturgy's location and with identifying the sex of the person at the center of the ceremony reflected a desire to contain heresy and to reinforce women's secondary status. Invariably the explanation offered for women's different treatment was womankind's association with Eve. Although most liturgical differences were marked by the words of the priest, in the case of funerals, it also meant that women's funerals were to be simpler than men's. Yet, when considered in light of the possible dynamics of households, and the fluid boundaries between house and church, the clergy also appear concerned with containing women's authority and influence. Whether this was solely in response to Lollardy, or just general concerns with women's behavior is difficult to say. Whatever the motivations were, the result was that the liturgies continually underscored women's subservience and offered priests numerous opportunities to admonish women to express no separate knowledge other than what the Church taught. In practice, clerical and liturgical proscriptions were not always followed. As we shall see, women's roles in the pararituals surroundings these sacraments and the identities they expressed while performing them were often more visible and complex than we might expect.

The Beginning of Life: Baptism and Churching

Documentation on the actual performance of the liturgies of baptism and churching is poor. What we do know of their celebration, however, suspects that the laity manipulated pararituals to emphasize family lineage, social status, and communal inclusion. As we saw in this chapter's opening vignette, proofs of age provide evidence for baptismal variations.[25] In a proof of age, jurors testified as to why they knew an orphaned heir or heiress was of age and able to come into their inheritances.[26] To be sure, the baptisms jurors remembered were those of the elite, but the types of variations noted were well within the reach of the less well-off. The variations we find speak to a family's desire for integrating the child into the local community, pride in family lineage, and display of status. None of these concerns were unique to the elite; it is not difficult to imagine peasants and lesser townspeople, as they purchased high-status clothing for themselves, and aspired to an improved social position, that they also adapted or emulated the kinds of variations they observed in the ritual celebrations of their betters. Nor is it unlikely they would impose their own meanings onto these pararituals in their own celebrations.

Fundamental to jurors' memories of baptisms were who participated in them and how. Unless the midwife had to baptize the baby, mothers were not part of the baptism. Still, she may have had input into who the godparents would be, and what the child would wear at the baptism.[27] The baptismal festivities started with fetching godparents and bringing the baby to church, an action that typically involved women. John Spensere explained he was

present when William Anketil came from his house at Leigh where Thomas was born and asked Katharine wife of Arnold Fauconer to be godmother. Consenting, she asked him to accompany her to the church at Wimborne Minster. He went, was present at the baptism and returned with her to her house where she gave him bread, cheese and good red wine and thanked him.[28]

Many jurors noted who carried the baby to the church. In 1319 Adam de Hope testified that "he was servant of William the father, and went to the church with the women who carried the said Griffin to be baptized."[29] William Martyn and William Gamman said they had gone to church together to hear mass "and met Christine de Ichene, the midwife, carrying Richard to the church.[30] These processions, large or small, stayed in the minds of the men who observed them because of their role in the festivities or the roles played by their family, friends, and neighbors. Jurors often remembered what the babies had worn. In 1407, Nicholas Turpyn commented on Henry de Lylburrn's baptismal wrapping of silk, while Thomas Gray had been wrapped in a red cloth.[31] Thomas Fox, a skinner, remembered he had sold John Mitford's grandfather a fur of pure grey for 100s. "in which John was wrapped when carried to church for baptism."[32] Although babies needed wrapping for warmth, the choice of material and its color displayed and maybe even asserted the family's status and marked the occasion as special. The social meaning of clothing was all the more significant after the attempts at sumptuary legislation, which defined cloth and personal adornment in terms of rigid social distinctions.[33]

Most memories of baptisms revolve around the varied roles played by participants within the community. Holding candles and the Bible, fetching water, and ringing bells all involved different people in the baptism, and helped to secure the event in people's minds. Walter Frenssh says "he saw a girl carry a silver gilt basin before Alice [de Sancto Mauro] to the church."[34] Thomas Dansey of Webton, remembered that "at the father's request [he] held a holy wax candle during the baptism.[35] John Ruyhale remembered that his role in Maud Dicleston's baptism was to carry "the basin and ewer to Besford church for the godfather and godmothers to wash their hands."[36] During John Botiller's baptism in 1387, John Skydemour "filled the font with water."[37] Other items needing portage to the church were the salt and the chrisom cloth, and carrying these items involved yet other members of the parish.[38] William Longe saw Alice Laceby carrying "le crysome" to the church for the said John Munson.[39] After the baptism, the proud father typically rewarded observers with a celebration at the church, followed by a larger party at the house. Providing for the party further involved the local community and enforced the father's role in the local hierarchy. William

Wryht remembered he was butler to Henry Heton at that time, and delivered bread and wine for the baptisms.[40] John de Leone said he saw the chaplain, the godfathers, and the godmother raise the infant from the font, and afterwards "drank red Gascon wine there."[41]

Non-elite families, like their social betters, also added and subtracted pararituals to baptisms as they saw fit. Some families in Westminster spent money for extra candles at their children's baptism. The variety of candles parents purchased ranged from two tapers to four torches, with costs ranging from 2d. to 48d. While individual families might have spent different amounts for christening boys and girls, there was no discernible code for how many torches or tapers represented a male or female child. Gerard Lumberd had two torches for the baptism of his son, while Thomas Staning only had two tapers for his.[42] Because torches cost more than tapers, Lumberd might have been making a statement about his wealth and respectability. As a probable foreigner, he might also have been incorporating Lombard traditions into his child's English baptism or asserting his piety in the face of antiforeigner sentiment.[43]

Elaborate ceremonies served the dual purpose of displaying a family's status and position in the community and fixing the date of an heir's birth in the minds of witnesses. The latter would prove valuable should the inheritance later be disputed.[44] But the former also meant something to those observing and participating. For jurors remembering long-ago baptisms, participation and their proximity to a noble or gentle family were central to their memories. Through their participation in the sacrament and then again as jurors, they accrued status themselves.

The mother's churching completed the rituals surrounding birth. After childbirth, women enjoyed a period of confinement that limited their work and their outside social interactions. Female neighbors, friends, and family members helped out with household obligations during this period. Wealthier women enjoyed a longer period of rest after the birth in more elaborate surroundings than their poorer counterparts.[45] Churching generally occurred four to six weeks after the birth, after women had recovered from the aftereffects of childbirth. First the new mother, sometimes called a childwife, donned a veil and processed to the churchyard, accompanied by a variety of women friends, neighbors, and female relatives, many of whom had probably attended the birth. She went up to the church door or porch where she knelt with a candle in her hand and received a blessing and a sprinkling of holy water from the priest. She then went into the church for mass. During the offertory, she processed to the altar with her attendants and presented an offering of a candle and a penny, and returned the baptismal or chrisom cloth. At the end of the mass, the women would receive the blessed bread before anyone else attending mass.[46]

Scholars have debated the meaning of churching because the ritual incorporated the dual notions of women's bodies needing purification and celebrating a successful delivery. Childbirth was a dangerous event, and many women and their babies died. Not only was thanksgiving appropriate, but in anthropological terms, reintegration into the community was necessary after confronting such a crisis.[47] Gail Gibson described medieval churching as women's theater, with a focus on women and the sanctification of women's bodies.[48] Even after the Reformation ended most pre-Reformation rituals and practices, women insisted on keeping churching, showing that it had some meaning and value to them. Early Modern scholars have thus offered a variety of interpretations of its significance. Keith Thomas saw it as a superstitious holdover that focused on women's inferiority and impurity, while others have seen it as a clerical imposition and a sign of medieval misogyny.[49] Those who have focused particularly on churching's meaning to women also present a range of interpretations. Adrian Wilson looking at women in the seventeenth century saw confinement and churching as a time when gender norms were reversed, raising the possibility of an alternative world where women were in charge.[50] Churching marked the mother's transition from the all-women's world of childbirth and her lying-in back to a world of subordination to men.[51] However, David Cressy downplayed women's independence during their confinement, viewing it instead as a time of women's sociability.[52]

The variety of opinions about churching comes, in part, from the varied roles laywomen could play in the ritual, and the obvious clash between ideas about sex as sinful and impure, children as desirable, and the marital status of the parents. The churching service for a woman who had suffered for many years from infertility would have differed in local and personal significance from one for a woman with too many children to feed, or who had given birth to an illegitimate baby.[53] Although scholars have focused less on the variety of pararituals, Becky Lee has shown the *Sarum Manual* left a great deal of room for local and personal variation, a mutability matching the multivalent meaning of the ceremony itself. By choosing the number of candles and members of the procession, and by wearing special clothing, women were able to interpret for themselves a liturgical celebration originating in clerical ideas of women's pollution and impurity.

The number and status of those included in the churching procession would have said something about the woman being churched. It exhibited a woman's network of friends and associates. Processional order must have mattered as it did in other contexts.[54] Even poor women had a chance to take center stage in the church. It is likely that the local midwife who helped with the birth would have been part of the churching procession as well. Other participants would have included female neighbors, friends, and family members. When the vicar of Woolaston (Hereford) "maliciously and without authority . . . refused to minister the purification to one Amiot Howel after child-bearing," the friends who would make up her churching processions interceded with the church authorities on her behalf.[55] The women's protest hints at the close relationship and mutual support of those in the churching ritual.

Both the birthing room and the church were decorated for the occasion.[56] Some parishes, such as St. Margaret's, Westminster, had a special churching pew for women to sit in when they were "to be purified."[57] Similarly, the parish of St. Mary's Dover (Kent) had a "childwife's pew" that they loaned out to other parishes.[58] The fact that other parishes borrowed it suggests it was special, perhaps carved with images appropriate to the liturgy. The childwife's pew served as a way of separating the childwife from the rest of the congregation before she returned to her accustomed place at the next service. Some parishes had special vestments, which further identified the childwife's liminal status. An inventory from the Cambridge parish of St. Mary the Great records a "cloth of tapestry work for the churching of wives lined with canvas."[59] The London parish of St. Peter Cornhill used special candlesticks for the occasion.[60] The decorations remind us of the special nature of the liturgy, the connections between women's domestic concerns and their parish ones, and the link between houses and churches. After these services, it would have been women who washed and scoured the special vestments, altar cloths, and candlesticks.

Part of the churching ritual was the mother's offering. In most parishes the offerings went to the priest; in Saffron Walden, Essex, however, the childwife's offering of a penny went into the parish's coffers.[61] The guild certificate for the parish's Corpus Christi guild also specified that any poor pregnant woman arriving in the town was to receive a chrisom cloth for her baby's baptism and a penny for her churching offering.[62] These local idiosyncrasies emphasize the communal aspects of this ceremony. By taking the churching offerings, the parish highlighted each woman's relationship with the parish community rather than to the priest. Her contributions became part of the revenue for maintaining the nave, an important aspect of parish membership.

Although there was no male equivalent to churching, it was not a ceremony performed in the absence of men and it was not without meaning for men. A priest presided over the liturgy, and his presence introduced moralizing and hierarchy into the ceremony. The contrast between his celibacy and the mother's fecundity emphasized the differences between the laity and the clergy. At Clunbury, Hereford, the vicar violated these boundaries when he refused to church Maiota Crowe "unless she offered what pleased him."[63] Many jurors in proofs of age testified that they had attended the mother's churching. In 1355, John Tymperson of Cumberland said he witnessed the churching of John de Eglesfeld's wife because he was at the church to bury his own mother.[64] Husbands may have also attended their wives' churching. In the London parish of St. Bride's, a certain Sir Nicholas Gryffyn attended his wife's churching outfitted with a new pair of hose. For him, the ceremony was clearly a celebration.[65] We might speculate that the celebrations were not only over his wife's survival and health, but also the resumption of sexual relations and her household duties. Whether confinement was a period of female rule or not, household routines were upset when the housewife was indisposed.

It was also customary for husbands to host a celebratory meal after the churching. Lee argues that among the elite, this feast "allowed the father of an heir to reinforce and enhance his social and economic ties and standing among his peers and neighbors through displays of material wealth and largess."[66] A medieval man attained social maturity when he married and produced an heir. Thus Lee concludes, "the customs and practices surrounding the birth of a child were as integral to men's lives as they were to women's."[67] It showed his new position within the community as a father and perpetuator of a lineage. Most evidence for this ceremony comes from the aristocracy and gentry, but it was practiced by those in the lower classes as well. In his modest will, Robert Rutter of the Lincolnshire parish of Burgh le Mash left half a quarter of malt, a bushel of wheat, and a ewe for his wife's churching feast.[68]

Baptism and churching liturgies were malleable enough for families to use them to express concerns for family ambition, a successful birth, promotion of lineage, and social status. The visible roles played by laywomen in both services underscored their central role in birth and the importance of the safe delivery of a child to every family. While the formal liturgies of baptism and churching emphasized women's impurity and secondary status, women and their families tempered these messages with the addition of pararituals. The pararituals chosen by families and women offered a means of contemplating women's relationship to their families and their roles within their household. Manipulation of the liturgy and the incorporation of celebrations after them suggest that women and their families saw a new birth as a time of joy and sociability, rather than yet another occasion to ruminate on the impurity of women.

Marriage

Even in this period of late age of marriage, most medieval men and women married. Marriage was the foundational relationship of medieval society and it was used as a metaphor to describe the relationship between God and the Church. Much scholarly debate surrounding medieval marriage concerns the age of marriage for men and women, the role of emotion or love, and legal issues.[69] Michael Sheehan argued that medieval marriage litigation in the late fourteenth century "reveals an astonishingly individualistic attitude to marriage and its problems."[70] This individualistic attitude was reflected in the ways that couples made marriages and the often incidental role played by Church and parish. Shannon McSheffrey, however, has argued that by the fifteenth century, marriage was less individualistic, because people received greater supervision and advice in choosing their spouse.[71] In fifteenth-century London, and possibly elsewhere, this greater supervision reflected a concern for civic order, social boundaries, and confidence in civic Christianity.[72] Yet greater supervision did not diminish the ability of families to create weddings that mirrored their concerns for the relationship.

Ideally, during the fourteenth and fifteenth centuries, the road to marriage required the couple to exchange promises of future intent before witnesses, followed by a priest reading the banns. The banns publicized the intended marriage and uncovered impediments to the union, such as bigamy or consanguinity. If no one objected after the banns, the couple would solemnize the marriage at their parish church, often at the church porch, and always before witnesses and a priest. There they exchanged vows in the present tense. Then the couple and witnesses moved into the church for the nuptial mass.[73]

In reality, however, all that was legally needed to make a binding marriage was the exchange of vows in the present tense, or the exchange of vows in the future tense followed by consumption.[74] Marriages, moreover, often took place outside the church. In one London case from 1470, witnesses stated the marriage between John Bedeman and Agnes Nicholas had taken place in a garden "beneath a vine."[75] In another, William Forster and Ellen Grey allegedly exchanged vows "in the tavern at the sign of the Greyhound in East Cheap, on a certain bench across from the door of the tavern."[76] Three-quarters of the alleged marriage contracts litigated in London's church courts took place in locations other than a church.[77] A similar situation prevailed in York as well.[78] Scholars have puzzled over the frequency of such marriages. Some argue such venues signaled the laity's attempts to circumvent clerical influence. McSheffrey, however, has argued that the laity intended no such duplicity. The laity had co-opted aspects of the proceedings in an effort to make the ceremony more meaningful. Exchanging vows outside the church was merely the ritual that preceded the solemnization of the marriage and was not an attempt to deny the liturgy.[79]

The location where a couple exchanged vows reflected their status and possibly their families' and friends' hopes and concerns for the marriage and the couple's relationship. In analyzing the different locations used by couples for their exchange of vows, McSheffrey observed that a location other than a church was not an obstacle to marriage, but that not all venues were equal. Marriages contracted in bedchambers or streets, for example, were of questionable propriety because of their association with sex and prostitution.[80] Those who were young, of lower station, or who had no domestic space of their own might contract their marriage in a tavern. These marriages were probably less supervised by elders, but they were not necessarily disreputable.[81] In London, where much of the marriage-age population were immigrants from other parts of the kingdom, working as servants and apprentices, employers often stood in for absent parents. The employer's role could also be reflected in the venue of the exchange of consent.[82] Robert Arwom and Joan Deynes, for example, exchanged consent in Richard Reynold's shop.[83] Halls and gardens where only invited people could witness the exchange of vows brought respectability to the proceeding, not only to the couples themselves, but to the hosts as well. In well-to-do houses, owners displayed their wealth and status with oak paneling, pewter and silver plates, and other luxury goods. A marriage conducted in this space allowed the family's or the employer's wealth and respectability to serve as a backdrop for the proceedings.[84] In the eyes of the laity, therefore, location reflected the couple's social standing, connections, and resources, but not necessarily a lack of respectability or legitimacy.

Although the *Sarum Manual* called for extensive gender-specific vows and actions, memories of weddings recounted in witness depositions recalled only the hand clasping, exchange of simple vows, and often a kiss afterwards. Deponents never commented on longer vows, the blessing of the ring, or the couple's prostration before the altar during the nuptial mass.[85] The pararituals over which the laity had control and which they chose for their personal significance were the things that lodged in the memories of witnesses. Like the jurors in proofs of age, deponents' personal role in the proceedings, the location, and the material trappings distinguished the event in their minds.

As witnesses vividly recalled, the occasion of a marriage meant giving gifts, special clothes, and exchanging rings. These objects had meaning beyond personal affection or liturgical requirement. Courtship rituals involved exchanging gifts, often coins, kerchiefs, or jewelry. Agnes Whitingdon claimed that John Ely had loaned her his first wife's coral beads as part of their marriage negotiations.[86] Coral, commonly believed to promote fertility and bring love, would have been an appropriate gift for a new bride on a number of levels.[87] When John Brocher courted Joan Cardif, he gave her "a certain kerchief which she gratefully accepted from him, kissing him and tying the kerchief around her neck."[88] That same kerchief worn on her head would identify her as a married woman to people who saw her on the street or at church. For the wedding itself, the bride and groom often wore special clothes. The parish of Westminster had a "circlet for maidens when they be married," to wear in their hair.[89] In a bigamy case, Arnold Snaryng stated Robert Grene wore "a gown of murrey," while Maude Knyff wore "a black tunic or kirtle with an apron" when they exchanged their vows.[90] For some, wedding clothes continued to have special meaning. As we saw in the last chapter, Elizabeth Tymprly of East Hamsted, Buckinghamshire, left her wedding dress to the church of Savret to remake into a vestment.[91]

The liturgy also called for a wedding ring for the bride, but many men apparently wore them too.[92] Thus, here is another example of ritual elaboration surrounding marriage. The larger significance of these rings is apparent in the numbers of men and women who left them to the parish at their deaths. In this gift, the deceased articulated a powerful marital-style relationship with the ring's recipients be they saints or parish communities more generally. Embedded in all the objects exchanged around the marriage were hopes for the future prosperity, economic security, health, family ambitions, expectations about gender roles, and personal affection.

The apparent frequency with which couples exchanged vows in places other than their parish churches caused Mirk to worry over the legitimacy of these marriages. In his *Instructions for Parish Priests*, he tells priests "to stand by them at their wedding; / So openly at the church door."[93] Mirk associated weddings held outside of church with secrecy and lack of supervision. As with a house baptism, he argued that errors could arise. Family and female supervision, implicit in a household setting, were not enough. However, the laity's choice of nonchurch locations for the exchange of vows reflects the context of the courtship, the status of the couple, and the proximity of friends and family. Indeed, if marriage contracts exchanged in homes, gardens, and taverns before friends, family, or employers were not attempts to circumnavigate the clergy, but a prelude to the solemnizing of the union at the church, then location was a way of introducing other concerns into the marriage relationship. Although the laity recognized the importance of marriage, they expressed these sentiments in different terms than the clergy. Like other church rites, the laity appropriated the marriage ceremony, added their rituals, and made it socially meaningful. The clergy could not completely dictate the meaning of the life-cycle sacraments to the laity, nor could they choreograph the look and feel of these events.

Funerals and Social Identity

Death required its own set of rituals. The high mortality rate in late medieval England made the deaths and funerals of friends, family members, spouses, and employers a common experience. The Christian belief in life after death provided the context for the rituals surrounding death—the preparation of the body, the funeral, and the burial. Fully articulated in the thirteenth century, the doctrine of purgatory further informed ritual behaviors. Since most Christians, so the Church taught, had not lived virtuous enough lives, they were to spend time in purgatory working off their sins. The prayers of the living could help shorten this time, and elaborate institutions evolved to facilitate these prayers in perpetuity.[94] Continental studies have argued that funeral practices grew more elaborate in the late Middle Ages, although scholars offer urbanism rather than purgatory and plague as explanations. Migration cut people off from ancestral graveyards and they compensated with elaborate funerals that identified them and their social position.[95] In Bury St. Edmunds, England, Robert Dinn found that late fifteenth- and early sixteenth-century wills had more funeral arrangements than those in previous centuries. He argued that this reflected a greater interest in planning their funerals.[96] Social pressure and local competition must also have contributed to an increase in funeral pomp.[97]

More than other liturgical celebrations, scholars have studied how funeral rituals manifested status. Vanessa Harding explained a funeral was "an event scripted by its central participant, or by those to whom he or she had delegated that power."[98] Although this could be said of baptisms, churchings, and weddings as well, parishioners left a great deal more written and physical evidence for funerals and other death rituals than other life-cycle liturgies. Observers did not generally comment on the funerals of the lower classes, but we have descriptions of royal or noble funerals that emphasized their long processions, large doles to the poor, huge funeral feasts, and elaborate tombs. Most funeral instructions come from wills, sources skewed toward a relatively elite and male segment of the population. The lower social orders were unable to afford elaborate funerals, but a careful reading of the evidence suggests that far down the social scale, men and women used funerals in much the same manner as the elites.

Because the non-elites left fewer records, we know little about differences between men's and women's funerals. In studies of burial locations both Vanessa Harding and Robert Dinn found that women were more likely to request burial locations near their spouses than men, but they do not assess the role of gender in funerals.[99] Sharon Strocchia found little difference between Florentine men's and women's funerals, finding that families focused on representing lineage in the funerals of both men and women.[100] After the Reformation, when individual funeral sermons became popular in England, sermons for women's funerals tended to celebrate the woman's motherhood and wifely devotion, sentiments inappropriate in men's funeral sermons.[101] This evidence then shows women's death rituals across the divide of the Reformation and geography revolving around their gender identities and their connections to their husbands.

We are fortunate in having a wealth of information about the funerals celebrated at St. Margaret's, Westminster, and at St. Mary's, Sutterton (Lincs.). In these parishes we can see the ways in which people of lower social status manipulated the funeral liturgy and its attendant pararituals and what meanings these variations had beyond simply aping their betters. These findings are suggestive of how they might also have shaped the other life-cycle liturgies. The parishes of St. Margaret's and St. Mary's both sold candles and other liturgical items or furnishings for funerals. Although many other parishes also sold funeral furnishings, they generally only sold them to the local elite. For reasons that are not entirely clear, the vast majority of parishioners in Westminster and Sutterton bought from the churchwardens at least a penny candle for their funerals. As a result, the churchwardens' accounts record funeral information on nearly everyone who died in the parish, rather than just those local elite who purchased a burial plot inside the church. Between 1460 and 1535, the Westminster accounts record 12,978 lay funerals, not including children, while between 1462 and 1534 Sutterton held 623 lay funerals, not including those for children.[102] This volume and consistency of funeral information makes it possible to study the funerals of those who generally left no wills: the poor, the middling sort, and married women. Although the accounts only provided information on what a family purchased from the parish for a funeral, they give some insight into what actually happened during these events, rather than what a testator hoped would happen, as stipulated in his or her will.[103]

The communities that produced these records are quite different. St. Margaret's, Westminster, was an urban parish, lying just outside of London, with between two and three thousand parishioners.[104] For a London-area parish, this was very large. In London the average parish size was probably closer to 300.[105] Westminster was the royal capital and the location of the wealthy and influential Benedictine abbey of St. Peter. London's close proximity made Westminster a highly urbanized place. Pilgrims to the shrine of Edward the Confessor, monks living in the Abbey, lawyers and petitioners to the king's court, and those accompanying the king and queen created an array of economic opportunities for those living in the parish. Most inhabitants worked in trade, manufacturing, and victualing.[106] London and Westminster also attracted many immigrants seeking economic opportunity. Householders, innkeepers, and taverns needed servants, and artisans and merchants had apprentices, while trade drew men and women from the continent. Westminster's population was diverse, including people from across the kingdom and the sea. Despite its proximity to wealth, though, Westminster was not a particularly wealthy community, and its permanent residents spanned the social and economic spectrum.[107] Sutterton, in contrast, was a small rural fenland parish in the western corner of the Wash, lying along the Witham River, in Lincolnshire. It contained approximately 75 to 100 households.[108] Sutterton was in the gift of Crowland Abbey. Although mentioned in *Domesday*, it had no salterns, castle, marketplace, or religious house. Its inhabitants made their living as farmers and had responsibilities for maintaining a portion of the Foss Dyke, to keep the river at bay.[109] The difference between the richest and poorest inhabitants, according to the 1524 lay subsidy, was not a broad as it was in Westminster.[110]

Despite social and economic differences, the records for these parishes compare well. Both sets of accounts cover nearly the same time period. St. Margaret's churchwardens' accounts begin in 1460 and Sutterton's in 1462. Sutterton's end in 1534, Westminster's continue up through the seventeenth century, but I have stopped my analysis in 1535, the eve of the Reformation.[111] Because of gaps, fifty-eight years of accounts for this period survive for Westminster and fifty-two years for Sutterton. These two parishes are a good comparison because the records cover the same time span and the settlements are so different. Differences in funeral practices relate to the ways parishioners incorporated local concerns and traditions into funerals, while similarities show how urban and rural dwellers shared many of the same family and economic concerns.

The sex ratio of the funerals for both parishes is somewhat problematic. In Westminster, 5,482 (42 percent) funerals were for women and 7,496 (58 percent) were for men, for a sex ratio of 135 males to every 100 females.[112] Male apprentice migration, the presence of the royal and law courts, and the fact that many women moved away when their husbands died makes it possible that more men than women died in the city, but men may be overrepresented in the records as well. The ratio is similar, however, to what Roger Finlay found for late sixteenth- and early seventeenth-century London.[113] Sutterton's sex ratio is more difficult to explain. The accounts record 262 funerals for women and 361 funerals for men, giving Sutterton the same sex ratio as Westminster.[114] Although unmarried rural women immigrated to towns and cities in greater numbers than men after the plague, the vagaries of recordkeeping combined with a small name pool and the records' periodic failure to explain whether the candles were for a funeral or a subsequent memorial mass make it likely that I have inadvertently counted some men more than once. Removing 151 questionable entries reduces the number of funerals and yields a sex ratio for Sutterton of 47 percent women and 53 percent men, a more reasonable figure if we assume women migrated out of the community in larger numbers than men.[115]

In either parish, the rituals surrounding death were similar. They began with the writing of a will if there was to be one. John Hore remembered in his proof-of-age testimony that "afterwards the chaplain who baptised came to his house to make a will for Margaret his mother, now deceased."[116] Once the testator died, women prepared the body for burial, sewing it into a shroud before it left the house.[117] In 1515, Mistress Brailles, a seamstress and supplier of cloth, provided the winding sheet for Mother Rogers, an almswoman dependant on the charity of Westminster's Assumption Guild.[118] A death knell from the parish bells would be tolled at this point, and those within hearing were to stop and pray for the departed.[119]

Liturgical celebrations were also held the day before the burial with the vespers office of the dead, called *placebo*. The next day, a procession led the body to the church for the matins office of the dead, called *dirge*. Accompanying the body were family, friends, and associates. Women seem to have been more likely to accompany a woman's corpse. In Lambeth, Surrey, the churchwardens paid John Tayler's wife 6d. "for bread and ale and for bearing of 3 torches to the burying of Mother Snow," another woman dependent on parish charity.[120]

After the liturgy, mourners processed the body to its burial location, usually the churchyard, but sometimes into the church itself, or to a local a monastery or convent.[121] Most people were buried in churchyards, but a handful of the better-off parishioners were interred inside the church, and they sometimes stipulated in their wills exactly where they wished to be buried. Alice Baron of St. Margaret's, Westminster, asked to be buried "in the parish church in middle isle by my pew side," while Elizabeth Abraham of Sutterton wanted to be buried "by my husband Robert Abraham within the church."[122]

Once the body was interred, the family was to pray for the soul of the departed in order to lessen its time in purgatory. The range and form of these intercessory prayers was broad.[123] The better off could afford to endow memorial masses at monthly and yearly anniversaries when the funeral was reenacted. Those who were wealthier still could endow a chantry and found a chapel, with a priest hired specifically to pray for the soul of departed.[124] For most parishioners, though, commemoration came either informally or communally when the parish prayed for all the dead at the community obit held each year on the feast of All Souls (2 November).

Westminster's churchwardens' accounts delineate in extensive, even tedious, detail the various tapers, torches, and bell ringings sold to parishioners for funerals. The ways parishioners combined candles and bell ringing made their funerals highly variable both in terms of their cost and their elaborateness. For example, a woman of middling means, Agnes Blacknall, had four tapers and two torches at her funeral, wealthy benefactor Henry Abingdon's funeral had twelve torches, a knell, and an in-church burial, and the poor woman, Isabel Albright, had only two tapers at her funeral, by far the most common funeral accoutrement.[125] Analyzing funerals in terms of overall cost, elaborateness, and variety of pararituals reveals interesting but subtle differences between men's and women's funerals. Sutterton's records are less detailed than Westminster's and they can only be used to analyze the cost of funerals and burial location of the dead. For example, when the wife of Robert Link died in 1462, her family paid 4d. on "her burial day," whereas William Alger's family only paid 1d. for his burial day in 1483.[126] We might assume the 4d. bought a more elaborate funeral, or more candles, but the records do not provide the specifics. Nonetheless, even with less fulsome record keeping, these churchwardens' accounts reveal how funeral arrangers both modified church liturgy and expressed anxieties surrounding family and social standing that the death of a family member brought to the fore.

Although visual cues unrecorded in documents may have alerted observers to the sexual identity of the deceased, a simple comparison of men's and women's funerals reveals broad similarities rather than differences. At Westminster, 60 percent of all funerals, male and female, had only two tapers. Even the funerals of those labeled "poor" generally had two tapers.[127] Thus, most men and women in the parish, whether working, living hand to mouth, or dependent on parish charity had funeral liturgies lit by two tapers. What is more, and perhaps more surprising, men and women whose families could afford more elaborate funerals received very much the same combinations of tapers, torches, or bells. As we see in Figure 2.1, 4 percent of men's (330) and 5 percent of women's (257) funerals used four or more torches, 9 percent used bells (389 female funerals and 499 male funerals), and 7 percent used two types of liturgical items, such as torches and tapers, or tapers and bells. When the wealthy gentleman brewer, John Pomfrett wrote his will in 1531, he asked that he be buried "in the example of Edward Stockwode's wife if it may please my lord Abbot and the parish of the same."[128] Bartelyn Stockwood had had a lavish funeral in 1528,[129] and apparently Pomfrett had no reservations about imitating a woman's funeral. Whatever message it sent to observers, gender was not strictly encoded

For those men and women in Westminster who were buried in the churchyard, there also appears to be little difference between the sexes in the costs of their funerals. Men's funerals cost on average 8.3d., and women's 7.6d. The ha'penny difference means that women's funerals on average cost 92 percent of men's. In Sutterton, families also generally spent the same amount on men's and women's funerals, men's funerals costing on average 4.8d. and women's 4.6d. Women's funerals here cost 96 percent of men's.

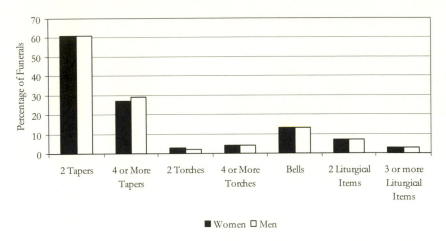

Figure 2.1. Men's and women's funeral accessories, Westminster (1460–1535).

A plurality of Sutterton parish, 34 percent or 177 individuals, also had the cheapest funerals. These funerals appear to be less elaborate than Westminster's ubiquitous two-taper funerals. At Sutterton the least elaborate funerals had only a 1d. candle. Thus, in both parishes, a basic comparison of men's and women's funerals reveals few differences in furnishings or in cost.

Some of these similarities disappear when we compare the funerals of men and women buried in the church itself. In both parishes, in-church burials cost 6s. 8d. and wealthier members of both communities exercised this option. The overall percentage of men and women buried inside St. Margaret's was similar—5 percent of women (272) and 6 percent of men (452). However, the composition of the funerals accompanying these in-church burials differed between the sexes. As Figure 2.2 shows, among the men and women buried in the church, women tended to have more elaborate funerals than the men, even though women's funerals cost slightly less, only 129.5d. compared to the average cost of men's funerals, which was 133.5d. Because so few Sutterton parishioners received an in-church burial, less than 1 percent of men and women (eight women and twelve men, respectively), they cannot really be compared. Yet 15 percent of women, compared to 11 percent of men, had expensive funerals, those costing between 5d. and 14d. Thus, in both parishes, a greater percentage of women than men had more elaborate funerals. These findings are difficult to reconcile

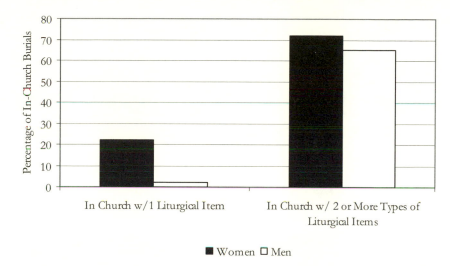

Figure 2.2. Funeral accessories for men and women buried in St. Margaret's Church, Westminster (1460–1535).

with clerical instructions that men's funerals should be performed with greater elaboration than women's on account of women's connection to Eve.

Some of the underlying motivations for these differences become clearer when we compare the funerals of married couples in Westminster, where the corroborative evidence of family relationships is more abundant.[130] This analysis also shows correlations between gender and marital status at death and family life cycle and funeral display. I have only been able to identify 150 couples who both had funerals in Westminster prior to 1536. Although they are only 2 percent of the funerals recorded in the churchwardens' accounts, the findings are suggestive of the interplay of gender, life cycle, and economic status in funerals.

Based on burial location, cost, and amount of funeral adornment, the funerals of Westminster couples fall into four groups: (1) in-church burials with two or more types of liturgical items, such as tapers, torches, and bells; (2) in-church burials with only one kind of liturgical item such as torches or tapers or bells; (3) churchyard burials with two or more types of liturgical items; and (4) churchyard burials with one kind of liturgical item. Of our 150 couples, 127, or 85 percent, had funerals different from one another. These differences can be further correlated to the couple's social status and

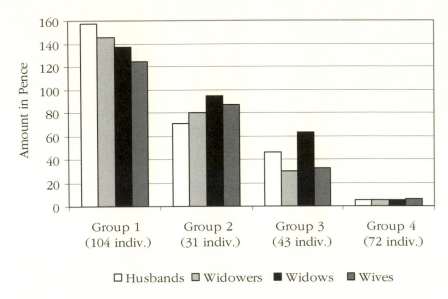

Figure 2.3. Cost of funerals for 127 married couples based on marital status at death, Westminster (1460–1535). A few couples in this sample buried two and three spouses, so the 127 couples include 250 individuals, not 254.

the marital status of the deceased at death; whether the woman was a wife or a widow and the man a husband or widower. This analysis reveals whether surviving widows spent more on their husbands' funerals than surviving widowers spent on their wives, or whether widows had more or less spent on their funerals than widowers. In the end, we will see that different segments of the population had different priories when staging the funerals of their spouses (see Figure 2.3).

The group with the most expensive funerals, costing on average £1 1s. 2d., were members of the local elite. Of the fifty-eight men in this group, fifteen left wills, eighteen held either parish or civic office, and six were described as gentlemen in their wills, leases, or by the churchwardens' accounts.[131] Eleven of these couples and four widows directly rented property from the Abbey. For those in this high-status group, funerals asserted family status, piety, and public visibility. Katherine Baynard's funeral instructions, for example, speak directly to these concerns. In her will, she specified that "23 children bear 23 tapers about my hearse the day of my burial." She also requested that thirty masses (a trental) be said the day of her burial.[132] The churchwardens' accounts show that when she died a few days after making her will, her funeral had knells, peals, and four torches accompanying her body for an in-church burial.[133] This amount of ritual would have attracted notice, and identified Katherine Baynard as prosperous, charitable, and respectable. The twenty-three children might also reflect her identity as a mother. Whatever her display meant to those who saw it, she hoped it would also bring prayers for her soul. Family members who survived her and remained in Westminster were no doubt making claims about themselves as they oversaw such an elaborate funeral. They could be sure of their own increased visibility within the parish community and perhaps even basked in the glow of their parents' piety.

Within this first group, men, whether they died as husbands or widowers, had the most expensive funerals, followed by widows and wives. This elite group appears to follow the liturgical expectations that men's funerals be more elaborate than women's. Felicity Riddy has noted that courtesy literature for the urban bourgeoisie deemed social climbing and public visibility acceptable for men, but not for women. Although this group would marry their daughters into the aristocracy if they could, girls and women were not to draw attention to themselves.[134] Perhaps the less elaborate funerals for wives and widows suggest an internalizing of this ethos.

The second and third groups, those buried in the church with one type of liturgical item or those buried in the churchyard with more than one kind of liturgical item, were clearly less wealthy and less socially important than the first group. A few in the second and third group could be found renting tenements directly from the Abbey, rather than subletting a portion of one, some left wills, and some paid taxes on the lay subsidy of 1524, but none seem to have held civic or parish offices. Among the more visible parishioners in the second group is Robert Stowell, master of the Abbey's masons from 1471 to his death in 1505. He was also the architect for several parish churches, including the new St. Margaret's, begun in 1487.[135] He was buried in the church, and his funeral had a knell costing 6d.[136] As Figure 2.3 shows, these two groups shared some of the same priorities in staging funerals. In both groups, widows had the most expensive funerals. Additionally, the wives in both groups had more spent on their funerals than the widowers would have spent on their own. These differences reflect a number of economic dynamics. Men had greater economic resources than women, and newly widowed men could afford more elaborate funerals for their deceased wives than newly widowed women could afford for their deceased husbands. Furthermore, widows' funerals, arranged by children and other heirs, might be incorporating prayers and rituals for predeceased husbands, now that money was available with the death of the widow.

The fourth group is the poorest. None of those dying just after the lay subsidy of 1524 were wealthy enough to be taxed and none rented tenements from the Abbey or held public office. Although one widow in this group, Lettice Fisher, became a parish almswoman after the death of her husband in 1515, the members of this group were not generally destitute.[137] Some may have been young couples at the start of family life. Two couples had children who went on to do very well, and two others appear to have been prosperous in their own right.[138] The funerals for this group were quite modest, costing on average 5d. Women who died as wives had the most expensive funerals, with their husbands' spending on average 5.6d. Widowers and husbands had the least expensive funerals, costing 4.8d, with widows having only slightly more expensive ones at 4.9d. The difference between wives and everyone else in this group again appears to be a function of their husbands' greater resources. Pragmatism, not greed or lack of religious fervor, could underlay the planning of these funerals. The hardworking, financially strapped families in this group, while not the poorest members of the community, could not take money for granted.

Wills frequently show couples collaborating on pious and charitable bequests, with husbands often deferring their spiritual concerns for postmortem prayers until their wives' deaths. In practice this meant some husbands gave their wives wide latitude in executing their wills. When Richard Hyland, a wheelwright in Westminster, wrote his will in 1504 he specified that his wife Agnes should "pay my debts and bring my body in earth and do for my soul as she may think to please God and profit my soul."[139] These instructions allowed Agnes to assess the family's finances before deciding on her husband's immediate intercessory provisions. She could add further intercessory services when she died, as a result of these calculations. Richard's funeral only had a knell.[140] In 1516, Margaret Wycam, also of Westminster, left money in her will for two trentals to be said for her soul and the souls of her two deceased husbands.[141] The executors in charge of a widow's funeral were potentially in a better position to honor her funeral requests because the death of a widow was typically bringing an end to a household, thus freeing up capital for both the funeral and the pious bequests. These strategies for intercessory prayers worked out between husbands and wives would help explain why widows in the second, third, and fourth groups had the most expensive funerals. They were making up for their economizing when they arranged their husbands' funerals.

The funerals of Westminster's widows point to life cycle and economic troubles shared by widows throughout medieval society. We can, for example, see the widows in Sutterton acting in similar ways to the Westminster women in the poorest group. In Sutterton 85 women died as wives and 160 died as either widows or single women. Of the wives, 26 percent (22), had the more expensive funerals, those costing between 5d. and 14d. compared to 11 percent (17), of widows or single women.[142] Moreover, 39 percent (62), of widows compared to only 17 percent (14), of wives had funerals with a 1d. candle, the cheapest funeral. Either way one looks at these figures, widows or single women had less expensive funerals. Christine Peters in her analysis of Sutterton suggests this difference was the result of "grief stricken husbands" spending more on their wives' funerals than those arranging widows' funerals.[143] This might be true, but it might also be equally true that the greater earning potential of husbands who oversaw their wives' funerals facilitated more expensive funerals. The overall poverty of widows, who had less remaining in their estates with which to finance their funeral, made their funerals less opulent than wives' funerals. Identifying couples in Sutterton is not easy, so we cannot compare the funerals of widows with those they arranged for their husbands. The records do not record men's marital status at death, but most men died married. The distribution of the cost of their funerals resembles those of the widows, with 38 percent of men's funerals costing 1d. This finding suggests again, that many new widows did not have extra resources to spend on their husband's funerals.

The experiences of poor and elite married couples in Westminster and Sutterton show that gender, family, and marital status played themselves out differently in funerals. For lower-status women, the death of a husband brought more financial worries than it did for the widows of elites. Many must have found themselves in the same position as the Kentish widow, Elizabeth Miller, who was unable to pay the 14d. for the "wax, use of the church, and other things at the burial of her husband."[144] Elite men, moreover did not need to wait for their pious displays to be folded into their wives' funerals; instead their families could afford to provide them during these men's funerals. Such displays figured prominently in strategies for the maintenance of social position or even the social advancement of their survivors. The different economic realities facing men and women when they lost a spouse also underlie differences between men's and women's funerals. The impact of a husband's death on his family was not the same economically as the death of a wife. The stage of the family's life cycle—a man leaving a young family, or a widow ending a household—also mattered.

Confronted with economic uncertainty and the need to keep a household together, new widows opted to conserve on their husbands' funerals, making up the deficit at their own if they could. Their relatively grander funerals, therefore, did not necessarily reflect an improved economic position or greater piety, but rather the need to fulfill delayed family obligations because of the economic uncertainty of widowhood. Widowers, with their greater earning power, did not typically have the same financial concerns and could spend more on their wives' funerals.[145]

By and large, the differing priorities men and women incorporated into the funerals of their spouses are only visible when we know marital status at death and when we have known couples. For most dying in Westminster, 60 percent, their funerals had only two tapers. Poverty hid distinctions within this large group. Yet the Westminster churchwardens' accounts, with their careful listing of each funeral candle's cost, also provide evidence of the pious strategies of the poorer members of the parish.

Candles are a ubiquitous but highly variable element in all funerals. According to Eamon Duffy, "the burning of candles around a corpse was an act of profound resonances. Blessed candles had an apotropaic power to banish demons. They were also understood as particularly eloquent examples of a whole vocabulary for light and darkness."[146] Some, however, did see them as adding unnecessary ceremony. In his will, Westminster parishioner, John Howell, equated them with pomp and requested none be used in his funeral.[147] The churchwardens of Westminster sold many different kinds of candles at different prices. There are half tapers, small tapers, great tapers, best lights, second best lights, half torches, candles for the candelabra of the guild of St. Mary, great tapers for Our Lady's candlesticks, torches of St. Cornelius' Guild, candles for small candlesticks, and one Westminster parishioner, George Crosby, even had "8 strange torches" at his funeral.[148] It is also possible the cheaper candles were made from tallow instead of beeswax.

In the late 1490s, the price of wax dropped and cheaper candles began to dominate. Although the cheaper tapers were 1d. instead of 2d. a piece, and the new torches were 12d. instead of 20d., the accounts do not identify or describe the less expensive candles as in any way different from the expensive ones except by price.[149] Ultimately the adoption of the new candles dropped the average cost of funerals for men and women buried in the churchyard by half. As Figure 2.4 shows, in the period between 1460 and 1490, men's funerals cost on average 12.4d., but in the period after 1490 they

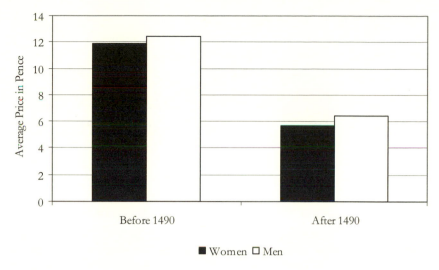

Figure 2.4. Impact of the price of wax on men's and women's funerals, Westminster (1460–1535).

were 6.4d. Similarly, the average cost of women's funerals declined from 11.9d. to 5.7d.

More important, the survivors in charge of men's and women's funerals adopted the cheaper candles at different rates. Women's funerals used the more expensive candles longer than men's. This pattern is most obvious when we look at the cost of torches for one year. In 1496, the mean cost of torches in men's funeral was 12d., while for women it was 20d. The average cost of torches for men's funerals was 18d., while for women it was 26.7d. There is a similar pattern in the use of tapers. Among those funerals with only two tapers, the cheaper tapers appear in funerals as early as 1475 and are the norm by 1478. As this group would include the poorest of the parish, it makes sense the cheaper tapers would emerge here first. Among those using four tapers for their funerals, the shift did not occur until 1504, and it was not complete until 1516. Similarly, women's funerals continued to have the more expensive kinds of tapers longer.

Why wax prices declined is unclear. It might be that the cheaper candles were simply smaller, made of inferior wax, or made from less expensive imported wax. Whatever the reason for the decline in price, the different rate at which men's and women's funerals adopted the cheaper candles may well reflect new widows' further attempts at economizing as they struggled to pay for their husbands' funerals. Although the statistics show that women did not compromise on the number of tapers and torches used at their husband's funerals, they saved money by purchasing cheaper ones when they were available. Maintaining the number of candles allowed them to uphold the message the number of candles implied, but purchasing cheaper ones allowed them to address their own fiscal concerns. Until the parish-wide adoption of the cheaper candles in the 1510s, both women's economic anxieties and their need to maintain their families' social status are visible in the funerals of their husbands.

In her study of Renaissance Florence, Sharon Strocchia argued that "pomp helped forge common, rather than gender-distinct, funeral styles, which were directed toward common family purposes."[150] Although family concerns certainly figured in English funerals, negotiating family life stage, economic resources, and marital status lay at the heart of the formation of gender-distinctive funerals. The role of gender, however, is not obvious from the simple inclusion or exclusion of symbols or adornments. We can only see the differences between men's and women's funerals when we compare them mindful of the marital and economic status of the deceased.

The Church expected funerals to reflect the "order, craft, and degree" of the deceased. Families and the deceased themselves, however, took the opportunity to elaborate on this social identity through the vocabulary of pararituals offered by candles, bells, and burial location. We usually think of social identity in terms of increasing wealth, power, and visibility, but in these English funerals we can also see that economic anxiety was a component of social identity. The lack of certainty confronting most widows meant that relative to their own social group, they had more elaborate funerals than their husbands. This behavior reflects their individual status, but it also reflects how their pious and economic concerns combined with those of their deceased husbands. In contrast, among the elite, where money did not inhibit the level of funeral display, families gave new meaning to women's funerals, perhaps picking up on ecclesiastical admonitions that women's funerals should be less elaborate because of their association with Eve or perhaps because of desires to limit women's visibility. Poor families, worried about both survival and salvation, could neither afford the luxury of clerical misogyny nor the modesty that rendered elite men's funerals more elaborate than women's. Both hampered larger family strategies for salvation. Observers would have seen funerals of the lower classes displaying their social identity in terms of the financial worries that went with being poor, and the financial worries that related to sex, marital status, and a family's life stage.

Conclusion

In the life-cycle liturgies of baptism and its associated churching, marriage, and death, the laity included pararituals that added to the meaning of the liturgy, and anchored it in a particular community, family, and moment of history. Although the completeness of the Westminster funeral data is unusual and difficult to integrate with material on the other life-cycle liturgies, the appearance of some of the same broad trends in Sutterton's funerals as well shows that Westminster's parishioners were not unique in their desire to use funeral pararituals to express economic and social concerns. The information on pararituals surrounding the other life-cycle liturgies—baptism, churchings, and weddings—is more episodic than comprehensive, but it is still clear that these liturgies included a variety of pararituals and that the laity also used them to express a variety of sentiments. Interpreting the pararituals' meaning is not straightforward. An austere funeral might be a sign of poverty, but it might also be a manifestation of extreme humility and piety, or it might be an acknowledgment of disinterest in the individual undergoing the liturgy or in the theology of the liturgy by those arranging it. There is some evidence that professed Lollards desired simple burials with few pararituals. One Thomas Walwayn of Herefordshire asked in his 1415 will to be buried "without pomp, which may not profit my soul."[151] Whatever the concerns, the laity were well aware of how to manipulate pararituals to express a variety of sentiments and the ability to do so was not limited to funerals alone.

By modifying life-cycle liturgies, the laity used them to reflect contemporary social and familial concerns. They became a means of manifesting and reinforcing newly acquired social status, but they were also a vehicle for attaining status in much the same manner as clothing. Pararituals, like clothing and food, became a means of imitating one's betters. Moreover, by adding important members of the community to a liturgical celebration such as baptismal, churching, or funeral processions, the family created, strengthened, and expanded social bonds and networks, which could benefit the family and help them fulfill their ambitions.

In their households, women were legally subordinate to their husbands and in these liturgies they were secondary to the clergy. Yet the nature of these liturgies was such that the priest's role was not tantamount; neither baptism nor marriage technically required a priest and last rites were done in the house, the women's domain. Moreover, women's importance to the successful running of a household meant that men remarried quickly after the deaths of their wives and in the crisis moments of birth and death, women played the dominant role and in marriage they were the center of much attention. Legal standing and reiteration of women's connections to Eve did not diminish women's importance to these contexts.

Because these life-cycle liturgies were connected to family and household, women played a significant role in them. The pararituals of the life-cycle liturgies provided women with the means to transfer their household prominence and importance to the life-cycle liturgies. In much the same way women ran their household, they ran these liturgies. Women's household obligations, like their liturgical obligations, involved choosing participants, economizing when necessary, and promoting the interests of their families and husbands to the best of their abilities. Women's willingness to discount clerical funeral instructions for economic and social reasons was matched by their willingness to contract a marriage in venues other than the church. The ability to mark family status with an elaborate funeral was similar to marrying in fine clothes or dressing one's baby for baptism in silk. Despite assertions and actions within the liturgies themselves that reaffirmed women's identity as the daughters of Eve and in need of supervision, the growing importance of the pararituals surrounding life-cycle liturgies gave women influence in these ceremonies well beyond what the clergy dictated.

Women's household and familial roles provided a template for their religious involvement. This religious involvement expanded beyond clerical expectations even when directed at maintaining and upholding clerically approved roles such as mother, wife, and widow. These life-cycle liturgies thus held in tension the social experiences of post-plague England and the desire to restore society to its theologically prescribed order.

Chapter 3
"My Pew in the Middle Aisle": Women at Mass

On 19 March 1535, the Friday before Palm Sunday, Bridget Stokes alleged that Sir Oswald Wylsthorpe and eleven others broke into the locked south chapel in the church of Bylton, Yorkshire, and destroyed the pews placed there.[1] In the melee that followed, the attackers injured her servant Anthony Wardell. Stokes brought a suit to Star Chamber, where she explained that her late husband "Robert Stokes and all his ancestors . . . of long time have had and used a pew or a seat for them and their wives and children at all such times as they were disposed to serve God in the same church without interruption of any man."[2] What is more, she explained, she "of late did bestow and lay out divers great sums of money for the building and reparation of the same chapel to the intent [that] she and her children might have the greater ease and comfort to serve God within the same."[3] The answering petition from John Carboit, one of the twelve defendants, challenged Stokes's account, explaining that, in fact, "divers other parishioners [as well] as the said Stokes used to sit or kneel within [the chapel] to hear the service of God,"[4] and that Bridget Stokes had recently taken it upon herself, to "keep the door of the said chapel, which she had newly made, always locked contrary to the custom and use of the said church." No one could now use the chapel, including the chantry priest accustomed to celebrating mass there.[5]

As with most Star Chamber cases, no texts describing the court's resolution survives. Nonetheless, the incident offers insights into the concerns and priorities women brought with them when they went to church.[6] Bridget Stokes's words tell us of her desire "to serve God . . . without interruption of any man," but her adornment of this high-profile seat also reveals that she had a proprietary view of where she sat at mass and that she cared about where and with whom she served God. Moreover, her repairs and embellishments to the chapel and its pew mimic the kind of interactions that women had with their houses. Bridget Stokes furnished the chapel for the comfort of her family, viewing the chapel and pew as a family space where outsiders should not intrude. For Bridget, church attendance was about more than the liturgy; it was about worshipping with her family in a high-profile space and in physical comfort.

The case of *Stolkes v. Wylsthorpe* should also make us wonder about those, like John Carboit, who did not have the seat in church they wanted or had no seat at all. Where one sat or stood augmented one's local reputation. Those sitting up front were closer to the high altar and the host, and they had a better chance to create an aura of piety as they reacted to the liturgy, which they could hear and see better than those in the back. Local elites usually sat in front of the nave connecting their high status with their piety. Poorly located seats were farther back and gave the occupant either an obstructed view of the liturgy or none at all. Poor seats also limited occupants' opportunities to mix with or impress better-off neighbors who were closer to the front.[7] Seating at mass, therefore, created visibility, making it an important display of social relations, which could be hotly contested. Seating was a sign not only of status or identity, but also of communal inclusion and exclusion. Those without seats held different positions in their parishes from those with seats.

Bridget Stokes's behavior also gives life to many clerical complaints about the laity's behavior at mass. The clergy complained about congregants who were inattentive to both the liturgy and priest in the chancel. Instead, the clergy complained that the laity talked about business, wandered about the nave, and gossiped with friends. Prescriptive literature particularly admonished women not to use the mass as an opportunity to compete with neighbors or flirt with men. In arguing about her seat location and in redecorating the chapel, Bridget Stokes sought to distinguish herself and her status from the rest of the parish, making her social identity a part of her agenda for mass.

Bridget Stokes's justification also provides some evidence that the laity and the clergy understood displays of piety differently. In closing the chapel to others, she not only identified her elevated social status, she claimed that she did not want her devotions distracted by others. In her petition Stokes tied her status and piety together into one set of actions. The clergy, however, understood status and piety as two separate concerns, arguing that attention to status distracted from true piety and devotion.

This chapter looks at parish seating arrangements as a reflection of the concerns parishioners, particularly women, brought with them to mass.

The parish church was first and foremost a venue for piety, but it also provided a backdrop against which the laity acted out their social, individual, and communal identities and status. Not only were parishioners interested in being close to the host, they also wanted to impress their neighbors, and show off their wealth. For many parishioners, such as Bridget Stokes, these two goals were not necessarily incompatible. Respectability and civic ambition required displays of piety.[8] For others, competition, self-aggrandizement, and social promotion were the primary goals of church attendance; piety and devotion were secondary. Whatever their interests in being in church, the nave's internal organization delineated spaces where individuals fashioned their social identities and where groups, even cliques, could act out their differences and boundaries. Seating arrangements, which marked both sex and social status, helped determine how and when men and women encountered one another in church.[9] In large urban parishes, seating may have helped forge social relationships and groups that grew into other associations both within and without the parish. A well-placed seat displayed the occupant, his or her fine clothes and adornment, religious demeanor, and social status. At the same time, seating arrangements, which the parish as a corporate entity officially created, reflected attempts by the parish to regulate behavior at mass and define the members of the parish community.

In seating arrangements, we can see another manifestation of how women's domestic identities and obligations to promote their family merged with their parish opportunities for participation to create visibility for women. Many women linked their social identity with their parish involvement and their piety. Piety could help promote or enhance a family's reputation, which wives were enjoined to protect as part of their family and household duties. In connecting piety and status, women created a vocabulary of piety, which challenged what the clergy taught, while at the same time conformed to the expectation that they would uphold family honor. Some women may have had little interest in piety, but the ability to act on social and family concerns through attendance at mass still gave parish participation meaning.

Clerical Opinions

Canon law dictated that the laity should attend three services on Sundays: matins at around six or seven o'clock in the morning, high mass at around nine or ten o'clock, and finally evensong between two and three o'clock in the afternoon.[10] The ecclesiastical year also included special holy days that commemorated the life of Jesus and the martyrdom of the saints. On these days, called *festa ferianda*, the laity also attended church. In addition, parish priests, along with the stipendiary priests, said a daily mass and the other canonical hours throughout the rest of the week. When and how depended largely on local custom; the priest might say the hours privately or fold them into the beginning and end of the daily mass.[11] Unlike the legislated Sunday mass, the laity could attend these other services, but they were not required to. In the fifteenth-century, clerically authored conduct poem directed at women called "How the Good Wife Taught Her Daughter," the mother character explains to her daughter that respectable young women went to church regularly.

Go to church when you may,
Even if it rains,
For you fare best that whole day
When God you have seen.[12]

The mass reenacted Christ's last supper, passion, and resurrection. This ritual was to be the laity's most frequent contact with sacramental grace, although they generally only received the Eucharist once a year at Easter. The rest of the year they might receive holy bread, which was blessed but not consecrated, or kiss a carved wooden board called a pax, which the laity passed through the congregation at the mass. Scholars debate how visible the liturgy was to the laity. An elaborately carved fence, called a rood screen, divided the priest and high altar in the chancel from the laity in the nave. The priest also said the liturgy in Latin with his back turned to the congregation. In large churches, with long naves, those in the back might have felt the service was far away. Yet many parish churches were quite small and priests also said mass at the many side altars throughout the nave, possibly making the liturgy familiar. Furthermore, at the moment of consecration, a bell rang to alert the congregation to this important moment. These factors might have mitigated some of this alienation.[13]

Interestingly, episcopal legislation provided different rules for when men and women should attend church. In the thirteenth-century diocesan statutes for Worcester and Canterbury, the bishop identified the feasts of St Agnes (21 January), St. Agatha (5 February), St. Margaret (2 July), and St. Lucy (13 December) as days when women were not to work but were, rather, to go to church.[14] The *Speculum Sacerdotale*'s Easter sermon betrays a similar notion that men and women were sometimes obliged to attend church on different days. The author of this sermon collection insists that "for three days after Easter, no one was to work. But in the fourth day, it is lawful for men to till and work the earth, but women ought to cease from their work. And why? Rural work is needed more than other work."[15] The sermon contains an anachronistic assumption that all men were involved with rural labor. Moreover, the sermon writer does not define women's work, or say that women should not prepare meals for their families. He does believe, however, that women's work was less important for the survival of the community; hence they were not to return to work as soon as men, but instead remain in church praying.[16] Such statements also implicitly valued men's and women's spiritual efforts differently. Women were to pray and attend church at times when men were not. These rules not only drew upon, but reinforced the belief that women were inherently more religious than men. Mirk similarly assumes in his *Instructions for Parish Priests* that men are often too busy with work for regular devotions.

For holy days you must pass
At hearing God's service and the mass
And spend the day in holiness
And leave alone all other busyness
For upon the week day,
Men are so busy in every way,
So that for their occupation,
They leave off much of their devotion . . . [17]

Although in the period between childbirth and churching the new mother might have stayed away from church, as Mirk recommended, churching required women to attend church. Although men too were sometimes present at churchings, it was primarily a women's liturgical obligation.[18] In another conduct poem directed at young men, "How the Wiseman Taught His Son," the clerical author only tells the boy to pray. The poem does not mention going to church as a component of good behavior.[19] If the laity actually practiced these clerical expectations then women may have attended church more often than men. The unintentional outcome of these mandates coupled with the demographic changes wrought by regular outbreaks of the plague may explain clerical complaints that greater numbers of women than men attended church.[20] Women may also have felt more at home in the church than men because they were obligated to attend more regularly and their work for the church made them familiar with its contents and layout. At the same time, when women were in church, they were under clerical supervision. The clergy sought to direct women's attention to appropriate gender roles and female virtues. By promoting church attendance for women particularly, the Church tapped into contemporary concerns about women's work, their growing amount of unsupervised time, and their need for governance.

The Church not only stipulated which services lay people were obliged to attend, it also laid down rules for how the laity should behave while at church. Late medieval clerical writings make it clear that men and women behaved differently while attending mass. The clergy fit their observations into their understanding of women's moral failings; they typically wrote that women's bad behavior showed their disrespect for the liturgy, which they had because of their frivolous natures and propensity for sin. Some women, no doubt, did disdain the clergy and the liturgy, but obvious clerical misogyny obscures other interpretations of women's behavior when they attended their parish churches.

The clergy also worried about the meaning that seating arrangements gave to the laity's church attendance. The Bishop of Exeter's episcopal statutes of 1287 stated that church patrons, those with the right to fill the parish's benefice, as well as nobles, could sit in or near the chancel, but others must remain in the nave, with seating on a first-come-first-served basis. The parish was not to sell seats either.[21] This statute recognized that the better seats were closest to the host, but makes no comment on the place of women in the nave. Later rulings make similar statements about the allotment of seats.[22] In practice, however, there seems to be some anxiety about where in the church women sat or stood. In the early fourteenth century, Robert Mannyng's instructional text, *Handlyng Synne*, asserted that when women stood among the clergy in the chancel they did greater harm by their presence: they distracted the clergy, and led the weak ones to temptation and sin. He wrote:

But women do greater folly
when they stand among the clergy,
either at matins or a mass,
by causing distress,
for they may bring temptation
and disturb devotion.[23]

In the fourteenth-century episcopal visitation for Hereford, the churchwardens of Brilly complained of women in the chancel.[24] In 1405, the dean of

Salisbury similarly had to reprimand the vicar of Lyme Regis for letting women into the chancel.[25] From these admonitions we might assume that parish priests were more accepting of women's presence in the chancel than their superiors, possibly because of women's extensive "churchkeeping" responsibilities.

The clergy not only expected the laity to attend church, but to behave themselves once there. The clergy admonished both men and women to pay attention to the liturgy, not talk with friends, not wander about the church, and not play games or conduct business. The popular fourteenth-century didactic work *The Book of Vices and Virtues* declares that, "when folks are at church, men and women should be still and calm and honest and do honor and reverence to God and his holiness. For the place is holy and consecrated to prayer therein and [they must] not talk or fidget."[26] Similarly Mirk enjoins priests to teach the laity

That when they are inside the church door
Then bid them listen to these words:
Give up idle speech and jokes they have heard,
And put away all vanity,
And say then the *Our Father* and then the *Hail Mary*
No one shall stand in the church at all
Nor lean on a pillar, nor against the wall
But pray on their knees, they cannot do more
Than kneeling down upon the floor.[27]

The clergy defined proper behavior for *both* men and women as attention to their prayers and the priest in the chancel.

Although correct behavior in church was the same for men and women, the clergy observed that men and women misbehaved differently. Prescriptive literature has a long tradition of condemning women's love of finery, and their use of the mass as an occasion to display it.[28] Accusations ranged from vanity and self-promotion by dressing well to using fine clothing to attract men and compete with neighbors. Fancy clothing was not only a sign of vanity, it could also lead to pride or lust. Accusations of dressing too well for church took on further significance in this era of sumptuary legislation because a conscious attempt at social climbing by means of fine clothes was also disobedience to the law. Although men were more typically the initiators of changes in fashion,[29] the clergy repeatedly targeted women's interest in clothing, accusing them, not men, of violating social bounds. *The Book of Vices and Virtues* specifically understood biblical injunctions against

women's interest in fancy dress in terms of sumptuary legislation. The author reminded its readers that

St. Paul teaches that good women should attire themselves when they go to church
to bid their beads to God; he says they should have honest clothing and attire and
not too much, that is to say in accordance with a women's estate. For what is too
much for one woman is not too much for some others. For much more behooves
to the queen than to a burgess' wife or to a merchant's or to a squire's or a simple
lady such as a knight's wife.[30]

The problem of dressing "dishonestly" for church conformed to other expectations about women's readiness to misbehave, while at the same time
recognizing that attendance at mass did display one's social status.

The poem, "How the Good Wife Taught Her Daughter," warns
against other kinds of misbehavior while in church. This didactic poem accuses women of using church attendance as an opportunity for gossiping
and sparring, implying that age was another source of tension and competition among women.

When you sit in church, attend to your beads and
your prayers;
Do not talk to friends or to
neighbors;
Do not laugh or scorn the old or the young
But be of fare baring and of good tongue.[31]

In didactic literature, the clergy accused women of inattention to the liturgy
or sermons because of their verbal and material displays. Church was too
often a social forum, not a spiritual one. Read in the context of fifteenth-
century social mobility and material acquisition, these criticisms respond to
the ways that parish life and liturgy had become forums for contemporary
behavior. The laity were increasingly using the parish church as a place to
express sentiments other than piety.

These clerical accusations were repeated so often that they became literary tropes, but there was a measure of truth in them. Bridget Stokes, for
example, did not explain what she meant by "building and repairing" so
she and "her children [would] have the greater ease and comfort to serve
God."[32] It is possible, however, that there were cushions to soften the hard
surfaces and blankets to keep the occupants warm in the cold weather. The
courtesy text "The Book of Nurture" instructs a chamberlain to supply his
master's pew with cushions, blankets, curtains.[33] Stokes might also have in-

stalled new images in the chapel and hired her own carver to carve special bench-ends adorned with pious images or family crests. Even women without private chapels could show off a variety of religious paraphernalia while in church, such as prayer books and rosaries.[34] When cleaning the church of St. Margaret's, Westminster, the sexton found a coral necklace and a variety of loose change all lost as people played with them during mass.[35] Looking out on the nave, the clergy saw women preening in their finery and fiddling with their rosaries and prayer books. Their movement spoke to the clergy of vanity and competition, not of pious contemplation and prayer. For some women, however, these accessories were manifestations of their identity and aids to devotion. The statutes for the parish guild of Moreton (Essex) instructed its members that they had to attend church wearing their best clothing.[36] For some, then, good clothing signaled the values of the guild: piety, sobriety, and respectability, presumably even if their clothing was grander than their social position.[37] These differences between clerical expectations and women's behavior suggest that the boundary between piety and self-promotion was not clear-cut in practice. Women understood the church was God's house, and they interacted with the space in the nave in ways reminiscent of their household interactions. Church attendance was an opportunity for expressing concern and care for family, which included the promotion and protection of a family's reputation through the wearing of nice clothing and the assertion of status.

Although the clergy's observations about women's behavior while at church were not necessarily wrong, they were interpreted through a prism of belief in women's inherently sinful natures. The clergy had little room to understand women's church behavior as their own vocabulary of piety, shaped by their social and economic experiences. Although church attendance did provide women with an opportunity to compete with neighbors, we can view some of this competition as a form of family promotion and protection. Moreover, even when women's church behavior was motivated by outright vanity instead of piety, their actions still expose women's priorities for church attendance and the opportunities for and nature of personal interaction among women.

These clerical observations can be separated further from their underlying misogyny when considered in light of how seating arrangements functioned within different communities. Seating arrangements illustrate some of the ways in which women connected their religious behavior to their social identity. Women, therefore, could invest church attendance with additional meaning over and above those expected or outlined by the clergy.

Conformity, Status, and Seating

There was a great deal of architectural variation among parish churches. As a result, seating arrangements were locally specific. They also tended to be dominated by women. Indeed, the noted antiquarian J. Charles Cox wrote that in the parish of St. Edmund's, Salisbury, the number of women in the nave "attained egregious proportions."[38] Until the fifteenth century, most laity attending the liturgy stood or brought their own stools. In the two hundred years prior to the Reformation, though, many parish churches underwent extensive rebuilding programs.[39] Often included in these projects was the building of permanent seats for the laity, or the rearrangment of older seating. Some scholars associate the introduction of fixed seats with the increase in preaching and the realization that the laity would not pay attention to long sermons if they had to stand.[40]

Seating arrangements recognized that some seats were better than others. Key to a good seat was a view of the high altar, or proximity to a cult site. In St. Lawrence's, Reading, for example, the best were close to the chancel. Or again, in Yeovil (Som.), parishioners John Short and John Tressher both had seats in the south side of the nave "under St. Christopher."[41] A good seat, however, did more than place the occupant close to sacred objects and places. A good seat usually cost more and so also implicitly advertised wealth, uniting the two concepts in the arrangement of the nave.

The resulting seating arrangements usually separated men and women, a practice that goes back as early as the third century.[42] These early churches apparently placed women in the back of the church, at the west end, to keep them as far as possible from the chancel. Some believed separating women and men confined women's impurity.[43] In medieval England, the more usual arrangement placed women on one side of the nave, usually the north side, and men on the other. The traditional explanation for this organization lies in the association of the north and women with things dark, damp, and demonic.[44] An alternate interpretation is that women sat on the same side as Mary relative to her position to Christ on the cross as depicted on top of most rood screens.[45] The association of Mary with the north side is also reflected in the positioning of females at baptisms and weddings and spatial arrangements within the nave. The Marian chapel was often to the north of the chancel.[46]

A women's section gave women visibility, but this visibility also allowed the community and the clergy to monitor their behavior more closely. Seating arrangements made it harder for women to "misbehave" and easier for authorities to identify absenteeism and inappropriate behavior. Sitting together also encouraged social conformity and particular types of behavior. Certainly it would be easier to monitor women's behavior if they were confined to a single section of the church.

Many clerics in the later Middle Ages continued to believe men and women should sit apart. Faced with seating irregularities, the late medieval clergy rarely resorted to arguments about the dangers of female pollution. They continued, however, to see women "out of place" as a problem, as apparently did many members of the lay community. Their concerns grew out of broader social concerns for controlling women. Parish communities and the clergy overtly cast their concerns about women's placement in the nave in terms of community membership and respectability.[47] When women moved out of their expected places or categories, many questioned their morality or propriety, assuming the worst motivations.[48] In the Lincoln parish of Grayingham, for example, churchwardens cited several women for sitting among the men and sharing the kiss of peace with them.[49] The wardens worried that the kiss of peace, a sign of Christian community and charity, would be sullied by the mixing of the sexes. The women were not participating in an act of Christian charity, but rather were behaving in a wanton and promiscuous manner. In another confrontation over seating, the churchwardens of the London parish of St. Martin Vintry brought suit against Maria alias Mariot Harington, a common bawd, for sitting in a seat during mass.[50] Harington's status as a prostitute made it inappropriate, the wardens argued, for her to sit among the respectable members of the parish. Respectable women, those who could afford a seat in the nave, should not have to mix with such company. They might have also feared that she would recruit other women to her line of work.[51] The wardens saw Harington's presence as both an intrusion and a threat to the moral order of their parish community, which their seating arrangement was to reflect.

Seating did not include everyone. In most parishes, a sizable number of men and women would have stood in the back or on the sides or brought stools from home. Gervase Rosser estimates St. Margaret, Westminster's population at between two and three thousand people in the early sixteenth century.[52] Even with a high death rate, there were not enough seats for everyone, nor were the poor likely to have afforded them. For example, the laundresses who worked for the parish do not appear to have purchased seats. They may have attended mass on a regular basis, and could have participated in the festivals sponsored by the parish, but they did not buy seats.

The presence of seating arrangements predicated on wealth and status made it more difficult for the poor to belong to the parish in a social or emotional sense, even though they did belong legally and morally.

Among women without seats, bad or disruptive behavior would have been harder to monitor on an individual basis, but it would have been easier to generalize to a group of women or women in a particular part of the nave and hence of a particular economic status. With their view of the high altar obstructed and their social visibility minimalized, there would have been little to hold their attention at mass and they may also have been less interested and less involved with the parish.

Bench-end carvings and the placement of wall paintings connect location of seats with the laity's behavior at mass. As pews became more prevalent, bench-ends sported their own genre of decorative carving.[53] The best surviving examples of medieval bench-end carving are in the West Country and East Anglia (see Figure 3.1). Many of the images are religious, such as the instruments of the passion, the saints, or the seven works of mercy and the seven deadly sins; other common images are animals. Many of the images are taken from books, especially wood-block prints from the *Biblia Pauperum*, printed in the Netherlands in the fifteenth century.[54] The presence of exotic animals and plants indicates that carvers had access to bestiaries and herbals.[55] Such images often had religious meanings and would remind both viewers who walked by and the occupants who sat by them of their Christian duty to charity or the punishments for sin. Initials, coats-of-arms, and family names in the form of rebuses were also common, probably matching the seat's original occupants, reinforcing in the carving the seating arrangements.[56] In Donyatt, Somerset, one bench-end sports carved initials tied together, denoting a marriage alliance between two families. Below the initials are four yokes and a plow, possibly representing the family's occupation and maybe even their wealth in land.[57] All the medieval bench-ends in Braunton, Devon, have either initials or heraldic devices, which identified their occupants. Those seats with the best view of the high altar and chancel have the heraldic devices, meaning those of highest status had the best seats.[58]

The location of wall paintings of the "Warning to Gossips" also ties seating arrangements to concerns about lay behavior at mass. This image shows two women sitting on a bench gossiping (Figure 3.2). They could be at church, since some images show them holding prayer beads, but this is inferred rather than explicit. If they were in church, they were not paying attention to the sermon or mass. Between the two women is the devil Tuti-

Figure 3.1. Bench-end with the instruments of the Passion, Trull, Somerset. Photograph by Katherine L. French.

villus writing down their conversation. This image was also a popular *exemplum* in sermons.[59] According to one version of the story, Tutivillus is discovered when he runs out of parchment and tries to stretch it with his teeth and hands. The parchment slips out of his hands and he smacks his head on the wall. The tears of the gossips' repentance wipe the scroll clean. This image survives in at least fifteen churches, and always shows women

Figure 3.2. Warning to gossips, Peakirk, Northamptonshire. Drawing by Patrick St. John.

as the protagonists.[60] Sandy Bardsley has connected the popularity of this image with the rise of scolding and general concerns with women's speech. By the late Middle Ages, women's speech was thought of as transgressive and associated with gossip, frivolity, and sexual promiscuity.[61]

Although the message to attend to one's prayers and not gossip would have applied to both men and women, the presence of women in the paintings and the paintings' location in churches suggests particular concern with controlling women's behavior in the church. Of the fifteen images of gossips in their original locations, nine are on the north wall.[62] Placement on the north side would offer all entering the church a reminder of how to behave, but its placement on the north side associates this behavior particularly with women. In Slapton, Northamptonshire, the image is on the south of the church. Miriam Gill argues it is likely that in this church the Marian altar and possibly the women's seats were all on the south side, as they were in St. Lawrence's, Reading.[63] Most of these images are also at the back of the church, farthest from the high altar, where the least attentive men and women probably sat or stood and where those left out of seating arrangements congregated.[64] The existence of seating arrangements by sex and images associated with women suggests a generalized concern to categorize and control women as they sat in the nave. The lessons taught in the warning to gossips paintings were to remind viewers that church attendance was supposed to be directed at spiritual concerns only. The information, self-promotion, and competition that underlay gossip were inappropriate in the church, and women should not link them to their devotional behavior and concerns.

In addition to gender, some parishes specifically included social status when creating seating arrangements. Some rural parishes based seat location in the church on land holding.[65] In Ashton-under-Lyne, Lancashire, the early fifteenth-century manorial custumal contains a detailed seating plan for the church, created when the tenants received new twenty-year leases.[66] The plan shows seats on the north and south sides of the church, with the south side containing six forms, or benches, and the north side containing a block of seven forms and then a block of at least five and probably more forms in the "nether-end" of the church.[67] The best seats were up front, where not only the local gentry but also other "gentle strangers" sat.[68] Ralph Assheton's tenants held the majority of seats. In a pew dispute from Minehead, Somerset, Giles Dobell explained because he held land in Minehead, he and his wife could also have seats in the church.[69] By using seating to display manorial status, these rural parishes inscribed social and tenurial differences into the liturgy, making attendance at mass a reflection of the manor's hierarchy. These methods of arranging seating made them relatively stable and eliminated personal choice or other issues as an aspect of seating decisions. This system of assigning seats also helped naturalize the connections between piety and local status.

Urban churches often sold seats to raise money to help maintain the nave. As a result, urban church seating reflected other more personal concerns, in addition to wealth, such as health, marital status, and friendship. Moreover, social status and wealth, which were a part of urban seating arrangements, were more mutable in urban communities.[70] As a family's ambitions or wealth grew or declined, seats could, therefore, be changed. Additionally, because the well-to-do, middling, and very poor could live in the same buildings, and social climbers could easily imitate high-status clothing, an individual's "real" status was difficult to identify visually.[71] As a result, in urban parishes seating arrangements both created as much as displayed social identity. Purchasing or changing one's seats was another means of claiming a higher social status. One could change pews to reflect or anticipate an increase or decrease in status. Because not everyone attending church purchased a seat, seating also divided the laity between those with and those without seats. The inability or the decision not to purchase a seat displayed yet another set of lay priorities, identities, and concerns. Whether in an urban or rural environment, seating arrangements reinforced and promoted local hierarchies at each service.

Parishes sold seats for three or four different prices, probably matching blocks of seats. Price structures reflected the wealth of the parish and parishioners. In both St. Edmund's, Salisbury, and All Saints', Bristol, seats sold for 4d., 6d., 8d., or 12d. with a plurality of parishioners buying the 8d. seats. In St. Ewen's, Bristol, a smaller and poorer parish, most seats sold for only 4d. Rebuilding a church or installing new pews could alter the status of those buying seats. After re-pewing the parish church in Bridgwater, Somerset, in 1454, local-elite males took up the new pews in the front, whereas elderly and infirm men and women had occupied the majority of the old seats.[72] In re-pewing the nave, Bridgwater changed the meaning of seating for the community from a comfort in old age and sickness to a sign of civic office holding and local status.

The ratio of men and women purchasing seats varied from parish to parish. These differences not only reflect real variation in seating practices, but variations in how parishes administered seats, which is often difficult to interpret. In the parishes of St. Edmund's, Salisbury, St. Margaret's,

Westminster, and St. Lawrence's, Reading, churchwarden's accounts record women purchasing the majority of seats. In 1515, the parishioners of St. Lawrence's agreed to new seating regulations. They stated "that all women that shall take any seat in the said church shall pay for the same seat 6d. except in the middle range and the north range beneath the font where they shall pay but 4d. And every woman is to take her place every day as she comes into the church except those who have been mayor's wives."[73] In 1545, new legislation again addressed women's seating, stating "it is ordered and enacted that all women of the said parish whose husbands now are or have been brethren of the Mass of Jesus, shall from henceforth sit and have the highest seats or pews next to the mayor's wife's seat towards the pulpit."[74] There was no comparable legislation about men's seating, nor did men purchase seats at the same rate as women.[75] In this parish, women's seating reflected their husbands' office holding, which in turn displayed the families' local position. When the wives of mayors processed to their seats once everyone else was in place, everyone understood their own place in the local hierarchy in relation to these prominent women. The custumal from Ashton-under-Lyne, which tied seating to land holding, only listed women as sitting in the church. The plan named 101 wives and four single or widowed women.[76] The lack of seats for men perhaps reflected the assumption that women went to church while men worked in the fields. There were also parishes where women did not purchase the majority of seats. In All Saints', Bristol, Sherborne Minster, Dorset, and Ashburton, Devon, women purchased a minority of the seats.[77] It is likely that husbands purchased seats for their wives, and that many of the women purchasing seats on their own were widows or single women. As we will see, these variations mean that the significance of seating varied from parish to parish.

Wealth and seating were related and the purchase of an expensive seat marked the occupant's high social and economic status. Nonetheless, seating arrangements signaled a variety of other identities, including marital status for women. In the London parish of St. Mary Woolchurch, the wardens paid 2s. to mend the maidens' pew, suggesting some unmarried women sat together.[78] In another London parish, St. Andrew Hubbard, the maidens had a pew in the loft.[79] In Maldon, Essex, some of the evidence in a marital dispute comes from the claim that the woman in question assumed a pew in the wives section, thus implying she was married.[80] When seating arrangements reflected marital status, the parish could also expect appropriate behavior based on that status. In the wives' section, newly married women could easily identify and emulate the demeanor, deportment, and dress of more experienced matrons or women from more socially prominent families. As we saw in the previous chapter, seating could also temporarily mark out a woman's successful childbirth as well, by placing her in the childwife's pew for her churching. Grouping the unmarried women together might have made it easier to supervise them as a group. It might also have reflected the large number of unmarried women working as servants who were without family affiliation or households of their own. In Ashton-under-Lyne, however, servants sat with their mistresses. Intentional or not, mistresses could keep an eye on them during the service.[81] The number of servants accompanying the housewife to church would also have signaled some local position. Church records do not designate men's sections by marital or reproductive status, suggesting that seating meant something rather different for men. Overall marital status was a less important marker in male identity.

Seating arrangements did more than simply separate the sexes. Through seating arrangements, parish members affirmed, created, and displayed social identities. Just as social identities were comprised of many things—gender, economic status, local office holding, marital status, and even birth order—so too did seating reflect a variety of factors, both creating and mirroring some ideal vision of local society. It created and re-created social hierarchies that included gender as an important constituent of parish order. Attendance at mass bound together notions of gender, deportment, status, respectability, and piety. However, seating arrangements did not reflect only clerical or elite notions of community order. Whatever the local traditions in seating, within the larger concern for community order, seating arrangements not only accommodated men's but also women's priorities. Some husbands and wives coordinated their seating as part of a strategy for family visibility and advancement, yet evidence also suggests that men and women often had separate goals, and that seating could mean different things to men and women.

Seating in St. Margaret's, Westminster

Most parish seating plans are difficult to reconstruct from the surviving documents. Even if we know where individuals sat, as we do in Ashton-under-Lyne, the more challenging issue, especially for urban parishes, where other issues besides the social hierarchy influenced seating, is to connect these other issues to buying or changing seats. The level of detail in the churchwardens' accounts from St. Margaret's, Westminster, that allowed for a detailed analysis of funerals allows similar analysis of seating. Seat sales were an annual part of parish revenue. In the fifty-eight years of accounts, 972 women purchased seats compared to only 316 men.[82] Women thus purchased about three-quarters of the seats sold in the parish.[83] Only about 12 percent of the men and women who purchased seats were married couples, and most did not apparently sit together.[84] Given the lack of seats and cost to a family budget, the seat purchaser would have been the sole member of their family with a seat, perhaps representing the family. Seats became available when the previous occupant died, moved to another seat, moved away, or when the parish built new ones. Prosopographical analysis of Westminster reveals connections between seat purchases and life cycle, increasing prosperity and public responsibility, and individual and familial concerns about health and ambition. In choosing seats, men and women integrated their own concerns into local religious life while still conforming to the social order created by parish leaders through seating arrangements. Westminster's seating practices gave women, either intentionally or inadvertently, more choices and greater opportunities to incorporate their own interests into church attendance than other parishes.

Between 1487 and 1523 the laity of St. Margaret's, Westminster, financed the demolition of their old church and the building of a new one. The new church with its long nave as wide as the chancel followed a design common to London' friary churches and seems to reflect an interest in preaching.[85] Part of this extensive rebuilding program was the gradual construction of pews for the new nave. In 1478, John Russell built eleven new pews in the south aisle.[86] Construction of pews continued on and off in this aisle until 1512.[87] Between 1502 and 1504, after the new north aisle was finished, a large crew of carpenters and joiners outfitted it with new pews as well.[88] In 1512 and 1526 joiners built more pews, but the accounts do not specify their location.[89] The ongoing construction may have been one of the factors giving women more seating choices.

Despite the unusual amount of documentation from this parish, there is only occasional information on the actual seating arrangements within the church. The churchwardens' accounts give the impression that most women sat in an all-women's section. In 1499, for example, twenty-nine women and no men purchased seats in the "new pews."[90] Women also seem to have sat in the north aisle, known variously as St. George's aisle or Our Lady's aisle (see Figure 3.3). Richard Fisher, who died in 1510, asked to be buried near his wife's pew in the Lady aisle.[91] Alice Baron wanted to be

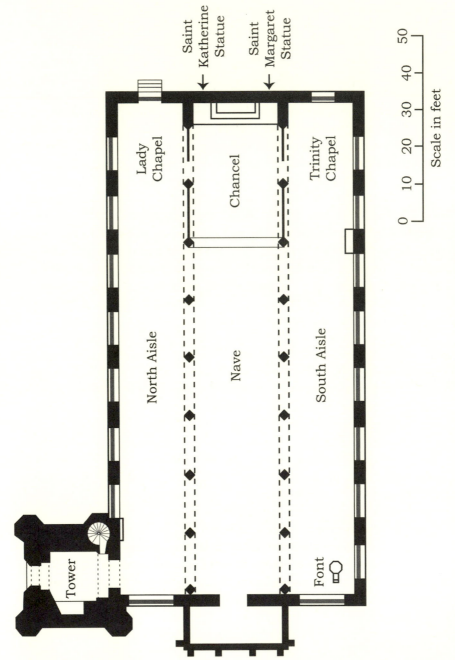

Figure 3.3. Floor plan of St. Margaret's, Westminster after the parish finished construction in 1523. Created by Stephen Hanna.

buried near her pew in the middle aisle, showing the presence of at least one woman in this part of the church.[92] Only men purchased seats in the south aisle, also called the Trinity aisle.[93] Thomas Peacock requested in his will that he be buried in the south part of the church, by his pew.[94] Finally, only men bought seats in or near the St. Cornelius chapel, suggesting that it, too, was located somewhere along the south aisle.[95] Although it is difficult to know how much to generalize from these occasional references, it seems that except for a few elite couples sitting together in the St. Erasmus chapel,[96] men and women at Westminster generally sat apart, with women, because of their sheer numbers, dominating the north and central parts of the nave. It also seems likely that the church could not hold the entire parish population. Many people may have chosen to go to one of the several chapels in the city or even the Abbey. Others may simply have not attended church regularly, especially if they were on the margins of the community. In 1593, when Westminster had become a more fashionable place, the parish still had problems with a lack of seats. It published seating ordinances directed at those with more than one residence, stipulating that anyone absent from church for more than three months lost their seat. The ordinances also took away seats from members fallen into poverty.[97]

In Westminster, seating marked social status, but it also allowed each sex to act out his or her own hierarchies and concerns. To be sure, women's status was predicated on the wealth of their husbands or fathers, but that does not lessen its importance to women. Because selling seats developed out of lay initiatives to raise money, seating arrangements were of institutional and financial interest to the community as a whole. The arrangements of seats and the priorities they reinforced thus received official recognition by the parish. The fact, moreover, that men and especially women were eager to purchase seats suggests that the practice was deeply appealing to members of the parish and that such purchases enabled lay people to turn church space into community space.

Even without firm knowledge of seat locations, we can see men and women made different decisions about their seats. The seats in the men's section tended to be more expensive than those in the women's section (see Figures 3.4a, b). Once the parish finished building the new church, the overall cost of seats increased and more men purchased seats. Before construction was completed, 30 percent of women (210 out of 695) compared to 17 percent of men (41 out of 239) bought the least expensive seats, those costing 12d. or less.[98] After 1523, the percentage of those men and women buying these inexpensive seats declined significantly. Of the seventy-three men who

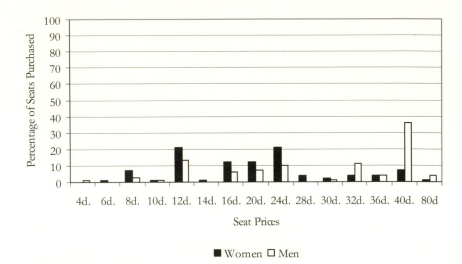

Figure 3.4a. Distribution of the price of men's and women's seats, Westminster (1460–1523).

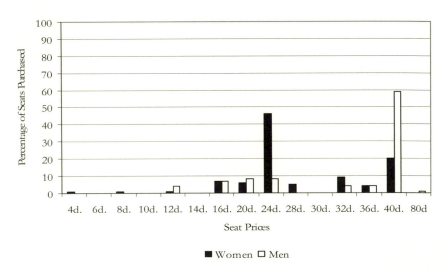

Figure 3.4b. Distribution of the price of men's and women's seats, Westminster (1524–1535).

purchased seats between 1524 and 1535, only three, or 4 percent, purchased inexpensive seats. Similarly, out of 182 women purchasing seats in the same eleven years only three, or 2 percent, bought the least expensive seats. The percentage of women purchasing the most expensive seats also increased from 18 percent before the end of construction, to 33 percent after construction. The increase among men was less pronounced, increasing from 56 percent of men to 68 percent. These changes all suggest that the parish diminished the number of inexpensive seats and increased the price of seats overall. There was probably a commensurate increase in the overall economic status of those with seats as seats became more exclusive.

Another difference between men's and women's seating is that women changed their seats more often than men. Prior to 1524, 132 women, or 17 percent, changed their seats, compared to only 27 men, or 11 percent. After construction was finished and seats were more expensive, men began changing their seats more often. In the post-construction period, 56 men changed their seats, 67 percent of all the men's seat changes. Women, in contrast, made only 41 percent of their changes during this later period. These figures show that, although seating remained dominated by women, after the new church was completed, men increasingly changed their seats. Both the rise in seat prices and the change in men's behavior imply that seating increased in importance among men. It is unlikely these changes were spontaneous. They probably reflect a conscious change in policy by the parish. With a new church to pay for, possibly seats needed to raise more money, which meant raising prices, and attracting those with the money to pay.

The range of prices and the option to change seats allowed those who were going to purchase them to incorporate a variety of personal concerns into their seat choices. Many different reasons prompted men and women to purchase or change their seats. The records occasionally provide an explanation and prosopographical analysis gives us further clues. Although these findings cannot be presented statistically, they are suggestive of the motives behind seating decisions. Several women requested seats with other women, possibly friends. In 1509, for example, Margaret Rosemund purchased a seat "with her fellows," and in 1517 Alice Lucas and Margaret Eldersham purchased seats next to one another.[99] Other women wanted seats with family members. Elizabeth Hovell purchased her seat in 1527, and then moved it in 1531 to sit with her daughter.[100] Her change seems to have been prompted by failing health that required her daughter's care. Within two years of her moving her seat, Hovell died.[101] Both Agnes Bird and Robert

Bette's wife died also within a year of purchasing their inexpensive seats, suggesting they, too, were in poor health, and that they purchased their seats as a physical aid because they could no longer stand for the whole mass, or carry a stool to sit in the back.[102] Marriage and widowhood also prompted seat changes or purchases. In 1517, Mistress Pen took over Mistress Morley's daughter's pew "from before her marriage," implying the daughter had moved to another seat or parish upon her marriage.[103] Seat location was also of interest to many women. Many wanted newly constructed seats, or seats perceived to be better than their current one, such as in the case of Mistress Pen, who took advantage of Mistress Morley's daughter's marriage.

Numerous women also purchased or changed seats when their husbands' died. This practice offers further insight into the policies and dynamics of Westminster's seating arrangement. Cicely Wardrobe purchased her seat in 1479, possibly when she got married, and changed it in 1483 when her husband John died.[104] Mistress Smyth, the locksmith's widow, purchased her first seat when her husband died in 1503.[105] Her husband, however, purchased his seat in 1485, at the time he started working for the parish.[106] As Wardrobe's and Smyth's behavior shows, some widows moved from a previous seat at the death of their husband, while other women purchased a seat for the first time when their husband died. The timing of the new widows' seat changes hints at the existence of a widows' section in the nave. The fact that not all women moved when their husbands died suggests there was an unofficial section, created by the women themselves to share their similar circumstances with other women. It is also possible that there were some couples who sat together, although the churchwardens' accounts did not register the fact, and once widowed, the women had to give up their seat in this section for husbands and wives. Mistress Smyth might have sat with her husband Simon when he bought his seat in 1485.

Many women took up seats or moved them accordance with development in their husbands' careers. Of the ninety-six named churchwardens and guild wardens, eighty-seven have traceable wives. Of these eighty-seven wives, fifty-nine, or 68 percent, had seats, and twenty-two, or 37 percent, moved in relation to their husband's parish office holding. For example, both Elizabeth Bough and Thomas Crane's wife changed their seats when their husbands became churchwardens.[107] While only 37 percent of churchwardens' wives changed seats in relation to their husbands' service, 47 percent of the wives of the wardens of the Assumption guild did, implying that the guild reserved some seats for the wives of its officers. If the wife did not already have an acceptable seat, the guild could provide one for her. For the wives of socially prominent men, seating could be a marker of their status, but it was not obligatory as it was in St. Lawrence's, Reading.

One of the most active women in the seat market was Ellen Attewell, wife of gentleman wax chandler John Attewell. Her five different seats reflect her family's increasing status in the community, her desire for visibility, and the recognition that some seats were better than others. Ellen Attewell purchased her first seat for a modest 8d. in 1498.[108] She then moved a second time in 1503 to a seat that cost 40d.[109] She moved a third time in 1513 into a seat made free by the death of Agnes Stephenson, who had owned it for the past ten years.[110] While Attewell only paid 12d. for the change, the seat originally cost Agnes Stephenson 40d. Her long-term use of this seat, Attewell's immediate purchase of it when Stephenson died, and its cost are all factors that suggest it was a desirable seat. In 1515, Ellen Attewell moved a fourth and final time to a seat vacated by Elizabeth Legh, who had moved with her husband to an even better seat in the Erasmus Chapel.[111] Ellen Attewell's last seat cost her 80d.

Ellen Attewell's successive seat changes moved her to ever more expensive and, likely to her mind, better seats. Her third and fourth seats had previously been occupied by wives of men in royal service.[112] While the availability of better seats explains her third and fourth seats, her second seat in 1503, which cost 40d., was possibly related to her husband's career in public services. John Attewell purchased his own seat in 1501.[113] That same year, she and her husband both gave money to the benevolence fund set up to raise money for building the new church.[114] In 1504 he served as one of the auditors of the churchwardens' accounts, and he started selling wax to the parish.[115] In 1505, he served as one of the wardens of the Assumption Guild.[116] Ellen's second seat, which was so much more expensive than her first seat, fits in with a larger family strategy for promoting the couple's visibility and status within the parish community.

Social aspirations often have a dark side. Rivalries and competition also influenced seating decisions. After sitting in the same seats for nearly twenty years, both Joan Pomfrett and John Henbury's wife suddenly moved their seats. Considering their seating changes in light of their families' histories reveals motivations other than life cycle, friendship, or public office. Both women were married to brewers. The Pomfretts were the wealthier family.[117] John Pomfrett styled himself a gentleman on his leases for the two taverns he ran in Westminster: the White Lion at Charing Cross and the Lamb on King Street.[118] John Pomfrett also held both guild offices and parish offices, culminating in his term as churchwarden from 1516 to 1518.[119] John Henbury, for his part, rented the Red Lion tavern or brew house next to Pomfrett's Lamb and also leased land in Charing Cross.[120] John Henbury also served as warden of two of Westminster's parish guilds, the St. Cornelius Guild and the prestigious Guild of St. Mary Rounceval, but he was never a churchwarden.[121] As befitted such active and prosperous members of the parish, both of these men's wives purchased seats in 1503, when their husbands were embarking on their careers. The men purchased their own seats a few years later—John Henbury in 1504 and John Pomfrett in 1509.[122] In 1515, on the eve of becoming churchwarden, John Pomfrett moved his seat, and then in 1517 he moved it again a second time.[123] In the same occupation and in business next door to one another, the men started out as business partners, but they eventually became fierce rivals. At about the time Pomfrett moved his seat for the second time this rivalry turned violent. Henbury accused Pomfrett of trying to force him out of his Red Lion tavern. According to Henbury's court petition, Pomfrett's servants seized Henbury's Thames wharf and "took up pavements, and stones of walls and glass of windows and so utterly destroyed the same [wharf]"[124] that it threatened Henbury with the loss of his leases from the Abbey. The dispute ended up in the Chancery Court, sometime between 1518 and 1529.[125]

During this conflict, both families moved their seats many times. Joan Pomfrett started the seat switching by purchasing a high profile seat "under our lady" in 1522. Possibly up in front of the Lady Aisle, by the Lady Chapel, she would have been very visible whenever she took her seat and as she sat to hear mass. Joan Pomfrett seems to have exerted some pressure to get this particular seat, because Mistress Clasy already sat there and remained there. The churchwardens' accounts suggest it was the location that Mistress Pomfrett wanted, not Mistress Clasy's company. John Pomfrett moved his seat again in 1523, and John Henbury moved his seat the year after that. John Pomfrett then moved a fourth time in 1525, and John Henbury's wife also moved her seat that same year. The settlement of the feud does not survive, but Pomfrett's greater wealth did not obviously vanquish Henbury, who was still active in parish life in the late 1520s and early 1530s, although problems with Pomfrett may have prompted Henbury to direct his new leases to London property. In 1530, he took out an additional lease on a brewery with shop in London, called the Cross Keys.[126]

Although the Pomfretts and Henburies tied some of this seat changing tied to their increasing social position in the community, this case also hints at the role women played in family visibility and feuding and how these concerns accompanied them to church. Initially, Mistress Pomfrett's and Mistress Henbury's behavior was typical of high-status women. They purchased their first seats just prior to their husbands' assumption of parish office, signaling their families' ambition and respectability. Yet the successive seat changes appear to be part of the performance of their feud. Although we only know the location of one of these many seats, improved locations and proximity to each other probably prompted seating decisions as both couples tried to outdo the other in displays of power and piety. Both wives' seats contributed to the public display and the posturing of the conflict. Not only were men and women concerned with the liturgy, but they were concerned with the political and social implications of attending mass.[127] Seat location played into all these issues.

An analysis of men's seating in Westminster reveals that they had some different concerns when purchasing seats. Friendships and business relations figured in men's seating decisions. Thomas Valentyne, also a brewer, changed his seat in 1515 to one with John Henbury.[128] The link between seating and the assumption of public or parish offices was also important to men: 18 percent of the churchwardens moved their seats when they assumed office. The location of the seat and/or enhanced prosperity, however, appears more prominent in men's decision making than in women's. Men appeared more willing to request a seat in a particular location, such as Master Hunt, who requested a seat in the Trinity aisle.[129] Yet marital status played no obvious role in men's seating. Men do not appear to have changed seats when they married or when their wives died. In 1521, when Ellen Attewell died, her husband John stayed in the same seat. By 1527 he had married a woman named Elizabeth. In 1529, when John died, Elizabeth moved her seat.[130] For men, seating brought visibility, but it also displayed legitimacy and respectability. Seats shared this meaning for women as well, but they were more obviously connected to their marital status and place in the life cycle.

Taken together, the similarities and differences between men's and women's seating shows that both recognized that seats gave visibility and could be tied to status, office holding, and social identity. Husbands and wives sometimes coordinated their seating movements in order to promote any number of family agenda. Women, however, marked more facets of their social and economic identities with their seating than did men, and they used seating to display more concerns and priorities than men. Because a wider range of women purchased seats, the dynamics in their section of pews would have been different from the men's section. Westminster women would have interacted, however briefly, with a wider cross-section of the community when they went to mass than did the men. This dynamic might further influence women's behavior at mass by heightening status tensions and the desire to flaunt family status and wealth. Yet the women's section might also have forged connections among women of varying wealth and position, giving them access to information on the condition of the church's goods and the needs of the liturgy.

Other Parishes, Other Priorities

Because the records for Westminster are so detailed, it is possible to connect seating purchases to a variety of other factors. Other, less-detailed, church-wardens' accounts suggest that not all parishes allowed women to act on their familial and social concerns as the women of St. Margaret's, Westminster, did. Even in those parishes where women could, the organization and layout of naves was locally specific, meaning that women would manifest the relationship between their seating and their marital, social, and economic position differently. By also establishing different rules or expectations for when individuals could change their seats, parishes expanded or contracted an individual's ability to incorporate other concerns such as ambitions or health into seating choices.

All Saints' was located in the center of the city of Bristol and had about 180 parishioners.[131] In this parish more men than women purchased seats. Of 213 seats purchased, women purchased only 47 percent, and of these women, 60 percent purchased seats at the same time as their husbands.[132] Men constituted 53 percent of the seat purchases, and 55 percent of these men also had wives sitting in seats. These figures mean that women attending mass at All Saints had a different social experience from women in Westminster. Women did not dominate the nave of this church, and by extension, the role women played in publicly marking their families' social identity also differed. Married couples were also the majority of men and women in this nave. Although the records do not say if seating was segregated by sex, we can see that sex and couple ratios alone created a very different dynamic in this nave than at St. Margaret's. In Westminster, women created visibility not only for their families, but also for themselves. In All Saints', women generally purchased seats when their husbands did, making the visibility accompanying seat purchases something husbands and wives shared, not something wives alone had.

The parishioners at All Saints' did not change their seats often, making seating less a reflection of social competition or changing social identity. Also different from Westminster was the fact that only two wives of All Saints churchwardens (2 percent) purchased or changed their seats when their husbands took office, compared to 37 percent in Westminster. In All Saints', with 98 percent of the churchwardens' wives already holding seats, seating appears as a necessary sign or precondition of respectability, status, and seriousness, qualities husbands and wives shared. It was not a privilege to be assumed and displayed when one's husband took parish office, as was the case in Westminster. Only two widows in All Saints', Bristol, purchased seats when their husbands died.[133] Instead of signaling the existence of a widows' section, these two women appear motivated by other concerns, possibly loss of wealth, declining health, or even remarriage. Thus, at mass in All Saints', women's seating more exclusively reflected their married status. What is more, the culture surrounding seating was not dominated by women, and thus was not as reflective of women's other concerns. Although competition and self-aggrandizement no doubt figured in some seating dynamics, the parish minimized them by limiting opportunities for changing seats. Again, this practice probably reflects a conscious policy rather than serendipity.

The seating arrangements in St. Edmund's, Salisbury, offer yet another variation. The surviving accounts start in 1469, but the parish only began to sell seats in 1477.[134] As in Westminster, women dominated seat purchases, but office holding appears to have mattered less in the decision to take a seat. St. Edmund's was one of three parishes located in the cathedral town of Salisbury. It was not as wealthy as the more centrally located parish of St. Thomas's, nor was it as implicated in town government as St. Thomas's.[135] In St. Edmund's, 291 women purchased seats compared to 177 men, making women 62 percent of the seat purchasers. Although we can assume that the majority of women were married, only 19 percent had a husband who purchased a seat as well.[136] This church also had a section of pews called "the wives' pews," implying that women and men sat apart.[137] As in Westminster, we see women trying to sit by friends, and we see attempts to move to better seats when they became available.[138] Life cycle also played a role. What we do not see are obviously elite men and women purchasing and moving seats commensurate with the acquisition of parish or public offices. Identifiable churchwardens and their wives did not generally purchase seats, either on their own or as part of a couple. Most couples, in fact (45 out of 60), purchased seats at the same time, while at Westminster most wives purchased seats in advance of their husbands, if their husbands in fact ever purchased a seat. Whatever seating meant to the women of this parish and however it fit into public displays of status, it was not obviously tied to their husband's office holding. This difference suggests that the health and social concerns evident among Westminster parishioners, and of which we see some evidence in St. Edmund's parish, were probably more important factors in women's choices of seat and that local status was not necessarily tied to parish office holding.[139] Office holdings' diminished role in this parish's seating arrangements may also reflect the parish's lesser status in the town. St. Edmund's was not as closely connected to the town government as St. Thomas's was.

Finally, in Ashburton, Devon, between 1489, when this parish started selling seats, and 1540, men purchased 89 percent (157 of 177) of the seats. Ashburton was a prosperous market town that served as one of the four stanneries in England. This meant that tin mined in the area was weighed, stamped, and taxed here. It was also an important center for the cloth industry.[140] While a few men purchased seats at the same time as their wives, most did not. Because there is less supporting documentation for this parish, it is difficult to create a social profile of these men. Of the 114 individuals serving as churchwarden, only 32 percent (36) also purchased seats. Most of them, however—64 percent (23)—purchased their seat prior to assuming office, suggesting some connection between the ability to attain an office and seat purchasing as a source of visibility and legitimacy. Eighteen of the men who purchased seats also appear on the lay subsidy of 1524.[141] Among these eighteen, those whose income fell below £4, generally had just purchased their seat. They were also at the beginning of their adult lives, and their seats were a sign of their expected prosperity. The remaining men were assessed at £8 or more, and had held their seats for many years, suggesting that they were at the end of their life and at their most prosperous. Although this still leaves a large number of men who purchased seats and did not hold office and a large number of prosperous men who never purchased seats, we can still see that for some, seat purchasing was a step on the way to local prominence.

Regardless of the other dynamics that seating arrangement created in the nave, seating gave women more visibility, even if they were a minority of those with seats. Women put this visibility in the service of their families' ambitions, but it could also be dangerous, if their husbands' ambitions clashed with others. Several plaintiffs pleading cases in Star Chamber accused the defendants of seeking out their wives in church and attacking them. This situation was what brought Giles Dobell of Minhead, Somerset, to court. He alleged that Robert Heyward, along with many others,

with force of arms that is to say with swords and daggers and other weapons . . . took out the said Margaret wife of your said orator of her said pew where she was kneeling in the said church and brought [her] out into an aisle in the said church against her will and then and there did beat and ill use her.[142]

This visibility also made women victims of bullying as Alicia Porter's husband alleged. He explained that a stranger, Richard Barowe, arrived at their Gloucestershire parish, sat down behind Alicia Porter and began to harass her. When asked to move he refused, even though there were other seats available. From this confrontation violence ensued.[143] Such obvious displays of status and inclusion aggravated many and made some women vulnerable as a result. Medieval society wanted women to keep a modest and low profile, but seating sometimes made this difficult.

The Pastons, never a family to hide their ambitions, had special seats in their parish church, but it did not insulate the Paston women from village politics or neighbor complaints. In 1443, William Paston bought licenses to divert a road in order to add a parlor and chapel onto his house. The change in the road meant a change in the parish's procession route. William's death a year later put the project in jeopardy as the parish and its churchwarden objected to the change. In 1451, William's widow, Agnes, was in conflict with the parish over this addition. While Agnes Paston sat in her pew in church on Sunday, many made their feelings known to her. In a letter to her son John, Agnes explains the physical dynamics of this interchange.

On the Sunday before St. Edmund, after evensong, Agnes Ball came up to me in my closet [enclosed pew] and bade me good evening, and Clement Spycer was with her. . . . And all that time, Warren Herman leaned over the parclose [half door to her pew] and listened [to] what we said.[144]

Clearly Agnes's pew separated her from her fellow parishioners physically, but her location did not isolate her from her neighbors or their ability to interact with her. Agnes Ball came into her pew with a man, and another man leaned over the partition to listen in on their conversation. Sex- and status-segregated seating did not put women or the elites in isolation as Bridget Stokes, discussed at the beginning of the chapter, had hoped.

Conclusion

Through seating arrangements, parishes could try to control women's behavior while they were in church. In doing so, seating arrangements reflect concerns about women's underlying motivations for attending church and late medieval society's belief that women needed governance. The clergy also expressed these concerns in their own writings. Yet in grouping parish women together and further delineating their seating in accordance with their local status or family ambitions, parishes further compelled women to connect their devotions to their family and household roles. Through seating, women joined their social, religious, and personal concerns to their parish participation. In parishes such as Westminster, where construction, lack of space, and local policies readily allowed parishioners to change their seats, women used their space in the nave to articulate further individual or collective identities. Women sat together because they were women, but smaller groups of women, as defined by social or marital status or pious interests or friendship, also sat together. For wealthy women with private chapels, such as Bridget Stokes, the space allowed them to re-create in physical and psychological ways their household roles. Most women did not have private chapels, but on a smaller scale, women such as Ellen Attewell, the Westminster wax chandler's wife, used their seating in similar ways. Shared conditions and identities brought women together in the nave in particular configurations. These arrangements had a number of implications. Ralph A. Houlbrooke has argued that women in preindustrial societies begin to act collectively when there is an infrastructure of specifically female social and economic contacts.[145] Through its seating arrangements, a parish church could enable or legitimized these connections or it could eliminate just such opportunities. But even for the large number of women who never held a seat, attendance at church would still have brought them into contact with other women, as they congregated in the back.

Comparing the seating arrangements of a number of parishes demonstrates the exceedingly local character of both spatial organization and parish gender relations. Parish leaders, aware of the potential dynamics in seating arrangement, established policies to shape these interactions. Westminster facilitated women's interaction, even if it was only an inadvertent consequence of rebuilding the church. All Saints', Bristol, limited these contacts among women. Women in All Saints' could forge relationships with those around them, but they could not readily, or at least did not, change their seating to create or enhance new relationships. Although gender was an organizing principle for many seating arrangements, it was more complicated than the mere separation of the sexes. Giving women space within the nave acknowledged their role in the parish community, even as it defined them as a group in need of regulation. Women could, in turn, use seating to act on their own priorities making them a part of their religious behavior and parish involvement.

When the churchwardens of Penhull, Lancashire, cited Agnes Atchyson and Johanna Bybby for failure to attend church, their excuse shows their priorities for church attendance. The women claimed they were too poor and had no clothes to wear to church.[146] It is unlikely the women were naked; more probably their clothes were in rags, and these two women thought them inappropriate relative to the standards and expectations of other women in church, so they stayed home.[147] Since some laity equated wearing nice clothes with devotion, the women may not have felt they could go to church because they could not behave appropriately. Behavior in this case was not simply sitting still, but going to church with the right clothing. They may also have viewed church attendance as a social, not a devotional, experience for a group that excluded them. In their excuse, however, we also hear the clergy's concerns that women used the church as a forum for their vanity, but beyond the clerical voices, we get a hint that attendance was also about women's culture, community belonging, and social identity.

Chapter 4

Maidens' Lights and Wives' Stores: Women's Parish Groups

Introduction

Sometime in the 1540s, Geoffrey Alsip, a parishioner of Chep-monger, Essex, went to the Court of Chancery on behalf of his wife Agnes.[1] In his petition, Geoffrey claimed that some twenty years earlier an old widow of the parish had left his wife a frontlet of gold, jewels, and pearls on the condition that she would "fit and put the said frontlet upon the image of Saint Margaret to garnish the same image . . . at every . . . feast."[2] Geoffrey claimed that Agnes had fulfilled this obligation faithfully until 1536 when Henry VIII ordered the removal of all saintly images from the parish churches. Agnes had continued to possess the wonderful decoration until its value drew the attention of the other parishioners. Led by the parish clerk and the churchwardens, the parishioners challenged Agnes's ownership in the local court. Unable to convince the judge of their ownership of the decoration, Geoffrey and Agnes turned to the royal Court of Chancery for their appeal.

The prominent role of women in this petition points to their particular interest in the cult of St. Margaret, the patron saint of childbirth, and to the collective religious activities of women more generally prior to the Reformation. The original owner of the decoration, the person who inherited it, and the saint who wore it were all women. What is more, the pearls, which embellished the frontlet, were believed to be beneficial against "running of blood and against the flux of the womb."[3] The frontlet's placement on an image of the patron saint of childbirth suggests that at least two women in this parish, and likely more, were concerned about childbirth and its dangers and prayed at the image of St. Margaret. The parish's challenge to Agnes's right to the frontlet may have involved Reformation politics; confiscating the frontlet was the parish's way of punishing her for

holding religious views at variance with the rest of the parish or that were
in conflict with the religious reforms being promulgated by Henry VIII. But
their challenge might also reflect the existence of an all-women's group
dedicated to St. Margaret and that Agnes did not really have a right to the
frontlet, it belonged to the women's group or the parish. Agnes may have
been the warden in charge the last year the women decorated the image,
and she kept the frontlet instead of turning it over to the parish.

Collective action was a hallmark of late medieval parish involvement.
Parishioners both raised money and worshiped collectively. By the middle
of the fifteenth century, collective action in single-sex groups had also become a commonplace of parish life. This chapter looks at how women organized themselves both temporarily to help their parishes raise money for
special projects and more permanently in associations that looked much
like parish guilds.[4] Whether these groups were fully constituted as guilds or
not, I argue that they contributed to the visibility that parish involvement
gave women. At the same time, these groups and their activities affirmed
and reinforced appropriate female behavior and interests for married
women and they helped socialized the large numbers of single women into
socially appropriate behavior. Women's abilities to create these groups
within their parishes speak as much to the atmosphere generated by parish
life as it does to women's interest in the parish's liturgical and cultic activities.

In the post-plague period there was tension surrounding women's visibility and mobility in society at large and these tensions were played out
in the parish. Didactic literature and sermons questioned the propriety of
women's behavior and activities within the church, yet medieval women
needed to go to church and parish membership required working to maintain and supply the church building. The means by which parishioners in
general fulfilled these goals and obligations often caused concern. Parish
fundraising frequently included excessive drinking, a manifestation of gluttony. Drunkenness could lead to violence, sexual permissiveness, and even
sacrilege. Seating, which as we have just seen filled the coffers of many
urban parishes, actively involved women in promoting familial displays of
status and wealth, which challenged Christian concerns for humility and
charity, but it also allowed women to form and act upon personal relationships. Parish maintenance offered women opportunities for public participation and collective action unusual in medieval society. The ability of
women to work together to forge common goals, exercise leadership, and
effect the community through their parish activities challenged prescribed

norms that women needed to be subservient, modest, and quiet. Indeed women's parish activities, although usually conducted to further religious and familial goals, propelled them to visibility, creating tensions that were difficult to reconcile with social expectations. It is impossible to determine whether these all-women's groups were an inevitable or at least expected consequence of their involvement in an institution that valued and promoted collective action, or whether they developed out of attempts by the parish to control women's behavior during a time when women's mobility and economic opportunities caused concern.

In the late medieval English parish, women began to develop collective consciousness cast in religious, marital, and gendered terms. Social theorists generally claim that medieval women did not share a common sense of identity. S. H. Rigby argues that "in terms of a *subjective* sense of social identity and immediate economic interests, membership of a household was more important than gender."[5] Ralph A. Houlbrooke, however, has remarked that the economic and social functions reserved for women brought them together "arguably facilitating the development of independent common opinions."[6] He adds further that women protesting in all-women or nearly all-women groups "were not feminist assertions of women's rights or interests against men, but rather expressions of shared or communal grievances which women, for one reason or another, felt best fitted to undertake."[7] While I would agree that the women acting in all-women's parish groups were not making recognizably feminist assertions, they were openly identifying and articulating their own parish and religious interests separately from men's and we have seen these interests grow out of gender-role expectations and identities.

Parish Fundraising

The laity had financial and physical responsibility for the nave and they organized themselves to raise and spend money to meet this responsibility. As we have already seen, testamentary bequests were one way the laity supported their parish. Yet testamentary bequests were only a fraction of a parish's income. Parishes relied on a variety of more predictable strategies for raising money. Urban parishes often rented out property, while rural parishes and town churches without property hosted ales and revels and held annual collections.[8] Some fundraising events were yearly, such as ales or wax collections. Documents rarely acknowledge women's individual contributions in such activities, but they did more than just attend. Women sometimes organized the event and brewed the ale, as Isabelle Wilmot and Margaret Stacy, of Tintinhull, Somerset, did in 1453.[9] Most parishes also raised some money through regular collections. Collections operated in a number of ways: collectors could go door-to-door, or "pass the hat" at the service. Occasionally women served as collectors. In 1514, Rosamond and Robert Hall collected money for St. Margaret's, Westminster, from those living in St. Stephen's alley and the tenement called Wool Staple.[10] Still, women's financial contributions remain obscure. Women's contributions, like their financial role in parish rents and ales, tend to be hidden by their memberships in households or in the parish more broadly.[11] We assume they gave less because they had less to give, but we cannot see through house doors to learn what influence wives had upon how much their husbands contributed. Only as widows or single women do their contributions become apparent in the documents.[12]

Occasional needs, such as a new chalice or a building project, such as a new aisle, called for special fundraising, and late medieval women frequently took an active role in these special endeavors by organizing and carrying out all-women's fundraising activities. Marital status usually defined participation in these groups. In the Cornish parish of St. Neot's, the "wives of the western part of the parish," "the sisters," and the young men all donated windows and the patrons had themselves depicted kneeling in a row. These three windows are dated 1528, 1529, and 1530 respectively[13] (see Figure 4.1). In Great Dunmow, Essex, the wives of the community raised money in 1529 for new surplices, and in 1536 to "redeem the pax," which the parish had used as collateral on a loan.[14] The maidens and young men of All Saints', Derby, organized themselves to raise money for a new bell tower.[15] In the urban parish of St. Ewen's, Bristol, the wives of former churchwardens organized and ran a collection in 1466 that raised 83s. for a new silver censer.[16] There women worked in pairs, possibly each pair in charge of a neighborhood or street.[17] Their connections to parish administration and their greater knowledge of parish issues would have helped them raise funds effectively. Not all such attempts were so successful, however. In 1521, the parish of St. Lawrence's, Reading, had to pay for painting the image of St. Leonard because the wives had left it unfinished.[18]

With these women's collections, we see something we do not generally see in medieval society at large: women working collectively on an economic venture. When confronted with a communal need, women organized all-women's groups arranged usually around marital status, but also

Figure 4.1. Stained glass window for St. Neot's, Cornwall, donated by the wives of the parish. Photograph by C. David Benson.

by neighborhood, to meet that need. Parish involvement afforded women the opportunity to work together for a common concern. One consequence of such collective action was that it led to greater female visibility within a parish, despite strictures against women calling attention to themselves.

Parish Guilds

English parishes had a variety of subparochial groups of greater or lesser permanence dedicated to supporting an endowment in the church, usually a chapel or a light. The most institutionalized were usually called parish guilds or confraternities, and these groups were a ubiquitous feature of late medieval religious life.[19] Less formalized groups also formed, usually to support a light. These smaller groups, although often headed by a warden, elude easy terminology and might be variously referred to by the property they held in common to support the light, such as a "store of St. Katherine," or by the object they maintained such as the "light of St. Mary in the Chapel." These groups might or might not render annual accounts of their finances. Guilds, with their more sophisticated organization, provided many of the same social and religious services as parishes, but on a more focused and often more intimate scale. What is more, they were voluntary associations, and although often tied to a parish, they were not, strictly speaking, based on geographical boundaries the way parishes were.[20] In 1389, afraid that parish guilds promoted treason and sedition, Richard II ordered an investigation of the functions, membership, and origins of all parish guilds. According to the more than 500 surviving guild returns, only a fraction of what must have been originally collected, many guilds originated in the period just after the Black Death.[21]

Traditionally, scholars understood guilds as burial societies. Members sought insurance for a Christian burial and quick salvation from purgatory during this period of social and emotional upheaval. Burials were, indeed, one aspect of a guild's concerns, but more recent research has emphasized shared devotion to a patron saint or Christ, conviviality, social and political networking, and financial help for members fallen on hard times.[22] Gervase Rosser has argued that guild formation was in part a response to parish inadequacies: in a guild, members could address social and spiritual concerns that the parish, for whatever reason, did not or could not meet.[23] Eamon Duffy has countered that guilds brought into greater relief concerns and issues already present in a parish.[24] Whether responding to local inadequacies or not, guilds gave members a forum for sharing a common devotion with other like-minded people. Members often organized their guilds around common identities such as status or occupation. The fullers and weavers in the tiny parish of Croscombe, Somerset, for example, each had a parish guild that supported a light in the parish church.[25]

Guild members directed their devotions toward an image of their patron, usually located in the parish church. According to the guild returns, three-quarters of these parish guilds burned candles in front of an image, certainly on feast days, but in some cases probably every Sunday as well.[26] The image might be freestanding, as in the case of Tintinhull, Somerset, where the Guild of St. Mary cared for a statue of the Virgin,[27] or painted on the wall, as in the case of the chapel for Chagford, Devon's Guild of St. Michael.[28] Wealthier guilds might have their own chapel with an altar, smaller or poorer ones typically had an image and a light somewhere in the nave. Freestanding images were dressed and could be carried in parish processions. Guild inventories also show that members marched in processions honoring their saint by carrying banners with the saints' image on them.[29] Ken Farnhill has argued that "through the cult of the patron, one can see the dual emphasis within the fraternities on their care for their living and the dead membership."[30]

Membership in parish guilds was typically open to both men and women. The guild returns show that in 1389, only five limited membership to men, and there were no guilds exclusively for women.[31] The membership list for the Guild of St. Peter in Bardwell parish, Suffolk, shows that women made up nearly 50 percent of its lay members. There were thirty married couples, thirty single men, and twenty-four single women.[32] Women were less prevalent in Wydmondham's Guild of the Nativity of the Blessed Virgin, perhaps only a third of the membership.[33] Farnhill's study of East Anglian guilds found that women made up a significant part of guild membership, but he could find no discernible pattern of membership based on gender.[34]

Guilds required their members to pay dues or make regular financial contributions. The Assumption Guild in Westminster required a quarterly payment.[35] Typically, guild wardens oversaw payment of dues and other fundraising activities. Like parishes, guilds relied on a variety of fundraising strategies. Some owned rental property, others hosted ales, and others had stocks of cash, grain, and livestock from which members could borrow, purchase, or lease. This gave many guilds functions akin to credit unions or banks, and those with stocks had more flexible finances than those with just property.[36] Some guilds split their stock between male and female members, giving each group responsibility for one aspect of guild life, such as supplying the wax. This is probably what the wives of St. Edmund's, Salisbury, were doing when they raised money for "the wives' light."[37] Similarly, the Guild of St. Peter in Swaffham, Norfolk, had a women's stock, and the "sisters" of this guild raised money together for the repairing of the steeple.[38]

The guilds used their funds to maintain the image of the patron saint, the lights, and the chapel, pay for a chaplain and guild feast, and to support indigent members. Westminster's Assumption Guild maintained several almsmen and women, who lived in guild-owned houses and who received an annual stipend. These men and women were not random poor people, but members fallen on hard times. Lettice Fisher, for example, was well-to-do enough that she purchased a seat in the nave in 1508 for 12d.[39] Her husband John died in 1515, after which point she became a guild almswoman, living in one of their tenements.[40] When almswoman Margaret Rogers died in 1515, the guild paid for her funeral, which included a vigil "with fire and candles for the one who watched her."[41] Some guilds also agreed to bring the body of a deceased member home for burial if it was not too far away. The activities and venerations supported by the guilds allow us to see the various interest groups at work within the parish. They organized themselves around issues of devotion, self-help, and social interactions, which were legitimate avenues of religious expression.

Both Farnhill and Rosser have argued that hosting a feast was central to the definition of a subparochial group as a guild.[42] At the feast, members from different social strata and groups met and forged an identity based on the shared concerns of the guild. These associations could be turned to social advancement both within the guild or parish, but also in the larger community. Some feasts were elaborate affairs, requiring many specialized cooks and exotic ingredients. The menu for Westminster's Assumption Guild feast included swans, herons, beef, wine and ale, and dishes flavored with pepper, saffron, cloves, mace, almonds, cinnamon, and sugar.[43] In keeping with the kinds of duties they had to their families and to the parish, female guild members supplied ale, milk, flour, calves' feet, table linens, and liveries for the servers.[44] At the feast itself, the guild also hired women to tend the buttery, kitchen, poultry, and to wash the dishes and scour the pots.[45] Cooking for such an occasion created further connections between women. So important was the guild feast that some guilds even owned a hall in which to hold it.[46]

At some point in the fifteenth or sixteenth centuries, parish guilds began changing their emphases and concerns, and parishioners started forming more permanent single-sex organizations. Studies of the better-documented mixed-sex parish guilds show that at this time, many existing guilds began limiting their membership by income level.[47] This strategy had the effect of curtailing social networks and contacts and limiting them to people of similar rank and interests. Charles Phythian-Adams has shown that membership in the town of Coventry's Trinity Guild was a prerequisite for holding an office in the city's government.[48] Guild membership provided people with the opportunity to learn skills necessary for further advancement, contacts to achieve promotion, and visibility to encourage public support. This move toward elitism is similar to the move toward defining religious involvement in terms of gender roles. These groups represented voluntary ways of meeting specific concerns about family, prosperity, class, occupation, geographic location, or gender within the larger and more diverse unit of the parish. Guilds had always promoted lay involvement in Christianity in ways that were both supportive of parish participation and reflective of different needs and concerns within the parish. With the active role women played in other areas of parish life, setting up their own all-women's groups was an obvious next move.[49]

The Rise of Women's Groups

It is impossible to know precisely how many parishes had women's guilds or women's groups, but women's organizations appear to be more common than previously thought. Because they were not as formal or as institutionalized as some of the older or wealthier mixed-sex guilds, they are poorly documented and difficult to classify. For example in Walberswick, Norfolk, the churchwardens' accounts usually note a sum of money for Our Lady's Guild although they rarely list a warden. Twice, however, individual women present money to the parish from the guild.[50] These brief entries might signal that women ran this group or that these two women were the widows of guild wardens. Similarly, in 1408 the churchwardens of Hungerford, Wiltshire, alleged that both Juliana Farman and Margery Coterall had stolen a chalice, a missal, a set of vestments, three altar cloths, a portable altar, sixteen sheep, and ten marks from St. Katherine's light.[51] Such a varied list of "stolen" items suggests an alternative explanation for their behavior, however. This list looks like an inventory of the light's goods and endowments and that these women might not have been common thieves, but had served as the light's wardens and, therefore, had charge of the light's property during their term of office. For whatever reason, when their term was over, they refused to relinquish the goods to their successors, and were thus charged with stealing these items. This too might have been a women's endowment. I have found thirty sets of churchwardens' accounts that mention a women's endowment of some kind.[52] Other sources such as wills, inventories, or dedications reveal the existence of similar women's associations in still more communities (see Appendix A). For example, the maiden's light in Long Sutton, Lincolnshire, is only mentioned in a single will, while the "Sisterhood of St. Anne" in the parish of St. Olave, Southwark, just appears in a parish inventory, although testators such as Johanna Hodson remembered the altar it supported in their wills.[53] The failure of these organizations to appear in churchwardens' accounts should not, therefore, be taken as proof that they did not exist nor that they were only temporary associations. Churchwardens were often capricious in their recordkeeping.[54]

Membership in such single-sex groups was organized around a number of interests. The most common one was marital status. There were groups for maidens and groups for wives. There is no evidence of groups for widows, but there is also no evidence that women left their wives' groups at the death of their husbands.[55] Membership could also be based on where one lived. Wimborne Minster had two such women's groups, one for the "wives of the town" and one for the "wives of the country or land."[56] At other times, all-women's groups organized themselves around occupation, such as in St. Martin-in-the-Fields, Westminster, where there was a light that "the midwives made."[57]

Many of the parishes with all-women's groups or activities are found in the southern and western parts of England in both urban and rural communities (see Map 4.1). That there are more examples in Devon and Cornwall than in any other county is probably in part the result of genuine regional differences and in part because of the serendipitous survival of sources, since about 20 percent of all pre-Reformation churchwardens' accounts come from these same two counties.[58] Most examples of women serving as churchwardens also come from the West Country, and this suggests that the region may have been more accepting of women's parochial leadership.[59] Parishes around the Wash in Lincolnshire, however, had maidens' lights, but no wives' lights, suggesting yet another regional variation.

The activities and organizations that catered specifically to women varied in their level of organization and autonomy. The "sisterhood" of St. Anne in St. Olave's, Southwark, appears as a separate organization; a church inventory from 1485 states that it had given the parish a chalice.[60] Some endowments, such as the light to St. Katherine in Horley, Surrey, or to the chapel of St. Mary in Chagford, Devon, also appear to be supported by permanent associations of women.[61] In other parishes, such as Swaffham and Holy Trinity, Cambridge, the women appear to have worked as a subgroup of a larger parish guild. In the city of Chester, the banns for the Corpus Christi play (c. 1467) list the town's wives as the producers of the Assumption play. Whether these women were part of a larger Assumption Guild, or had formed their own independent group, they routinely produced a play. It required working together and providing both time and financial commitment to the project.[62] In St. Edmund's, the wives hosted an annual Whitsuntide dance to raise money for the parish. Some of the proceeds supported a "wives' light," but the women apparently did not have a fully independent organization. The churchwardens oversaw the management and maintenance of the light, repaired the cross that the wives used in their processions, and even paid for a minstrel to play at the wives'

Map 4.1. Known women's and maidens' groups. Created by Stephen Hanna.

dance.[63] Their dance was one event in a larger program of entertainment-oriented fundraising sponsored by this parish. At the same time, the women of St. Edmund's parish had a processional cross, which suggests that they marched together, giving them some parish recognition as a separate group.

Several sets of churchwardens' accounts seem to reveal the initial appearance of women's groups, and in the process they betray a growing interest in gendered devotions. Often, however, several years of accounts pass before there is even a limited explanation of what sort of endowment the women supported. This may reflect either the group's relative independence from the parish or the group's occasional nature. In Ashburton, Devon, and St. Margaret's, Westminster, the appearance of women's groups coincided with the expansion of other parish activities. In the 1480s St. Margaret's parish began purchasing more church decorations for the feasts of St. Margaret and St. Katherine, and the St. George's procession began including a dragon.[64] By 1512, after a few false starts, the parish maidens finally established their own annual collection that helped support the chapel of St. Margaret located in the chancel.[65] Although the maidens participated in the parish-wide cult of St. Margaret, there was no guild or store dedicated to overseeing devotion to St. Margaret. Some support came from the maidens, but individuals and the parish as a whole also contributed significant sums of money on different occasions. In Ashburton, the number of parish guilds also began increasing in the late fifteenth century. In 1507, the accounts list twelve separate groups contributing to various endowments within the church: included in this list were several guilds dedicated to saints, one group called the "green torches" and another listed as the "wives' store."[66]

The details surrounding the development of the women's group in Chagford, Devon, are unusually vivid, and the organization appears to be quite permanent. The accounts for this parish start in 1480.[67] Several parish guilds and stores supported the church and its endowments, including one called the store of St. Mary in the Church, which had two male wardens. Starting in 1500, women became the wardens, and by 1517, in a move that reflects some sexual humor, they changed the date of their audit from the Feast of the Conception to the Feast of the Purification.[68] These changes suggest that the women took over the organization and refocused it to reflect their concerns and experiences. Although, both the Feast of the Conception and the Feast of the Purification would have been celebrated by the whole parish, as we have seen, purifications or churchings were an opportunity for an all-women gathering, and it seems an appropriate holiday for an all-women's group to audit their accounts. At about the same time, Chagford's St. Katherine's Guild may have become an all-male organization. Initially the accounts mention both the brothers and sisters of the guild, but by 1499 the accounts begin referring only to the brothers of the guild.[69]

Variations in organizational structures probably reflect different moments in the development of all-women's groups. Some groups seem to have had less independence from the parish than others. The groups in Chagford and Horley appear to be permanent and independent, even if we do not have evidence of a feast. Both groups rendered accounts, and in Chagford they had a chapel. Yet the wives in St. Edmund's, Salisbury, were a subgroup of a wider parochial devotion.

Only in the Devon parishes of Broadhempston and Woodland did the women's groups disappear before the Reformation. In Broadhempston, the men took over the women's St. Mary's Guild in 1520, and in Woodland the women's accounts for their guild of St. Mary disappeared after 1531.[70] When the Woodland store of the Virgin Mary reappeared in 1537, it was being run by men. As is typical of churchwardens' accounts, they offer no explanation for the changes, but these stops and starts illustrate the occasional nature of some of these groups. For some groups, the initial enthusiasm probably waned when the founder died and the group withered away. Other groups might have suffered the disapproval of the parish. Medieval society by and large distrusted women in groups, fearing they would lead women to acts of disobedience or even rebellion.

Literature provides some sense of the distrust and low opinion that many had for all-women's groups. In the morality play *The Castle of Perseverance*, the author writes "Go forth, and let the whores cackle! / Where women are, are many words: / Let them go hopping with their finery! / Where geese sit, are many turds."[71] As Sandy Bardsley points out, these lines tap into late medieval anxiety about women's speech; women's words are waste. But these lines are no more complementary about women in a group. Together they produce dung while preening in their fine clothes. These types of literary complaints see groups of women as challenging men's authority and social position. Women will reveal their husband's failings and encourage each other to defy their husbands. In groups, the influence that housewives gained through knowledge of family needs and weaknesses could be turned into more potent forms of rebellion.

The character of Mrs. Noah, in both the Wakefield and the Chester mystery plays about the great flood, would rather stay with her friends than follow Noah to the ark. In the Chester play she declares,

For without fail
I will not leave this town
Because I have all of my friends
One foot further I will not go;
They shall not drown by St. John,
And I may save their life.
They loved me full well, by Christ;
So you must let them into your boat.
Or else row forth, Noah wherever you will go,
And get yourself a new wife.[72]

In the context of the play, Mrs. Noah's disloyalty to Noah and love for her friends is misguided and humorous, an inversion of the expected household order. It is nevertheless a strong statement about the relationships of women to each other, and what those relationships meant to women. These examples all express anxiety about what women say and do when they are together and away from men's supervision. Women in groups challenged male authority, not only with their words, but with their collective actions. The parish church as a source of much social interaction by women posed a challenge to medieval society in this respect.

In contrast, a late fifteenth-century ballad "Wives at the Tavern," which imagines the conversation of six women gathered at a local tavern, gives a fuller sense of what might have attracted women to all-women's groups, while at the same time affirming the rebellious potential of such associations. In this ballad, the women challenge society's good order, although the anonymous author is not altogether unsympathetic to these women's plight. At the tavern, the women to drink too much expensive wine, gossip loudly, discuss their husbands, and encourage each other to neglect their households, their families, and their work.

How say you friends, is the wine good?
"That it is," quoth Elinor "by the cross;
It cherishes the heart, and comforts the blood;
Such junkets among shall make us live long!"
. . .
This is the thought the friends take,
Once in the week merry will they make,
And all small drink they will forsake;
But wine of the best shall have no rest.[73]

The poem goes on to illustrate just why such occasions were of interest to women. Within this supportive and nurturing atmosphere, these women shared the food that they had brought, wished absent friends were with them, comforted those who were victims of domestic violence, denounced men's power and authority over them, and argued for a household order that put women in charge.

Each of them brought forth their dish;
Some brought flesh, and some brought fish.
Said Margaret meek, now with a wish,
"I would Anne were here, she would make us cheer.
. . .
Would God I had listened to your counsel!
For my husband is so wrathful
He beat me like the devil of hell;
and the more I cry the less mercy!"

Alice with a loud voice spoke then
Truly she said "it is little good he does
Who beats or strikes any woman,
And especially his wife; God give him short life!"

Margaret meek said, "as I may thrive
I know no man that is alive,
That give me two strokes, but I shall have five;
I am not afeard, though I have no beard!"[74]

Their momentary escape from their household duties temporarily released them from their husband's control, and their shared values and experiences serve as fodder for further rebellion. Moreover, audiences hearing this ballad would have recognized that women at a tavern were not working for their families, were talking to strangers, and were spending family money.[75]

The tavern and church were oppositional places, the former a place of sin, and the latter of prayer. Parishioners avoiding church often found refuge in the tavern. However, the ballad "The Wives at the Tavern," with its more sympathetic treatment of women's relationships, blurs the boundary between church and tavern when considered in light of the new women's groups. Both could foster rebellion, but both could also provide women with a support group. The dynamics outlined in this ballad are similar to the ones created by an all-women's parish group. In all-women's groups, women were in charge, they worked together, made financial decisions, may have shared food, and probably found comfort in their shared experiences. The ballad of the "Wives at the Tavern" offers an elaboration on the kinds of interactions fostered by women's groups and the challenges that they posed to medieval society.

Patron Saints

Although the patron saint was an important figure in all-women's groups and guilds, many accounts are vague about exactly which saints women's groups supported (see Appendix A). In Croscombe, Somerset, and Holy Trinity, Exeter, we are told only that the women raised money for a maidens' light, but not the saint to whom the light was dedicated. In an early work on English parish guilds, Herbert Westlake posited that women were more involved with guilds devoted to Mary than others.[76] While he offered no empirical evidence for this claim, other than that there were more parish guilds dedicated to Mary than any other saint, he is still correct in his basic evaluation of women's interests within the late medieval cult of the saints.[77] Of the nearly fifty women's groups examined in this study, twenty-five have no specified patron, seventeen were dedicated to Mary, two to St. Anne, and one each was dedicated to St. Katherine, St. Margaret, St. Ursula, and St. Stephen. One other women's group supplied the taper to the Easter Sepulcher.[78] All of these saints were very popular in the later Middle Ages, and their images adorned parish rood screens, walls, and side altars.[79] So important was the patron saint to the guild that celebrations of the patronal day were often the largest single expense in mixed-sex guilds. Not only did the guild celebrate a mass for the saint in the chapel, but it also had a procession and a banquet. For those guilds where accounts are still extant, we see that devotion to the patron constituted a major focus of annual guild activity and expense. Although we do not have the same vivid records for all-women's groups, it is likely that the patron saints were still important, and that they were the focus of both financial activities and iconographic displays.

In parishes where women's groups were part of parish-wide devotions, we can sometimes piece together their activities from the churchwardens' accounts. For example in St. Edmund's, Salisbury; Ashburton, Devon, and St. Ewen's, Bristol, the women's groups were part of larger parochial Marian devotions centered on a chapel and an image. In 1491, John Brigge, a wealthy clothier from Salisbury, asked to be buried in St. Edmund's by the north altar, called the wives' altar, under the image of the Blessed Virgin Mary. He also left 20s. for the maintenance of the altar.[80] As we have seen, the wives of this parish marched together in parish processions. The maidens of St. Ewen's raised money to support a light before an elevated image of the Virgin. The statue was on a tabernacle and a colored curtain could be drawn around it.[81] The altar attracted offerings from individual parishioners of both sexes. In Ashburton, St. Mary's altar received support from both men and women acting within their own groups. The men were in a group called the Hogens, who were probably a variation of the Hogglers found in other parishes.[82] Both groups contributed money to St. Mary's altar, located in one of the church's aisles. The wives' group contributed more money than the men's group, appeared more regularly in the accounts, and seemed more enthusiastic than the Hogens. In 1491, when the carved panel behind the altar (the reredos) needed repainting and gilding, it was the women who put out a coffer before the altar to collect donations.[83]

The Virgin Mary also had a prominent place in the Devonshire parish of Chagford. By 1480, there were two stores devoted to her cult, each supporting a separate endowment: the store of St. Mary in the Church and the store of St. Mary in the Chapel. In the early 1500s, the store supporting St. Mary in the Chapel closed, leaving only St. Mary in the Church and an empty chapel. Soon after women took over the store of St. Mary in the Church and moved their devotional attention to the empty chapel, reports of repairs then began to appear in their accounts. They first bought a new key for the chapel door, and they then had the roof fixed, new tiles laid, the walls repaired and replastered, and the glass replaced.[84] They seem to have finished their repairs by the late 1520s. Although repair work of this kind was a regular part of parish life, the concentrated activity on the chapel after the women took it over suggests that the women were doing more than maintenance work after a few years of neglect. They were also updating the images and decorations to suit their own devotional interests. With the closing of the store of St. Mary in the Chapel, the women were able to establish their own space within the church; looking after it in much the same manner they would have their houses.

The maidens of St. Margaret's, Westminster, also participated in the parish's cult of St. Margaret, the parish's patron saint. To celebrate her day, the parishioners decorated the church with rose garlands and rushes, held a vigil, and instituted a collection for candles and processional expenses.[85] With the added income, the parish hired minstrels for the maidens' section of the procession, provided garlands for the priests, clerks, and wardens to wear, and began paying the "singing men" a small stipend.[86] By 1523, the maidens received new clothes to wear during the procession, which suggests that they, too, marched as a group.[87] Inside the church, there was an elaborate altar dedicated to St. Margaret. The parish had a silver and coral bead necklace that the wardens were to hang around the saint's neck "everyday or else every holy day as the wardens of the church see best."[88] Starting in 1526, the parish began work on a new tabernacle for the image of St. Margaret. Her tabernacle had twelve gilded and painted images and scenes from her vita and a martyr's crown suspended from above.[89]

The elaborate contents and images of Westminster's Margaret Chapel, along with many other medieval chapels, disappeared in the Reformation or in subsequent remodeling or rebuilding. The fragments that still survive suggest that many such chapels sported iconography that specifically addressed women's concerns for fertility and motherhood. One of the most famous of these chapels is the Mary chapel at Ranworth, Norfolk, which Duffy has identified as a focus of women's offerings and prayers.[90] The images on the chapel's screen show a concern for childbirth, children, and motherhood. On this screen are St. Margaret, the patron saint of childbirth, and the Holy Kindred, the three daughters of St. Anne: Mary Salome, Mary Cleophas, and the Virgin Mary, and their children. The image of the Holy Kindred affirmed and sanctified motherhood, fertility, and family.[91] The three Marys are surrounded by their children, the young saints James the Great, John the Evangelist, Jesus, James the Less, Jude, Simon, and Jose, who all play with toy versions of their attributes: John has a toy eagle and James the Less' fuller's club becomes a bubble pipe (see Figure 4.2). The child saints also appear as adults elsewhere on the screen suggesting the hope that children would grow up. Taken together, these images betray concerns for safe and successful childbirth and child rearing.

The surviving wall painting in the Mary chapel in St. Thomas's, Salisbury, may have also been directed at concerns for fertility. The one surviving image shows Mary visiting Elizabeth. Both women are visibly pregnant, and reach out to touch each other's swollen bellies (see Figure 4.3). The restored version of the painting shows both women looking very pleased with themselves. None of the chapel's other wall paintings survive, so it is difficult to place this one in context, but fertility and family are easily read into this particular painting. The missing images probably portrayed other scenes from the Virgin's life, which could also address fertility and family concerns.

Children seem to be a central theme of the mid-sixteenth-century rood screen at Loddon, Norfolk. The surviving screen panels show the annunciation, the nativity, the adoration of the Magi, the circumcision, the presentation at the temple (partially destroyed), the martyrdom of William of Norfolk, the Ascension, and a red-cloaked figure with a cowl over his head holding an upright dagger by the point (see Figures 4.4a and 4.4b).[92]

Figure 4.2. Marian altar screen, Ranworth, Norfolk. Photograph courtesy of the Conway Library, Courtauld Institute of Art.

William was believed to be a child martyr ritually murdered by Jews. As both a local and a child martyr, his inclusion in the screen fits in with the theme of childhood. According to his vita, he was especially solicitous of women's and children's prayers.[93]

Wall paintings and screens are only a fraction of the imagery that would have promoted a guild's cult. Stained-glass windows, altar cloths, vestments, and statues would also be likely trappings in a chapel. The variety of artistic media gave artists and their patrons numerous ways of promoting women's devotions.

While we might associate childbirth most obviously with women, men also cared about the survival of their wives and children. Many men lost wives and infants during this dangerous event, and many were patrons of these images and chapels. Miriam Gill suggests that a likely patron of the Ranworth screen is Robert Iryng whose will left money for the painting of the screen above the St. Mary Altar.[94] Men certainly cared about the fertility of their wives, childbirth, and the survival of both their wives and their children. Separate religious groups for women that focused on childbirth did not exclude men's prayers, money, or concerns.

Figure 4.3. Mary's visit to Elizabeth, wall painting, St. Mary Chapel, St. Thomas's, Salisbury. Photograph by Lydia Murdoch.

Maidens and Single Women

The presence of patron saints in the local liturgy encouraged pious behavior and opened up access to divine intervention through female saints. Although the cults of female saints drew the participation of both men and women, the images of these particular cults drew inspiration from the fe-

Figure 4.4a. Presentation at the Temple, rood screen, Lodden, Norfolk. Photograph by Katherine L. French.

Figure 4.4b. Adoration of the Magi, rood screen, Lodden, Norfolk. Photograph by
Katherine L. French.

male body and life cycle. Mary conceived immaculately, and the virgin martyrs suffered physical torments often directed at their female anatomy. The tendency of women's groups to venerate female saints suggests that through these images, medieval women gained strength and comfort. As Patricia Crawford has written "women saints provided a feminine influence on religion."[95] Episcopal constitutions for both Canterbury and Worcester made the connection between women and women saints when they prohibited women from working on the feasts of Agnes, Margaret, Lucy, and Agatha.[96]

The virgin martyrs in particular served as models for young women.[97] The virgin martyrs were a group of young women, most commonly, Dorothy, Katherine, Lucy, Apollonia, Agnes, Cecilia, and Barbara, who purportedly lived in the second and third centuries, when Christianity was illegal. They refused to marry pagan Romans and suffered gruesome tortures in an effort to remain chaste and single. Ultimately they died for their faith. Their cults were tremendously popular in late medieval England and numerous collections of saints' lives recounted their legends.[98] Their images appeared throughout parish churches, their saints' days were cause for celebration, and their stories informed many didactic texts. They served as role models for young medieval women because moralists tried to match role models to women's life stage.

In the late Middle Ages, characterizations of the virgin martyrs in literature and art changed in order to make them more appropriate role models for young women of the era. This new style of virgin martyr fostered submissive and courteous behavior among young women, instead of the defiance so central to earlier portrayals.[99] The *Golden Legend* and the *South English Legendary*, both popular collections of saints' lives from the thirteenth century, portrayed the virgin martyrs as triumphant, defiant, heroic, and confrontational as they endured their tortures.[100] Yet in the late fourteenth, fifteenth, and early sixteenth centuries, depictions of these young female martyrs, such as those found in the two fifteenth-century English translations of *The Book of the Knight of the Tower*, Mirk's *Festial*, and other sermon collections, as well as elite collections of saints' lives, were not defiant. When the knight recounts the life of St. Anastasia to his daughters, he portrays Anastasia as a pious and charitable wife, not an insubordinate and defiant one. She aided those wrongly imprisoned, but the knight does not explain that Anastasia angered her pagan husband by dispensing charity without his permission or that he imprisoned her for defying him.[101] The knight similarly recommends to his daughters emulation of Saints Lucy and

Cecilia "and many other ladies" who gave charity to the poor. He is not promoting defiance against either a husband or king. Instead, he edits their stories to turn them into models of decorum and passivity.[102] Katherine Lewis, who has looked particularly at St. Katherine, has argued that the clergy promoted this saint as a particular paradigm of maidenhood, the ideal age of a woman.[103] St. Katherine was a very popular cult in late medieval England. Her story appears in wall paintings, windows, and sermon cycles.[104] In Somerset, Yorkshire, and Cambridgeshire she was the most popular saint after the Virgin.[105] Late medieval versions of her life present Katherine as "demure, lovely and practical," attributes that fit well with the behavior promoted in conduct literature, and make her a particularly appropriate model for maidens.[106]

Late medieval parents, clergy, and employers all promoted passivity and silence as particular manifestations of women's Christian behavior. Mirk's story of the Annunciation in his sermon for that feast day emphasizes Mary's silence during Gabriel's speech. Mirk explains, "Wherefore a maiden must be of few words, and see that she speaks honestly and courteously to her parson, for it is an old English saying that 'a maid should be seen, but not heard.'"[107] A sermon for the second Sunday in Lent tells the Gospel story of the Canaanite mother with the possessed daughter (Matt. 15:21–28). The sermon writer explains that Jesus healed the woman because she had faith and because she asked meekly.[108] Even housewives in charge of servants and raising daughters probably advocated such behavior; we should not, therefore, assume that these were simply men's values imposed on women.

The late fourteenth- or early fifteenth-century wall painting at Sprole, Norfolk, is one of the most detailed depictions of the life of St. Katherine. It not only shows Katherine refusing to obey Maxentius's order to sacrifice to an idol, it vividly paints her preaching to the fifty pagan philosophers sent to confound her. Yet, later fifteenth- and sixteenth-century depictions, especially those on rood screens—the wooden fence that divided the nave and chancel—promoted modesty and courtesy. The virgin martyrs wear sumptuous contemporary clothing and hold themselves and their symbols demurely with cast-down eyes in the manner of well-bread, modest women (see Figure 1.1).[109] Their defiance is elided and the presence of their devices—such as the wheel for Katherine or the tower for Barbara—only implies their tortures, they are not depicted.

In Mirk's late fourteenth-century accounts of the virgin martyrs, they are not only meek, they suffer. For Mirk, one of the saints' big attractions was their suffering. In his sermons, he tells the laity they were to venerate the saints for three reasons: their holiness, miracles, and passion or suffering.[110] In his account of the life of St. Margaret, Mirk altogether eliminates Margaret's confrontation with her pagan suitor-tormentor Olibrius.[111] The compiler of the fifteenth-century sermon collection, the *Speculum Sacerdotale*, dwells on St. Katherine's suffering and teaching, not her defiance of Maxentius, her pagan suitor-tormentor.[112] By shifting their focus to the virgin martyrs' suffering, late medieval preachers emphasized what Karen Winstead has called the "transferable qualities" of courtesy, patience, diligence, humility, piety, and charity, which would make the saints suitable models for laywomen.[113] The virgin martyrs became heroic examples of gracious comportment.[114] Winstead believes that this shift was a consequence of the bourgeois audience's increased consumption of books. Authors wrote for paying customers who did not want saints' lives that would challenge their social positions or promote immodest and unruly behavior among women.[115]

The stories of the virgin martyrs as they appear in Mirk and other sermon collections begin with the saint as a young girl. A key moment in the story is her learning about Christianity and then converting. According to Mirk,

when Margaret was born, the father sent her into the country to a nurse, so while she was there among other maidens, she heard speak of God and of our Lord Jesus Christ, how he bought mankind with his death out of servitude of the devil, and how he loved specially all who would live in chastity and serve him in simplicity and poverty. Then, when Margaret heard of this, she made a vow in her heart that she would never have part of a man's body, but live with her maidenhood all her life.[116]

St. Winifred, a popular British saint, converted to Christianity after hearing a hermit preach.[117] These stories reinforce the idea that young girls could learn about and then adopt Christian behavior. Moreover, both Margaret and Winifred learn through hearing, a more passive form of education than reading or debate. Late medieval parents and clergy did not want to teach young girls about defiance and rebellion, therefore, these sermons reconfigured the stories of the virgin martyrs emphasizing female styles of learning and conformity to contemporary behavioral ideals.

Maidens' groups gave women a chance to socialize with other women of similar social status. Often parishes with maiden's groups, such as Long Sutton and Winthorpe (Lincs.) also had groups for young men, or bachelors as they were sometimes called.[118] Women married late in fifteenth- and sixteenth-century England. Jeremy Goldberg has argued that the age of marriage could be as late as between twenty and twenty-five years, although it declined somewhat by the end of the fifteenth century.[119] Such a late age of marriage prolonged the time between childhood and marriage, and many women used this period of their lives to work as servants. In Croscombe, Somerset, and Stratton, Cornwall, two leaders of the maidens are specifically described as servants.[120] Especially in towns and cities, such as Westminster or Bristol, but in the rest of northern Europe as well, many young servants were far from home and probably lonely and vulnerable.[121] Organized groups of maidens offered comfort and support from others in similar circumstances.

Maidens groups also instilled notions of proper conduct as promoted in the lives of the virgin martyrs. Maidens' groups socialized unmarried women by promoting behavioral norms of both submission and activity.[122] The unmarried women of St. Margaret's, Westminster, had a special role in the parish-wide cult of St. Margaret. They worked together annually to raise money to further the veneration of St. Margaret, and they marched as a group in the annual St. Margaret's Day procession wearing special robes. Women's groups then were far more than just a source of income for the parish. It may be that the visibility offered to the maidens helped them to attract husbands. Group activities displayed their piety in a public way, showed off their economic sense, and allowed them to meet a variety of eligible men. In 1534, the maidens' and young men's groups of Morebath, Devon, joined together to help out the parish after someone broke into the church and stole the money in the church box and the chalice on St. Sidwell's altar. "So upon this, the young men and maidens of the parish drew themselves together and with gifts and provisions they bought another chalice without charge for the parish."[123] The effort to earn enough money to replace the chalice not only developed the organizational skills of both groups, but put marriageable men and women into close proximity, in carefully supervised conditions.

The collective nature of women's groups in general and maiden's groups in particular allowed for greater public action and visibility. In the parish of St. Lawrence's, Reading, the maidens collected money "at the tree at the church door."[124] In St. Ewen's, Bristol, the maidens held a dance and in other parishes, such as Westminster, the maidens seem to have gone door-to-door during fundraising drives.[125] However they raised money, the records show that young unmarried women could go out and solicit money for the parish without compromising their virtue and reputations. Without parish affiliation though, such actions would have been unacceptable. The women's groups, therefore, provide another example of how the parameters of women's acceptable behavior changed in the context of the parish, permitting actions that were otherwise inappropriate.

Maidens' groups were led by a warden picked from their own group, probably one of the older and more experienced members. Compared to the wives' groups or guilds, however, maiden's groups received greater support and advice from the rest of the parish. When his daughter Christina became one of the wardens of Morebath's maidens' guild, John at Courte gave 26s. 8d. "to help to pay for the gilding of our Lady as the maidens be concerned with."[126] His gift helped assure the success of her term in office. When St. Margaret's, Westminster, initiated the maidens' collection, some married women helped out. In 1498 the parish "received from Simon Smith's wife and Symken Barber's wife of money by them gathered with [the] virgins upon May Day—7s. 7½d."[127] That same year, Mistress Russell supervised the maidens who went collecting on St. Margaret's Day.[128] Under the supervision of the older and more experienced women, the maidens gained experience in organizing themselves, raising money for the parish, and participating in the spiritual life of the community.

The maidens of St. Ewen's parish, Bristol, needed such supervision. Each year, the maidens held either a dance or a collection to maintain a light dedicated to the Virgin Mary.[129] In 1464, the father of one of the maidens, John Nancothan, had to pay the parish 10s. 1d. because his daughter Margaret had not turned over all of the proceeds from the previous year's dance.[130] The St. Ewen's maidens seem to have continued to have problems: in 1478 Jonet ap Howell turned in 2s. 2½d. raised by the maidens for wax, but the next year the parson turned in the maiden's money.[131] Finally, in 1535, the parish decided that the churchwardens should be allowed 6s. 8d. for maintaining the women's light. This move apparently took financial responsibility out of the hands of the maidens, who had repeatedly mismanaged it.[132] These older women had also helped oversee the maiden's behavior during the May Day celebrations and other parish festivities.

Looking at songs and carols sometimes performed at parish revels, Judith Bennett argues that they contain warnings, jokes, and stories about the sexual behavior of young men and women.[133] The songs portray three kinds of unmarried women: lusty maidens, abandoned maidens, and victims of rape.[134] These images all warned of the consequences of sexual misbehavior and suggest some of the concerns that adults had for the unmarried women

of the parish. The freedom and visibility these groups gave unmarried adolescents could also bring unwanted attention, especially to those living away
from their parents. Parish fetes or fundraising activities brought unmarried
adolescents together, and adults worried that these situations could become
scandalous without proper supervision. Within this context it is under-
standable why maidens' guilds had so much oversight. Parents wanted their
daughters to find suitable marriage partners and employers wanted female
servants who would not bring shame to the household. They did not want
them to end up pregnant by an unreliable man or married to an unsuitable
one. These songs thus reflect the numerous sexual threats and situations
confronting young women even as they sang these songs at moments of
high visibility. Inherent in membership in maidens' groups was a tension
between expectations for good behavior and the self-promotion and public
display that membership fostered.

Not all the maidens involved in the maidens' guild would marry. Life-
long single women comprised about 30 percent of the English population
in the late Middle Ages.[135] They were more prevalent in towns and cities
than the countryside. The late age of marriage in England and northern
Europe in general meant that women did not marry as soon as they reached
childbearing age. Many young Englishwomen moved to towns or to London in search of work to help build their dowries. Although most married
and returned home, some stayed either because they married local men or
because they did not marry at all, and it was easier for them to support
themselves in a town or city. Single women supported themselves often by
working as servants or in some other occupation. The separate religious
interests of these women, if they had them, are difficult to see because their
single status is rarely identified in the documents. One woman who seems
to have tried to start a group, perhaps for other life-long single women of
the parish, was the seamstress Anne Malte, who lived in Cambridge and
attended Holy Trinity parish.[136]

Anne Malte is unusual in that we see her both working for the parish
and participating in identifiable ways in the parish's religious life. She was
particularly active in the parish's guild life. Holy Trinity had several guilds,
including the Holy Trinity and Assumption Guilds, which dated back to the
1380s.[137] By the time the churchwardens' accounts start in 1504, there were
also organizations supporting the sepulcher light, the rood light, St. Erasmus's light, and Our Lady's light.[138] The parish also had guilds or stores
dedicated to St. Clement, St. George, St. Katherine, and St. Ursula and the
11,000 virgins. In 1518, Malte had been in charge of money for an unnamed

group.[139] The next year she, along with Katherine Grabeley, collected 13s. 2d. for St. Erasmus's light.[140] In 1525, both women again worked together, this time for the light to St. Ursula and 11,000 virgins, although with limited success. They reported no money and their altar was moved before the image of St. Mary Magdalene.[141]

On the surface, it is difficult to distinguish Anne Malte's involvement from that of other women of this parish, but there were some important differences. Unlike the wives who supported the guild of the Virgin Mary, Malte also worked for the parish. As a single woman, she may have been excluded from their association.[142] These fragmentary records leave more questions about her religious involvements than they answer. What we do know is that she did more than sew for the parish. She also participated in the voluntary religious activities sponsored by the parish, and she worked with other women as part of her involvement with her parish. Her relationship with Katherine Grabeley was long standing. She was able to assume some guild responsibilities and her status as a single woman may have helped mold her religious involvement, drawing her toward devotion to St. Ursula and the 11,000 virgins.

Guild and Store Fundraising

To maintain their organizations and appropriately celebrate their patron saint's feast day, women's groups had to raise money. While all these groups accepted gifts and legacies, they did not generate sufficient income on their own. At most, women's groups generated a few pennies from the occasional will, but no more.[143] Of the twenty-two wills for Horley, all of which are from men, only six mention St. Katherine's light by name, while another nine leave money to "all four common lights in the church."[144] None, however, mention that the women of the parish ran St. Katherine's light. Moreover, John Chelsham, whose wife had been a light warden in 1525 and 1533, only left money to St. Nicholas's light.[145] The relative rarity of testamentary bequests to maiden's and wives' lights suggests that they were activities and associations that one left behind when one moved on in life. Even former leaders of women's groups or parents of maidens' wardens did not necessarily remember these associations in their wills. In Croscombe, Somerset, Joan Carter served as a leader of the maidens in 1493–94 and Joan Maiewe in 1491–23.[146] Joan Carter left a will, as did Joan Maiewe's mother, but neither contains bequests to the maidens.[147] Parishioners might also

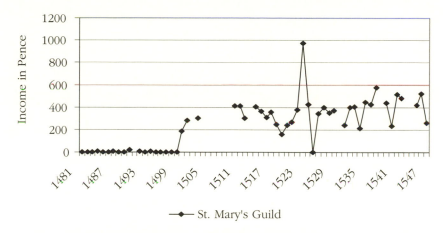

Figure 4.5. Income from St. Mary in the Chapel, Chagford, Devon. The large amount of money raised in 1523 comes from the sale of wool, but the accounts do not explain why it was such a profitable year.

have seen these groups as not only driven by a particular stage of life, but as impermanent, and were not willing, therefore, to direct bequests to organizations that might not survive to pray for their souls. In this respect, the women's groups are different from guilds, which routinely received testamentary bequests.

To raise money, groups used a variety of methods. When the wives in St. Edmund's, Salisbury, and in St. Ewen's, Bristol, needed to raise money, they held dances. More commonly, however, women's guilds raised money by holding collections. Collection activities usually took place in the spring when the weather was fair. The women of both St. Thomas's in Salisbury and Holy Trinity in Exeter held their activities during Whitsun.[148] The most permanent and highly developed organizations, such as those in Chagford and Woodland in Devon, earned part of their income from rental property or stocks of sheep.[149]

It is the women's guild in Chagford, Devon, that again provides the most complete information on sources of income. When men ran the Guild of St. Mary in the Church, they generated their income by leasing out a flock of sheep, occasionally selling wool, and from gifts. The accounts are sketchy and the income recorded is quite low, between 2d. and 6d. a year. As Figure 4.5 shows, when the women took over leadership in the sixteenth century, they expanded their sources of income. In addition to increasing

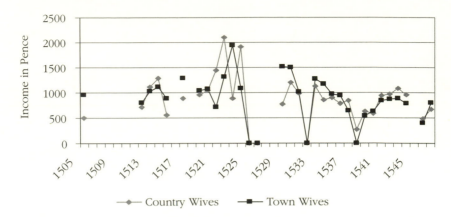

Figure 4.6. Income from the wives of the town and the wives of the land, Wimborne Minster, Dorset.

wool sales, the women began to rent out brewing equipment, and to hold a yearly ale.[150] Their financial strategies took advantage of women's domination of brewing, and as a result, their finances flourished, and they were able to raise on average more than a pound a year.

Overall income raised by the women's groups remained fairly steady until the Reformation, and the income levels during this period sometimes reveal interesting parish dynamics. The two wives' groups in Wimborne Minster, Dorset, appear for the first time in 1498, and the income, which both groups earned by selling cakes, remained consistently high throughout the rest of the pre-Reformation period.[151] The amount each group collected suggests a competition between the country and town wives. Neither group clearly dominated the other. As Figure 4.6 shows, between 1520 and 1525, first one, then the other, earned the most money each year.[152] Until 1540, the town wives then were the greater fundraisers, but they gave way to the country wives again in 1540.

Most parishes had only one women's group, so the sense of competition came not from women living in different sections of the parish, but from the existence of a guild for men. The parish of Horley, Surrey, had one group for the women who raised money for a light dedicated to St. Katherine, and one for the men who raised money for a light dedicated to St. Nicholas. The women raised twice as much money as the men.[153] The guilds in Ashburton, Devon, show a similar pattern. One possible explanation for this phenomenon is that men, who ran more of the parish and who had more opportunities to participate in parish life, spread out their money and fundraising efforts among a variety of guilds and groups. Women had only one outlet specifically for them, and concentrated their efforts on their one guild or group.

Because income levels from these single-sex groups reflect a number of possible social dynamics, they do not necessarily provide an accurate gauge of popularity, but growth in revenue does suggest increasing interest. Morebath, Devon, had both a maidens' and a young men's group, but in this parish the young men earned far more money—between two and three times as much. Despite the greater amount of money earned by the men, income for the maidens' group grew steadily until Henry VIII's religious reforms began moderating local religious practices. In 1538, the maidens earned a healthy 12s. 6d. for their maidens' light. The next year, when the churchwardens finally removed images from the church, the maidens only reported earning 22d. from their collection. The next year, 1540, it was down to 16d., and the maidens ceased to report to the churchwardens after that.[154] Income from the maidens' collection in St. Margaret's, Westminster, showed similar growth prior to the Reformation and a subsequent decline and disappearance with the removal of the saints from that church. The loss of images diminished the guild's interests, suggesting that commitment on the part of members was closely tied to veneration of the patron saint.[155] The sudden appearance of a midwives light in St. Martin's, Westminster, in 1540 might have been an attempt to maintain some female collective association in the face of religious changes, but the accounts only record it once.[156]

Leadership, Membership, and Local Status

There are no membership rolls for any of the all-women's groups. The names of the groups specify the life stage of the membership, but not much else.[157] Without membership lists, we can only speculate on whether these groups attracted just the wealthier members of the parish or all parish women. Analysis of who led these groups suggests that while they drew members from some of the most active parish families, it was not the sole qualification. Membership itself conferred some status and allowed women to create their own hierarchies, based on less visible qualities such as personality, leadership ability, and piety.

While many women leaders came from socially prominent families, this was not the only criteria. The women who attained office in Chagford's women's group and Stratton, Cornwall's maidens' group came from families who served the parish in leadership capacities. In Morebath, however, where the population was so small, almost everyone took turns at the numerous parochial offices.[158] In Croscombe, Somerset, another small rural parish, only six of the fifteen named wardens for the maidens' group shared surnames with the churchwardens, although two came from the powerful Branch family, who monopolized the office of churchwarden for more than twenty years.[159] Thus in large, well-organized parishes, there was a relationship between women's leadership and their family's overall parish involvement in parish administration. But in tiny rural parishes, such as Morebath, with flatter social hierarchies, women may have involved themselves in such groups less because of who their families were, and more simply to get the work of the parish done.

Although there was a connection between being a warden in a women's group and one's husband's or father's parish involvement, women used the office to create their own hierarchies. In Horley, nine of the twenty-three women (39 percent) who served as wardens for St. Katherine's light between 1518 and 1542 had husbands who served as churchwarden. Only four (17 percent) had husbands who served as wardens of St. Nicholas's light. These figures suggest that within Horley the women's group was more prestigious than its male counterpart. Office in this women's group was more frequently an outlet for churchwardens' wives than those of the guild wardens. Yet we can read these statistics another way. Nearly two-thirds of the women who led the St. Katherine's women's group did not have husbands who served as churchwardens, showing that the criteria for serving as warden was not solely dependent on one's husband's parish involvement.[160]

This situation is even clearer in the women's group in the Cambridge parish of Holy Trinity.[161] Between 1504 and 1525, twenty-two women served as wardens for the light of Our Lady. The husbands of nine of these women never served as churchwardens, and an additional six served as churchwardens only after their wives had been wardens of the light of Our Lady. Although their family's wealth and position contributed to the women's likelihood of being elected warden, their candidacy was neither determined solely by their husbands' involvement in the parish, nor by his prior service as churchwarden.[162] With the husband's involvement removed from the scenario, we can hypothesize that women's desire to lead and manifest administrative skills and status brought them to leadership roles. Office holding not only conferred status, but it could also be construed as a pious act and a way of demonstrating one's commitment and interest in the Church, as well as one's general respectability.[163]

A comparison of the lay subsidy records for 1524 with a list of wardens helps to tease out the economic status of wardens. Unlike previous subsidies, the one in 1524 listed individual heads of households and their assessed wealth, whereas previous taxes had only listed the amount collected by vill or town. Cross-referencing leaders with their tax assessment shows that most came from a relatively broad range of the upper-middling parish women, and membership must have been equally as broad or broader. The parish with a women's group most easily analyzed in terms of the lay subsidy is the Surrey parish of Horley.[164] The accounts for the St. Katherine light list all the female wardens as "the wife of" a male parishioner.[165] This readily identifies the women with the male head of house listed on the tax role. Between the years 1518 and 1530 fourteen different women served as wardens (in pairs), generally for two-year terms. Four of these women do not appear on the tax list. Although it is reasonable to think that these single-sex groups might have attracted membership from outside the parish, the missing wardens do not appear listed on the tax roles for neighboring parishes either.[166] Their families could have been too poor to tax. The wealthier members of the parish are slightly better-represented in leadership roles than the poorer ones, but the wealthiest parish women did not appear to serve in this capacity at all. During the same years, twelve men served as wardens for St. Nicholas's light, and only two of them are not listed on the subsidy role. By contrast, however, the men drew their wardens from a slightly lower social strata. As Table 4.1 shows, more people were assessed at £2–5 than at any other income level, yet more female wardens came from a higher income level (£10–19), while more male wardens were from the lowest.

The Chagford figures for the wardens' status are less precise because there are several families with the same last names, and it is not always clear to which families the wardens for the women's store belonged. As Table 4.2 shows, the majority of the parishioners on the subsidy roll (60 percent) earned between £1–3.[167] For the same period, 1518–1530, twenty-four women served as guild wardens, six of whom are not on the tax list. Compared to Horley, more Chagford women from the lower income levels served as wardens of the women's guild. The guild of St. Katherine, which may have become all male in 1499, drew from a similar economic group.

It is difficult to get these kinds of figures for Morebath, because the accounts do not start until 1526/1527, and there are no young men's wardens

TABLE 4.1. ECONOMIC STATUS OF LIGHT WARDENS, HORLEY, SURREY (1518–1530)

Assessment	Distribution of wealth	No. of St. Katherine's Wardens	No. of St. Nicholas' Wardens
not appear		4	2
£1	8 (14%)	–	3
£2–5	19 (33%)	2	2
£ 6–9	13 (23%)	2	2
£ 10–19	12 (21%)	4	2
£20 +	5 (9%)	–	1
total	57 (100%)	12	12

Most clearly the Subsidy shows the economic status of those wardens serving in 1524, but to expand my analysis I have looked at those wardens who served six years on either side of the Subsidy. I am assuming a modest amount of economic stability.

TABLE 4.2. ECONOMIC STATUS OF ST. MARY'S AND ST. KATHERINE'S WARDENS, CHAGFORD, DEVON (1518–1530)

Assessment	Distribution of wealth	No. of St. Mary's Wardens	No. of St. Katherine's Wardens
not appear		6	9
£1	71 (40%)	3–8	2–3
£2–5	64 (36%	4–7	5–8
£6–9	13 (7%)	2–4	2
£10–19	21 (12%)	3–6	2
£20 +	8 (5%)	1	–
total	177 (100%)	24	24

named until 1529. If we compare names of wardens serving between 1527 and 1540 (when the maidens' collection disappears from the accounts), the data again suggests that women serving as wardens came from families across the social spectrum of the village, except the gentry.[168] Many shared last names, a fact that makes it difficult to identify the wardens' families. The different figures for the young men's guild reflect the different expectations for men and women in the parish. Young men's groups could serve as training grounds for future parochial and other public offices, whereas maiden's groups did not as clearly lead to service in other sectors. As Table 4.3 shows, men from the poorest families typically did not serve as jurymen and parish officers or in manorial offices. There were more maidens from

TABLE 4.3. ECONOMIC STATUS OF MAIDENS' AND YOUNG MEN'S WARDENS, MOREBATH, DEVON (1527–1540)

Assessment	Distribution of wealth	No. of Maidens' Wardens	No. of Young Men's Wardens
not appear		3	10
£1	16 (29%)	4–6	1
£2–5	27 (49%)	4–8	4
£6–9	5 (9%)	2–5	1
£10–19	7 (13%)	2–7	8
£20 +	0	–	–
Total	55 (100%)	25	38

the lowest income bracket serving as wardens, but in both youth groups, the majority of the wardens came from the families of husbandmen and lesser yeomen.

It appears that although there are more women from the better-off families in the parish serving as wardens, economic status was not any more of a determining factor in attaining office than one's family's parish involvement. Women from the poorer families were also represented. Furthermore, the parishes' wealthiest women and the local gentry were not very interested in serving as wardens in these local groups, nor were their husbands or fathers generally interested in serving as churchwardens.[169] Leadership in women's guilds attracted the middling parish women and allowed them to draw upon their domestic economic experiences. Thus we can see that women were creating their own hierarchies out of their membership in these groups.

The female wardens from the town parish of Holy Trinity, Cambridge, had a different social profile than the rural wardens just described. Because the lay subsidy was collected by ward and not by parish, and because there were several other parishes in Cambridge, it is not possible to compare the female wardens' personal wealth with that of the parish as a whole. Nonetheless, these women do not come from families assessed anywhere near the lowest income level.[170] The lowest assessment for a family of a woman serving as warden of Our Lady's light was 10 marks, paid by Thomas Knyghton, whose wife was warden in 1515.[171] The next lowest were Robert Robynson, an inn keeper, whose wife served in 1513 and 1520 and John Goodwyn, a cook, whose wife Katherine served as warden in 1519 and 1526.[172] Both families paid taxes on 20 marks of income. On the other end of the social spectrum were the wives of Robert Smith, master wax chandler, and Robert Cobbe, a free mason. Their wives served as wardens in 1518 and 1520, and they were assessed at £19 and £40 respectively.[173] The women who supervised this group were far wealthier and came from a more elite segment of the parish's population than their rural counterparts. The wealth of this group's leaders may explain Anne Malte's attempt to found another women's group. Both she and Katherine Grabeley were significantly poorer than those women who served as wardens for Our Lady's light. According to the city's poll tax return for 1512, Anne lived with her servant Alice Sympson, and paid taxes on an income of £1 a year.[174] The 1524 lay subsidy assessed her on the same income level, the lowest level taxed. There is no mention of her servant. Katherine Grabeley may have been married to John Grabeley who also paid taxes on £1 of income on both subsidies.[175] Social status as much as marital status might have influenced their efforts to found another women's group. Anne and Katherine's lower status suggests that the St. Ursula veneration was intended to attract a different group of women.

For most parish women, leadership of a women's group was the highest public position they could hold. Although women did serve as churchwardens, this was less common and did not necessarily happen in parishes with women's groups. In some parishes, the maiden's groups offered the only leadership positions available to women. In these parishes, once women married, their participation in all-female groups ended and involvement in the parish came through their families, mixed-sex guilds or stores, seating, and labor for the parish. The wives in Croscombe, Somerset, tried to expand their options and organized a dance in 1482 that earned the parish 6s.[176] They did not repeat their efforts in later years, and the maidens remained the only visible women's group within this parish.

Women's opportunities for parish leadership did not always end with their marriage. In both Morebath and Westminster, after membership in the maidens' group there were some leadership opportunities for married women. Married women in Westminster supervised the maidens, and as we will see in the next chapter, celebrated Hocktide. In Morebath, Devon, women joined other guilds, raised money for the church, and were able to hold other parish offices. Throughout the twenty-five years of pre-Reformation accounts, woman occasionally served as either guild wardens or churchwardens. Margaret Borston and Lucy Scely were churchwardens in 1528 and 1548, respectively; in 1538 Johanna Morsse was warden of the alms light, while Joan Goodman served the following year; and for the Guild of St. Anthony, Johanna At Pole served with John Done in 1531.[177] Unfortunately the accounts only start in 1526, and we do not know if these women had been wardens of the maidens' guild earlier in their lives, although this seems likely. In other communities, such as Horley, Chagford, and Wimborne Minster, which only had wives' groups, marriage created the opportunity for greater visibility and action within the parish.

Conclusion

The records for women's groups are fragmented, making them difficult to reconstruct. It appears clear, however, that they are a development of the mid-fifteenth century and part of the overall increase in parish activities during this period and an increased concern for women's behavior at a time when women married late. Variations among the groups suggest that some were independent, taking on many of the attributes of full-fledged guilds. Others were tied into preexisting guilds or saints' cults, but their creation meant that members valued the ability of women to work together on behalf of their guild or parish. These variations also suggest that what we see in the mid-fifteenth century was part of an evolutionary process that would be halted by the Reformation. We will never know how they would have continued to evolve or how much more common they would have become. Certainly the evidence we have suggests they were already quite popular. Women's groups in England, whatever their form, appear to be unique in late medieval Europe in providing women of different ages and marital statuses the opportunity to join single-sex organizations that were openly sanctioned by the parish community.[178]

In the end, it matters less whether these groups were fully articulated guilds or not, than that they allowed women to support the parish in substantial, positive, and socially approved ways. Regardless of these groups' constitutions, within their confines, women filled the coffers of the parish and furthered community goals. These groups fill a social role, offering women the companionship of women in similar positions, but within an approved context. Women's groups also gave women chances to serve in leadership positions. Maiden's groups in particular served social needs in providing a guarded and religiously sanctioned organization for what were probably fairly large numbers of unmarried young women. They helped supervise and socialize young women living away from home and parental oversight. The existence of wives' organizations indicates that these groups also played a part in ushering women through different stages of the life cycle. We can imagine that in wives' groups, women found both comfort and advice to help them through difficult marriages, the birth and death of children, and the running of a household. Through these groups women could create their own hierarchies, based somewhat on family status and wealth, but also on less visible criteria, such as piety, fertility, or personality. Embodied in these opportunities was the tension between the empowerment of women and their role as enforcers of patriarchal norms. Single-sex groups gave women much more visibility but ultimately channeled their behavior into what was considered the "proper" direction.

Chapter 5

"To Save Them from Binding on Hock Tuesday": The Rise of a Women's Holiday

When the parishioners of St. Margaret's, Westminster, decided to rebuild their parish church in the 1480s, they needed to raise large sums of money.[1] Although well-to-do community members did front much of the cost, parish leaders still created fundraising strategies that specifically included the middling and poor and the women of the parish community. In addition to regular door-to-door collections, the parish began celebrating a new holiday and revel activity called Hocktide in 1497 that specifically facilitated women's participation.[2] Hocktide fell on the second Monday and Tuesday after Easter. In its fullest form, celebrations of Hocktide started on Monday with women trying to catch the men, tying them up, and releasing them upon payment of a forfeit. On Tuesday, they reversed roles and the men captured and tied up the women. The parish coffers received the forfeit money.[3] In Westminster's initial celebration, only women did the capturing, and their efforts earned the parish 11s. Mistress Moreland, wife of gentleman draper Hugh Moreland, ran the event. The next year the parish held both a male and a female collection, and prominent couples again led the activities.[4] That year the parish "received of Mistress Bough, Mistress Burgess, and Mistress Morland for Hokkyng money—3s. 4d [and] received of Master Bough, Master Morland, and Master Raby for Hokkyng money—16s. 7½ d."[5] Both Masters Morland and Bough were gentlemen, had been churchwardens, and would serve the parish in various capacities in subsequent years.[6] Raby was well-to-do and in the employ of the Abbey.[7] That same year, the parishioners also experimented with celebrating May Day. Two women from artisan families, Mistresses Smyth and Barber, both wives of blacksmiths, organized and led the young women in the parish in a May Day collection and earned 80d.[8] Information on the parish's third Hocktide celebrations suggests that the parish had introduced an element of competition among the wards or streets to increase interest in the celebrations. Mistress Morland who lived in Charring Cross[9] "and her company" contributed 5s. 1d. "in hokking money," while Mistress Hachet, who lived on King Street[10] "and her company" gave only 3s. 10d. "The women of the palace" outdid both of these groups. Led by Walter Gardener's wife, they raised 13s.[11] As a result of this organization, the holiday doubled its proceeds. Like the couples who had run the festivities the previous year, the Gardeners and the Hachets were local elites active in parish life.[12] A few years later, in 1502, the parish again celebrated both Hocktide and May Day.[13] The need to create both enthusiasm and legitimacy for this new celebration apparently played into decisions over which holiday to celebrate and who would run it. After 1502, May Day disappeared from the accounts, but Hocktide remained an annual event.[14] Although the accounts do not continue to include information on who ran the Hocktide celebrations, the amounts raised suggest that the holiday increased in popularity, reaching a peak in 1518 when the collections raised nearly £3.

Scholars have often connected Hocktide to medieval courtship rituals, youth culture, and May Day celebrations.[15] In many respects they were similar kinds of holidays. Neither Hocktide nor May Day commemorated an ecclesiastical occasion, both fell in the spring, and both dealt with sexual concerns.[16] Medieval literature seems to have ignored Hocktide in favor of the more picturesque May Day celebrations of Maypoles and Robin Hood revels held in the spring. In more generic terms, however, binding, capturing, and forfeits appear in medieval romances such as *Sir Gawain and the Green Knight* as part of the dalliance and courtship between noble ladies and their knights.[17] Lawrence Clopper also suggests that John Lydgate's antifeminist mumming debate between husbands and wives that he wrote for Herford Castle drew upon knowledge of Hocktide.[18]

Antiquarians, struck by the sexual nature of Hocktide's activities, have used words such as "quaint," "merry," "amusing," and "sportive" to describe the holiday.[19] E. K. Chambers, in his classic study of medieval drama, ends his discussion of the holiday with the dismissive statement: "The central incident of 'hocking' appears therefore to be nothing but a form of that symbolic capture of a human victim of which various other examples are afforded by village festivals."[20] Antiquarians also found women's greater financial successes at the holiday's end inexplicable and surprising. Charles Kerry in his study of St. Lawrence's, Reading, wrote that "the ladies always appear to have been more successful than the men on these occasions."[21] Even as recently as the 1990s, scholarship on parish festivals remained largely interested in the financial aspects of the holiday. Ronald Hutton de-

Figure 5.1. Wife beating husband. Misericord, Stratford on Avon, Warwickshire. Photograph courtesy of National Monuments Record.

scribed the holiday as a "great moneyspinner," and Andrew Brown referred to it as a "ubiquitous" way of raising money.[22] These characterizations ignored gender by discussing the holiday only in terms of parish fundraising.

Hocktide was a different type of holiday from May Day. In general, its celebrations took place in town or borough parishes, and generally the principal actors were married couples or married women, not the rural youth more typically found leading May Day celebrations. Thus it drew upon urban and adult concerns of marriage and wifely influence, rather than the courtship and fertility themes found in May Day. These themes may have made it more attractive to urban Westminster parishioners.

As a parish fundraising opportunity, Hocktide shared many features with other parish fundraising activities, such as ales, collections, plays, and revels. Yet, the celebration's actual activities show that unlike many other fundraising occasions, Hocktide was a carnivalesque holiday that temporarily upset male-female relationships: women captured men, tied them up, and forced them to pay for their freedom.[23] In these activities, Hocktide shared concerns with the artistic and literary motifs of Phyllis riding Aristotle and the wife beating her husband. All overturned expected relations between men and women, where women were submissive and men were in charge (see Figure 5.1).

Traditionally scholars have understood rituals of inversion in one of two ways; it was either a safety valve that temporarily allowed the oppressed to let off steam, so as to prevent real rebellion, or it promoted social change by offering a vision of an alternative social order. With respect to games involving sexual role reversal and separate male and female activities, Natalie Davis has argued that they specifically expressed a number of communal concerns: they "gave a more positive license to the unruly women,"[24] they affirmed a traditional ordering of sexual relations during times of change in the "distribution of power in family and political life,"[25] and they negotiated the world outside and reinterpreted it through a prism of local understanding.[26] Games and rituals of inversion played during periods of misrule called attention to, defined, and ultimately preserved the status quo.[27] More recently Chris Humphrey in a broad study of carnival and misrule in England has called for more locally specific treatments of carnivalesque rituals, so as to move beyond seeing them simply as social safety valves or containment of rebellion and locate these activities in local politics.[28]

Certainly Hocktide could be analyzed along these many lines. The activities did provide women with temporary license to capture and control men. As a result, Hocktide allowed participants to explore a world with women in charge, an inversion of the patriarchal and misogynistic world of late medieval England. With the end of each Hocktide season's festivities, traditional gender roles were restored. In restoring order, Hocktide affirmed traditional patriarchal control at a time when many women delayed or gave up marriage. Such an argument, however, does not go far enough in explaining the holiday's attraction to late medieval English parishes. It does not consider the holiday in the context of the prominent role women already played in the parish. Moreover, only viewing rituals through a lens of local concerns ignores the shared interests that parishes across England had in this holiday, and the broader social themes that it addressed. Literary scholar Pamela Allen Brown in her study of Early Modern jesting classifies Hocktide as a manifestation of jesting, a wide-ranging genre that included literature, drama, proverbs, and songs.[29] Jesting was satirical, clever, and humorous. Although often associated with virulent misogyny, Brown argues that women jested and in looking for jests that "appeal for women's laughter," we can find sources and forms of women's rebellion, humor, and action.[30] Women's jests show how even for a moment a woman could gain control of her superior. Within a parish context then, Hocktide as a form of women's jest reveals women working together in opposition to men, in a parody of their other parish involvement that often supported and collaborated with men.

This chapter argues that the timing of this holiday's rise in popularity, the late fifteenth century, is significant. Hocktide became popular as a parish holiday at the same time that women's groups were increasing, permanent church seating was becoming more common, and interest in parish liturgies and their enhancement was more popular. The capturing of men by women in Hocktide celebrations, I would argue, not only addressed larger social issues surrounding women's behavior, mobility, and influence, but served as a controlled way of examining the implications of their parish participation and the tension surrounding it. Hocktide did not stop the expansion of women's parish activities, nor did it propel parishes to adopt new gender roles. Rather, it affirmed women's expanding position within the parish by exploring it within the defined context of marital relations. Even as the holiday ultimately reasserted women's secondary status vis-à-vis men, it furthered women's opportunities for participation and influence within the parish. Leading and organizing the holiday gave women an official economic role to play in parish fundraising, offered them sanctioned leadership roles within the parish administration, and provided them with a recognized slot in the parish calendar. Women derived status from participating in the Hocktide, just as they did from participating in the women's parish groups discussed in the last chapter. Under the auspices of Hocktide, women organized themselves and raised money to help meet community needs. However, the holiday's specific activities of capturing and releasing a quarry make the holiday more than another manifestation of women's collective action, it was a parody of women's parish activities, which grew out of their roles as housewives.

Parishes used the holiday as a way of raising money, and its success as a fundraiser had implications for women's relations with men beyond the period of the holiday. Although it did not bring about changes in the social order of the parishes, collective action created moments of solidarity among women, and raising and spending money for the church created a permanent physical demonstration of the power of this collective action.[31] The women of Westminster, for example, could see their new church building as a result of their combined fundraising efforts. As the moral arbiter of sexual and marital behavior, the Church told women to be good wives and to support their parishes. Within the context of Hocktide, however, the second message potentially contradicted the first. By letting women run Hocktide, earn money, and make purchases for the church with that money, the parish was encouraging them to exercise their own financial and cultural prerogatives. These practices tried to reconcile contradictory ideas of mandated parochial involvement and medieval gender roles.

The division of Hocktide into male and female halves should not be understood as only a conflict between the sexes, however. Parishes sponsored gender-related activities for married couples because conviviality, gender identification, and life stage—issues that all figure in the Hocktide celebrations—were important concerns to parish communities. As parishes experimented with how to celebrate this holiday, parishioners also explored what women's parish involvement and their domestic vocabulary of piety meant to parish life. In the end, the holiday affirmed the importance of women's contributions to the parish. The holiday had no single meaning within parish culture; instead it offers historians the means to find the intersection of a number of issues relating to local religious participation. Hocktide forces us not only to read gender back into parochial life, but to assess how concerns surrounding gender were inherent in medieval parochial interaction.

The Rise and Celebration of Hocktide

Hocktide's origins are obscure and the earliest references to its celebration do not connect it to parishes. John Rous, a fifteenth-century chronicler, believed that it commemorated the death of Harthacunute and the accession of Edward the Confessor.[32] When Coventry hosted Queen Elizabeth in 1566 at a revival of its Hocktide festivities, city leaders claimed that Hocktide commemorated a victory by Anglo-Saxon women over a Viking army on St. Brice's day (13 November) in 1012. Whatever its initial inspiration, locating the origins of Hocktide in the distant past helped tame its subversive activities of the sexes acting out of form.[33] Women's visibility, power, and authority become old and familiar issues, not new threats or sudden changes.

Descriptions of Hocktide's activities are frustratingly vague. Some manorial courts held session on Hocktide betraying a familiarity with the day, if not the celebrations.[34] Between 1406 and 1419, the mayor of London repeatedly forbade an activity called "hokking" carried out on the Monday and Tuesday after Easter. The mayor demanded that

no person of this city, or within the suburbs thereof, of whatsoever estate or condition such person maybe, whether man or women, shall, in any street or lane thereof, take hold of or constrain, any person of whatsoever estate or condition he maybe, within house or without.[35]

In 1446, in advance of Queen Margaret's arrival in London, the mayor again banned "hokking" in an effort to clean up the city and improve public behavior.[36] These proclamations link "hokking" to gambling, riotous games, and social upheaval that threatened the city's peace, decorum, and social hierarchy.

In 1450, a fuller description of Hocktide's activities associated the holiday with both parish fundraising and sexual licentiousness. In a letter to the almoner of his cathedral, John Carpenter bishop of Worcester soundly condemned the holiday, considering it a "noxious corruption" and a sign of "spiritual illness."[37] His denouncement, however, provides the fullest description of its celebration:

(For you must have known) how on one set day usually, alas, when the solemn feast of Easter has ended women feign to bind men, and on another (or the next) day men feign to bind women, and to do other things—would that they were not dishonorable or worse!—in full view of passers-by, even pretending to increase church profit but earning loss (literally damnation) for the soul under false pretenses. Many scandals arise from the occasion of these activities, and adulteries and other outrageous crimes are committed as a clear offence to God, a very serious danger to the souls of those committing them, and a pernicious example to others.[38]

The bishop demanded that all parishioners must "cease and desist from these bindings and unsuitable pastimes on the hitherto usual days, commonly called 'hock days'."[39] Anyone caught participating in the holiday was to be brought before the bishop's consistory court, the appropriate venue for sexual infractions. Around the same time, Rous provided a similar description of the holiday's activities. He explained that "on the day called in the vulgar 'Hox Tuisday' villagers played at capturing one party with cords and with other jokes."[40] An early sixteenth-century description reveals how some parishes modified festivities, by blocking entrance to the churchyard. An Oxford student complained:

As I went yesterday to St. Mary's church there came a great many women about me and [they] began to stop me at the gate, so that I could neither go forward nor backwards from them. And when I asked them what they meant, they answered that it was the rule to let no man pass that day, unless they had something of him. And so whether I would or not, I was fain to give them something. And I did see afterwards that I was not the only one so treated, but many other men were similarly treated as well as I. For there was no man who passed by then but that they got something from him by hook or by crook.[41]

The student's indignation also shows a lack of familiarity with the holiday and the cultural division between town and gown. In one way or another, these early descriptions understood capturing a quarry as central to the holiday's celebrations. Whether women were at the center of celebrations or not, the holiday challenged good social order.

Although a recognized feature of the calendar, not all communities celebrated it. From its earliest appearances in the fifteenth century to its widespread disappearance in the Reformation, Hocktide appears most commonly as a parish celebration in parishes in or near towns and cities rather than in rural ones: four parishes in London celebrated it, as did those in Reading, Salisbury, Oxford, Westminster, and Canterbury. Thirty (or 12 percent) of the 250 parishes with surviving pre-Reformation churchwardens' accounts record celebrations of Hocktide at least once. Geographically, these communities are concentrated in central and southern England (see Map 5.1).[42] Anecdotal evidence, however, suggests that Hocktide had a wider popularity. In 1549, Shrewsbury's Hocktide activities turned tragic when two men seeking refuge from the women hid in a cave that collapsed on them.[43] Hocktide was not solely the purview of parishes. Several towns—as opposed to parishes—celebrated Hocktide, such as Coventry's elaborate Hocktide festival.[44] The city first held what became the annual Hock Tuesday play in 1416. According to the city's *Annals*, "the pageants and Hox Tuesday [were] invented, wherein the King and Nobles took great delight."[45] The celebrations continued to expand until reformers shut it down in 1561. In 1566, however, the city revived it and invited Queen Elizabeth to their celebration. Hocktide's popularity among urban rather than rural parishes may also reflect late medieval urban preoccupations with mobile and independent women. As the holiday evolved as a parish celebration, it involved married couples, signaling that marriage and women's roles within it were of issue. In post-plague England, where as many as a third of women never married and where women routinely delayed marriage, marriage and women's independence were of concern to the Church. As the local representatives of the Church, the parish was most immediately confronted with the changes the demographic crisis brought to women and the institution of marriage.

At about the same time Bishop Carpenter wrote his letter, the parishes of St. Margaret's, in the London suburb of Southwark, and All Hallows', London Wall, began to incorporate Hocktide into their fundraising schedule.[46] When Westminster first celebrated the holiday in 1497, it was still, therefore, relatively new to parish calendars. The spread of Hocktide ap-

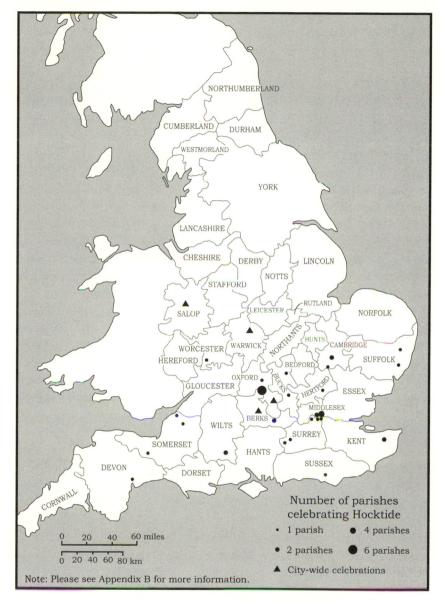

Map 5.1. Known Hocktide celebrations. Created by Stephen Hanna.

pears as part of a general expansion of parochial celebrations that started in the fifteenth century.[47] Not only were the Westminster churchwardens overseeing the construction of a new church, they were expanding their celebrations of the feasts of St. Margaret and St. George.[48] Hocktide's growing popularity kept pace with women's overall expanding parochial involvement. Most information on Hocktide's role within parish life comes from churchwardens' accounts. Many document Hocktide's earliest celebrations, their subsequent growth, and their financial success. Only in those accounts that start in the sixteenth century does Hocktide appear as an established holiday (see Appendix B).[49]

On a number of levels, the holiday created a certain amount of unease. As we have already seen, Bishop Carpenter condemned what he saw as the sexual nature of the festivities, and the mayor of London thought the activities too violent to permit. The language of many churchwardens' accounts implies that parish leaders wanted to sanitize the holiday as well. The accounts for St. Mary at Hill, a wealthy London parish, refer to the women who "gathered" at Hocktide. "Gathered" was the term frequently used in churchwardens' accounts for parish-wide collections, a common form of fundraising. This wording opens up the possibility that parishioners of St. Mary at Hill had modified the celebrations in keeping with the mayor's desire to control the rowdiness on the holiday, or it was glossing over the activities with rhetoric. However the women raised their money, the term links their activities to tried and true forms of parish fundraising. The 1499 churchwardens' account for St. Edmund's, Salisbury, bluntly recorded that parish coffers "received of diverse wives and maidens to save them from binding in Hock Tuesday in all this year—5s."[50] A subsequent account, however, attributed the Hock money to the "devotion of the people."[51] By adding pious motivations to raucous activities, parish leaders may have hoped to legitimize further Hocktide's place in their fundraising cycle. There is evidence that these attempts to gloss over Hocktide activities were more than merely rhetorical attempts to merge the holiday with other forms of parish fundraising, parishes also struggled to find acceptable forms of celebration. Changes in celebration suggest a struggle between the desires of some to maintain standards of behavior and others who recognized the popularity of the holiday's bawdy activities and their use as a fundraising tool.

At many initial celebrations of Hocktide, parishes included a supper for the female participants. It did not become a permanent feature, nor was there a dinner for the men. When St. Mary at Hill in London first celebrated Hocktide in 1498, the parish contributed 16d. "for 3 ribs of beef to the wives on Hock Monday & for ale & bread for them that gathered."[52] The next year, there were only two ribs of beef, and in 1500 only bread and ale.[53] Although the women continued to celebrate Hocktide with considerable financial success, the parish no longer provided a dinner for them after this point. Two years after Kingston-Upon-Thames started its celebrations in 1508, the parish paid 12d. for "meat and drink at Hocktide."[54] In 1510, St. Edmund's, Salisbury, paid 3s. 10d. for a meal for the women "on the day of 'le Hockes.' "[55] Since the women in this parish had only earned 4s., the celebrations did not raise much money that year. In 1527, the women of St. Giles's, Reading, took over the Hocktide festivities, and the parish occasionally, but not regularly hosted a supper for them.[56] Although the cost of the supper to the parish was much less than what the women had earned, this supper never became permanently associated with the celebrations either. The London parish of All Hallows', Staining, bluntly called the women's feast they held after Hocktide a "drinking" and supplied the women with bread, meat, cheese, and a harper.[57] Including a feast implies that parishes were, at least initially, equating women's Hocktide activities to the collective actions of parish guilds. As we saw in the last chapter, Gervase Rosser regarded "Feasting and drinking . . . as defining activities of the guilds."[58] During a guild's annual dinner, which could range from simple to extravagant, participants formed new social relationships. The meals integrated members of potentially disparate social backgrounds into the community of the guild and allowed for the development and expansion of common ideas and attitudes.[59]

    The dinners fit well with other forms of parish activities and by being fed by the parish, women's suppers inverted their household obligations to feed members. Moreover, the capturing and binding united the women as they reenacted, in comic form, their shared experiences with men. Maintaining the feasts as a permanent form of celebration, however, could further unite the women and could expand the atmosphere of conviviality to one of solidarity and defiance,[60] much like the wives conversation in the ballad "Wives at the Tavern," discussed in the last chapter. As the wives relaxed with food and alcohol, they shared experiences and challenged men's treatment of them. If such a situation persisted, it would permanently undermine the subordination of women to men that the Church upheld. The feast was such a potent forum that parishes could not allow it to become a permanent part of the holiday revelries, in case they could not control them. Solidarity among women had to be rechanneled into more acceptable directions that would reestablish women's interests within traditional limits of behavior.[61] The failure of suppers to remain a part of Hocktide celebrations suggests that the holiday's attendant activities did not sit comfortably with all parish leaders.

Some parishes experimented with other forms of celebrations. Bishops Stortford, Hereford, started its Hocktide celebrations in 1479.[62] Although the parish did not initially celebrate it every year, Hocktide celebrations became a regular part of parish fundraising, raising a consistent amount of money. In 1517 profits started to decline; in 1521 the parish added a bonfire to the festivities and the profits plummeted ever further.[63] They hosted a bonfire again for the next two years of the Hocktide celebration and had even lower profits.[64] In 1524 there was no celebration; in 1525 and 1526 Hocktide returned to the parish calendar with no bonfire and the profits rebounded.[65] By and large, Hocktide remained a constant part of this parish's annual celebrations, but the apparently unpopular bonfires did not. Typically the accounts provide no explanation for the bonfire's failure. Given the concerns of other parishes celebrating Hocktide, it may be that the bonfires attracted violent and disreputable people to the parish celebration, who were either unwilling or unable to pay money. Those who paid money stayed away. Eliminating the bonfires reasserted the holiday's decorum.

In the rural Somerset parish of Yatton, Hocktide was an occasion for a parish ale, held as early as 1459 and possibly earlier.[66] Yatton was a large parish with three hamlets. Each sponsored an ale to benefit the parish church. Hocktide was apparently the ale for Claverham, the "west part" of the parish.[67] The Hocktide ales usually had two ale wardens, occasionally one of whom was a woman, suggesting that the festivities involved gendered activities, but perhaps not the chasing and capturing of more urban parishes.[68] Still other parishes, such as St. Giles's, Reading, eliminated the men's collection altogether, but retained the women's one, while Westminster added the men's collection after having only the women's.

These examples all show that despite the holiday's popularity, parishes found it difficult to settle on acceptable forms of celebration. Parishes appear to be continually modifying either descriptions of the holiday or the actual activities. The failure of either suppers or the bonfire in Bishops Stortford to become permanent implies that the central role of women and sex and the potential for violence in the festivities made it difficult to fit Hocktide into the parish calendar.

Fundraising

Hocktide fit into the cycle of revels and celebrations used by parishes to raise money to maintain their church buildings and their contents.[69] Many parish entertainments and revels were modest affairs, earning only a few shillings each year. Grander entertainments that would earn large profits required hired actors and minstrels to attract large crowds. In Yatton (Som.), when the churchwardens began including music and professional performers in some of their ales profits grew.[70] In an effort to maintain the interest of visitors, parishes frequently changed the kind of entertainment they offered on these occasions.[71] The desire for variety may have inspired churchwardens at Bishops Stortford to add the bonfires. Parish gatherings, many of which involved drinking and convivial behavior, took place on ecclesiastical holidays. This marriage of social gatherings and religious acts encouraged financial support of the parish and its endowments, and the festivities that resulted constituted a vibrant part of local religious culture. As Hocktide became a regular feature of the calendar, it earned more money, making women's financial contributions a significant portion of some parish's revenue.

Within any given parochial fundraising calendar, parish leaders generally paired Hocktide with one of a number of male-oriented celebrations. The most common one was Whitsun, the seventh Sunday after Easter, which communities celebrated in a number of different ways, such as with a King Play or a Robin Hood revel.[72] King Plays, like Hocktide, were another form of ritual inversion. Its activities inverted social status by holding mock courts, run by individuals outside the local political elite. King Plays might also include comic battles and other games that drew on local politics and personalities.[73] Reenacting Robin Hood stories could also play into local issues, such as when the parish of Yeovil (Somerset) cast their churchwarden in the role of Robin Hood as a way of raising money.[74] May Day was another male-centered holiday that fell at the same time of year. Some parishes conflated May Day and Whitsun. Celebrations of May Day included dances and May poles. As May Day was also the feast of Saints Philip and James, some parishes held an ale in their honor. Men also had two wintertime celebrations: a Christmas or New Year's activity called Hoggling and Plow Monday, the first Monday after Epiphany, which celebrated the start of the growing season.[75] The origins of Hoggling and its activities are obscure. It was predominantly a rural event that involved men going door-to-door soliciting beer or ale and food in addition to requesting money for the church. Failure to contribute may have meant some retribution, in the fashion of modern Halloween's "trick or treat." Pairing Hocktide with male-oriented festivals, such as Robin Hood revels, focused Hocktide more explicitly on women and, indeed, as we have seen, some parishes dropped the men's Hocktide collection altogether. Still a parish's sponsorship of these male-centered entertainments was no guarantee that it would also celebrate Hocktide. Both the Somerset parishes of Banwell and Nettlecombe, for example, had Hoggling, but neither had obvious all-women's collections or activities.[76]

As individuals and as part of a family, men had more economic resources and could contribute more money and labor to the parish than women; women's groups generally raised only modest amounts of money. Hocktide momentarily reversed this trend. When women organized themselves into a coherent group with the goal of capturing men and raising money for their parish, they breached both their usual sexual and economic roles within the parish. Although the end of the day restored normal relations, the parish's coffers permanently benefited from this reversal of gender roles. In this respect the holiday permitted both a temporary and a permanent expansion of women's power and influence within the community.

Comparing Hocktide's financial success to other parish festivals reveals some general trends. Consistent income levels suggest that parishes enjoyed Hocktide, and that women were committed to running it. Generally, it brought in less money than May Day, but was more financially successful than the winter holidays. Similarly, when parishes hosted both a men's and a women's Hocktide collection, the women's half consistently earned more money than the men's. As Figure 5.2 shows, in the London parish of St. Mary at Hill, the women regularly raised between two and three times as much money as the men, and in some years men failed to bring in any money at all. Similar situations prevailed among the Hocktide celebrations at St. Mary's in Lambeth, the Canterbury parishes of St. Dunstan and St. Andrew, and Croscombe, Somerset.[77]

One probable explanation lies in the economic resources available to late medieval men and women. If the women were catching the men and making them pay a forfeit, they could expect their quarries to pay higher sums, whereas the women had less money to pay out, and so the men's collection earned less. Both collections, however, relied on some form of involvement by women. When the women were not paying for their own

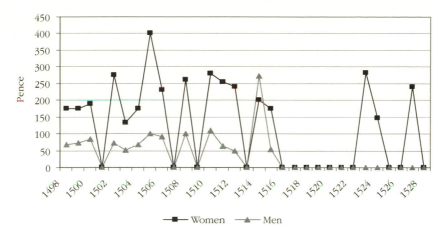

Figure 5.2. Hocktide income, St. Mary at Hill, London.

release, they were attracting donations from the men. Although they may have been drawing on the greater earning power of men, women still used their wiles, charm, and persuasion to draw on that earning power. They were not taking money from random men, but fundraising and doing so with great effectiveness.

Separating the sexes also linked fundraising and sexuality, and the ability to influence members of the opposite sex. By doing so, the holiday addressed the implied concerns surrounding the maidens' fundraising discussed in the last chapter. Under the supervision of the parish, the unmarried women raised money for the parish. Such behavior was acceptable within the context of the parish, but must have raised uncomfortable associations with prostitution. In Hocktide, the connection between money and sex was overt but controlled by limiting involvement to married couples. Hocktide created a situation where wives could be capturing their husbands, men who were bound to support them financially, and with whom they could legitimately have sex. At the same time, it would be naïve to assume that couples only focused on capturing each other, so the holiday explored issues of fidelity as well.

In St. Michael's, Oxford, and St. Giles's, Reading, Hocktide evolved as a women's holiday paired with a male-focused Whitson celebration. Both parishes used these festivals as a way of supplementing income earned from parish-owned rental property, their primary source of income. The first surviving churchwardens' account for St. Giles's is from 1518, and it shows

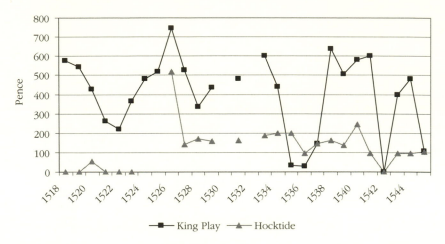

Figure 5.3. Hocktide income, St. Giles's, Reading.

that the men ran both a profitable Whitsuntide King Play and the male half of the Hocktide collection.[78] The Hocktide collection was small and it disappeared from the accounts after 1520. In 1526 Hocktide reappeared, only now run by the parish wives.[79] As Figure 5.3 shows, their first attempt at raising money was quite successful, raising 12s. 4d. It was at this point that the parish also experimented with holding a wives' supper. Hocktide never garnered the same support as the King Play, a larger production that probably attracted outsiders. Yet Hocktide did earn an average of 13s. 6d. a year, once the women took it over, so it was not insignificant as a source of revenue. In Oxford, St. Michael's parish started a male-run Whitson ale in 1457 and added the female component in 1464.[80] Not until the 1470s were either an annual or significant source of income, and neither Hocktide nor Whitsun was as profitable as those celebrations hosted by St. Giles's, Reading. St. Michael's Hocktide festivities earned on average 8s. 8d. a year, compared to Whitsun's annual average of 32s. 4d.[81] Ultimately, however, both festivals in both parishes contributed between 15 and 20 percent of the parishes' annual income, although the male Whitson activities regularly earned twice as much as the women's Hocktide.[82]

Kingston-Upon-Thames, Surrey, celebrated Hocktide along with the popular but sporadically held Robin Hood revels and Mummers' dances.[83] The Robin Hood revels and Mummers' dances were part of Kingston's large Whitsun fair and part of a moving cycle of plays and festivals held up and down the Thames Valley.[84] Kingston's Whitsun fair reportedly attracted thousands of visitors, who bought paper badges or "liveries" to show they had paid admission to the festivities.[85] The summer lords who presided over the fair traveled to other nearby parishes for their fairs as part of this cycle of parish festivities. The effort to produce these celebrations demanded a high level of commitment and organization. The parish not only needed to coordinate their calendar with those of other communities, but they also had to assess their own financial needs and determine how to raise funds for projects such as a new bell tower. Comparing their relative financial successes to Hocktide events underscores Hocktide's small-scale and local nature even as it drew on the skills and resources of parish women.

The repetition of these trends in different communities helps separate the local economic concerns from the more general themes that the holiday addressed. In strictly economic terms, Hocktide did not compete successfully with the other springtime festivals. Too many financial demands on parishioners at the same time meant that they had to choose which activities they would support. The added splendor of drama, costumes, music, and visitors from other communities that accompanied Robin Hood revels and King Plays attracted more financial support than Hocktide. The relative weakness of Hocktide compared to the male celebrations underscores women's more limited economic options. Nonetheless, Hocktide could still earn upwards of 15 to 20 percent of a parish's annual income. In one parish, Hocktide was a major moneymaker, perhaps because it competed with a winter holiday. In Boxford, Suffolk, the parish celebrated both Plow Monday and Hocktide.[86] The Hockpot, as the Hocktide ale was called, generated more enthusiasm and greater profits, regularly earning upwards of £2, or 25 to 45 percent of the parish's annual income. Although not made explicit in the churchwardens' accounts, Hocktide's economic stability and importance in this parish might have given women a prominent role in this parish, even if they shared their revels with men. These constant income levels show sustained support for the holiday among both male and female parishioners. Enough participants remained willing to contribute to make it financially viable.

The churchwardens typically spent the money raised at Hocktide on the kinds of activities supported by women in their wills and in their other fundraising efforts. By using the holiday's proceeds in this fashion, the churchwardens and the parish reaffirmed the existence of women's spiritual interests, but focused them on family and motherhood, and thereby reinforcing women traditional gender roles. In St. Mary the Great, Cambridge, part of the Hocktide money supported a light in the church dedicated to the Virgin Mary.[87] In 1518, the women also raised money outside the confines of Hocktide for the same light and for a new tabernacle for the St. Mary statue.[88] In 1535 when there was no Hocktide collection, the women still collected 37s. 6d. for St. Mary's light.[89] The Hocktide collection for St. Mary Steps, Exeter, went to the "damelight."[90] In both St. Edmund's and St. Thomas's of Salisbury, some of the Hocktide revenue supported the "wives light."[91] In these instances, it becomes difficult to distinguish Hocktide from the all-women's groups or "proto-guilds" run by women.

Hocktide money not only supported lights, it also provided needed furnishings for the church. In 1497 the women of St. Edmund's, Salisbury, spent the Hocktide income on new windows for the church.[92] In 1509, at St. Margaret's, in Westminster, the Hocktide proceeds purchased a new banner for the St. Margaret's altar in the nearly completed new church.[93] In 1532, the women of St. Martin-in-the-Fields, in Westminster, spent their money on a satin altar cloth and two curtains.[94] Once again, we see traditional women's interests funded by Hocktide profits.

As the early disappearance of the Hocktide suppers suggests, however, many parishes had an ambivalent attitude toward women's collective action during this festival, and their activities did not form the same kind of permanent associations found in parish guilds. Hocktide was an opportunity for women to support an endowment that already existed, and churchwardens, rather than the women themselves, typically handled the money.[95] Hocktide and its proceeds remained under the control of the parish, which channeled some of the proceeds into endowments catering to women. This arrangement further helped to reorder the "topsy-turvy" world created by Hocktide.

Leadership

As we saw in Westminster, Hocktide provided some women with leadership opportunities and enhanced the status of those who participated in the holiday. The women in charge of Hocktide were usually members of prominent families in the parish or the wives of either current or past churchwardens. Organizing Hocktide gave the churchwardens' wives some official duties within the parish. Much like guild wardens, these women collected the money raised at the celebrations and turned it over to the churchwardens.

These women probably also had responsibility for organizing and managing the festivities.

We find churchwardens' wives involved in Hocktide in many parishes. In the London parish of St. Mary at Hill, the churchwarden's wives turned over £1 3s. 6d. in Hocktide money to their husbands in 1523.[96] In the parish of St. Andrew's Lewes, Sussex, the account from some time between 1537 and 1539 states that the parish "rec' of Thomas Pokell's wife of hock money—20s." Thomas Pokell had been churchwarden in 1536.[97] In All Hallows', London Wall, where the churchwardens' wives ran Hocktide, their efforts only earned 3–5s., but they extended their organizational capacity by raising money on other occasions.[98] In 1482–83, when the church was undergoing major renovations, the churchwardens' wives organized a collection to help pay for the work.[99] In 1527–28, when the parish was again renovating the church, the wives of the parish used their fundraising skills and contributed £2 toward the building project and another £2 for glazing the windows the next year.[100] Women's contributions, which began with Hocktide, later continued with greater success at other occasions.[101]

Not all women ran Hocktide successfully or cooperated with the parish leadership. In the parish of Lambeth, the churchwardens' wives ran the festivities, but in 1517, when William Bever's and John Skyner's wives ran it, they refused to turn over the proceeds to the wardens. The churchwardens' accounts record these women's failure to turn over the hock money as a parish debt until 1522, when William Bever's wife finally paid the parish.[102] The churchwardens of Little Mongeham grew so irritated at Johanna Hornys's refusal to turnover 8d. in Hock money that they cited her to the bishop at his visitation in 1511. She also refused to turn over money from a parish collection from the sale of parish wood.[103] Once women played administrative roles in the parish, they were subject to its discipline as well.

Organizing Hocktide not only gave women further visibility in the parish, it gave them official roles within parish administrations. They were hosting a parish fundraising activity and the money was to help fulfill lay obligations to the parish. In many instances, parishes drew upon women who were already prominent, such as the churchwarden's wives. Giving churchwardens' wives responsibility for overseeing the Hocktide celebrations was another way of bringing an air of respectability to the holiday and gave churchwardens' wives a quasi-official status within the parish. At the same time this assignment of leadership to particular women based on their husbands' status helped limit the authority that women in general wielded in the parish. It may also be that the churchwardens' wives assumed leadership of Hocktide, and that the rest of the parish accepted them in this role. If this were the case, then we can see that women's hierarchies and social priorities were not too different from their husbands'. Women per se did not gain parish authority, only some women who might rightly claim it through their husbands did. Thus, while Hocktide temporarily overturned women's subordinate position vis-à-vis men, parish administrations seem to have been careful about how far this official reversal of gender roles would go. Realizing that the holiday provided women with opportunities for solidarity and leadership, they ended the suppers, and confined leadership of the celebrations to respectable women, already connected to parish organization.

End of a Medieval Holiday

Although some parishes grew tired of celebrating Hocktide and ceased to hold it, the holiday was by and large a casualty of the Reformation. As a critique of parish gender dynamics that were also coming to an end, it had no place in reformed local religious life. To end the holiday, reformers tapped into older clerical critiques of the holiday by denouncing it as a manifestation of licentiousness and wantonness, a characterization that was more successful in the sixteenth century than it had been a century before. In another example of what Peter Burke has called the "triumph of Lent," the reformers stressed social conformity, deference to authority, and patriarchy replacing what they saw as disorderly and exuberant displays that challenged patriarchy, and supported the cult of the saints and other ceremonies of the Roman church.[104]

Interest in Hocktide flagged in those London parishes where it had appeared earliest. In both St. Mary at Hill and St. Margaret's, Southwark, declining proceeds apparently reflected declining interest.[105] Both were sophisticated urban parishes, where trends came earlier and disappeared sooner. St. Margaret's, Southwark, which has the earliest recorded parish celebrations of Hocktide, stopped holding it in the mid-fifteenth century; and St. Mary at Hill, which was also early in incorporating it into parish fundraising, stopped celebrating it in 1527. As Figure 5.1 shows, St. Mary at Hill had only held the holiday sporadically since 1515. Although the income earned in 1523 was at the same levels as previous celebrations, there was no men's holiday and subsequent events were ever less profitable.

In many parishes with Hocktide celebrations, the holiday remained a regular and popular yearly event until the Reformation forced a rearrangement of the parochial calendar for the kingdom. St. Mary's, Lambeth, only dropped it with the accession of Edward VI, celebrated it again during Queen Mary's reign when Catholicism was again permitted, and stopped yet again with the accession of Protestant Elizabeth.[106] Those parishes that brought it back in Mary's reign did so with little sign of dampened enthusiasm, and certainly revenues immediately returned to their pre-Reformation levels.[107]

The demise of Hocktide ended an officially sanctioned forum for women's parish leadership, organization, and collective action. Protestants sought to strengthen respect for authority while emphasizing humility, penance, and the submission by women. Hocktide's celebrations offered up a diametrically opposite vision of parish gender relations in service of the Catholic Church. The fact that the holiday ultimately restored and affirmed women's submission made little difference to reformers. They distrusted these parish celebrations, which were overly familiar and disorderly. They ended not only Hocktide, but also May Day, Hoggling, and any other parish activity to which they ascribed pagan roots and popish themes.

A few parishes, such as those in Oxford, did continue to celebrate Hocktide throughout the sixteenth century, although the accounts do not explain what activities they hosted or had eliminated.[108] The city of Coventry was another exception; it continued to hold its Hock-play until 1561 when reformers stopped it. Coventry's Hocktide celebrations, however, were not connected to parish support, but were instead a civic holiday and used to promote the city's civic identity. This difference may account for the city's success in holding on to its Hock-play; it was not recognizably associated with Catholicism. The city managed to revive it in 1566 and then again in 1573 for Queen Elizabeth.[109] The play, which apparently reenacted an Anglo-Saxon women's defeat of a Viking army, fed on budding nationalist sentiments and excitement over their own female monarch. In a letter describing the event, a member of the court, one Robert Lanehame, enthusiastically wrote: "And for because the matter mentioned how valiantly our English women for love of their country behaved themselves: expressed in actions & rhymes after their manner, they thought it might move some mirth to her Majesty."[110]

The demise of Hocktide did not banish from English culture the theme of sexual role reversal. The image of the wife beating her husband or pulling his beard and Phyllis riding Aristotle remained popular images in jest books and stories and jokes about women working together to best abusive or foolish men continue to appear as well. As this theme moved out of the parish, however, it took on new significance.

Conclusion

In 1622, a woman testified in court that a Wiltshire man tried to induce her to commit adultery with him as part of his own private Hocktide revival. He told her "he must bind her [and then] they would do as their forefathers had done."[111] Divorced from its role as a parish fundraiser, the celebrations leave only a legacy of titillation and voyeurism. To learn something of what this holiday meant to those who celebrated it, we need to think about how it fit into the context of the late medieval parish, and question how issues of sexual interactions combined with concerns for parochial support and late medieval social concerns.

Despite our limited descriptions of how the laity celebrated Hocktide, the information that does survive suggests that its celebration presented the occasion to flirt with and perhaps even engage in surreptitious physical contact with someone else's spouse or exact physical retribution for mistreatment. It is difficult to bind up someone without actually touching them. But these activities might just as well allow women a chance to punish a violent husband or overbearing churchwardens. These activities then implicitly and explicitly invoked concerns for marital fidelity, male dominance, and sexual relations within the context of marriage, allowing parishioners to express their anxiety about and interests in, such issues. The Church, as the arbiter of moral behavior, was committed to upholding proper behavior between the sexes and between spouses. The parish tried to assure an appropriate outcome for each sexual interaction by providing a moral context for the issues expressed in Hocktide.

Hocktide provided more than an occasion to explore marital relations. Its appearance in parish calendars in the mid-fifteenth century implies its celebrations tapped into parochial concerns for gender roles, particularly those exercised by women. By the late Middle Ages, parish activities did not fit comfortably with the gender roles of society at large. Participation in local religious life included not only receiving the sacraments, but a whole range of other parochial activities designed to promote lay support of their parish. Parish involvement was also linked to pious work for the benefit of one's soul, something in which both men and women could partake. Women found it easy to adapt their housekeeping roles and behaviors to

God's house. In a parish context, however, this behavior fostered women's collective action. Consequently the development of parish responsibilities had inadvertently expanded women's opportunities and made relations between men and women within the parish less clear. Parishioners thus needed a means of trying to reconcile expected gender roles with actual parochial experiences by parodying women's parish involvement.

Hocktide was a latecomer to the parish calendar. Yet because its form of celebration was a carnivalesque consideration of gender roles, it allowed celebrants to think about what the status quo meant to them and how they felt about the expanding role of the parish and the opportunities it offered men and women. In its fundraising capacity, Hocktide mixed well with other accepted parish activities. As a forum for women and an occasion for their increased visibility and financial success, it allowed communities to explore temporarily the outer bounds of their expanding gender roles and imagine a parish run only by housewives. Sexual relationships, the foundation of medieval gender roles, were, therefore, inextricably linked to issues of communal participation and local religious involvement.

Chapter 6
A Cross Out of Bread Crumbs: Women's Piety and Impiety

In the early fifteenth century, a cleric composed a set of devotional instructions for a pious English layman. The instructions explained how the man could turn his daily activities in and outside his house into occasions for prayer and religious meditation.[1] In the background of these instructions is the man's house and household, including his wife. Her only appearance in these instructions is at dinner when the instructions admonish the man to "let the family be silent at table and always as far as possible expound something in the vernacular which may edify your wife and others."[2] After dinner, the instructions recommend the man "make a cross on the table out of five bread-crumbs; but do not let anyone see this, except your wife; and the more silent and virtuous she is, the more heartily you should love her in Christ."[3] Husband and wife share a pious and domestic moment centered on food and food practices that invoke Eucharistic devotion.[4] The silent wife learned about Eucharist and Christ's sacrifice on the cross through the bread she served her family.

This text, although written for a literate urban man, idealized women's pious behavior, their pastoral care needs, and their deportment. In this vision of domestic life, the wife remained in the house tending to her family, while her husband left the house, went to church, met with business partners, and then returned for dinner and pious family time. The clerical author identified the wife's pious behavior as "silent and virtuous," while he described the man's in active and constructive terms. The man could manifest his piety both at home or in the world, while the woman's pious practices were to derive from her home, her household responsibilities, and her subordination to her husband. Moreover, the wife required vernacular and verbal instruction, while the husband's were written and in Latin. The man could read his instructions in the absence of his clerical mentor, yet his wife's instruction and pious actions required her husband's presence. In assuming that the husband and wife had different daily activities the instructions also assumed that they had different manifestations of piety.

This cleric's gendering of pious behavior was not unusual, even if it was unrealistic. Similar descriptions appear in numerous other clerically authored didactic texts, from sermons to courtesy literature.[5] As a layman commissioned and used these instructions, he apparently found its assumptions and descriptions acceptable and appropriate. Felicity Riddy and Karen Winstead have argued that late medieval urban bourgeois culture actively promoted this gendered approach to piety. Silence, courtesy, and modesty became the hallmarks of proper behavior for late medieval urban women.[6] This behavior complemented other values of "stability, piety, hierarchy, diligence, ambition, and respectability" also held by the medieval urban bourgeoisie. Riddy explained that these qualities were crucial for those making a living at crafts and trade in late medieval English towns and cities.[7] Consequently, these values permeated late medieval male-authored texts for women and they informed how the clergy interacted with, ministered to, and taught women. Failure to live up to these expectations, therefore, defined women's bad behavior as well.

Although based in urban culture, these assumptions and expectations surrounding women's behavior were not entirely absent from the countryside. As rural women migrated into towns and cities in large numbers to work as domestic servants, knowledge of these values would have helped them make the transition form a rural home to an urban one. After a few years in the city, many women also returned home to the countryside, bringing with them urban behavior and expectations. As a result rural women would have received some of these same instructions in modesty and humility as their urban counterparts.

Whether urban or rural, the laity learned these lessons in a variety of ways. If they were literate and of sufficient means, they purchased and read didactic texts. Images on the walls and in the windows of their churches also promoted submission and modesty in women and industry in men. Their priests taught these lessons at confession and in their sermons. By the late Middle Ages, preaching had become more frequent and central to the laity's religious education. Mendicant friars traveled around England and bishops increasingly encouraged the local parish clergy to preach to their flocks on a weekly basis.[8] Surviving sermon collections, such as John Mirk's late fourteenth-century *Festial*, or the fifteenth-century Ross Collection, served as models for preachers to imitate or copy, and they give us an idea of what preachers said to their audiences.[9] These lessons were conveyed through Bible stories, lives of the saints', and homey analogies intended to inspire, instruct, threaten, or chastise listeners, readers, and observers.[10] Whatever the medium, we are discussing, in effect, piety taught through association. The Christian would become closer to God through the imitation of the saints, good works for the community and the Church, and repentance of sins.[11]

The story of Eve and her role in the Fall informed opinions about women's inherently sinful nature, but it did not teach women Christian behavior or recognize their piety, it merely explained their failings.[12] Preachers and Church officials had to do more than illuminate women's propensity for sin; they had to teach women how to identify sin and virtue and how to transform this knowledge into meaningful Christian action. As a result, medieval men and women of all classes received gender-appropriate lessons in pious behavior. John Bromyard, a fourteenth-century Dominican, noted that "It pleases men when [preachers] preach against women, and the converse. It pleases husbands, when they preach against the pomp of wives, who perhaps spend half of their goods on their ornaments. It pleases wives, when they preach against husbands, who spend their goods in the tavern."[13] Bromyard, and indeed most didactic works, assumed women's primary identities would be as wives and mothers and that their interests, activities, and obligations centered on the home and their families.[14] The clergy, therefore, tied descriptions of women's Christian behavior to their gender roles and implied that failure to conform either led to sin or was sinful in and of itself. Pious women were like the silent wife in the opening vignette—submissive, humble, and quiet, not noisy, active, or worldly.

Although men apparently valued the virtues of modesty, courtesy, and silence in women, women also strove to inculcate this behavior in their daughters and maids. Young women who lacked good governance did not reflect well on either the master or mistress of the house. As hallmarks of social hierarchy, both men and women would have drawn value and meaning from this behavior. At the same time women within their own homes were unlikely to be perpetually submissive and meek. The intimacy and familiarity fostered by caring for a household helped level personal interactions between husbands and wives and male householders and their housekeepers.[15] As we have already seen, women transferred their housekeeping skills to the parish church and in the process assumed the easy familiarity that came with caring for a space and its inhabitants.

Women's piety as manifested in the parish did not, therefore, match descriptions found in didactic works. How then did parish communities react to women's parish involvement when it fell so far outside the ideal? Did women's parish involvement make the parish church a forum for widespread disobedience, or did the parish make other accommodations to women's behavior? This chapter argues for the latter; in the context of the parish, the laity accepted as piety a wider range of behavior by women. Although the clergy denounced much of women's parish behavior as impious, lay leaders were more tolerant in practice. Women's familiarity with God's house did not compromise lay goals and religious concerns, even as parishioners accepted, encouraged, and promoted women's submission.

To understand how the parish reacted to women's parish activities, we must read the ideals and instructions that women confronted on a weekly, if not a daily basis, in the context of their actual wide-ranging and visible parish involvement. We can do this by being attentive to the chronology of the development of women's parish activities vis-à-vis late medieval didactic texts. Neither the need to clean and furnish the church, nor the life-cycle liturgies were new in the late fourteenth or fifteenth centuries. Women's labor for the church, their choice of bequests, and the life-cycle liturgies probably did not change dramatically in the wake of the fourteenth-century demographic crisis. What did change was the availability of material culture with which women worked, and the meaning and significance of that material culture in a world of social mobility. Also new to the parish in the fifteenth century were permanent seats, all-women's groups, and the attendant opportunities for collective action created by these changes. Thus, although sermons and didactic literature written in the post-plague period, such as Mirk's *Festial*, or "How the Good Wife Taught Her Daughter," relied on many "tried and true" themes, stories, and complaints, they took on new meaning in the context of the post-plague parish. Moreover, these sources responded and adapted to women's mobility and activity both inside and outside the parish, by emphasizing the virtue of women's submission in new ways.[16]

Teaching Piety to Women

Contemporary medical and religious theories held that women were less capable than men of understanding abstract concepts; women were more emotional and associated with the corporeal or physical, while men were more rational and associated with the spiritual. Therefore, women had information presented to them in ways that reflected their more emotional and less developed natures.[17] One method was to emphasize learning as a submissive activity, such as the silent wife who learned from her more knowledgeable husband. In two courtesy texts written by men for urban women, the poem "How the Good Wife Taught Her Daughter," and a compendium of stories, advice, and moralities, *The Book of the Knight of the Tower*, parental figures dispense the advice, making the female listeners obedient and servile daughters with respect to the authoritative text.[18] Sermons set up a similar dynamic, with women passively listening to a cleric expound on Christian doctrine for the good of their souls.

Not only were women supposed to be subservient to more knowledgeable and authoritative figures, their subservience should also include passivity and if not silence, at least measured speech. In the post-plague period, medieval society found women's speech increasingly problematic.[19] The rise of scolding and its attendant concern that women be quiet reflected post-plague desires to reinforce social and gender boundaries in this period of social mobility. Certain types of speech became a measure of gender conformity and status. If outright silence was impossible for secular women to achieve, then at least controlled speech was the ideal.[20]

The poem "How the Good Wife Taught Her Daughter" contains a great deal of advice about the speech and public conduct of both unmarried and married women. The mother tells her daughter that fair speech, mild manners, and true words and deeds will keep her from sin. When in public, at the market, church, or on the street, the girl is not to laugh loudly, be wild, or walk quickly down the street with her face up and shoulders back, "for such behavior comes to an evil end." Once she is married, she is to turn these lessons to the treatment of her husband. She must answer her husband meekly, not be shrewish with him, "so that you calm his mood, and be his dear darling."[21] The clerical author of this poem clearly equated women's bold behavior and loud speech with sin.[22] Well-behaved women were to be quiet because silence was virtuous.[23] In contrast, young men who heard or read "How the Wiseman Taught His Son," a similar courtesy text for boys, received no such deportment instructions nor were silence and passivity promoted as means of avoiding sin. For a boy, sin came from gambling, heavy drinking, arguing, lack of industry, and bearing false witness. While a girl's presence in taverns and streets raised concerns, the boy's did not. He was warned to avoid some forms of behavior associated with these places, but was not admonished to avoid them altogether. Moreover, he was instructed that the ideal wife was not rich, but "meek, courteous, and wise."[24]

While modesty, silence, and humility characterized the demeanor of good Christian women, charity was the central action of a good Christian, man or woman. Charity included giving food and money to those in need, but also being in harmony with one's neighbors and fellow Christians. Charity received a great deal of emphasis in late medieval Christian pedagogy, even if outright donations declined in the late Middle Ages as a consequence of increasing concerns about the unworthy poor.[25] Contemporary concerns notwithstanding, the medieval imagination particularly linked women and charity.[26] According to the Book of Proverbs, charity was among the qualities of a good wife: "She opens her hand to the poor and reaches out her hand to the needy" (31: 20). So important was charity that a wife did not have to consult her husband to dispense it, charity temporarily qualified women's subservience to her husband. Thomas Aquinas argued that a wife could give charity without her husband's permission, provided that she did not reduce the family to penury.[27]

Because charity was an extension of good household management, lessons on the importance of giving charity focused on women's household activities. The sermon for Sexagesima Sunday (second Sunday before Ash Wednesday) in the Ross Collection includes a story drawn from Jacques de Vitry that argues that managing a house put women in a good position to dispense charity. According to the story, a nobleman, who hated lepers and would not allow them near his house, went hunting.[28] While he was away, a leper approached the man's house. The nobleman's wife, full of compassion, invited the leper in for food and drink. The leper insisted on first lying down in the nobleman's bed. When the nobleman returned home tired from hunting, he went to rest. Upon entering the bedroom, he saw no leper, but rather smelled the sweet odor of sanctity. When his wife explained what had happened, he was so glad of her charity he turned over the management of his affairs to his pious wife.[29] Although other versions of this story focus on the sexual component of the story—lepers were believed to be especially lascivious—this version explicitly links household management to charity. When the wife prepared food for her husband, she also prepared food for the poor and hungry who passed by her door. Once her husband turned over his affairs to her, she had even greater opportunities for charity.

Fundamental to Christian charity were the seven works of mercy. These consist of welcoming strangers (receiving the poor), giving food to the hungry, drink to the thirsty, clothing to the naked, visiting the sick, comforting the imprisoned, and burying the dead. They grew out of Jesus' teachings on the Last Judgment and the conditions for salvation.[30] In accordance with the Gospel of Mathew (25: 35–45), medieval preachers taught that those who performed these acts would inherit the Kingdom of God.[31]

The seven works appear individually in many *exempla*, including the one just discussed, but they are also discussed collectively, such as in the longer of Mirk's two sermons for the Feast of the Assumption.[32] Mirk first explains that Martha, who prepared food while Jesus preached to her sister Mary, embodied the seven works of mercy (Luke 10: 38–42). Mary represented the contemplative life, the life of monastic men and women who had given up worldly concerns for a life of reading, praying, writing, and contemplation.[33] Martha symbolized the active life, those involved in the business of the world.[34] The world was fraught with temptation, but there was work that should be done for God's sake. Mirk specifically connected the active life to the seven works of mercy:

By these two sisters, holy church understands that there are two manners of living, one is active the other is contemplative. Active in business of the world you may not be without trouble and great business. But it shall be done only for God's sake, that many may receive the poor, and give to those in need of food, drink, clothing, shelter and help for the sick and succor to those in prison and burial of the dead. This is what is understood by Martha.[35]

Late medieval theologians saw the active life not as a rejection of the monastic world, but as an alternate way to please God.[36] The mendicant orders and the religious laity associated with them lived this active religious life. The Dominican constitutions stated that manual labor kept laziness and leisure away, a dangerous state that led to other sins such as gluttony and sexual excitement.[37] Dominican penitent women, such as Catherine of Siena, performed housework and charity as religious acts.[38] Judy Ford has argued that Mirk shaped his sermons to address the crises England faced in the 1380s. He wrote after the Rising of 1381 and in the face of Lollardy's growing popularity. His sermons, therefore, tried to provide parishioners with alternatives to rebellion and heresy by making their own circumstances religiously meaningful.[39] Most women hearing his sermons could not have chosen monasticism, but would have remained housewives in the world. The example of Martha thus gave religious significance to their daily activities as housewives.

Mirk's discussion of Mary and Martha provide background for his central discussion of the Virgin Mary on the feast of her Assumption. Mirk argued that the Virgin lived both an active and contemplative life. When the Virgin Mary carried Jesus in her womb, fed him and nursed him, clothed him, comforted him when he was sick, visited him while he was on the cross, and helped to bury him when he had died, she performed the seven works of mercy. She also lived the contemplative life in attending to Jesus' teachings, thinking about them after his death and resurrection, and, according to medieval legend, teaching the gospel writer St. Luke.[40] In comparing the Virgin to the two sisters Mary and Martha, Mirk explained that the Virgin Mary was "the first Martha."[41]

Preachers such as Mirk did not intend Mary and Martha to represent women per se, but to promote Christian behavior and values in both men and women.[42] Yet through his comparison of Martha and the Virgin, Mirk implicitly directed medieval parishioners to understand the works of mercy in terms of the experiences of women. It was Martha's food preparation and Mary's mothering, both tasks intimately associated with women, that enacted the works. The sermon directed audiences to understand that the tasks and cares of motherhood and household responsibilities could be transformed into the seven works of mercy. In the courtesy book, *The Book of the Knight of the Tower*, the knight explicitly tells his daughters to emulate Martha, "Every good woman ought to take her (Martha's) good example of how it is good to give shelter and feed the servants of God, that is to say the preachers and those who preach the faith and discern good from evil, also the pilgrims and the poor people of God."[43]

Promotion of charity as a behavior for women was not without its dangers. The woman who took in the leper defied her husband, decided on the disposition of family resources without consulting him, and threatened her own chastity. Such behavior directly challenged the values and ideals of urban households.[44] Moreover, talking to strangers, visiting prisons and the sick, and touching strangers further compromised the lessons on deportment, passivity, and humility that didactic texts also taught. Murals of the seven works of mercy found in parish churches across Britain explore this tension, and attempt to bring the lessons of charity for women into line with contemporary thinking on the correct behavior for women.

Images were an important part of a parish church and central to medieval religious practice. As we have seen, parishioners dressed statues of the saint and carried them in processions. The laity also decorated chapels dedicated to the saints with scenes from their lives. Theologians taught that images aided memory and inspired religious commitment, because viewers would identify with the scenes they were observing. The author of the fifteenth-century didactic text *Dives and Pauper* explained that

[Images] serve three purposes. They move men's minds to think of Christ's incarnation and of his passion and of holy saints' lives. Also they stir man's affection and his heart to devotion for often man is more moved by sight than hearing and reading. Also they are a token and a book to the lewd people, that they might read in the imagery and painting what the clerks read in books.[45]

Parish churches offered many surfaces for adornment. As part of their mandate to maintain the nave, the laity covered the nave walls with paintings and filled windows with stained glass.[46] As perpendicular gothic became the preferred architectural style in the fifteenth century, windows became more prominent and images filled the newly enlarged windows, while smaller decorative paintings and depictions of individual saints filled in between the windows.[47] The relative cost of wall paintings and windows may have made wall paintings more common than stained-glass windows in most parish churches. Skilled glaziers generally lived in urbanized centers, such as York or London, so importing artisans added to the cost of outfitting a church with windows.[48] Complete glazing schemes were rare even in the late Middle Ages. Poor communities could only have afforded leaded glass with occasional bits of color rather than elaborately painted scenes.[49] Windows also broke easily and many an original artistic program disappeared long before the Reformation. Those that did survive suffered extensively in the hands of reformers. Surviving windows, however, show that they had greater diversity of subjects than wall paintings.

Although the laity by and large determined what images would adorn the walls of the nave and fill the windows, they received advice from clerics and the artists, and drew inspiration from sermons and saints' lives. The subject matter of British parish wall paintings and stained-glass windows fall into seven obvious categories: lives of the saints, Last Judgments, biblical scenes, liturgical scenes, decorative and heraldic images, and moralities, such as the seven works of mercy and the seven deadly sins.[50] Usually a Last Judgment scene, called a doom, covered the chancel arch facing the congregation in the nave.[51] St. Christopher typically appeared on the wall opposite the door, often accompanied by St. George, the patron saint of England. Many believed that seeing St. Christopher would protect one from harm the rest of the day.[52] His placement opposite the door facilitated a quick peek at him, without entering the church. Most parish churches also had a Marian Chapel or Lady Altar, often at the east end of the north aisle, decorated with scenes from her life in windows and wall paintings (see Figures 4.2 and 4.3).

For the laity, images in wall paintings and glass were both explanatory and didactic. The choices that individuals and groups made when they commissioned art for walls and windows reveal that they connected them to their religious interests. In the parish church of Yatton, Somerset, the parishioners instructed their wardens to hire someone to paint a picture of the Virgin Mary. Support for this project appears widespread among both men and women in the parish.[53] When the wardens added a picture of St. Christopher, the parishioners balked. The wardens had to reimburse the parish the cost of the second painting, and the painter had to repaint it.[54] Hoping to influence future parishioners, William Wytteney of the Bristol parish of All Saints' left £18 for an image of the Dance of Death "so that every man should remember his own death."[55] Patrons, whether individuals or groups, thought about the composition, location, and meaning of their donations.

David Park has observed that pictorial depictions of moralities, such as the good works, the seven deadly sins, and the warning to gossips, appear more often in churches than in manuscripts. While manuscripts were typically directed at individuals, hundreds of people saw wall paintings and windows, which gave them a larger didactic role in communal life.[56] Wall paintings and windows of the seven works of mercy portray both men and women as charity givers, however, comparing differences in representations of the seven works reveals that many surviving images were directed specifically at women. Although the clergy preached that both men and women should practice the seven works, visual renderings presented this lesson in particularly gendered ways. Some versions explicitly tie the seven works to women's work around the house so that charity would not lead women into sinful situations. These images show that modesty and courtesy, so much a part of the vision of piety promoted by urban conduct literature, was not limited to urban audiences who had greater access to them. These virtues were a part of a broader conception of women's piety in late medieval England.

The survival of parish wall paintings is generally a matter of luck. Mariam Gill has identified thirty-nine paintings with the seven works of mercy theme.[57] She has identified the sex of the charity givers in twenty-six of them: ten are of women, ten are of men, and six have both men and women performing the labors.[58] These images are not unusual or regional. They come from twenty-two different British counties.[59]

A variety of conventions informed decisions about which sex the charity worker in the paintings should be. Latin grammar dictated that the per-

Figure 6.1. Seven Works of Mercy, Wickhampton, Norfolk. Photograph by Katherine L. French.

sonification of charity should be a woman. As we have also seen, the Book of Proverbs listed charity among the qualities of a good wife. However, the willingness of artists to substitute men for some or all of the works in many versions suggests artists had either lost this knowledge or were responding to local concerns and the personal preferences of those commissioning the painting. The female figures in the partially destroyed mural at Potter Heigham, Norfolk, all wear the same veil and clothing, suggesting it is the same woman, possibly the donor of the painting. Similarly, the male charity giver in the widow at All Saints', North Street, in York has the same bushy white beard.

Some versions made an explicit statement to viewers about the relationship between charity and gender roles.[60] At Moulton St. Mary and Wickhampton, both in Norfolk, the female figures wear different headdresses and clothing denoting different ages or marital status (see Figure 6.1).[61] They correspond to the three ages of women: maiden, wife, and widow.[62] Gill suggests that this variation was "a deliberate attempt to promote charitable behaviour by women, not simply through the presentation of a female personification, but through a scheme that demonstrated the appropriateness of charity to every stage of a woman's life."[63] Use of the ages of women motif directs these paintings particularly to a female audience, because men and women had different ideal life cycles. Although male figures might be called to represent humanity, female figures did not play this role. The ages of women motif did not represent the human life cycle, but the female one.[64]

Paintings with both male and female charity givers make the most obvious statements about gender because the artist or patron assigned certain works to men and others to women. At issue was how to promote charity among women without inadvertently promoting inappropriate behavior. Suggesting that women go out in public and talk and touch strangers directly challenged the lessons that instructed women to be meek and modest.[65] Variations in the assignment of the works show different solutions to this problem.

One of the best-preserved paintings of the seven works of mercy is in Trotton, Sussex. Financed by Sir Thomas Camoys (d. 1421), the elaborate murals include morality scenes, depictions of various family members, and several coats-of-arms. The family images emphasized both lineage and family connections. It is on the east wall opposite the door used by the Camoys family to enter the church. The morality scenes, located on the west wall opposite the door the villagers used, promoted Christian behavior among the parishioners.[66] Women perform all the works except for welcoming of strangers (see Figure 6.2). With the exception of those visiting prisoners, the figures are in half-timbered houses. This arrangement of the figures provides a very specific context for the acts of mercy. The houses frame and protect the female figures, encouraging the viewer to understand the works as an extension of women's housework and the house as the locus of women's work. They make a statement about the kind of behavior and movement to which women should aspire. Women could give charity while remaining safely and respectably at home.

The details of Trotton's painting share the sentiments of the poem, "How the Good Wife Taught Her Daughter." The poem admonishes women to avoid talking to strangers:

Acquaint yourself not with each man that goes along the street;
If any man speak to you; Swiftly greet him
And let him go by the way: do not stand by him.[67]

According to this poem, it was inappropriate for a woman to talk to strangers. The poem also stresses houses and the work done in them are the proper and respectable place for women's activities.

Go not to wrestling, nor to shooting at cock,
As if you were a strumpet or a wanton woman:
Stay at home, daughter, and love your work much . . .[68]

The Trotton painting makes a connection between women's deportment and piety similar to that in sermons and conduct literature.

In the version of the seven works of mercy found at Wickhampton, Norfolk, the artist or patron gendered the works differently than the Trotton painting.[69] Women perform all the works save burying the dead. A priest, a clerk, and a man stand over a shrouded body (see Figure 6.3a).[70] In most parishes, the sexton or clerk, a male employee of the parish, buried the dead, making it a work of mercy easily associated with men. In order to reconcile women's work with burying the dead, the Trotton painting depicts a different moment in the preparation of the dead. Although blurred, the image depicts two or three women surrounding a body. In the middle stands a priest sprinkling holy water with his asperges. This scene depicts women's traditional responsibility for caring for the dead body, sewing it into a shroud, and readying it for burial (Figure 6.3b). The badly preserved

Figure 6.2. Seven Works of Mercy, Trotton, Sussex. Photograph by C. David Benson.

Figure 6.3a. Burying the Dead, detail of Seven Works of Mercy, Wickhampton, Norfolk. Photograph by Katherine L. French.

Figure 6.3b. Burying the Dead, detail of Seven Works of Mercy, Trotton, Sussex. Drawing by Kimberly Ruth.

Figure 6.4. Seven Works of Mercy, Ruabon, Clwyd, Wales. Engraving from D. R. Thomas, *The History of the Diocese of St. Asaph*, vol. 3 (Oswestry: Caxton Press, 1913), 277.

version of the seven works at Hardwick, Cambridgeshire, presents yet another alternative. It shows a group of women walking to a funeral, another appropriate way for women to bury the dead.[71]

In the now-destroyed mural at Ruabon, Clwyd, Wales, men perform all the works except providing drink. Instead, a woman offers a man a covered tankard (Figure 6.4). This image juxtaposes a man giving away a coin with a woman giving away drink, making the traditional association of women with brewing and reflecting the economic reality that men had greater access to cash.[72] The paintings at Trotton and Hardwick show women with flagons as well.[73] These charitable alewives have a counterpart in the popular stereotype of the fraudulent and lascivious alewife.[74] Such an alewife appears in the Doom wall paintings at St. Thomas's, Salisbury, and Holy Trinity, Coventry, where demons carry them off to hell.[75] By choosing to depict an alewife giving charity, the Ruabon painting specifically included women in its audience.

Windows in parish churches also depict the seven works. Windows showing women performing the works survive at Quidenham, Lammas,

Figure 6.5. Feeding the Hungry, stained-glass window, Combs, Suffolk. Photograph courtesy of National Monuments Record.

and Guestwick in Norfolk; windows showing men as the charity givers are at All Saints', North Street, in York; Chinnor, Oxfordshire, and Tattershall, Lincolnshire.[76] The version at Combs, Suffolk, where only two of the works still survive, has both a man and a woman feeding the hungry and giving drink to the poor. Yet, even in these windows, the figures accommodate expectations about men's and women's behavior. When the couple dispenses drink, the woman is in the background pouring drink from a barrel into a cup (Figure 6.5). The man hands the cup to a thirsty man. Similarly in giving bread to the hungry, the woman has immediate control of the food, while the man interacts with the hungry stranger.[77] Although arranged differently from the wall paintings, these windows also argue that charity must fit into acceptable female behavior and that charity should never become an occasion for immodesty.

Concern with apportioning the seven works of mercy between men and women appears in the fourteenth-century poem *Piers Plowman*. The author writes about work in the ideal world. Drawing on the seven works, he divides them between what is proper for men and what is proper for women. What is more, he relates some of these divisions back to work for the parish.

"What should we women work on meanwhile?
I appeal to you for your profit," said Piers to the ladies,
"That some sew the sack to keep the wheat from spilling,
And you worthy women with your long fingers
That you have silk and sandal to sew when you've time
Chasubles for chaplains to the church's honor
Wives and widows spin wool and flax;
Conscience counsels you to make cloth
To benefit the poor and for your own pleasure.
For I shall see to their sustenance, unless the land fail
As long as I live, for love of the Lord of heaven.
And all manner of men who live off the land
Help him work well who obtains your food."[78]

David Benson argues the theology expressed in parish wall paintings is an important and overlooked context for this poem.[79] The author of this poem was not socially well enough placed to draw upon manuscripts in the hands of the elite. Wall paintings, however, were a readily available source of inspiration. The gendering of the seven works of mercy in *Piers Plowman* suggests that this idea was widespread, and that the poet was drawing upon broader and more ingrained assumptions about men's and women's piety.[80]

The delegation of different works of mercy to different sexes acknowl-
edges the threat that giving charity could pose to women's virtue. The images deflect this challenge by embedding the seven works in women's
prescribed housekeeping activities. The paintings with both male and female charity givers pay particular attention to the physical location of wom-
en's charity. The women of the Hardwick mural bury the dead in the
company of other women by going to a funeral; the husband in the Combs
window protects his wife from direct interaction with strangers. Pictures of
women performing the seven works of mercy, therefore, express a more
intimate connection between women's work and piety than those pictures
of men doing the same actions. Women do not have to seek out charity;
charitable opportunities will come to them while they observed proper behavior. When artists portrayed men performing the works, they stand out
in greater relief from their daily labors as acts of religious charity. Men had
to seek out charitable opportunities. These paintings, like the instructions
for a pious layman that opened this chapter, all connect women's piety or
charity to housekeeping, but they locate that piety at home. Men can more
readily leave their houses to seek out pious actions. The paintings and windows, like the sermons and conduct literature, acknowledge a specifically
gendered understanding of spiritual practices operating within late medieval life. These images seem to conform to clerical and male expectations for
women's behavior. They also reflect an idealized vision of the household
where women were always home and ready to meet the needs of those who
come to them.

We should not assume, however, that all who saw them necessarily
interpreted them in the same way priests intended. The charitable alewife
in the Ruabon mural points to the economic and labor opportunities and
obligations of most women. The sick person tended by a female figure at
Trotton could be a paying lodger. Women may have passed prisoners in
either jails, as in the Trotton image, or stocks as at Wickhampton on their
way to and from the market. Most women worked at a variety of occupations to help support their families or themselves.[81] Although much of this
work did grow out of their domestic labors, it did not keep them at home
or away from interactions with strangers. Women viewing these paintings
could see them as reflections of a more varied work life than that endorsed
by sermons and conduct literature. These paintings are thus ambiguous
enough to allow for a number of possible interpretations.

Because the emphasis of medieval Christian education was on behavior, people living in the late Middle Ages assumed men and women would receive different lessons on Christian piety. Sermons, didactic works, and wall paintings all employed pedagogies designed specifically to reach women. They used examples from women's daily life to explain theological concepts and employed female role models to exemplify female Christian behavior. By promoting the biblical image of the charitable housewife, preachers affirmed the connections women made between their obligations to their families and housekeeping, and their piety. Yet these messages were not without their dangers. Encouraging charity and promoting the seven works of mercy potentially undermined the expectation that women would remain close to home and avoid strangers. These lessons of charitable behavior needed to be reconfigured so they matched contemporary social norms. The result was that medieval society expected women's piety to differ from men's in practice, just as their behavior was to differ. For women, Christianity was to reinforce mandates for modesty and courtesy. Men received no such instructions. Like the unnamed wife who learned about Christian doctrine from breadcrumbs manipulated by her husband, women's piety was to blend into their family and household obligations, and reflect their status and gender.

Defining Women's Impiety

The belief that women's pious behavior needed to be focused on her home and include submission, humility, and silence clashed with most women's actual religious activities and behavior and indeed with most women's lives in general. The parish, where most women practiced religion, was, as we have seen, a venue where women gathered together in planned or serendipitous groups and shared experiences and promoted their families. Sharing experiences included talking, working, and fundraising. All these activities could bring women into contact with strangers and could impel women to be persuasive, committed, forceful, and flirtatious, none of which fit well with the Christian ideals outlined by the "Good Wife." This contradiction produced a great deal of anxiety about women's parish behavior in proscriptive literature.

Among the seven deadly sins, theologians most often associated lust with women.[82] In John Bromyard's *Summa Predicantium*, a very popular fourteenth-century compendium of *exempla*, Ruth Karras found more *ex-*

empla addressing lust than any other sin, and of these *exempla* 50 percent of them have female protagonists, far more than any other sin. Because fewer *exempla* contain women, women were also five times as likely to be represented as lustful as men.[83] Although not all women in Bromyard's work were sinful, just as not all men were virtuous, Karras points out that women were represented as sinful because they were women, while men were individually sinful or sinful because they were human, not because they were men.[84]

According to late medieval sermons, the parish church was often a venue for women's sins and lust was only one of the many temptations facing them when they went to mass. Indeed the assumption behind many of the images of women performing the seven works is that charity could specifically become an opportunity for sexual sin.

In the imagery found in parish churches, the seven works are usually part of a larger scene. For example, at Trotton, the works were coupled with a later painting of the seven deadly sins. Both works and sins are in medallions, which surround the man of mercy and the man of sin. The works of mercy and the sins are below Christ in judgment. Pairing the seven works of mercy with the seven deadly sins seems an obvious choice. Alan Caiger-Smith writes in his study of medieval mural paintings that

Although theology places the seven deadly sins against the seven virtues, in popular teaching, the sins were very concretely visualized and were therefore usually contrasted with the works of mercy. These two practical schemes of human conduct were taken to be the chief criteria for the separation of the sheep and the goats at the last day.[85]

Parishes, however, did not automatically pair the two morality scenes. Miriam Gill found that only about half of the mercy murals are in such pairs (20 out of 39).[86] Stained-glass artists more commonly matched the seven works with the seven sacraments.[87]

John Bromyard's schema notwithstanding, women are less common in wall paintings of the seven deadly sins than they are in painting of the seven works.[88] When women do appear they often perform sins associated with their work as mothers and housekeepers. Instead of the house as a place of charity and piety, the house is a place of sin. These images of the seven sins, then, maintained a connection between women's religious behavior, or lack thereof, and their domestic roles. In the badly damaged paintings in Bardwell and Hessett, Suffolk, and in Ingatestone, Essex, the figures of gluttony are all alewives, underscoring the opposition between giving drink to the thirsty and drinking to drunkenness.[89] As distributors of food to their families, women were in a position to hoard food and overeat. Images of women committing the sin of pride, such as those at Ruabon, Clwyd (Wales), and Chelmsford, Essex, show women prideful about their clothes.[90] This manifestation of pride is contrasted against images of clothing the naked and drew upon condemnations of women wearing fancy clothing to church in order to attract men.

Such pairings of the works and the sins are also echoed in the conduct literature. In *The Book of the Knight of the Tower*, the knight explicitly contrasts the sin of pride with the good work of clothing the naked in a story about a woman with too many clothes. The devil took her to hell when she died because she had not given her extra clothes as charity:

And the enemy or devil cried with a high voice and said "sire this woman had ten pairs of gowns long and short and you know well that she had enough with half that much, that is a long gown, two skirts, and two coats or two short gowns and with that she might have been pleased and satisfied."[91]

The devil went on to add she should have given some of this clothing to the poor to keep them warm. The knight is trying to teach his daughters to manage their households and lives charitably. Although this message could apply to men, the knight directed his message at his daughters by employing stereotypes of women's bad behavior.

Viewing women as inherently lustful, vain, and greedy has a long history that draws upon theological beliefs in women's connection to Eve. However, by the late Middle Ages, many of these associations reflected further anxiety about women's behavior and visibility in church. One sermon in the Ross Collection tells the story of a woman praying in church who looked up from her prayer book every time a man passed by her. A man finally reprimanded her greater interest in the people than her prayers. The story ends with a warning for churchgoers to look into their own hearts for sins and trespasses and not count who was coming late or leaving early.[92] This story assumed that women went to church to meet men. It complemented the accusation that going to church was a social occasion that women dressed up for in order to attract men. Another sermon warned about the dangers of using the line to receive the Eucharist as a form of self-promotion and individual grandstanding. In this story a woman had hated a poor woman for seven years, and finally the priest warned that unless she forgave this woman, he would not let her receive communion. "For the shame of the world rather than the awe of God she forgave her the trespass, for she would not that Easter day be without her rights (communion)."[93] When the woman admitted to her neighbors that her forgiveness was only half-hearted and that she was more interested in appearing pious to her neighbors, the devil strangled her. Among the many morals in this sermon is that women should not treat receiving communion as an opportunity for visibility and social competition. The clergy wanted the laity to attend to their spiritual failings while in church, not to what their neighbors thought of them. Perhaps the most famous story of women's bad behavior in church is of the story of two women gossiping during mass. A devil sat on their shoulders writing down their words.[94] In some versions, the women discover the devil, because his parchment tears when he tries to stretch it with his teeth. He hits his head loudly against the wall. In other versions, the priest sees the devil and makes him read out loud the gossip he has recorded. The woman's tears of contrition wipe clean the scroll. Most obviously this story condemns women's speech, but it also denounces women talking to each other, instead of listening to the (male) priest. These images of women's church behavior are not limited to didactic literature or sermons. Geoffrey Chaucer similarly mocks this kind of behavior, when he describes the Wife of Bath, who while at church both competes with her neighbors and flaunts her clothing.

> In all the parish not a dame dared stir
> Towards the altar steps in front of her,
> And if indeed they did, so angry was she
> As to be quite put out of charity.
> Her kerchiefs were fine in texture;
> I dare swear they weighed ten pounds
> That on a Sunday were upon her head.
> Her hose were of fine scarlet red,
> Closely laced and shoes supple and new.[95]

These stories and descriptions all negatively interpret the opportunities that parishes offered women. In all these sermons and in Chaucer's description of the Wife of Bath, women are using church attendance for something other than spiritual improvement. During the liturgy, women displayed lust, pride, and vanity, not piety, silence, or humility. Also noteworthy is that these women are unattended by either husbands or fathers. Seating arrangements made this a likely scenario, but these stories also imply that the parish church was a place where women were on their own in unsupervised groups. In these sermons, women were not using the church as a sacred place, but as a meeting spot. These sermons appear particularly uncomfortable with women's interactions with each other while in church. They interpret women's interactions as manifestations of vanity, lust, and insincerity. In groups women competed with each other. These sermons could be read as criticism of lay parish organization, which fostered this freedom of action among women.

In a few *exempla*, Mirk reconfigures women's church behavior as models of pious action. Yet, these stories are still implicitly critical of women's involvement with other women in church. In his sermon for the Nativity of the Virgin Mary, John Mirk likened devoted motherhood to Christian devotion in his version of the story of a widow whose much beloved son was incarcerated.[96] The mother went to church repeatedly to pray to the Virgin that she might deliver her son from prison.[97] When the Virgin did not restore her son to her, the woman went up to the statue of the Virgin and child in her church and said, "Blessed maiden, I have often prayed for the deliverance of my son, and I am not helped. Wherefore, as you will not help me have my son, I will take yours instead of mine, until you send mine home."[98] The woman then took the Christ child off the statue's knee and took him home with her. She wrapped him in white cloth and put him in a locked chest. Mary then appeared to the son in prison, unlocked his chains, and sent him home saying "Go home to your mother, and say I ask her, as I send to her her son whole and sound, to bring my son again to me without harm."[99] The woman did as she was bidden and promised life-long devotion to the Virgin.

At first glance, this woman's behavior does not sound like the pious behavior preachers would promote. It does illustrate, however, how real the saints were supposed to be to the people who venerated them, and how constant the laity were to be in their devotion. Just like living people, the saints could be bargained with and chastised. The laity were to enter into relationships with the saints by visiting them and caring for them much like they interacted with each other. By showing a mother using her devotion to the Virgin as a component of her mothering, the story served as a model for women and promoted maternal zeal as a Christian goal. Although Mirk and others who told this story might have understood it as showing that good mothers went to church and regularly venerated the saints, it also validated women's familiarity with the parish church's contents.

In his sermon for Candlemas, the feast of the Purification of Mary (2 February), Mirk reworked the clerical obsession with what women wore to church. Mirk tells of a woman who gave away all her clothes as an act of charity. Mirk enthuses over the woman's actions, exclaiming that she

was so devout in service to Our Lady, that she gave out of her love for Our Lady, all the clothes she had except for the worst, which she kept for herself.[100]

However, no proper clothing was also a problem.

When Candlemas fell she should have gone to church. But because she was not well attired, she dared not out of shame; for she had no honest clothes as she should have had. While others went to church, she was truly sorry; for she would be without mass on that holy feast.[101]

The woman then fell asleep and dreamed she was participating in Mary's heavenly Candlemas procession. At the end of the procession the woman refused to give up her candle, the traditional Candlemas offering. When she awoke, she was still holding the stub of the candle, as a holy reward for her devotion and charity. This *exemplum* tries to negotiate the politics of women's clothing and church attendance. It is interesting to read Mirk's description of the woman's relationship to clothing against the passage from the *The Book of Vices and Virtues* previously discussed.

St. Paul teaches that good women should attire themselves when they go to church to bid their beads to God; he says they should have honest clothing and attire and not too much, that is to say in accordance with a women's estate. For what is too much for one woman is not too much for some others. For much more behooves to the queen than to a burgess' wife or to a merchants or to a squires or a simple lady such as a knight's wife.[102]

Mirk's version of this Candlemas story recognized the reality of how women's clothing marked social position. Appearing in church in rags was as inappropriate as dressing above one's station. Mirk's version of the Candlemas story argued that women should dress for church honestly, not above or below their stations. The woman's excessive charitable zeal, while laudatory, also had pitfalls, in that it would bring shame to her and her family. A housewife was to protect and support her family, not squander its resources or ruin its reputation. This woman had gone beyond the acceptable level of charity a wife could dispense without her husband's permission. She had reduced the family to poverty and public embarrassment. Because her motives were pure, Mary rescued her from her shame.

Mirk wrote his sermons in the 1380s, when social status was much more fluid as a result of the plague's impact on the population. It was more difficult to look at someone's clothing and know their status. Both social climbing and social advancement were an economic reality of this period. The social mobility enjoyed by some of lower and middling status in the late fourteenth and early fifteenth century upset the social expectations of elites. Sumptuary legislation was one such attempt to contain such social climbing.[103] People were to wear clothing appropriate to their position, not ape their betters. Women who had benefited from these economic changes found themselves in a difficult position vis-à-vis dressing for church. They could not dress down because it would shame their families, yet to the clergy, what women wore to reflect improved social circumstances looked like vanity.

In both of Mirk's attempts to model good church behavior for women, the women are only interacting with the Virgin Mary; they are not involved with other parish women. In practice, however, collective action was central to both the cult of the saints and Candlemas. Both provided women with opportunities to gather together. As we have seen, women often worked together in informal or formally constituted groups to attend to the saints and care for their chapels, lights, and images. The Candlemas liturgy involved a parish-wide procession with blessed candles. This ceremony reenacted the *Nunc Dimittis* hymn that Simeon sung when receiving the infant Jesus at the Temple (Luke 2: 29–35). Simeon's song calls Jesus "the light of the Gentiles." The ceremony also reenacted on a larger scale the churching processions of individual parish women, which as we have also seen was a liturgy that brought women together.[104] Mirk's description of these devotional moments carefully avoids collective action by anyone but the angels in the heavenly Candlemas procession. Although Mirk promotes an active form of Christianity for the laity,[105] the group behavior of women, so central to most of their parish involvement and piety, is explicitly absent from Mirk's portrayal of women's appropriate church behavior.

The clerical assumption that women were flighty or sinful influenced how the clergy interacted with women at confession and the sins they looked for when hearing women's confessions. Parishioners had to go to confession once a year before receiving the Eucharist, usually just prior to Easter. Over the course of the Middle Ages, numerous confessors' manuals elaborated on the dynamics of confession and the different moral needs of men and women.[106] Using the Ten Commandments and the seven deadly sins as guides, priests were to probe the behavior of the penitent since his or her last confession. Priests were to assign penance in accordance with the severity of the sin. Mirk warned in his *Instructions for Parish Priests* not to give too harsh a penance lest he drive the sinner away from the Church altogether.

> For if it was too hard the penance to maintain
> That the law specifically ordains,
> Therefore by your good discretion
> You must show in confession
> Join penance both hard and light
> As you hereafter will learn is right.
> But surely penance without shrift
> Help little the soul's thrift. . . . [107]

When hearing a man's confession, Mirk directed the priest to inquire if the man confessing to him belonged to the parish. If not, the priest should send him away or demand proof of the bishop's permission to confess in a parish other than his own. Mirk's concerns for hearing a woman's confession are quite different and he thought it could be a difficult situation. Despite the mobility of women in the late fourteenth century, when Mirk wrote his manual, he was not worried about whether women were in their own parish. Instead, he feared that women's modesty and bashfulness would make them reluctant to confess their sins. His description of a woman coming to confession is a paragon or parody of courtly deportment where Mirk goes so far as to enjoin his priests to imitate a maiden's modest demeanor so as to not scare away the woman. He warned priests,

> But when a woman comes to you,
> To see her face you must eschew
> But teach her to kneel down by you
> And turn her face away from you
> Still as a stone she must sit
> And be sure that on her you do not spit
> Cough you not, I give you thanks
> Nor move about on your shanks
> Lest she believe you will go away
> Instead of waiting for what she has to say.
> But sit you still as any maid
> Until you've heard all she has said,
> And when she becomes quiet or meek
> See if there's more that she might speak,
> Then speak to her and be precise

And say "take you this my good advice,
And what manner of thing are you guilty of,
Tell me boldly and do not bluff.[108]

If women internalized the admonitions to be demure and modest, then discussing their sins with a man should be difficult. However, if they did not, then they posed a sexual threat to the priest's celibacy. In either case, women's souls were in jeopardy.

In the fifteenth century, John Gybson, a canon at the Premonstratensian monastery at Coverham in north Yorkshire, wrote a confession manual that not only addressed men's and women's different moral failings, but also differentiated between married and single women's sins. Probably modeled on the anonymous *Memorialle Presbiterorum* written around 1344, Gybson's manual listed specific questions for confessors to ask single and married women, married men, and servants, either male or female when they went to confession.[109] His questions were based upon clerical assumptions about the lives of single and married men and women. Gybson's different questions illustrate the sins he associated with gender and marital status. Six of the ten questions to be posed to single woman involved issues of sexual promiscuity and vanity in the pursuit of men. The confessor was to ask, "Have you made yourself more beautiful with kerchiefs or any other raiment at any time for the pleasure of young men rather than God?"[110] For married women, only seven of the eighteen questions are about sex and vanity, two about her children, and three about her relationship with her husband. Gybson worried that married women would cheat on their husbands and fail to "obey [their] husband at all times as [they] are bound."[111] For a husbandman, only one of the seventeen questions is about sex, four are about church attendance, and one about work. For servants, seven of the fifteen questions are about work.

Gybson's assumption that most of women's sins would be related to sex was typical. His different questions for single and married women and the different emphasis he placed on sex are worth noting, however. While Gybson's questions clearly assumed that women had a greater proclivity for sexual sins than men, he also understood women's potential sins as related to their marital status or stage of life. He asked married women if they had sex for money, while he asked single women if they had contracted a marriage but failed to solemnize it or if they had slept with either a married or single man. Gybson also assumed that both married and single women were prone to loving nice clothes, but he ascribed different motives to married and single women. For single women nice clothing was "for the pleasure of young men rather than of God," while for married women it was "for the pleasure of the world or of the people."[112] Three questions later, Gybson then asks the married woman if she has envy against women who are more beautiful, connecting married women's vanity to competition with other women, instead of lust.

Women's relationships with each other and their participation in community life were important themes in Gybson's questions for married women. Associating with other women led married women to sin. He asked married women if they had any unpaid tithes, entered into a sworn agreement with other women, if they have "back bited or slandered any man or women," become jealous of other women's looks, and made a pilgrimage vow.[113] He asked none of these questions of single women. These differences reflect Gybson's assumption that married women's contact with other women created competition, jealousy, and sin and challenged her husband's authority. Gybson, like many others, distrusted women's collective or group behavior, although he did not specifically situate it in the parish church. Although both Mirk and Gybson understood pious behavior as gendered, they did not understand it as collective. To both clerics, collective action bred backbiting and competition. To be sure, Gybson does not disassociate married women from sexuality, but communal problems and relationships with other women figure more prominently in his assumptions about married women's sinful behavior. For single women, more than half the questions were related to sex and he presumed no relationships with other women or community involvement on their part. Although Gybson's only questions relating to the parish per se have to do with attending mass, receiving the Eucharist, and paying tithes, we can read his assumption that married women's sins revolved around their interactions with other women as an implied criticism of the parish. Women's piety was to be individual behavior, impiety happened in groups.

Regulating Women's Impiety

Women's parish involvement and the growing popularity of women's parish groups and Hocktide suggest that the laity ignored many of the clergy's denunciations of women's church behavior. However, the popularity of sermons and courtesy literature and the prevalence of themes of courtesy and modesty in wall paintings directed at women would imply otherwise. What should we make of this apparent contradiction? How did the laity understand or act on women's impiety? Did they, like the clergy, understand women's impiety as manifestations of collective behavior? Ecclesiastical oversight in the form of visitations provided opportunities for the laity to hold women accountable for their actions and behavior. Analysis of visitation reports reveals that the laity did not find women's visibility and activity within the parish as problematic as the sermons taught, but the laity were concerned about regulating sexuality, especially in single women. The reason for the laity's acceptance of women's parish involvement probably has more to do with their understanding of the parish's role in their lives than it did with disavowal of the values of modesty, charity, and courtesy.

Ecclesiastical statues stipulated that the bishop or his substitute inquire on a regular basis into every parish's physical and financial condition, the laity's and clergy's morality, and the regularity and uniformity of the liturgy.[114] By the fifteenth century, episcopal visitations were generally in the hands of professional administrators, such as the vicar general, and the bishop involved himself only in the most serious cases. Far more regular were smaller visitations conducted by the archdeacons and their rural deans.[115] Visitations were one of many mechanisms for controlling what Marjorie McIntosh has identified as an increased concern for misbehavior and social order in late medieval England.[116]

Visitors dealt with both individual and collective accusations. Individual accusations were of sexual misconduct, financial misdealings against the church, or erroneous religious beliefs and behavior. The clergy were not immune; they too could be cited for failure to perform their liturgical duties adequately, failure to maintain the chancel, sexual incontinence, or financial corruption. There were also collective citations against the laity. Most of these concerned failure to maintain the nave, inadequately supplying or maintaining liturgical items, and collectively defaulting on tithes. Visitors handled most accusations at the visitations, but more serious offences were referred to the episcopal courts.[117] Most citations are terse, without much extra information. There is some moralizing, but it generally just denounced the accused for setting a bad example to all.

Rather than physically visit each parish, visitors typically set up court in a central location in their district and had the churchwardens, parish clerks, and the clergy come to them. The visitor presented to the wardens and clergy a standardized set of questions designed to reveal problems. Some parishes did declare, "all is well."[118] Although things might indeed be well, the visitor might not have probed too deeply into the parish's affairs or the churchwardens and clergy were unwilling to discuss problems with outsiders.[119] The questions varied from diocese to diocese, from visitation to visitation, and from deanery to deanery, so the reports resulting from this process also varied in their findings.[120]

Comparing four episcopal visitations, chosen for their geographic and chronological distribution, reveals both shared concerns and locally and chronologically specific issues. The bishop of Hereford in 1397 was very concerned with sexual misconduct and as a consequence, there are detailed and extensive citations regarding sexual behavior. This visitation in 1397 was a generation after the second visitation of the plague. The population was greatly reduced, women were marrying later than they had a generation before, and they were more mobile. We should expect to see these social changes reflected in the bishop's findings. The Archbishop of Canterbury, who oversaw the visitation in Kent in 1511–12, had greater interest in the fiscal health of the parishes, and his questions revolved around the financial and physical condition of parishes. In this visitation, the clergy also appear to have played a bigger role than the churchwardens and as a result, the report is far more critical of their performance of their duties. Of the 260 parishes involved, 20 percent reported problems with the laity's maintenance of the nave and 6 percent specifically claimed problems with the churchwardens. In contrast, the churchwardens played a bigger role in the Lincoln visitation of 1518–19 and answered more wide-ranging questions.[121] Of the 1,143 parishes and chapels reporting, only 3 percent declared problems with the nave and only 1 percent noted inadequacies among the churchwardens. Conversely there were far more complaints against the clergy and how they conducted themselves. We should not discount real differences arising out of different episcopal administrations, or even different moments in history, but the questions and the participants also shaped the outcome.

Because the visitation process set up a potentially adversarial relationship between the laity and the clergy, we should not take each accusation as a necessarily truthful account of a parish's condition. Some accusations were hearsay and the accused acquitted themselves. Yet these accusations, whether true or false, reveal some communal expectations and assumptions about misbehavior and impiety. Some parishes exploited the process to argue among themselves. In Edmondthorpe, Lincolnshire, for example, the rector accused the laity of neglecting the bell tower, while the parishioners countered that the chancel's wall paneling and window needed repair.[122] This adversarial relationship helps distinguish lay and clerical priorities and concerns. In Kent, the churchwardens of Luddenham complained that "the parson deals not fairly with the vestments when he puts them on."[123] This accusation sounds like the complaint of the seamstress tired of repeatedly mending vestments ill-used by the priest. The wardens also complained that the priest was making a hedge out of branches from trees growing in the churchyard. Although seemingly another petty issue, the parson's activities gave him access to resources the churchwardens felt were theirs, while they were also paying to mend the vestments. These two accusations hint at larger personality problems between the parson and his parish. The authorities did not address the first complaint, but even though the parson denied the parish's claims to the churchyard's trees, bishop's commissary court awarded the churchwardens some of the trees for their own use. This sort of careful reading of claims and counterclaims illuminates the competition inherent in many visitations. Not every accusation was serious or of interest to the visitor, but taken together complaints can shed light on parish dynamics and local expectations. Similarly, not every individual who committed a sin was cited, and many individuals appear more than once, suggesting that like the parson of Luddenham, their bad behavior was cumulative.

As ecclesiastical authorities did not physically visit most parishes, we must also, therefore, recognize that male parish clergy and male churchwardens mediated the vision of the parish's health and well-being to male clerks accompanying the visitor, who recorded this vision. Although some kinds of women's actions were well represented in reports, women's opinions about parish conduct are not. When deciding how to answer the visitors and what issues to bring before them, both the clergy and the wardens had to decide on how they understood the clergy's and laity's behavior back home. Women's behavior must be understood then as a reflection of men's abilities to maintain good governance in their parish. In some instances, especially with regard to sexual behavior, the laity and the clergy shared the same priorities, the very concerns expressed in didactic texts and in Gybson's confessional manual. In other instances, however, the laity appear to give wider latitude to women's behavior.

As Table 6.1 shows, we can group individual accusations into five categories, with sexual misconduct the most commonly cited problem. In three of the four visitations, men were cited more frequently than women. The fact that more women than men appear in the Hereford visitation may be a reflection of both demography and anxiety about changes in women's behavior, real or imagined. However, men and women were not accused of the same crimes at the same rate. Sexual misconduct, such as adultery, for-

TABLE 6.1. INDIVIDUAL ACCUSATIONS IN FOUR EPISCOPAL VISITATIONS

		Hereford 1397	Salisbury 1405	Kent 1511–12	Lincoln 1518–19
Clergy & Monks	Sexual misconduct	(83)	(25)	(5)	(77)
Men (not clergy)	Sexual misconduct*	80% (495)	40% (69)	6% (21)	26% (118)
Women		94% (592)	86% (97)	34% (35)	72% (133)
Men	Missing church	9% (57)	4% (7)	11% (35)	17% (76)
Women		3% (18)	–	11% (6)	6% (11)
Men	Financial misconduct	8% (47)	41% (71)	80% (300)	49% (221)
Women		1% (5)	7% (8)	36% (20)	9% (17)
Men	Scolding/defaming/ talking in church	1% (6)	6% (10)	1%(3)	7% (33)
Women		1% (8)	5% (6)	11% (6)	11% (20)
Men	Violence	1% (9)	3% (5)	1% (6)	(1)
Women		–	(1)	–	–
Men	Other**	(6)	6% (10)	2% (6)	1% (6)
Women		(8)	(1)	9% (5)	1% (2)
Men	Total cited	620	172	376	455
Women		631	113	56	184

*Includes clandestine marriages, abandonment, and bigamy as well as fornication, and adultery.
**Other includes failure to provide holy bread, heresy, magic, and other colorful, but atypical accusations.

nication, contracting a marriage without solemnizing the union, or couples living apart, was the largest accusation leveled against women in three of the four visitations, while for laymen, financial misdealings were the most frequent accusation. These differences reflect opportunity as much as social expectations. As fewer women held parish offices and probably received greater supervision when they did, we might expect that they would not be in the same position as men to be financially negligent or criminal with church funds. Similarly, women received supervision when they served as executors of their husbands' wills. The household could also have masked women's religious or fiscal misbehavior in much the same way it hid their financial contributions to parish fund-raising.

The preponderance of accusations against women for sexual misconduct reflects a number of dynamics. Most obviously they suggest that parish leaders and clergy were attuned to the expectation that women were more prone to lust, and so prosecuted them for sexual misbehavior more than men. These figures also imply a large number of women had not internalized the moral standards imposed on them. However, the numbers of men and women accused of sexual misconduct balances out more if we add the clergy to the numbers of men accused. In the Lincoln visitation, the church-wardens were especially critical of the clergy's sexual incontinence, and frequently cited only the cleric, and not the woman accused of living with him. Of the seventy-seven rectors, vicars, and curates cited for sexual misconduct, only 32 percent had women cited with them, whereas in Hereford, nearly all of the women involved with clerics or monks were cited. The conviction rate for these Hereford women was about 26 percent, while for the clerics and monks it was only 17 percent. The Lincoln material does not include convictions. However, accusations, even if false, tell us that church-wardens and parishes were impatient with sexually active clerics, so were willing to accuse the clergy, but at least in Lincoln, by the early sixteenth century, the laity were more tolerant of the clergy's female partners.

Further analysis reveals a more complex situation.[124] As Figures 6.6 and 6.7 show, most of the lay men and women cited for sexual misconduct were single. Most sexual misconduct was adultery (sex with a married man or woman) and fornication. The other forms of sexual misbehavior committed by single men and women were related to problems contracting marriages, such as failure to solemnize it, or contracts with more than one person. The preponderance of single men and women is especially pronounced in Hereford (Figures 6.7a and 6.8a), where the parishes were only a generation away for the second plague outbreak, and young people were delaying marriage until their twenties. Of the 592 women charged with sexual misconduct in Hereford, 68 percent were single.[125] Of these, 75 percent were charged with fornication or adultery and 69 percent received some punishment. Among the men, 63 percent of the 495 men cited for sexual misconduct were single, and of them, 95 percent were charged with fornication or adultery and 85 percent were convicted. Punishment often consisted of being beaten around the church and or through the market place three times. Unrepentant offenders were beaten six times and suspended, a milder form of excommunication. If the evidence from Wiltshire is any guage, however, many of these beatings were commuted to fines.

These statistics show that single men and women were routinely having sex before marriage, although it is impossible to say whether this rate had grown since the plague. Among the single men and women charged, 10 percent either left the parish and escaped punishment or lived outside its

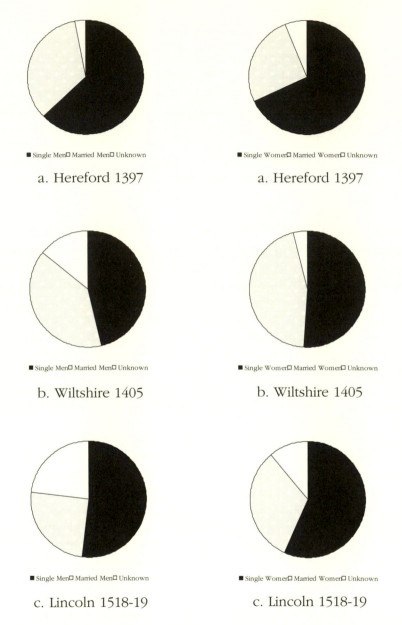

■ Single Men☐ Married Men☐ Unknown

a. Hereford 1397

■ Single Women☐ Married Women☐ Unknown

a. Hereford 1397

■ Single Men☐ Married Men☐ Unknown

b. Wiltshire 1405

■ Single Women☐ Married Women☐ Unknown

b. Wiltshire 1405

■ Single Men☐ Married Men☐ Unknown

c. Lincoln 1518-19

■ Single Women☐ Married Women☐ Unknown

c. Lincoln 1518-19

Figure 6.6. Marital status of men cited for sexual misconduct: (a) Hereford, 1397; (b) Wiltshire, 1405; (c) Lincoln, 1518–19.

Figures 6.7. Marital status of women cited for sexual misconduct: (a) Hereford, 1397; (b) Wiltshire, 1405; (c) Lincoln, 1518–19.

boundaries. Thus a significant proportion were mobile enough to flee the parish's correction or to contract relationships farther afield than their own community. The high rates of prosecution and conviction show that parish leaders and the church court system were trying to cope with this sexual behavior, much of which must have been the result of demographic changes coming from the plague.

Although married women committed adultery, it was not as big a problem for parishes, and the Church and the community seem more concerned with married men's behavior than married women's. The church-wardens in Hereford cited more married men than women for adultery, 24 percent compared to 19 percent. A greater percent of these men were also convicted, 36 percent of men compared to 31 percent of married women. Only 3 percent of married men were either not prosecuted or the record was left blank, compared to 27 percent of women. These statistics all show that married women were not the primary sexual offenders in these late fourteenth-century communities. The behavior of single men and women was more apt to violate community norms and communities acted on men's sexual behavior more readily than women's.[126]

The records for the other three dioceses are not as detailed or as voluminous as those for Hereford, nonetheless they shared similar concerns and behavior. As Figures 6.6b, c and 6.7b, c show, in the Wiltshire parishes visited in 1405 and the Lincoln parishes visited in 1518 most men and women cited for sex misbehavior were single. Moreover, most of the single men and women were accused of fornication or adultery.[127] Conviction and punishment rates in Wiltshire were also much higher for men than for women, with 60 percent of single men convicted and punished compared to only 36 percent of single women. As Table 6.1 shows, the visitation for Kent was not by and large concerned with sexual behavior and the numbers of men and women, married or single, charged for sexual misbehavior was very low.

These visitations demonstrate that sexual misbehavior concerned parishes, but the sexual misbehavior of the unmarried worried and threatened communities more than the sexual behavior of the married. Economic conditions and demographic factors made it difficult or unattractive for young adults to marry when their sexual urges were strongest. Their mobility also made it more difficult for communities and families to supervise their moral behavior and reinforce Christian sexual norms. Based upon the visitation evidence, communities were only marginally more willing to prosecute women's sexual misbehavior than men's. Most of this concern, however, was directed at single women. In Hereford, 31 percent of married women compared to 69 percent of single women were convicted and slated for punishment for their sexual misbehavior. Among laymen, 36 percent of married men compared to 86 percent of single men were convicted and set for punishment. Similar statistics appear for Wiltshire. According to these findings, communities across England shared Gybson's concern with single women's sexuality. However, communities did not appear to be solely guided by the belief that women were more lustful than men. In both Hereford and Wilshire, the Church convicted men more often for sexual misbehavior than women.

While prosecuting the sexual conduct of single men and women at visitations was one solution to violations of community sexual norms, the creation of maidens' and young men's groups directed at maintaining a parish endowment was another. In creating parish-based groups for young women and men, parishes sought to integrate this mobile and relatively independent population into the community. The supervision that maiden's groups received kept their leisure time under greater control, but this supervision also helped foster community standards of behavior. The activities these groups hosted recognized the need for social outlets, but tried to direct this social interaction toward appropriate behavior.

The lower levels of married women cited for sexual misconduct suggests changes in women's sexual behavior after marriage. The regulatory process of visitations and indoctrination by women's groups may have played a role in changing this behavior. In those Lincolnshire parishes with young men's and maiden's groups, the accusation rate of unmarried men and women for fornication and adultery is much lower than the diocesan rate as a whole. No young women were accused of adultery or fornication in any of the ten parishes with maiden's groups (see Appendix A). In Swineshead, the churchwardens complain about a suspicious tavern, but they do not accuse any individual.[128] Yet other factors were surely just as important, if not more so. Marriage provided a legitimate sexual outlet for both partners. Husbands may also have more effectively supervised their wives' behavior than parents or employers did their children or servants. The responsibilities of marriage and motherhood probably limited the time and energy available for sexual dalliances. Married women caught sexually misbehaving also had more to lose than unmarried women. The causes for changes in women's behavior after marriage were numerous, but once married, they had more invested in maintaining these standards of behavior, even if they had not followed them previously.

Married men and women were not exempt from parish scrutiny, however, and they faced different accusations than single men and women. With the responsibilities of households, families, land, and businesses, came different opportunities for immorality and misbehavior. Membership in a parish required attendance. Failure to attend church was another frequent complaint in visitation reports. Accusations ranged from simple nonattendance to not attending on feast days, not receiving the sacraments, or working on the Sabbath. Although the visitations cite both men and women, men appear more often.[129] Of the eighteen women appearing in the Hereford report for nonattendance at mass, seven of them were cited with their husbands.[130] In Lincoln, six of the eleven women cited are cited with their husbands.[131] Other visitation reports show similar ratios. On their own, women do not appear to have missed church as often as men. Indeed, Gybson was more concerned about men's attendance at church than women's. Most men and women accused by the churchwardens of not attending church were working. While the Church generally assumed that violators were greedy, economic necessity probably stood behind lack of attendance for the poorest members of any parish. Not all who missed mass, however, could plead poverty. Some did not attend because business was too attractive. In the Canterbury parish of St. Dunstan's, Agnes and John Green and Alice and Richard Woode were accused of "keep[ing] the tavern and ale house on holy days and at the time of divine service," while several male and female parishioners from the Canterbury parish of St. Alpheg's went to fairs rather than church, and the butchers of St. Mary Magdalene's parish sold meat on Sundays.[132] These parishioners found it difficult to resist the economic opportunities that markets and customers offered. Moreover, meat would spoil, and butchers might have been trying to sell theirs before it went bad. Some excuses reflect outright hostility to the church, without falling into heresy. The wife of John Clark of Sandey, Lincolnshire, "continu[ed] to gamble with dice in her house during services on Sunday to the bad example of all," while James Jasper and John Fokare of Canterbury's St. Alpheg's "are common card [players] and . . . revelers at the ale house and so [on] all the holy days and time of divine service they continue in this fashion to which wanton women resort."[133] Presumably the prostitutes were not at church either. Infirmity and age also made it physically difficult for some to go to church. In Forest Hill (Lincs.), Henry Thurston did not go to church, but the wardens noted he was very old.[134]

In these excuses, we can glimpse the lives of those who did not find parish religion or parish participation very meaningful. Poverty seems to have played a role in alienating people from the parish, but the cliquishness of long-established members, personal conflict, and religious skepticism played roles as well. Seating arrangements and guilds fostered group identification but it was identification that usually cost something and assumed some financial stability. Those who did not or could not go along with these social standards must have found the parish and its activities alienating.

Both men and women could find church obligations onerous, time-consuming, and dull, and the taverns' attractions or the need to put food on the table led both men and women to miss church. However, we should not automatically attribute women's better attendance records to greater religiosity, although the parish setting and social attitudes toward women's parish participation helped interpret women's behavior as greater piety.[135] Seating arrangements might also have been more difficult for women to absent themselves from church. The opportunities for involvement, self-promotion, and visibility that the parish offered women could also have encouraged them to attend more regularly, regardless of their personal interest or piety. Husbands and wives might also have divided responsibility for church attendance, in the manner of family strategies for salvation, observed in wills and funerals. The wife would go to church, while the husband worked. In Kent, for example, it was butchers, not their wives, who the visitors cited for missing church.[136]

Perhaps the citations most revealing about attitudes toward women's parish behavior are those of speech crimes, whether talking in church, or scolding, or defaming neighbors. The growing proportion of speech crimes over the course of the more than one hundred years covered by the four visitations reflects the growing concern with speech in the late Middle Ages.[137] Generally scolding, a crime associated with women, went to secular courts, but talking in church belonged in the visitations and the two complaints were often combined. As Table 6.1 shows, in Kent the visitors cited a greater proportion of women than men for some form of wrongful speech. This pattern generally conforms to the patterns Sandy Bardsley found in nonecclesiastical courts.[138] The Salisbury and Lincoln visitations, however, cite more men than women and these accusations make up nearly the same proportion of citations for men and women. The disparity between these three dioceses is notable, and is probably related to the different roles played by the churchwardens and clergy in the process. In the Kent visitation, where the clergy dominated the proceedings, women were cited with greater frequency. In Lincoln, where the churchwardens were more central to the process, speech crimes were 7 percent of men's citations compared to 11 percent of women's citations. The *exemplum* of the gossiping women notwithstanding, the visitation for Lincoln accuses sixteen men of talking or "jangling" in church and only one woman.[139] As husbands and wives are not cited together, seating arrangements presumably separated them, so the women were talking to other women and the men to other men. With women and men sitting apart, the male churchwardens would have been in a better position to hear men rather than women talking in church. Another possibility is that the churchwardens found women's talking in church less disturbing or more appropriate, therefore, they did not raise it as an issue with the visitor. The clergy in Kent, however, were perhaps more familiar or accepting of the assumptions made in the story of the gossiping women. Moreover, they had a different visual perspective on the congregation during mass. Standing in the chancel, the clergy could look out on the whole congregation in the nave and may have really seen more women talking, or the clergy may have noticed women's conversations more than men's.

While both the wardens and the clergy would have understood adherence to gender roles as signs of Christian behavior, the differences between Kent and Lincoln suggest that the laity understood women's behavior at mass somewhat differently than the clergy. The parish church was God's house and as such offered women opportunities and experiences analogous to those in their own households. In the parish, women assumed a greater visibility and agency than in other public contexts, but this visibility and agency benefited the parish. From this standpoint, it would be harder for churchwardens to ascribe impious behavior to women. While sexual misbehavior was a clear-cut violation of patriarchal norms and household order, woman's talking, leading, acting, and opining within the parish were expected and maybe even "natural." Therefore, it was more difficult for the laity to identify these behaviors to the episcopal visitors as problematic. The churchwardens who brought complaints to the visitor had wives who organized parish collections, played in Hocktide, joined wives' groups, supervised maidens' groups, washed the parish's laundry, and helped keep track of the church's goods and money. Churchwardens would not have seen such behavior, which asserted the family's respectability and social status as impious. Indeed such behavior could have meshed well with the hopes and prayers of many families. To the churchwardens, their wives were acting as women should act within the parish.

Most women accused of scolding or other speech violations in the visitations were also cited for sexual misconduct, absence from church, or other misbehavior, suggesting that these women were difficult or marginalized on a number of levels. In Kennington, Kent, Elizabeth May was cited first for having an illegitimate child by Richard Ricard, a man cited numerous times for violence, rape, sexual misconduct, and other manifestations of "evil rule." Elizabeth May and her husband Robert along with Richard Ricard were then accused of being "common slanderers of their neighbors and back biters." Elizabeth was then cited for "living suspiciously" and trying to seduce the parish clerk. Finally Elizabeth's husband Robert was accused of attacking the vicar, "keeping evil rule at the ale house," denouncing the images in the church, and mocking the Eucharist.[140] The accusations of slandering and backbiting were nestled in among other more serious accusations of violence and heresy. Elizabeth associated with unsavory men, and may have lived a sexually promiscuous life. It was probably these actions that got her noticed. The accusations of slandering and backbiting added to the impression she was an ungovernable woman. Men, however, were often simply accused of scolding or talking in church. These accusations were not as frequently paired with any other misbehavior. This pattern also suggests the different attitudes toward men's and women's behavior while in church, the different meaning of women's speech, and the lack of proximity of the churchwardens' to women while at mass.

In the end, the laity were probably not blind to the vanity and self-promotion that women brought with them to church. Although this behavior was condemnatory or amusing, it still fit into the lesson that being a good Christian also meant being a good woman. Fine clothing could be a manifestation of pride, but it could also display a family's status, hard work, and economic advancement. A man with civic ambitions needed to be outwardly pious, but so too did his wife; piety included dressing the part. Women without proper clothes stayed home. Similarly, talking during service might be gossip, but it might be prayers or an inquiry into the health or needs of a neighbor. With the exception of sexual misbehavior, the women cited in the visitations were rarely guilty of the impious behavior preachers described in their sermons. Churchwardens did not share Gybson's concerns with women's interactions with each other. The laity and the clergy looked for different clues when interpreting women's behavior in church. Although men and women might both laugh at the *exempla* that parodied women's church behavior, their amusement did not mean that they had internalized these values as the clergy hoped. Communally then, women's sins and impieties, especially among married women, were less visible to the churchwardens because women were an identifiable group associated with Christian behavior and expected to be comfortable in the church.

Conclusion

Late medieval men and women valued modesty in women. Moreover, most probably agreed that parish visibility, activity, and charity should not become occasions for sin. Women should remain demure and courteous so as not to threaten their father's or husband's authority. Both men and women in positions of authority or influence cared about the sexual behavior of those under their care. Married women in charge of servants had much to lose by the promiscuity of their maids, as husbands did by their wives' and daughters' sexual misbehavior. Through education, supervision, and punishment, parishes tried to control the behavior of women.

Collective action promoted among and by women as Christian behavior challenged the demure and courteous deportment advocated by didactic texts as Christian behavior. While the "Good Wife" admonished her daughter not to speak to strangers, the churchwarden's wife organized the parish maidens to go door-to-door to raise money for their parish. The "Good Wife" advised her daughter when she married, she should be meek and mild toward her husband, yet parish wives instructed the churchwardens on how to spend the money they had raised. Although some of this discrepancy grew out of the laity's and clergy's different values, the laity sought out sermons, and purchased religious didactic texts, so we should not make too much of this divide. Instead, I suggest that in transferring their domestic skills and household behavior onto the parish, women created a space where the authority of the housewife expanded as it met up with her desire for salvation. In the parish, women also met up with other women who had similar assumptions, goals, and interests. Together they created opportunities for collective action and created visibility in the name of salvation. Respectable women participated vigorously in their parish and probably equally as sincerely listened to sermons and lectures or read books if they could, advocating quiet contemplation and meek demeanor. Reconciling this contradiction lies in viewing modesty as a mutable behavior that manifested itself differently in different contexts and spaces.

Women's pious practices did draw upon their household responsibilities, but not in the manner idealized by the laymen's instructions described in the beginning of the chapter. Rather, women's household obligations gave them influence, which they brought to their parish churches. Moreover, parish leaders understood the reality of what their domestic vocabulary of piety meant in practice and did not challenge it in ecclesiastical courts.

Epilogue: Women and the Reformation

In 1536, Henry VIII ordered the closure of many small monasteries and hospitals. In response, a group of women in Exeter went to the Priory of St. Nicholas and assaulted the Breton workmen hired to dismantle the rood screen. Reportedly the women grabbed the two men and carried them out of the priory, temporarily halting their work. Later, the mayor of Exeter in a communiqué to the marquis of Exeter reported that he had interrogated "a great number of women which were among others the chief evil doers of the said unlawful assembly and also diverse of their husbands ... [the women denied] ... there were any men disguised or wearing women's clothing among them ... [or that] they were commanded, procured, counseled or abetted by their husbands or by any other men."[1]

In this event, we see women acting collectively in defense of their religious beliefs. We also see the mayor's doubt that women could have acted on their own in this fashion. While women were routinely involved in both peaceful and violent collective actions, such as parish fundraising and bread riots, we have few such examples of their involvement in anti-Reform agitation.[2] Given women's education to be submissive and passive, we might not be surprised at this, but given women's prominence in the parish and local religion, their silence and passivity in the face of such change might also be surprising.[3] The impact of the Reformation on women, especially its impact on their corporate and communal activities, has received limited treatment, and generally the topic is fraught with as much partisanship as any other Reformation issue. Recently Christine Peters has looked for the continuities across this great religious change, arguing that both Catholics and Protestants saw women as naturally more prone to religiosity.[4] In the short term, Peters argues, women might have resisted Protestantism in greater numbers, but this had as much to do with their legal position as their religious identities or sentiments. For Peters, the congruence between pious virtues and household obligations played more of a role in determining women's religious actions than identification with "gender-specific religious role models."[5]

No definitive answer is possible for the question "was the Reformation good or bad for women?" Some women, such as those in Exeter, found it upsetting and took action into their own hands; but others, such as the London women who denounced Queen Mary's Catholic chaplain, Dr. Bourne, in 1553 as he preached at St. Paul's Cross, had clearly found meaning in Protestantism.[6] Christine Peters argues that for women the Reformation was not a rupture with the past, but gave new prominence to themes already present in pre-Reformation religious practice and repressed others. The Reformation offers scholars many opportunities to weigh change and continuity, and this epilogue is no different. What this epilogue aims to do, however, is not so much offer a new interpretation of the Reformation's impact on women as provide a path for future research in light of the findings of this book. For a new interpretation of the late medieval parish surely offers some opportunity to reconsider the course of religious reform and its impact on the laity.

If women found any meaning in the communal activities of all-women's seating, all-women's guilds and stores, female saints, and the transformation of household goods into items of religious and liturgical significance, then they lost much, for the reform ended most of these practices. Reformers may have diminished the amount of laundry and dusting women did for the parish when they removed its images, vestments, altar cloths, and liturgical items, but they also narrowed women's opportunities for parish participation. As we balance continuity and change, women's actions vis-à-vis their parishes changed, but their social and family identities remained largely the same. The Reformation did not alter gender roles or women's legal and economic status, so women still came to church as widows, wives, and daughters, and still worked as housewives, servants, and small-time entrepreneurs.

Although there were pockets of Protestantism in England in the early sixteenth century, the English Reformation was more the product of parliamentary legislation and royal decree than popular agitation. Henry VIII's search for a way to divorce his barren wife, Catherine of Aragon, first drove him to split with Rome and then pass the Act of Supremacy, which made him head of the English church in 1534. This break, while perhaps emotional, did little to change daily routines at the parish level.[7] That same year, however, English translations of the Bible were not longer outlawed. In 1536, when Cromwell reduced the number of saints' days and suppressed small monasteries, religious routines at the parish level began to change. In 1538, Cromwell oversaw much more radical changes when he abolished all lights before images, including the Easter Sepulcher and the rood screen, dissolved all pilgrimage shrines, and ended the veneration of images. That same year, parishes were also required to purchase English Bibles, although most dragged their feet on this until 1541, when they faced stiff fines. In 1542, parishes were mandated to purchase a new English processional. Henry's Reformation was piecemeal and incomplete. He did finish dissolving all monasteries by 1540, and undermined the doctrine of purgatory, but he still left in place much of the rhythm of local religious life including the old liturgy.

Henry's death in January of 1547 ushered in a radical reorganizing of parish life. Edward VI and his protectors were sincerely Protestant, and by July there were injunctions to destroy all shrines, images, and paintings of saints that had had candles burned before them. The laity and the clergy were also to cease all processions at mass. The crown then started seizing parish property as it closed chantries, guilds, obits, and other endowments that provided masses for the dead. By February of 1548, there was to be no more blessing of candles for Candlemas, ashes for Ash Wednesday, palms on Palm Sunday, creeping to the cross on Good Friday, and burning the Paschal candle at Easter. At this point many churches also had their wall paintings whitewashed and rood screens removed, ceased to use the Easter Sepulcher at Easter, and stopped celebrating Corpus Christi. In 1549, Parliament passed the Act of Uniformity and imposed the first Book of Common Prayer. Parishes gradually removed their altars and replaced them with communion tables. In 1552, the government imposed the second Book of Common Prayer. This one had an overtly Protestant communion service. In 1553, the government set up another commission to seize remaining church property. Parishes could keep linen, chalices, and bells, but plate, jewels, and money had to be sent to London, and robes, base metal, and cloth sold locally and the proceeds sent to London. Margaret Mathew, widow of a wealthy Bristol draper, bought three copes for 4s. when the parish sold off goods related to the old liturgy in 1548.[8] Sometime around 1540, when Mother Davy's parish of Great Halingbury (Essex) sold off its goods, she bought an old Lent cloth.[9] Both women found bargains, as these items would have cost much more when their churches purchased them. In the space of fifteen years, the government had undone hundreds of years of tradition, material culture, and local organization. While Edward's death in July 1553 brought his Catholic sister Mary to the throne, her restoration of Catholicism was short-lived, ending with her death five years later. With the accession of Elizabeth in 1558, England was again Protestant, although not in the rigid form implemented by her brother and his proctors.

The removal of lights and images from churches in 1536 and the closure of the guilds in 1547 meant great changes in how women participated in local religion. Although churches still needed to be cleaned, there were no longer saints to be dressed and adorned with their handiwork. When this happened, women lost an outlet for pious expression. Their responsibilities to their families and their domestic roles, which had readily become ways of venerating the saints and asking for God's intercession, were no longer acceptable practices in the reformed religion of the early 1550s. Moreover, they lost the ability to influence the aesthetics of the mass or the church by transforming their clothes and household objects into vestments, and altar cloths. The new liturgy had no need for them. Although women still cleaned the church and mended the communion cloths and vestments, there were fewer of these goods in parish inventories. Women may have maintained their easy familiarity with the church and its contents that they gained from "churchkeeping" but the space of the church no longer had the same sanctified status that transformed their actions into prayer or put their household goods in proximity to the sacred.

Scholars have long noted that the Reformation included a shift from collective piety to individual piety.[10] Yet, while the Reformation may have implemented this shift, the sentiments were not new. John Gybson, the Premonstratensian monk discussed in the last chapter, distrusted women's collective actions, seeing it as an opportunity for sin, not piety. Regardless of these clerical sentiments, however, the growth of women's guilds and stores only ended with the Reformation. The abolition of saintly images from the parishes took away the focus of most such groups and when the Crown confiscated their property, it was difficult for communities to continue their activities. The virgins' collection from St. Margaret's in Westminster disappeared once the wardens removed the St. Margaret statue.[11] Initially the maidens in Morebath switched their support from the maidens' light at the altar of St. Mary to the light kept at the Easter Sepulcher, but interest waned nonetheless and ultimately the Easter Sepulcher was also removed.[12] Income declined and after 1540, the maidens' guild disappeared from the churchwardens' accounts altogether, although the young men's guild was not similarly so affected. In Chagford, the women's group survived the loss of their saint, but once the Crown confiscated all guild and chantry lands, that women's group also disappeared.[13]

Seating arrangements were not the first physical change the Reformation brought to churches, but as parishes refurbished and renovated their churches following the Reformation, seating often changed. Many parishes no doubt felt compelled to remove old pews because bench-ends frequently contained Catholic images that were no longer appropriate. New arrangements increasingly placed families together instead of separating the sexes.[14] This change was not, however, mandated by reformers, and indeed many reformers felt that keeping the sexes segregated was a good idea. However, many parishioners, including the carpenters working in West Bowden (Durham), countered that segregated seating would lead women to promiscuity and that proper sexual decorum would be maintained only when women were under the watchful eyes of their fathers and husbands.[15] In making this argument, the carpenters picked up on pre-Reformation clerical complaints about women's behavior in church, but reconfigured them to connect pre-Reformation practices with fostering promiscuity instead of controlling women. Women now sat with their husbands and children, not with their friends. It not only became easier for husbands to monitor their wives' and daughters' behavior, but family seats emphasized the family as a religious unit and limited the interaction among women while at church.

Because women still remained connected to housekeeping and domesticity, their ability to shape the life-cycle liturgies with pararituals and clothing remained even as the liturgies and their theology changed. Even though outlawing of processions and purgatory cut into some of the laity's ability to shape these liturgies and destroyed some of the attendant meaning, babies, newly delivered mothers, and corpses still needed to be brought to the church, thus not all processions disappeared. Women could still choose who to include and exclude. Until the government instituted the Book of Common Prayer in 1549, not much had changed in the liturgy and its accompanying ceremony either. The Rationale of Ceremonial produced in 1540 by a council of bishops largely defended the old Sarum rituals.[16] In 1552, when the second and avowedly Protestant prayer book was introduced, much then changed in the life-cycle liturgies. In the baptism rite, priests no longer exorcised the infant in preparation for baptism. There was no longer a chrisom cloth nor did the priest anoint the infant with oil. Women, however, insisted on retaining their churching liturgy, although there remained much debate about what it meant.[17] Even when some Protestant reformers denied the sacramental nature of marriage, much of the variation in weddings still revolved around place and material culture.[18] This still left women's ability to shape their weddings largely in tact.[19] The loss of purgatory and the need to pray for the dead, however, dramatically transformed the rituals surrounding death. Funerals were no longer a moment of intercession, but instead became an affirmation of faith by the living. While bell ringing remained, it no longer meant the same thing, and families no longer needed to strategize over how to afford intercessory prayers and actions the deceased wanted.

Ironically as the Reformation was gaining force, parishes deployed women in greater numbers to manage it or to resist it. During the early phases of the Reformation, many parishes sought to appoint or elect women churchwardens.[20] Although not unheard of prior to the Reformation, women churchwardens became more common thereafter. In one sense, appointing female churchwardens was a continuation and expansion of women's parish leadership positions. In another sense, female churchwardens were evidence of resistance to these changes.

In many parishes, female churchwardens broke with traditional leadership patterns, thus reflecting the confusion and tension that the religious reforms produced. Parishes changed the number of churchwardens they had, introduced female wardens where previously they had never had one, and altered their appointment procedures. Perhaps in part because many men even refused to serve. For example, in Nettlecombe, Somerset, and Morebath, Devon, the office of churchwarden rotated among a certain number of families on the basis of landholding. This rotation allowed widows to serve, in order to maintain their family's turn in the rotation after their husbands' had died. Not all women agreed to serve when their turn arose. In 1540, with both William Poole and Geoffrey Smith, the next churchwardens, dead, their widows refused to take their place in Morebath's churchwarden rotation.[21] Similarly, in 1546, Ellen Norman refused to serve.[22] She had to pay the parish four pounds of wax to escape her obligation. In 1544, Nettlecombe parishioner Alice Harper was added as a third warden, from outside the normal rotation of two wardens.[23] Other parishes, such as Trull, also in Somerset, had always elected three churchwardens, but in 1542 only two served—Master Cogwyll and Agnes Shorter.[24]

The Reformation also introduced women into the office of churchwarden who were of a different social status than those who served previously. Sybil Smith, who was Tintinhull's (Som.) churchwarden in 1547–48, was poorer than most of those who had served before her. She was assessed on the lay subsidy of 1524 at 40s. The other identifiable churchwardens for Tintinhull paid taxes on between £4 and £12 of goods or income.[25] At the other end of the social scale was Dame Elizabeth Copley. When she served as churchwarden for her parish of Gatton, Surrey, in 1546–47, she combined local privilege and religious politics.[26] Elizabeth's family dominated this tiny parish. As churchwarden, she could both protect her family's religious interests and the religious artifacts that the crown was about to confiscate. By 1584, her family members were known recusants.[27] Although some, like Elizabeth Coply, were dedicated to one side of the religious reform issues, others had probably been pressured to serve. Parishes may have hoped that legal authorities would excuse their actions if the parish failed to comply with mandated reforms. There were no precedents for how parishes and churchwardens should proceed through this crisis, and for female wardens the expectation that they lacked experience and wisdom might have been useful, even if false.

Like their male counterparts, female churchwardens presided over the repair of the church fabric, but they also helped manage the Reformation. As churchwardens they purchased the necessary new liturgical books, acquired copies "of the king's commandments," arranged meetings with the king's commissioners, and dealt with an increasing number of visitations, as the Crown sought to enforce compliance with new rules.[28] Lucy Scely, churchwarden of Morebath in 1548, had a particularly difficult time because the parish had no money. Religious reforms had abolished several stocks that had previously funded the parish's upkeep.[29] To raise money, Lucy sold off the Lent cloth, various hangings and altar frontals, some banners, and numerous basins and candlesticks that religious reforms had outlawed.[30] She did this apparently without consulting the parish and earned her vicar's ire.

Although we know Elizabeth Copley's religious politics, we do not know how Lucy Scely felt about these changes. Her family was poorer than the other families in the rotation of the office of churchwarden.[31] While the reforms were financially draining, some might have embraced them. Lucy Scely's willingness to sell off her parish's liturgical items might stem as much from religious ambivalence or Protestant conviction as the parish's financial crisis.[32]

The Reformation did not end the need for parish churches to be cleaned, babies to be baptized, or the liturgy performed for an attendant congregation. What it did do was to change the meaning of the space in which these actions happened. Women could still dress their babies in fine clothing to show off their social identity and celebrate the continuation of the lineage, but they could not then return to clean the church afterwards, certain in the knowledge that their actions were pious good works that would benefit their soul. The church also ceased to be an official and accepted place for women to work together collectively. While attending the liturgy, women sat with their friends less often, nor could they meet in their all-women's groups to share common concerns, religious or otherwise. The anxiety that the pre-Reformation clergy had repeatedly expressed in their sermons and in their courtesy texts about women's church behavior carried through to the other side of the Reformation. Even as the reformers altered the theology of the English Church, they fulfilled the pre-Reformation clergy's desires to regulate women's behavior while in the church, by curtailing their activities, agency, and visibility. The lay agency that was at the heart of women's ability to turn the parish into a forum for their own spiritual practices ended, as the family became increasingly a religious unit that was on display in the parish.

As scholars of the Continental Reformation have pointed out, an important component of the reformers agenda was the domestication of Christianity and the inculcation of proper Christian behavior among family members according to their place in the family.[33] Yet as we have seen, this equation of gender roles with Christian behavior was by no means new. Prior to the Reformation, pious behavior for women involved concerns for marriage, childbearing, and motherhood, and this continued after the Reformation. The parish had been the place to articulate and address these concerns and it was still true after the Reformation, although in a more attenuated form. Through their parishes, women were still socialized to become proper Christian women and Christian wives, and married women were encouraged to focus on their familial role as mothers and wives as a form of piety. What the Reformation did accomplish was an alteration in the manifestations of gender relations in the parish. Housewives may still have exercised emotional and physical influence over their households that somewhat mitigated the patriarchal order, but this influence was no longer a prelude to their agency and action in parish corporate life. The imposition of the Reformation on English parishes redefined appropriated religious behavior for women. It was still predicated on household tasks and concerns, but it was no longer as collective, visible, and active.

To be sure, some women rejoiced at the abolition of guild dues, the veneration of saint images, and the pomp and ritual of the Sarum Manual. However, those who were going to find meaning in this new Church needed to develop a new set of skills and actions from which to create religious meaning. For some literacy, a personal relationship with God, and the increased role of faith rather than works were the new skills and actions. For others, unable to read, and unable to hear the Word of God with their friends who supported them through difficult times, it was not enough.

Appendix A. All-Women's Groups

County	Parish	Earliest date	Membership	Saint	Source
Buckinghamshire	Wexham	1523	Maidens	Mary	Will
	Burnham	1523	Maidens	Mary	Will
Cambridgeshire	St. Mary the Great, Cambridge	1518	Wives	Mary	CWA
	Holy Trinity, Cambridge	1518	Single women?	Ursula	CWA
Cheshire	Chester[1]	1487	Wives	Mary	Civic records
Cornwall	Bodmin	1469	Maidens	?	CWA
	Bodmin	1472	Wives	?	CWA
	Stratton	1513	Maidens	Mary	CWA
	Poughill[2]	1534	Wives	?	CWA
Devon	Ashburton	1489	Wives	Mary	CWA
	Chagford	1500	Wives	Mary	CWA
	Holy Trinity, Exeter	1515	Maidens	?	CWA
	Broadhempston	1517	?	Mary	CWA
	Morebath	1520	Maidens	Mary	CWA
	Woodland	1527	?	Mary	CWA
Dorset	Wimborne Minster	1459 (1x)	Maidens	?	CWA
	Wimborne Minster	1498	Wives of the Town	?	CWA
	Wimborne Minster	1498	Wives of the Country	?	CWA
Gloucestershire	St. Ewen's Bristol	1465	Maidens	Mary	CWA
Kent	Biddenden	1518	Maidens	?	Will
	Frittenden	1519	Maidens	?	Will
Leicestershire	St. Martin's, Leicester	1498	Maidens	Mary	CWA
Lincolnshire	Long Sutton	1528	Maidens	?	Will
	Spilsby	1530	Maidens	?	Will
	Swineshead	1530	Maidens	?	Will
	Whitton	1531	Maidens	?	Will
	Winthrope	1531	Maidens	?	Will
	Hundelby	1532	Maidens	?	Will

	Gosberton	1532	Maidens	?	Will
	Bennington in Holland	1532	Maidens	?	Will
	Horbling[3]	1533	?	Dorothy	CWA
	Ingoldmells	1534	Maidens	?	Will
Middlesex	St. Margaret's, Westminster	1497	Maidens	Margaret	CWA
	St. Martin-in-the-Fields, Westminster	1542	Midwives	?	CWA
Oxfordshire	Spelsbury	1525	?	Trinity	CWA
Norfolk	Swaffham	1509	Wives	Peter	CWA
	Swaffham	1515	Wives	John the Bapt.	CWA
	Sale[4]	?	Maidens	?	Will
Nottinghamshire	Wollaton[5]	1521	Women	Mary	Household account
Somerset	Croscombe	1474	Maidens	?	CWA
Suffolk	Walberswick	1464	Wives	Mary	CWA
Surrey	St. Olave's, Southwark	1482	Sisterhood	Anne	Inventory
	St. Margaret's, Southwark	1485	Wives	Anne	CWA/ Will
	Horvey	1518	Wives	Katherine	CWA
Warwickshire[6]	Polesworth	1521	Women	?	Household account
	Middleton	1521	Women	Mary	Household account
	Middleton	1526	Women	Stephen	Household account
Wiltshire	St. Edmund's, Salisbury	1491	Wives	Mary	CWA/ Will
	Winterslow[7]	1542	Maidens	?	CWA
	St. Thomas's, Salisbury	1545	Women	Mary	CWA
Worcester	Badsey	1533	Little maidens	?	CWA
	Badsey	1533	Great maidens	?	CWA
Yorkshire	Doncaster[8]	1430	Wives	?	Will

[1] Mary Wack, "Women, Work, and Play in an English Medieval Town," in *Maids and Mistresses, Cousins and Queens: Women's Alliances in Early Modern England*, ed. Susan Frye and Karen Robertson (Oxford: Oxford University Press, 1999), 35–51.

[2] Joanna Mattingly, "The Medieval Parish Guilds of Cornwall," *Journal of the Royal Institution of Cornwall* 10, 3 (1989): 322.

[3] Christine Peters, *Patterns of Piety: Women, Gender and Religion in Late Medieval and Reformation England* (Cambridge: Cambridge University Press, 2003), 34.

[4] Eamon Duffy, "Religious Belief," in *A Social History of England: 1200–1500*, ed. Rosemary Horrox and W. Mark Ormrod (Cambridge: Cambridge University Press, 2006), 313.

[5] From P. J. P. Goldberg, *Women in England, c. 1275–1525: Documentary Sources* (Manchester: Manchester University Press, 1995), 261.

[6] Goldberg, *Women in England*, 261.

[7] Peters, *Patterns of Piety*, 28.

[8] Goldberg, *Women in England*, 287.

Appendix B. Hocktide Celebrations

County	Town	Parish	Earliest date	Source
Berkshire	Reading	St. Giles	1518	CWA
	Reading	St. Lawrence	1528	CWA
	Wallingford[1]	Citywide	until 1538	Civic records
Buckinghamshire	Amersham	St. Mary	1529	CWA
	Wing	Holy Trinity	1539	CWA
Cambridgeshire	Cambridge	St. Mary the Great	1470	CWA
	Bassingborn	SS. Peter & Paul	1498	CWA
	Cambridge	Holy Trinity	1508	CWA
Devon	Exeter	St. Mary Steps	1530	CWA
Herfordshire	Bishops' Stortford	St. Michael	1479	CWA
Kent	Canterbury	St. Andrew	1485	CWA
	Canterbury	St. Dunstan	1485	
Middlesex	London	All Hallows, London Wall	1457	CWA
	London	All Hallows, Staining[2]	1491	CWA
	London	St. Mary at Hill	1498	CWA
	Westminster	St. Margaret	1498	CWA
	London	St. Andrew Hubbard	1522	CWA
	Westminster	St. Martin-in-the-Field	1525	CWA
Oxfordshire	Thame	St. Mary	1457	CWA
	Oxford	St. Michael at the Northgate	1463	CWA
	Oxford	St. Peter le Bailey[3]	1465	CWA
	Oxford	St. Peter in the East[4]	1474	CWA
	Henley on Thames	Citywide	1499	Civic records
	Oxford	St. Mary[5]	1512–17	Student complaint
	Oxford	St. Aldate[6]	1535	CWA
	Oxford	St. Martin's[7]	1543	CWA

Somerset	Croscombe	St. Mary's	1473	CWA
	Yatton	St. Mary's	1512	CWA
	Trull	St. Mary's	1525	CWA
Shropshire	Shrewbury	Citywide	1549	Civic records
Staffordshire	Walsall	St. Mathew	1462	CWA
Suffolk	Boxford	St. Mary	1530	CWA
	Bungay[8]	St. Mathew	1523	CWA
Surrey	Southwark	St. Margaret	1452	CWA
	Guildford[9]	Holy Trinity	1509	CWA
	Kingston-Upon-Thames	All Saints	1504	CWA
	Lambeth	St. Mary	1504	CWA
	Shere	St. James	1512	CWA
Sussex	Lewes	St. Andrews	1532	CWA
Warwickshire	Coventry	Citywide	1416	Civic records
Wiltshire	Salisbury	St. Edmunds	1490	CWA
	Salisbury	St. Thomas	1545	CWA
Worcestershire	Badsey	St. James	1533	CWA

[1] Sally-Beth MacLean, "Hocktide: A Reassessment of a Popular Pre-Reformation Festival," in *Festive Drama*, ed. Meg Twycross (Woodbridge: D.S. Brewer, 1996), 237.

[2] MacLean, "Hocktide," 240 n. 19.

[3] *REED-Oxford*, vol. 2, ed. John R. Elliott, Allan H. Nelson, Alexandra F. Johnston, and Diana Wyatt (London and Toronto: British Library and Toronto University Press, 2004), 918.

[4] *REED-Oxford*, vol. 2, 921

[5] *REED-Oxford*, vol. 1, ed. John R. Elliott, Allan H. Nelson, Alexandra F. Johnston, and Diana Wyatt (London and Toronto: British Library and Toronto University Press, 2004), 56.

[6] *REED-Oxford*, vol. 1, 78.

[7] *REED-Oxford*, vol. 1, 86.

[8] Ronald Hutton, *Rise and Fall of Merry England: The Ritual Year 1400–1700* (Oxford: Oxford University Press, 1994), 300 n. 68.

[9] Alexandra F. Johnston and Sally-Beth MacLean, "Reformation and Resistance in Thames/Severn Parishes: The Dramatic Witness," in *The Parish in English Life: 1400–1600*, ed. Katherine L. French, Gary G. Gibbs, and Beat A. Kümin (Manchester: Manchester University Press, 1997), 184 n. 17.

Abbreviations

BL—British Library
CRO—Cambridgeshire Record Office
CWA—Churchwardens' Account
DHC—Dorset History Centre
DRO—Devon Record Office
EETS—Early English Text Society
ERO—Essex Record Office
GA—Guild Account
GL—London Guildhall Library
KBA—Kingston Borough Archive
LMA—London Metropolitan Archive
NRO—Norwich Record Office
PRO—The National Archive: Public Record Office
REED—Record of Early English Drama
SARS—Somerset Archive and Record Services
SHC—Surrey History Centre—Woking
SRO—Suffolk Record Office—Ipswich
VCH—Victoria County History
WAC—Westminster Archive Centre
WAM—Westminster Abbey Muniments

Notes

Introduction

1. Martin Riesebrodt and Kelly H. Chong, "Fundamentalisms and Patriarchal Gender Politics," *Journal of Women's History* 10 (1999): 63; Kelly H. Chong, "Agony in Prosperity: Conversion and the Negotiation of Patriarchy Among South Korean Evangelical Women," *Harvard Divinity Bulletin* 32, 3 (2004): 11.

2. G. R. Owst, *Preaching in Medieval England* (New York: Russell and Russell, 1965), 173; Peter Biller, "The Common Women in the Western Church in the Thirteenth and Fourteenth Centuries," in *Women and the Church*, ed. W. J. Sheils and Diana Wood (Oxford: Blackwell, 1990), 140. See also Christine Peters, *Patterns of Piety: Women, Gender and Religion in Late Medieval and Reformation England* (Cambridge: Cambridge University Press, 2003), 4, 11.

3. Pentecostal churches in Latin America have attracted large numbers of lower-class women who have used their church membership to "restructure and remoralize the patriarchal family against the destructive forces of machismo." Riesebrodt and Chong, "Fundamentalisms," 56; see also John R. Burdick, *Looking for God in Brazil* (Berkeley: University of California Press, 1993) and Elizabeth E. Brusco, *The Reformation of Machismo: Evangelical Conversion and Gender in Colombia* (Austin: University of Texas Press, 1995).

4. Chong, "Agony and Prosperity," 11; Felicity Riddy, "Authority and Intimacy in the Late Medieval Home," in *Gendering the Master Narrative: Women and Power in the Middle Ages*, ed. Mary C. Erler and Maryanne Kowaleski (Ithaca, N.Y.: Cornell University Press, 2003), 212–28.

5. Jim Bolton, "'The World Upside Down': Plague as an Agent of Economic and Social Change," in *The Black Death in England*, ed. Mark Ormrod and Phillip Lindley (Stamford, Lincs.: Paul Watkins, 1996), 17.

6. Herbert Grundmann anticipated much of this work when he argued that there was a distinctive women's religious movement in the twelfth and thirteenth centuries. Herbert Grundmann, *Religious Movements in the Middle Ages*, trans. Steven Rowan (Notre Dame, Ind.: University of Notre Dame Press, 1995). Carolyn Bynum in *Jesus as Mother: Studies in the Spirituality of the High Middle Ages* (Berkeley: University of California Press, 1982), 3–5 discusses the importance of this work to the study of women's spirituality. See also her *Holy Feast and Holy Fast: The Religious Significance of Food to Medieval Women* (Berkeley: University of California Press, 1987); Richard Kieckhefer, *Unquiet Souls: Fourteenth-Century Saints and Their Religious Milieu* (Chicago: University of Chicago Press, 1984); Elizabeth Alvilda Petroff, *Body and Soul: Essays on Medieval Women and Mysticism* (Oxford: Oxford

University Press, 1994). Although much of this initial scholarship focused on the writings of mystics, the further quest for women's writings has led scholars, particularly literary scholars, to the writings and reading practices of individual laywomen. Typically only noble- or gentlewomen had the financial means to learn to read or to employ a private confessor, so most studies of lay women's piety have focused on these classes of women. See in particular Susan Groag Bell, "Medieval Women Book Owners: Arbiters of Lay Piety and Ambassadors of Culture," *Signs* 7 (1981–82): 742–68. For England, see C. A. J. Armstrong, "The Piety of Cicely, Duchess of York," in *England, France and Burgundy in the Fifteenth Century* (London: Hambledon, 1983), 135–56; Michael Hicks, "The Piety of Margaret, Lady Hungerford (d. 1487)," *Journal of Ecclesiastical History* 38 (1987): 19–38; Michael Jones and Malcolm G. Underwood, *The King's Mother: Lady Margaret Beaufort, Countess of Richmond and Derby* (Cambridge: Cambridge University Press, 1992); Carol M. Meale, "'. . . alle the bokes that I haue of latyn, englisch, and frensch': Laywomen and Their Books in Late Medieval England," in *Women and Literature in Britain: 1150–1500*, ed. Carol M. Meale (Cambridge: Cambridge University Press, 1993), 128–58; Felicity Riddy, "'Women Talking About Things of God': A Late Medieval Sub-Culture," in *Women and Literature in Britain*, 104–27; Rebecca Krug, *Reading Families: Women's Literate Practice in Late Medieval England* (Ithaca, N.Y.: Cornell University Press, 2002).

7. Bynum, *Holy Feast and Holy Fast*.

8. Andrew Brown states after two-hundred-some pages of discussion of "popular piety" that he could have discussed women, but that this was not a book about gender. Brown is assuming that gender has no place in a discussion of collective action or lay religious behavior. Parish life and lay activity are gendered male, and gendering it male is taken as gender-neutral. Andrew Brown, *Popular Piety in Late Medieval England: The Diocese of Salisbury, 1250–1550* (Oxford: Oxford University Press, 1995), 256–58; Eamon Duffy, *The Stripping of the Altars: Traditional Religion in England, c. 1400–1580* (New Haven, Conn.: Yale University Press, 1992), has a short discussion of women's parochial activities, but he does not believe that gender made any difference in religious practice. He writes "within the diversity of medieval religious options there was a remarkable degree of religious and imaginative homogeneity across the social spectrum" (3; see also 131–54, 265, esp. 153). Clive Burgess argues a different point when he questions just which people constituted parishioners in parish records. "Wives, younger of dependent family, apprentices, resident servants, and the poor were not considered in parish memoranda at least to be 'significant parishioners'; not apparently liable for levies, they were presumably ineligible to contribute to parish business and decision-making because they were neither householders nor leaseholders. Although we use the term 'parishioner' loosely, contemporaries may well have approached it with important distinctions in mind." Clive Burgess, "Shaping the Parish: St. Mary at Hill, London, in the Fifteenth Century," in *The Cloister and the World*, ed. John Blair and Brian Golding (Oxford: Oxford University Press, 1996), 259–60.

9. J. J. Scarisbrick, *The Reformation and the English People* (Oxford: Blackwell, 1984); Duffy, *Stripping of the Altars*; Beat A. Kümin, *The Shaping of a Community:*

The Rise and Reformation of the English Parish, c. 1400–1560 (Brookfield, Vt.: Scolar Press, 1996); Peters, *Patterns of Piety*.

10. Judy Ann Ford has also argued for this position in her study of John Mirk's sermon collection, *The Festial*. Ford argues that in an effort to combat the attractions of Lollardy and rebellion in the 1380s, Mirk created a vision of active lay participation in religion that was essentially new. The popularity of Mirk's work up into the mid-sixteenth century suggests that Mirk's vision for parish life continued to have relevance. See Judy Ann Ford, *John Mirk's* Festial: *Orthodoxy, Lollardy, and the Common People in Fourteenth-Century England* (Cambridge: D.S. Brewer, 2006).

11. Marjorie Keniston McIntosh, *Controlling Misbehavior, 1370–1600* (Cambridge: Cambridge University Press, 1998).

12. Ibid., 54–107.

13. Felicity Riddy, "Mother Knows Best: Reading Social Change in a Courtesy Text," *Speculum* 71, 1 (1996): 66–86.

14. Lawrence R. Poos, "Social Context of Statute of Labourers Enforcement," *Law and History Review* 1 (1983): 36, 52.

15. Carlo M. Cipolla, *Before the Industrial Revolution: European Society and Economy, 1000–1700*, 2nd ed. (New York: Norton, 1980), 4.

16. J. L. Bolton, *The Medieval English Economy, 1150–1500* (London: Dent, 1980), 121.

17. Ibid., 182–83; William C. Jordan, *The Great Famine: Northern Europe in the Early Fourteenth Century* (Princeton, N.J.: Princeton University Press, 1996), 50–52.

18. Studies of individual manors, such as Halsoewen (Worc.), show the population declined by 10 to 15 percent between 1316 and 1318. Ibid., 102–4, 118.

19. "A Fourteenth-Century Chronicle from the Grey Friars at Lynn," quoted in *The Black Death*, ed. Rosemary Horrox (Manchester: Manchester University Press, 1994), 63.

20. Some historians have questioned whether the disease was in fact plague, or another disease, such as anthrax. See G. Twigg, *The Black Death: A Biological Reappraisal* (New York: Schocken Books, 1985); more recently Samuel Cohn has also challenged the belief that it was plague in his article "The Black Death: End of a Paradigm," *American Historical Review* 107 (2002): 703–38. Whether it was plague or not seems outside the scope of this study, the extreme mortality is not in question even if there are quibbles in the details.

21. The bishop of Bath and Wells permitted laypeople to hear confessions in this time of crisis if no priest were available. He did not explicitly prohibit women from this task. *Black Death*, 271–72

22. "*Eulogium*," quoted in ibid., 64.

23. "*Polychronicon*," quoted in ibid., 85.

24. "Chronicle of John of Reading," quoted in ibid., 87. For information on John of Reading see p. 74.

25. Bolton, "The World Upside Down," 30.

26. For example, the outbreak in 1432 hit Newcastle in the north, but not the southern portions of the country. East Anglia was spared the outbreak of 1466, but York's mortality rate reached its peak at the same time. Ibid., 32.

27. Ibid., 33; see also John Hatcher, "Mortality in the Fifteenth Century: Some

New Evidence," *Economic History Review*, 2nd ser. 39 (1986): 30–31; Christopher Dyer, *Standards of Living in the Later Middle Ages: Social Change in England, c. 1200–1520* (Cambridge: Cambridge University Press, 1989), 262–63, 265.

28. Gervase Rosser, *Medieval Westminster, 1200–1540* (Oxford: Oxford University Press, 1989), 170.

29. R. A. Davies, "The Effects of the Black Death on the Parish Priests of the Medieval Diocese of Coventry and Litchfield, *Historical Research* 62 (1989): 85–90; Lawrence R. Poos, *A Rural Society After the Black Death: Essex, 1350–1525* (Cambridge: Cambridge University Press, 1991), 107, see also note 20.

30. S. H. Rigby, *Medieval Grimsby: Growth and Decline* (Hull: University of Hull Press, 1993), 131.

31. John Hatcher, *Plague, Population and the English Economy, 1348–1530* (London: Macmillan, 1977), 14.

32. Bolton, "The World Upside Down," 28.

33. Poos, *Rural Society*, 118; Barbara Harvey, *Living and Dying in Medieval England, 1100–1540: The Monastic Experience* (Oxford: Oxford University Press, 1993), 128

34. Bolton, "The World Upside Down," 28.

35. Poos has provided the most compelling evidence of decreased fertility in his analysis of the churching records for Saffron Walden, Essex. Poos, *Rural Society*, 121–29. Manorial records also report fewer male heirs assuming their father's land-holdings implying reduced fertility. In Coltshall, Norfolk, Bruce Campbell found that the ratio of inheriting son to deceased father was 1.2 in the sixty years before the plague. Between 1351 and 1370 it dropped to 0.56, and then rose slightly between 1376 and 1400 to 0.69. Zvi Razi found similar rates for Halesowen. Although out-migration accounts for some of these findings, lack of male heirs, due to higher mortality or reduced fertility on the part of women also figures into this equation. Bolton, "The World Upside Down," 35; see also B. M. S. Campbell, "Population Pressure, Inheritance and the Land Market in a Fourteenth-Century Peasant Community," in *Land, Kinship, and Life-Cycle*, ed. R. M. Smith (Cambridge: Cambridge University Press, 1984), 87–134.

36. P. J. P. Goldberg, *Women, Work, and Life Cycle in a Medieval Economy: Women in York and Yorkshire, c. 1300–1520* (Oxford: Oxford University Press, 1992), 225–32.

37. Ibid., 368–75. See also Maryanne Kowaleski, "Singlewomen in Medieval and Early Modern Europe," in *Singlewomen in the European Past, 1250–1800*, ed. Judith M. Bennett and Amy M. Froide (Philadelphia: University of Pennsylvania Press, 1999), 46, 326. Goldberg's studies confirmed assertions made by other scholars. Hallam found that in Lincolnshire between the mid-thirteenth and later fifteenth centuries, men married at an average age of twenty-five years and women at 22.4 years. While his methods at arriving at these figures have been much criticized, more recent work confirms his overall findings. Poos estimated that in Essex, laborers, servants, and craftsmen, who made up a significant percent of the population, were less likely to marry than agriculturalists. Moreover he hypothesized that when they married, the former group married later. Phillip Schofield, *Peasant and Com-*

munity in Medieval England (Houndsmills: Palgrave/Macmillan, 2003), 98; Poos, *Rural Society*, 154–58.

38. Goldberg, "'For Better or Worse,'" 112; see also Goldberg, *Women, Work, and Life Cycle*, 98–99.

39. Poos, *Rural Society*, 172–79, argues it was difficult for women to find husbands; P. J. P. Goldberg, "'For Better or Worse': Marriage and Economic Opportunity for Women in Town and Country," in *Women in Medieval English Society*, ed. P. J. P. Goldberg (Stroud: Sutton, 1997), 112–13, argues that women delayed marriage by choice.

40. Goldberg, *Women, Work, and Life Cycle*, 72–81, 337.

41. John Hatcher, "England in the Aftermath of the Black Death," *Past and Present* 144 (1994): 3–35.

42. "Rochester Chronicle," quoted in *The Black Death*, 173; see also Hatcher, "England in the Aftermath of the Black Death," 13–19.

43. Mark Baily, "Rural Society," in *Fifteenth-Century Attitudes: Perceptions of Society in Late Medieval England*, ed. Rosemary Horrox (Cambridge: Cambridge University Press, 1994), 153.

44. Goldberg, *Women, Work, and Life Cycle*, 325; Caroline Barron, "'The Golden Age' of Women in Medieval London," *Reading Medieval Studies* 15 (1989): 35–58.

45. Judith M. Bennett, "Medieval Women, Modern Women: Across the Great Divide," in *Culture and History, 1350–1600*, ed. David Aers (Detroit: Wayne State University Press, 1992), 147–75; Judith M. Bennett, "Confronting Continuity," *Journal of Women's History* 9 (1997): 73–94.

46. Bolton, "The World Turned Upside Down," 45–48; Chris Given-Wilson, "The Problem of Labour in the Context of English Government, c. 1350–1450," in *The Problem of Labour in Fourteenth-Century England*, ed. James Bothwell, P. J. P. Goldberg, and W. M. Ormrod (York: York Medieval Press, 2000), 85–100.

47. Dyer, *Standards of Living*, 151–87.

48. Charles Phythian-Adams, *Desolation of a City: Coventry and the Urban Crisis of the Late Middle Ages* (Cambridge: Cambridge University Press, 1979), 125–27; David Gary Shaw, *The Creation of a Community: The City of Wells in the Middle Ages* (Oxford: Oxford University Press, 1993), 157–74.

49. Hatcher, "England in the Aftermath of the Black Death," 14.

50. Quoted in ibid., 16.

51. Anonymous poem quoted in *The Black Death*, 126–27.

52. Chris Given-Wilson found that more than a third of the seventy-seven parliaments held between 1351 and 1430 passed some form of labor legislation. "The Problem of Labour," 85.

53. Françoise Piponnier and Perrine Mane, *Dress in the Middle Ages*, trans. Caroline Beamish (New Haven, Conn.: Yale University Press, 1997), 77.

54. Quoted in *The Black Death*, 340–41.

55. Quoted in ibid., 341.

56. P. J. P. Goldberg, "Women," in *Fifteenth-Century Attitudes: Perceptions of Society in Late Medieval England*, ed. Rosemary Horrox (Cambridge: Cambridge University Press, 1994), 112.

57. Ibid., 118.

58. Sandy Bardsley, *Venomous Tongues: Speech and Gender in Late Medieval England* (Philadelphia: University of Pennsylvania Press, 2006).

59. Ibid., 84–89.

60. Charles Drew, *Early Parochial Organisation in England: The Origin of the Office of Churchwarden*, St. Anthony's Hall Publications 7 (York: Borthwick Institute of Historical Research, 1954).

61. Katherine L. French, *The People of the Parish: Community Life in a Medieval English Diocese* (Philadelphia: University of Pennsylvania Press, 2001), 44–67; Clive Burgess, "Pre-Reformation Churchwardens' Accounts and Parish Government: Lessons from London and Bristol," *English Historical Review* 117 (April 2002): 306–32.

62. Kümin, *The Shaping of a Community*, 265–66; Ronald Hutton, *Rise and Fall of Merry England: The Ritual Year 1400–1700* (Oxford: Oxford University Press, 1994), 263–93.

63. Burgess, "Pre-Reformation Churchwardens' Accounts."

Chapter 1. "My Wedding Gown to Make a Vestment": Housekeeping and Churchkeeping

1. SARS D/P/tin 4/1/1, fol. 85.

2. Ibid., fol. 4.

3. Ibid., fol. 18, 24.

4. Katherine French, *People of the Parish: Community Life in a Medieval English Diocese* (Philadelphia: University of Pennsylvania Press, 2001), 29–31.

5. Charles Drew, *Early Parochial Organisation in England: The Origins of the Office of Churchwarden*, St. Anthony's Hall Publications 7 (York: Borthwick Institute of Historical Research, 1954).

6. Andrew Brown, *Popular Piety in Late Medieval England: The Diocese of Salisbury, 1250–1550* (Oxford: Oxford University Press, 1995), 92–110; Clive Burgess and Beat Kümin, "Penitential Bequests and Parish Regimes in Late Medieval England," *Journal of Ecclesiastical History* 44 (1993): 610–30.

7. Clive Burgess, "'A Fond Thing Vainly Invented': An Essay on Purgatory and Pious Motive in Late Medieval England," in *Parish, Church and People: Local Studies in Lay Religion, 1350–1750*, ed. S. J. Wright (London: Hutchinson, 1988), 56–84.

8. Barbara A. Hanawalt, *The Ties That Bound: Peasant Families in Medieval England* (New York: Oxford University Press, 1986), 141–56.

9. Ibid., 37, 141–45.

10. Derek Keene, "Issues of Water in Medieval London to c. 1300," *Urban History* 28 (2001): 161–79; Jennifer Ward, "Townswomen and Their Households," in *Daily Life in the Middle Ages*, ed. Richard Britnell (Thrupp, Gloucestershire: Alan Sutton, 1998), 36–38.

11. Felicity Riddy, "Looking Closely: Authority and Intimacy in the Late

Medieval Home," in *Gendering the Master Narrative: Women and Power in the Middle Ages*, ed. Mary C. Erler and Maryanne Kowaleski (Ithaca, N.Y.: Cornell University Press, 2003), 222.

12. Venantius Forunatus, "The Life of Holy Radegund," in *Sainted Women of the Dark Ages*, ed. and trans. Jo Ann McNamara and John E. Halborg with Gordon Whatley (Durham, N.C.: Duke University Press, 1992), 71.

13. Dorothy Whitelock, ed., *Anglo Saxon Wills* (Cambridge: Cambridge University Press, 1930), nos. 3, 21. I am grateful to Robin Fleming for this citation. For more on Anglo-Saxon women and their pious bequests see Patricia A. Halpin, "The Religious Experience of Women in Anglo-Saxon England" (Ph.D. dissertation, Boston College, 2000), esp. chap. 6, "Chattel, and Patronage: Women's Gifts to the late Anglo-Saxon Church," 279–320.

14. Herbert Grundmann, *Religious Movements in the Middle Ages*, trans. Steven Rowan (Notre Dame, Ind.: University of Notre Dame Press, 1995); Carolyn Walker Bynum, *Holy Feast and Holy Fast: The Religious Significance of Food to Medieval Women* (Berkeley: University of California Press, 1987).

15. *The Sarum Missal*, ed. J. Wickam Legg (Oxford: Oxford University Press, 1916), 202; *The Sarum Missal in English* pt. 1, trans. Frederick E. Warren (London: Alexander Moring, 1911), 414, 418, 423.

16. "In it is the habitacion of God, concourse of angels, reconsiliacion of man, and the lowenes of ear is in it fellaschipid to the hyenes of heuene. And this place is holy hous of God and ȝate of heauene." *Speculum Sacerdotale*, ed. Edward Weatherly, EETS 200 (1936), 163.

17. Also wyth-ynne chyrche & seyntwary / Do ryȝt thus as I the say, / Songe and cry and suche fare, / For to stynte þow schalt not spare; / Castyng of axtre & eke of ston, / Sofere hem þere to vse non; / Bal and bares and suche play, / Out of chyrcheȝorde put a-way; / Courte holdynge and suche maner chosts, / Out of seyntwary put þow most; / For cryst hym self techeth us / at holy chyrche ys hys hows, / þat ys made for no þynge elles / But for to praye In, as þe boke telles; / Þere þe pepulle schale geder with Inne / To prayen and to wepen for here synne. John Mirk, *Instructions for Parish Priests*, ed. Edward Peacock, EETS 31 (1868), 11.

18. Riddy, "Looking Closely," 218.

19. Susan Powell, "What Caxton Did to the *Festial*, the *Festial*: From Manuscript to Printed Edition," *Journal of the Early Book Society* 1 (1997): 48.

20. Judy Ann Ford, *John Mirk's* Festial: *Orthodoxy, Lollardy, and the Common People in Fourteenth-Century England* (Cambridge: D.S. Brewer, 2006), 5–15.

21. Jacobus de Voragine, *The Golden Legend: Readings on the Saints*, vol. 1, trans. William Granger Ryan (Princeton, N.J.: Princeton University Press, 1993), 179–80.

22. John Mirk, *Festial*, ed. Theodor Erbe, EETS o.s. 96 (1905), 173.

23. Ibid., 173.

24. Like Mirk, the compiler of the *Speculum Sacerdotale* drew his information on the saints from the *Golden Legend*, although there are fewer *exempla* than in *Festial*. The discussions of the liturgy are direct quotes from Joannes Belethus's *Rationale Divinorem Officiorum*.

25. Denis Renevey, "Household Chores in *The Doctrine of the Hert*," in *The

Medieval Household in Christian Europe, c. 850–c.1550, ed. Cordelia Beattie, Anna Maslakovic, and Sarah Rees Jones (Turnhout: Brepols, 2003), 167–68; for similar housekeeping metaphors, see 173.

26. "clene þe howse all wythyn, beryng out þe fure and strawyng floweres, ryȝt soo ȝe schull clanse þe howse of your soule, doying away þe fyre of lechery and of dedly wraþ and of envy, and straw þer swete erbes and flowers." Mirk, *Festial*, 129–30.

27. R. N. Swanson, *Religion and Devotion in Europe, c. 1215–c. 1515* (Cambridge: Cambridge University Press, 1995), 66.

28. A lawndur in weshyng of cloþes worcheþ on þis wize: First she takeþ lie and casteþ cloþes þer-in and suffurs þem to be longe þer. Aftur she draweþ hem owteþ, turneþ, betes, and washes hem, and hanggeþ hem vp, and so is þe clothe clene. Þis lie is mad with askes and watur, and it is right bitter, þe wiche shall not faile to clense þe ȝff þou dispose þe of þi parte. Þe askus, þat causeþ bitturnes, signifieþ þe bittur consideracion of þe paynes of hell. In þis lie shuld mans soule lie eternally, how bittur þe peynes, be like as oure feþ3th teacheþ vs. And by þis consideracion I trust God þou shalt mow gett þe freshe watur to washe þi cloþes owte of þis lie. And þis watur shal be þi nown freshe teres. *Middle English Sermons*, ed. Woodburn O. Ross, EETS 209 (London, 1940), 274.

29. "Sir, þou must shryve þe like as a woman clenseþ hur hous. She takeþ a besom and dryveþ to-geþur all þe vnclennes of þe household. And lest þat þe duste ascende and enowmbure þe place, she spryngeþ it watur. And whan þat she haþ gadred all to-þeþeur she casteþ it with gret violence owt of þe dore. So must þou do alike-wyse. Þou must clense þin hous of þi soule, and make it holy in þe siȝth of God." *Middle English Sermons*, 279.

30. "A man þat commeþ to shrifte as it fareþ by a mans howse. For on Satirday at after-none, þe seruuantes shall swepe þe hous and caste all þe donge and þe filth be-hynde þe dore on an hepe. But what þan? Commeþ þe capons and þe hennes and scraþeþ it a-brode and makeþ it as il as it was be-fore." *Middle English Sermons*, 310.

31. Prior to 1355, the church of St. Benet Sherehog was known as St. Sitha's. Sebastian Sutcliffe, "The Cult of St. Sitha in England: An Introduction," *Nottingham Medieval Studies* 37 (1993): 85.

32. Ibid., 86.

33. Ibid., 85.

34. Marian C. Gill, "Late Medieval Wall Painting in England: Content and Context, 1350–1530" (Ph.D. thesis, Courtauld Institute of Art, University of London, 2002), 121.

35. Sutcliffe, "The Cult of St. Sitha," 84.

36. Ibid., 86; Eamon Duffy, "Holy Maydens, Holy Wyfes: The Cult of Women Saints in Fifteenth and Sixteenth Century England," in *Women in the Church*, ed. W. J. Sheils and Diana Wood, Studies in Church History 27 (Oxford: Basil Blackwell, 1990), 175–96.

37. Gill, "Late Medieval Wall Painting in England, 122.

38. Ibid.

39. BL Add Ms. 24202.

40. Sutcliffe, "The Cult of St. Sitha," 88 n. 34.

41. *The Book of the Knight of the Tower,* trans. William Caxton, ed. M. Y. Offord, EETS supp. ser. 2 (Oxford: Oxford University Press, 1971), 16.

42. George Ovitt Jr., *The Restoration of Perfection: Labor and Technology in Medieval Culture* (New Brunswick, N.J.: Rutgers University Press, 1987), 151.

43. See Pallas Athena Reiss, "The Sunday Christ" (Ph.D. dissertation, University of Chicago, 1995), 61; Constantine, "De feriis," in *Corpus Juris Civilis II: Codex Iustianus,* ed. Paulus Krueger (Berlin: Weidmannsche, 1954), 127; Book III: xii, no. 2.

44. C. R. Cheney, "Rules for the Observance of Feast Days in Medieval England," *Bulletin for the Institute of Historical Research* 34, 90 (1961): 117–47; Barbara Harvey, "Work and *Festa Ferianda* in Medieval England," *Journal of Ecclesiastical History* 23, 4 (1972): 289–308.

45. For more on the Church's attitudes toward money, wealth, and labor, see Jacques Le Goff, "Labor, Techniques, and Craftsmen in the Value Systems of the Early Middle Ages," in *Time, Work, and Culture in the Middle Ages,* trans. Arthur Goldhammer (Chicago: University of Chicago Press, 1980), 71–86; Aaron J. Gurevich, "Medieval Attitudes to Wealth and Labour," in *Categories of Medieval Culture,* trans. G. L. Campbell (London: Routledge and Kegan Paul, 1985), 211–85; Ovitt, *The Restoration of Perfection.*

46. Sigfried Wenzel, *The Sin of Sloth: Acedia in Medieval Thought and Literature* (Chapel Hill: University of North Carolina Press, 1960), 83–94.

47. Quoted in *The Peasants' Revolt of 1381,* 2nd ed., ed. Barrie Dobson (Houndsmill: Macmillan, 1983), 64.

48. Christopher Dyer, "Work Ethics in the Fourteenth Century," in *The Problem of Labour in Fourteenth-Century England,* ed. James Bothwell, P. J. P. Goldberg, and W. M. Ormrod (York: York Medieval Press, 2000), 21–42.

49. J. Charles Cox, *Churchwardens' Accounts: From the Fourteenth Century to the Close of the Seventeenth Century* (London: Methuen, 1913), 271–73.

50. *Cambridge Gild Records,* ed. Mary Bateson, Cambridge Antiquarian Society 39 (1903), xxi, 37.

51. Drew, *Early Parochial Organisation in England*; Beat A. Kümin, *The Shaping of a Community: The Rise and Reformation of the English Parish, c. 1400–1560* (Brookfield, Vt.: Scolar Press, 1996), 265–69; French, *The People of the Parish,* 68–98.

52. Maryanne Kowaleski, "Women's Work in a Market Town: Exeter in the Late Fourteenth Century," in *Women and Work in Preindustrial Europe,* ed. Barbara A. Hanawalt (Bloomington: Indiana University Press, 1986), 145–64; Marjorie Keniston McIntosh, *Working Women in English Society, 1300–1620* (Cambridge: Cambridge University Press, 2005).

53. Market-town parishes: Stogursey and Bridgwater, Somerset; Ashburton, Devon; Louth, Lincolnshire; Bishops Stortford, Hertfordshire. Urban parishes: St. Margaret's, Westminster; All Hallows, London Wall, St. Andrew Hubbard and St. Mary At Hill in London; Lambeth, Surrey; St. Ewen's, Bristol; St. Martin's, Leicester. Cathedral or university town parishes: Holy Trinity and St. Mary the Great, Cambridge; St. Edmund's, Salisbury; St. Michael's without the North Gate, Bath; St. Andrew and St. Dunstan, Canterbury. Rural parishes: Tilney, Norfolk; Nettlecombe, Pilton, Tintinhull, Yatton, and Banwell, Somerset; Great Dunmow, Great

Hallingbury, Essex; Walberswick, Suffolk; Prescot, Lancashire. My designations are based in part on whether the settlement had been incorporated. See Maurice Beresford and H. P. R. Finberg, *English Medieval Boroughs: A Hand-List* (Totowa, N.J.: Rowman and Littlefield, 1973.)

54. Kay E. Lacey, "Women and Work in Fourteenth and Fifteenth Century London," in *Women and Work in Pre-Industrial England*, ed. Lindsey Charles and Lorna Duffin (London: Croom Helm, 1985), 24–82; Judith Bennett, *Ale, Beer and Brewsters in England: Women's Work in a Changing World, 1300–1600* (Oxford: Oxford University Press, 1996).

55. For women and urban work see S. H. Rigby, *English Society in the Later Middle Ages: Class, Status and Gender* (Basingstoke: Macmillan, 1995), 270–78; Marjorie Keniston McIntosh, *Working Women in English Society, 1300–1620* (Cambridge: Cambridge University Press, 2005).

56. Mirk, *Instructions for Parish Priests*, 58, 60.

57. "Visitation of Parishes by John Trefnant, Bishop of Hereford, 1397," typescript from original in Hereford Cathedral Archives MS 1779, transcribed by Christopher Whittick, no. 20.2.5, p. 61 (unpublished English translation by Christopher Whittick, p. 32). Used with permission.

58. WAC E1, 422.

59. PRO Prob. 11/19 fols. 9–13v.

60. Ibid., fols. 10v–11v.

61. The Early Churchwardens' Accounts of Bishops Stortford, ed. Stephen G. Doree, Hertfordshire Record Society 10 (1994), 79, 86; St. Andrew Hubbard in London, GL 1279/1, fols. 51, 86; Yatton and Banwell in Somerset, SARS D/P/yat 4/1/1, fols. 82, 86, 89, 92, 101, 104; D/P/ban 4/1/1, fol. 11, 79; and Great Dunmow in Essex, ERO D/P 11/5/1, fols. 6v., 11v. 19, 20, 21.

62. SARS D/P/pilt 4/1/1, fol. 53; "Accounts of the Churchwardens of St. Dunstan's, Canterbury," ed. J. M. Cowper *Archaeologia Cantiana: Transactions of the Kent Archaeological Society* 17 (1887): 82; "Churchwardens' Accounts of the Parish of St. Andrew, Canterbury," ed. Charles Cotton, *Archaeologia Cantiana: Transactions of the Kent Archaeological Society* 33 (1920): 5, 18; GL 1279/1, fol. 19v; *The Transcript of the Churchwardens' Accounts of the Parish of Tilney, All Saints, Norfolk: 1443–1589*, ed. A. D. Stallard (London: Mitchell, Hughes and Clarke, 1922), 18, 45, 47, 51, 97, 99.

63. Both St. Mary at Hill in London and St. Andrew's, Walberswick had longterm laundresses. That the accounts name them rather than identify them as someone's wife suggests that laundering was an important source of income for these women, not occasional work. GL 1239/1 part 2; SRO FC 185/E1/1.

64. *Accounts of the Wardens of Morebath, Devon, 1520–1573*, ed. J. Erskine Binney, *Devon Notes and Queries*, supplementary volume (Exeter, 1904), 162.

65. *Churchwardens' Accounts of the Parish of Tilney*, 102, 103. Other churchwardens worked this way as well.

66. *Lambeth Churchwardens' Accounts: 1504–1645*, ed. Charles Drew, Surrey Record Society, 40 (London: Surrey Record Society, 1940), 7, 8.

67. SARS D/P/bw 39.

68. Ruth Mazo Karras, *Common Women: Prostitution and Sexuality in Medie-*

val England (New York: Oxford University Press, 1996), 54–55; David Herlihy, *Opera Muliebria: Women and Work in Medieval Europe* (New York: McGraw-Hill, 1990), 4–5.

69. SRO FC 185/E1/1, fols. 33, 50, 55, 61, 68, 73, 79, 84, 88, 92, 96, 102, 116, 125, 138, 145, 159, 164.

70. Ibid., fol. 164.

71. Judith Middleton-Stewart argues that she retired, but it is just as likely that she died. See *Inward Purity and Outward Splendour: Death and Remembrance in the Deanery of Dunwich, Suffolk, 1370–1547* (Woodbridge: Boydell, 2001), 212; SRO FC 185/E1/1, fols. 138, 184.

72. Ibid., fols. 184, 188.

73. Ibid., fols, 206, 212.

74. Ibid., fol. 217.

75. Ibid., fols. 230, 251.

76. Ibid., fol. 127.

77. Ibid., fol. 249.

78. Ibid., fols. 1–8; 51.

79. Ibid., fols. 35, 39.

80. Ibid., fols. 125, 182.

81. *Churchwardens' Accounts of the Parish of Tilney*, 130, 133, 134.

82. Ibid., 133.

83. Ibid., 138.

84. Thomas King held the property until 1541. The account names Margaret for the last time in 1539. Ibid.,147, 149, 151, 155, 158, 161.

85. Ibid.,124.

86. Ibid.,130.

87. *The Register of John Chandler Dean of Salisbury, 1404–17*, ed. T. C .B. Timmins, Wiltshire Record Society 39 (1983), no. 82, p. 41.

88. *Churchwardens' Accounts of Tilney*, 5, 11, 45, 47, 51, 61; SARS D/P/ yat 4/1/1, fols. 150, 177, 260, 264; D/P/ban 4/1/1, fols. 36, 45, 71, 80, 97; ERO D/P 11/5/1, fols. 9, 26, 27v.; SRO FC 185/E1/1, fols. 5, 46, 55, 138, 164, 180, 217, *The Churchwarden's Accounts of Prescot, Lancashire: 1523–1607*, ed. F. A. Bailey, Lancashire and Cheshire Record Society 106 (1953).

89. Rural parishes: 7 of 10; market-town parishes: 4 of 11; city parishes: 2 of 7.

90. SARS D/P/yat 4/1/1, fol. 90; *Churchwardens' Accounts of the Parish of Tilney*, 4, 5, 11, 18, 45, 47, 51.

91. At the time of the 1512 poll tax there were 136 household and 324 adults of fifteen or older living in Market Ward. *Cambridge Borough Documents*, vol. 1, ed. William Palmer (Cambridge: Bowes and Bowes, 1931), 108. Geographers have worked on the issue of urban parochial boundaries and believe that membership was often determined by which church was closest. Although historically this part of town was thought to include the parishes of St. Mary, St. Edward, and probably St. Bene't, with Holy Trinity further east. The boundaries of Holy Trinity parish abutted Market Ward, and Anne Malte's house was probably closer to Holy Trinity than the other parish churches. See Nigel Baker and Richard Holt, "The Origin of Urban Parish Boundaries," in *The Church in the Medieval Town*, ed. T. R. Slater

and Gervase Rosser (Aldershot: Ashgate, 1998), 209–35; *VCH: Cambridge*, vol. 3, ed. J. P. Croach (London: University of London, Institute of Historical Research, 1959), 113. Unlike the other women on these lists, Anne Malte had no designation of widow after her name. *Cambridge Borough Documents*, vol. 1, 120; PRO E179/81/144.

92. CRO P22/5/1, fol. 26v. The accounts start in 1504, so she had not been working for the parish regularly before 1509.

93. Ibid., fols. 45v, 53, 91.

94. She either died or moved. She apparently left no will. *Index of the Probate Records of the Consistory Court of Ely: 1449–1858*, part 2 (F-P), comp. Clifford and Dorothea Thurley, ed. Elisabeth Leedham-Green and Rosemary Rudd, British Record Society 106 (1994), 698.

95. WAC E1, fol. 86; GL 1239/1 part 2, fols. 307, 319v. For example, in St. Margaret's, Westminster, Parnell Bennett not only washed everything in 1491, she also mended a chasuble. WAC E1, fol. 290.

96. SARS D/P/yat 4/1/1, fol. 264.

97. Both the parishes of All Saints and St. Ewen's included silk women in their congregations. In All Saints parish, Margery Money was a silk woman. *The Pre-Reformation Records of All Saints' Church, Bristol*, pt. 2, *The Churchwardens' Accounts*, ed. Clive Burgess, Bristol Record Society 53 (2000), 53, 61, 64, 67, 71, 75, 79; In St. Ewen's, Alice Arnold was described the same way. *The Church Book of St. Ewen's, Bristol: 1454–1485*, ed. Betty R. Masters and Elizabeth Ralph, Bristol and Gloucestershire Archaeological Society 6 (1967), 28, 33.

98. WAC E1, fol. 422.

99. Kay Staniland, *Embroiderers* (Toronto: University of Toronto Press, 1991). For more on women silk workers see Marian K. Dale, "The London Silkwomen of the Fifteenth Century," *Economic History Review* 4, 3 (1933): 324–35. She does not discuss women's work in making liturgical vestments. See also Anne F. Sutton, "Alice Claver, Silkwoman (d. 1489)," in *Medieval London Widows: 1300–1500*, ed. Caroline M. Barron and Anne F. Sutton (London: Hambleton Press, 1994), 129–42. For more on how embroidery was done, see *Catalogue of English Ecclesiastical Embroideries of the Thirteenth and Fourteenth Centuries* (London: Victoria and Albert Museum, Department of Textiles, 1930), xii–xiii; A. F. Kendrick, *English Embroidery* (London: George Newnes, 1905); A. F. Kendrick, *English Needle Work* (London: A. and C. Black, 1933).

100. SARS D/P/stogs 4/1/1, fol. 26v.

101. *The Medieval Records of a London City Church (St. Mary at Hill): 1420–1559*, ed. Henry Littlehales, EETS 125 (1904), 199.

102. Mirk, *Instructions for Parish Priests*, 58.

103. GL 1239/1 part 2, fols. 310, 419, 441v, 453v.

104. WAC E2, 1514, 1521[no folio numbers]. See also Gervase Rosser, *Medieval Westminster: 1200–1540* (Oxford: Oxford University Press, 1989), 368–69. A similar situation prevailed in St. Andrew Hubbard. See GL 1279/1.

105. *Churchwardens' Accounts of the Parish of Tilney*, 18.

106. SARS D/P/tin 4/1/1, fol. 36.

107. Ibid., fol. 37.

108. The Churchwardens' Accounts of Prescot, 19–20.

109. Ibid., 20.

110. Hanawalt, "The Host, the Law, and the Ambiguous Space of Medieval London Taverns," in *Of Good and Ill Repute: Gender and Social Control in Medieval England* (New York: Oxford University Press, 1998), 104–23.

111. SRO FC 89/A2/1.

112. CRO P11/5/2, fol. 23.

113. ERO D/P 11/5/1, fols. 24v., 27v., 36v., 40.

114. I am grateful to Shannon McSheffrey for supplying this example. LMA, MS DL/C/205, fols. 166r–170r, 172v–177r, 182v.

115. For more on women in the food and food retail business see Kowaleski, "Women's Work in a Market Town," 145–64; Rosser, *Medieval Westminster*, 133–42.

116. McIntosh, *Working Women*, 210.

117. *Churchwardens' Accounts of St. Edmund and St. Thomas, Sarum: 1443–1702*, ed. Henry James Fowle Swayne, Wilts Record Society 1 (1896), 13. See also Audrey Douglas, "Salisbury Women and the Pre-Elizabethan Parish," in *Women, Marriage, and Family in Medieval Christendom: Essays in Memory of Michael M. Sheehan*, ed. Constance M. Rousseau and Joel T. Rosenthal (Kalamazoo, Mich.: Medieval Institute Publications, 1998), 102–7.

118. Charles Kerry, *A History of the Municipal Church of St. Lawrence, Reading* (Reading: privately printed, 1883), 67.

119. *Lambeth Churchwardens' Accounts*, 48–50.

120. Caroline M. Barron, "Johanna Hill (d. 1441) and Johanna Sturdy (d. c. 1460), Bell Founders," in *Medieval London Widows*, 99–111, see esp. 101 for map of their known bells.

121. St. Andrew's, Canterbury; Great Dunmow and Great Hallingbury, Essex; Banwell, Somerset; Tilney, Norfolk; St. Margaret's, Westminster; St. Martin's, Leicester, and Bishops Stortford, Hertford.

122. An earlier version of this section appeared as an article, "'I Leave My Best Gown as a Vestment': Women's Spiritual Interests in the Late Medieval English Parish," *Magistra* 4, 1 (1998): 57–77.

123. Will Coster, "Community, Piety, and Family in Yorkshire Wills Between the Reformation and the Restoration," in *Life and Thought in the Northern Church, c. 1100–1700: Essays in Honour of Claire Cross*, ed. Diana Wood (Woodbridge: Boydell, 1999), 511–31.

124. For women and English Law, see Lacey, "Women and Work in Fourteenth and Fifteenth Century London." For the rational behind how women disposed of their goods, see Giovanna Benadusi, "Investing the Riches of the Poor: Servants and Their Last Wills," *American Historical Review* 109 (2004): 825; Martha C. Howell, "Fixing Movables: Gifts by Testament in Late Medieval Douai," *Past and Present* 150 (1996): 28.

125. Scholars have used the universality of religious donations in wills to argue for the interest and commitment of the laity in the church prior to the Reformation. They have also used them to argue for the fear of purgatory and the coercion and influence of the clergy who wrote down most of the wills as the testator lay dying. See Christine Carpenter, "Religion of the Gentry of Fifteenth-Century England," in *England in the Fifteenth Century: Proceedings of the 1986 Harlaxton Symposium*, ed.

D. W. Williams (Woodbridge: Boydell, 1987), 53–74; Colin Richmond, "Religion and the Fifteenth-Century Gentleman," in *The Church, Politics and Patronage*, ed. R. B. Dobson (Gloucester: Alan Sutton, 1984), 193–208.

126. *The Book of Vices and Virtues*, ed. W. Nelson Francis, EETS 217 (1942): 213.

127. For a discussion of the problems in using wills, see Clive Burgess, "Late Medieval Wills and Pious Conventions: Testamentary Evidence Reconsidered," in *Profit, Piety and the Professions*, ed. Michael Hicks (Gloucester: Alan Sutton, 1990), 14–33; Clive Burgess, "'By Quick and by Dead': Wills and Pious Provision in Late Medieval Bristol," *English Historical Review* 142 (1982): 837–58. He argues that some of a testator's goods and chattels were predetermined by law and others might be negotiated and settled long before the death of the testator. A wealthy individual, therefore, might have left a modest will, because the property had been distributed prior to writing the will.

128. Howell, "Fixing Movables," 36.

129. Christopher Dyer, *An Age of Transition: Economy and Society in England in the Later Middle Ages* (Oxford: Oxford University Press, 2005), 172.

130. *Lincoln Wills*, vol. 4, ed. David Hickman, Lincoln Record Society 89 (2001), 132.

131. Diana O'Hara has a similar discussion of tokens given as a sign of betrothal. *Courtship and Constraint: Rethinking the Making of Modern Marriage in Tudor England* (Manchester: Manchester University Press, 2000), 57–98.

132. Nearly 50 percent of the wills from Bath and Wells were proven in the Prerogative Court of Canterbury, rather than the bishop's consistory court, making this a wealthier group of testators than those from Lincolnshire. Those not proved in the Prerogative Court only survive in published form, the originals were bombed in World War II. In contrast, 14 percent of the wills from Lincolnshire were proven in the Archdeacon of Buckingham's court, making this group of testators slightly poorer than those from Bath and Wells. The majority of Lincoln wills were proven in the bishop's consistory court. *Somerset Medieval Wills: 1383–1500*, vols. 1–3, ed. F. W. Weaver, Somerset Record Society 16, 19, 21 (1901, 1903, 1905); *Lincoln Wills: 1427–1532*, vols. 1–3, ed. C. W. Foster, Lincoln Record Society 5, 10, 24 (1914, 1918, 1930); *Lincoln Wills*, vol. 4; *The Courts of the Archdeaconry of Buckingham: 1483–1523*, ed. E. M. Elvey, Buckingham Record Society 19 (1975). PCC wills are at the PRO, and are searchable by place. See http://www.nationalarchives.gov.uk/documents online/wills.asp

133. Benadusi, 811 n. 15; Howell, "Fixing Movables," 28.

134. Coster, "Community, Piety, and Family in Yorkshire Wills."

135. Of the remaining 7 percent of women's wills, 3 percent or seven wills, are likely from single women and 4 percent or 10 wills are from married women.

136. I have counted candlesticks as liturgical items rather than household goods.

137. See for example *Lincoln Wills*, vol. 4, 101–2, 119–22.

138. Judith Bennett, *Ale, Beer, and Brewsters*, 34; Howell, "Fixing Movables," 26, 28.

139. Martha Howell, *The Marriage Exchange: Property, Social Place, and Gen-*

der in Cities of the Low Countries, 1300–1550 (Chicago: University of Chicago Press, 1998), 153.

140. Riddy, "Authority and Intimacy," 226–28.

141. *Lincoln Wills*, vol. 1, 109.

142. *Ancient Deeds Belonging to the Corporation of Bath*, ed. C. W. Shickle (Bath: Bath Record Society, 1921), 90.

143. SARS D/P/pilt 4/1/1, fol. 26.

144. Kathleen Kamerick, *Popular Piety and Art in the Late Middle Ages: Worship and Idolatry in England, 1350–1500* (New York: Palgrave, 2002), 87–91.

145. Colin Richmond, "Halesworth Church, Suffolk, and Its Fifteenth-Century Benefactors," in *Recognitions: Essays Presented to Edmund Fryde*, ed. Colin Richmond and Isobel Harvey (Aberystwyth: National Library of Wales, 1996), 259–60; see also Douglas, "Salisbury Woman," 101–2.

146. "unto the church of Savret my weddyng gown to make a vestment therof," PRO Prob 11/19 fol. 70v.

147. "red damaske mantell and [her] mantell lyned with silk . . . to the Mary Magdalene play," *Somerset Medieval Wills*, vol. 2, 52–57.

148. "gown of blew feluett, [her] kyrtll of blew damaske, . . . and a coverlet of tapstry werek with eglis," which were to "ley before the hyght auter in principal festes and other tymes," were not in use, they were to "be occupied on a bedde in the chauntry house to kepe [them] from mothes," *Somerset Medieval Wills*, vol. 1, 244–45.

149. *Lincoln Wills*, vol. 3, 79–80.

150. Ibid., 143.

151. Ibid., vol. 1, 5–7.

152. *Bridgwater Borough Archives*, vol. 3, ed. Thomas Bruce Dilks, Somerset Record Society 58 (1945), 9–11.

153. *Somerset Medieval Wills*, vol. 2, 249–52.

154. For example, those wills proven in the Court of the Archdeanery of Buckingham were poorer than those proven in the Prerogative Court of Canterbury. Fewer wills proven in the lower courts record material items left to the church.

155. Jennifer Ward, *English Noble Women in the Later Middle Ages* (London: Longman, 1992), 50–65.

156. Katherine L. French, "Women Churchwardens in Late Medieval England," in *The Parish in Late Medieval England: Proceedings of the 2002 Harlaxton Symposium*, ed. Clive Burgess and Eamon Duffy (Donington, Lincs.: Shaun Tayas/Paul Watkins, 2006), 302–21; Clive Burgess, "Shaping the Parish: St. Mary at Hill, London, in the Fifteenth Century," in *The Cloister and the World: Essays in Medieval History in Honour of Barbara Harvey*, ed. John Blair and Brian Golding (Oxford: Oxford University Press, 1996), 259–60.

157. WAC E1, fol. 50.

158. Ibid., fol. 407.

159. Based on the number of candles at White's funeral, she was not one of the parish's well-off people, see chapter 2 for more details. WAC E2, 1515, 1529 [no folio numbers].

160. SARS D/P/yat 4/1/1–2.

161. Ibid., fol. 94.

162. See also Robert A. Wood, "Poor Widows, c. 1393–1415," in *Medieval London Widows*, 61.

163. "Accounts of the Churchwardens of St. Dunstan's Canterbury," ed. J. M. Cowper, *Archaeologia Cantiana* 16 (1885): 312–17.

164. "In the walle are cortynes and palles of silke to be hongen and reysed. In the quere are to be sett dosers, tapytes, and bankers and the veyle that was before the curcifix schal be remouyed and put behynde hym a palle for that þat was first helyd afore the passion of Crist are now opyned and schewyd. Þe banners þat betokeneþ the victorie of Crist are rerede vp in-to the heyȝt. Þe autere is honowrid with his ornamentis as with crosses sette in ordre and on rewe with the corporax case, þe box with Godis body, textis of the euaunglii, and the tablis of the commaundmentis." *Speculum Sacerdotale*, 122.

165. In the late Middle Ages, there was a tremendous variety of belts, girdles, chains and other accessories that could adorn women or images of saints. This variety would be an apt medium for displaying social status and personal taste. Geoff Egan and Frances Pritchard, *Medieval Excavations in London*, vol. 3, *Dress Accessories, 1150–1450* (Woodbridge: Boydell, 2002).

166. Christian Peters, *Patterns of Piety: Women, Gender and Religion in Late Medieval and Reformation England* (Cambridge: Cambridge University Press, 2003), 51–52.

167. "Item a paire of Coral beds gauded wt silver and gilte wt a litill ryng given to the worship of god and oru ladi and Seynte Margarete to be hanged upon the ymage of Seynte margarete everyday orels every j haly day, as the wardyns of the chirch shall seme beste." WAC E1, fol. 386.

168. Albertus Magnus, *Book of Minerals*, trans. Dorothy Wyckoff (Oxford: Oxford University Press, 1967), 81; "North Midland Lapidary," in *English Medieaval Lapidaries*, ed. Joan Evans and Mary S. Serjeantson, EETS 190 (London: Oxford University Press, 1933), 53; "The Peterborough Lapidary," 77; "Sloan Lapidary," 125.

169. *Ancient Deed Belonging to Bath*, 90; *Kacabre* in Latin. Magnus, *Book of Minerals*, 93; "London Lapidary," in *English Medieaval Lapidaries*, 32.

170. *The Register of John Chandler*, no. 207, 80; Magnus, *Book of Minerals*, 121.

171. Egan and Pritchard, *Dress Accessories*, 305–17.

172. SARS D/P/yat 4/1/1, fols. 77, 88, 91, et passim.

173. Ibid., fol. 147.

Chapter 2. Hatched, Matched, and Dispatched: Life Cycles and the Liturgy

1. *Calendar of Inquisitions Post Mortem*, vol. 22 (1–5 Henry VI: 1422–1427), ed. Kate Parkin (London: Boydell Press and the National Archives: Public Record Office, 2003), 237.

2. Edward Muir, *Ritual in Early Modern Europe* (Cambridge: Cambridge University Press, 1997), 49.

3. Rosemary Horrox, ed., *Black Death* (Manchester: Manchester University Press, 1994), 271–72.

4. Bede, *Ecclesiastical History of the English People*, trans. Leo Sherley-Price (Harmondsworth: Penguin, 1990), 83; Becky R. Lee, "'Women ben purifyid of her childeryn': The Purification of Women After Childbirth in Medieval England" (Ph.D. dissertation, University of Toronto, 1998), 10.

5. Vanessa Harding, *The Dead and the Living in Paris and London, 1500–1670* (Cambridge: Cambridge University Press, 2002), 208–9.

6. Margaret Aston, "Lollard Women Priests?" in *Lollards and Reformers: Images and Literacy in Late Medieval Religion* (London: Hambledon Press, 1983), 49–70, esp. 52. While authorities may have feared that women were more susceptible to heresy, and there were notable female Lollards, they did not wield unusual power in the sect. See Shannon McSheffrey, *Gender and Heresy: Women and Men in Lollard Communities, 1420–1530* (Philadelphia: University of Pennsylvania Press, 1995).

7. Christine Peters, *Patterns of Piety: Women, Gender and Religion in Late Medieval and Reformation England* (Cambridge: Cambridge University Press, 2003), 19.

8. Nicholas Orme, *Medieval Children* (New Haven, Conn.: Yale University Press, 2001), 27–28.

9. "And yf a woman wer delyuerd of a mayden-chyld, scho schuld dowbull þe dayes of comyng to chyrch, and to hur husbonddys bed, and comyng ynto þe tempull." John Mirk, *Festial*, ed. Theodor Erbe, EETS o.s. 96 (1905), 57.

10. "Eve vexed God more þen dyd man, þerfor scho ys more lengyr yn forming þen þe man." Ibid., 57.

11. Quoted in Shannon McSheffrey, *Marriage, Sex, and Civic Culture in Late Medieval London* (Philadelphia: University of Pennsylvania Press, 2006), 44.

12. Ibid., 44–45.

13. Ibid., 44.

14. "And when he is ded, þenne owe belles to be rongen that the heare[r]s mowe praye for hym, *scilicet* for a womman twyes. Why? For sche made an alterite and an oerhede in that tyme that sche made alienacion and partyng bitwene God and man. And for the man it is ronge þries. Why? For the man was first i-founden, and woman was founden in man. For the firste was Adam made and formyd of the erþe, and the woman came of Adam, and man come of hem bothe, so there was a trinite." The original quote uses "he" and "him" in the first line to mean a person. *Speculum Sacerdotale*, ed. Edward H. Weatherly, EETS 200 (1936), 234.

15. "And the dede oweþ to be borne to the erþ of hem that are moste like to hym in order, crafte, or degree . . ." Ibid., 234.

16. And teche the mydewyf neuer the latere, / That heo haue redy clene watere, / Thenne bydde hyre spare for no schame, To folowe the chylde there at hame, And thaghe þe chylde bote half be bore, / Hed and necke and no more, / Bydde hyre spare never þe later / To chrystene hyt and caste on water; / And but scho mowe se þe hed, / Loke scho folowe hyt for no red; / And ȝef the wommon thenne dye, / Teche the mydwyf that scho hye / For to undo hyre wyth a knyf, / And for to saue the chyldes lyf / And hye that hyt crystened be, / For that ys a dede of charyte. / And ȝef hyre herte ther-togrylle, / Rather þenne the chylde scholde spylle, / Teche hyre thenne to calle a mon / That in that nede helpe hyre con./ For ȝef the chylde be so y-lore, / Scho may that wepen euer more. / Bote ȝef the chylde

y-bore be, / And in perele thow hyt se, / Ryght as he byd hyre done, / Caste on water and folowe hyt sone. John Mirk, *Instructions for Parish Priests*, ed. Edward Peacock, EETS 31(1868), 3–4.

17. Silvano Cavassa, "Double Death: Resurrection and Baptism in a Seventeenth-Century Rite," trans. Mary M. Gallucci, in *History from Crime*, ed. Edward Muir and Guido Ruggiero (Baltimore: Johns Hopkins University Press, 1994), 12.

18. Teche hem alle to be war and snel / That they conne sey e wordes wel, / And say the wordes all on row; / As a-non I wole ʒow schowe; / Say ryʒt thus and no more, / For non othere wymmenes lore. Mirk, *Instructions for Parish Priests*, 4–5.

19. Ibid., 4.

20. ʒef a chylde myscheuth at home, / And ys I-folowed & has hys nome, / ʒef hyt to chyrche be broʒt to þe / As hyt oweth for to be, / Thenne moste þou slylt / Aske of hem at were þere by, / How ey deden en in at cas / Whenne þe chylde I-folowed was, / And wheþer þe wordes were seyde a-ryʒt, / And not turnet in at hyʒt; / ʒef e wordes were seyde on rowe / As lo here I do þe schowe. Ibid., 17–18.

21. God seynt Ioun / Crysten e child boþe flesshe & boun." Robert Mannyng of Brunne, *Handlyng Synne*, ed. Idelle Sullens (Binghamton: Center of Medieval and Renaissance Studies, State University of New York, 1983), 240, lines 9635–36.

22. Quoted in Orme, *Medieval Children*, 26. Orme explains "Christendom" as baptism, but I think it must mean blessing, given Mirk's instructions to priests.

23. "Visitation of Parishes by John Trefnant, Bishop of Hereford, 1397," unpublished typescript from original in Hereford Cathedral Archives MS 1779, transcribed by Christopher Whittick, no. 53.2.3, p. 179 (unpublished English translation by Christopher Whittick, no. 53.2.3, p. 88), used with permission.

24. Loke also þey make non odde weddynge, / Lest alle ben cursed in that doynge. / Preste & clerke and other also, / That thylke serves huydeth so, / But do ryʒt as seyen the lawes, / Aske the banns thre halydawes. / Then lete hem come and wytnes brynge / To stonde by at here weddyng; So openlyche at the chyrche dore / Lete hem eyther wedde othere. Mirk, *Instructions for Parish Priests*, 7.

25. Proofs of age were legal proceedings to determine whether a royal ward was of age and could come into his or her inheritance. John Bedell, "Memory and Proof of Age in England," *Past and Present* 162 (1999): 4–5.

26. Joel T. Rosenthal, *Telling Tales: Sources and Narration in Late Medieval England* (University Park: Pennsylvania State Press, 2003), 59, 26–35. See also Becky R. Lee, "Men's Recollections of a Woman's Rite: Medieval English Men's Recollections Regarding the Rite of the Purification of Women After Childbirth," *Gender and History* 14 (2002): 226, for a similar justification.

27. I am following Joel Rosenthal's method in talking about proofs of age, but whereas he concentrated on describing baptisms, I am interested in the variety of pararituals these memories describe.

28. *Calendar of Inquisitions Post Mortem*, vol. 19 (7–14 Henry IV), ed. J. L. Kirby (London: HMSO, 1992), 359.

29. Ibid., 6 (Ed. II) (London: HMSO, 1910), 116.

30. Ibid., 19 (7–14 Henry IV), 322.

31. Ibid., 118.

32. Ibid., 22 (1–5 Henry VI: 1422–1427), 324.

33. Lee, "Men's Recollections of a Women's Rite," 234–35.

34. *Calendar of Inquisitions Post Mortem*, 22: 337.

35. Ibid., 19 (7–14 Henry IV), 280.

36. Ibid., 22 (1–5 Henry VI: 1422–1427), 228.

37. Ibid., 19 (7–14 Henry IV), 280.

38. *Calendar of Inquisitions Post Mortem*, vol. 2, (Henry VII) (London: HMSO, 1915), 3.

39. Ibid., 13.

40. *Calendar of Inquisitions Post Mortem*, 19 (7–14 Henry IV), 115.

41. Ibid., 280.

42. WAC E1, fol. 551; E2, 1521 [no folio numbers].

43. For foreigners and aliens in Westminster, see Gervase Rosser, *Medieval Westminster* (Oxford: Oxford University Press, 1989), 182–96; for Italians and baptism, see Muir, *Ritual in Early Modern Europe*, 23.

44. Sue Sheridan Walker, "Proof of Age of Feudal Heirs in Medieval England," *Mediaeval Studies* 35 (1973): 306; Lee, "Men's Recollections of a Woman's Rite," 227.

45. Kay Staniland, "Royal Entry into the World," in *England in the Fifteenth Century: Proceedings of the 1986 Harlaxton Symposium*, ed. Daniel Williams (Woodbridge: Boydell, 1987), 297–313; William Coster, "Purity, Profanity, and Puritanism: The Churching of Women, 1500–1700," in *Women in the Church*, ed. W. J. Sheils and Diana Wood (Oxford: Basil Blackwell for the Ecclesiastical History Society, 1990), 381; Adrian Wilson, "The Ceremony of Childbirth and Its Interpretation," in *Women and Mothers in Pre-Industrial England: Essays in Memory of Dorothy McLaren*, ed. Valerie Fields (London: Routledge, 1990), 75–77.

46. Lee, "Men's Recollections of a Women's Rite," 227.

47. Lee, "Women ben purifyid of her childeryn,"35–43; Gail McMurray Gibson, "Blessing from Sun and Moon: Churching as Women's Theater," in *Bodies and Disciplines: Intersections of Literature and History in Fifteenth-Century England*, ed. Barbara A. Hanawalt and David Wallace (Minneapolis: University of Minnesota Press, 1996), 139–54; Susan Karant-Nunn, *Reformation of Ritual: An Interpretation of Early Modern Germany* (London: Routledge, 1997), 72–90.

48. Gibson, "Blessing from Sun and Moon," 149.

49. Keith Thomas, *Religion and the Decline of Magic* (New York: Scribner's, 1971), 38–39; Wilson, "Ceremony of Childbirth," 84.

50. Wilson, "Ceremony of Childbirth," 68–107.

51. Adrian Wilson, arguing in agreement with Natalie Zemon Davis. See Natalie Zemon Davis, "Women on Top," in *Society and Culture in Early Modern France*, ed. Natalie Zemon Davis (Stanford, Calif.: Stanford University Press, 1965), 145, 313; Wilson, "Ceremony of Childbirth," 68–107.

52. David Cressy, "Purifications, Thanksgiving and the Churching of Women in Post-Reformation England," *Past and Present* 141 (1993): 111.

53. Lee, "'Women ben purifyid of her childeryn'," 106–29.

54. Muir, *Ritual in Early Modern Europe*, 237–39.

55. "Visitation of Parishes by John Trefnant, Bishop of Hereford, 1397," unpublished typescript from original in Hereford Cathedral Archives MS 1779, tran-

scribed by Christopher Whittick, no. 19.1.10, pp. 59–60 (unpublished English translation by Christopher Whittick, no. 19.1.10, p. 31), used with permission.

56. Wilson, "Ceremony of Childbirth," 75.

57. WAC E1, fol. 380; in 1511, it was repaired E2, 1511 [no folio numbers].

58. BL Egerton Ms. 1912, fol. 6a, 10. "pd for the pullyng down of the chylde-wyffes pue of saynt Martyns Churche an for the bryngyng of hit home—3d.

59. *Churchwardens' Accounts of St. Mary the Great, Cambridge from 1504–1635*, ed. J. E. Foster, Cambridge Antiquarian Society 35 (London: Cambridge Antiquarian Society, 1905), 8, "Item a Clothe of Tappestry werek for chirchyng of wifes lined with Canuas in Ecclesia."

60. Charles Pendrill, *Old Parish Life in London* (Oxford: Oxford University Press, 1937), 33.

61. Lee, "Women ben purifyid of her childeryn," App. B, 179–84. See also ERO D/DBy Q18.

62. Lee, "Women ben purifyid of her childeryn," 29. See also PRO C47/39/59.

63. "Visitation of Parishes by John Trefnant, Bishop of Hereford, 1397," unpublished typescript from original in Hereford Cathedral Archives MS 1779, transcribed by Christopher Whittick, 53.2.7, p. 179 (unpublished English translation by Christopher Whittick, no. 53.2.7, p. 88), used with permission.

64. Lee, "Men's Recollections of a Women's Rite," 229.

65. Ibid., 229; Pendrill, *Old Parish Life in London*, 33.

66. Lee, "Men's Recollections of a Women's Rite," 231–32.

67. Ibid., 236.

68. *Lincoln Wills*, vol. 4, ed. David Hickman, Lincoln Record Society 89 (2001), 150.

69. For age of marriage in England, see P. J. P. Goldberg, *Women, Work, and Life Cycle in a Medieval Economy: Women in York and Yorkshire, c. 1300–1520* (Oxford: Oxford University Press, 1992). For the issues of emotion, see Lawrence Stone, *The Family, Sex, and Marriage in England, 1500–1800* (New York: Harper Torchbooks, 1979), and Alan Macfarlane, *Marriage and Love in England: Modes of Reproduction, 1300–1840* (Oxford: Blackwell, 1986). For marriage litigation, see Richard Helmholtz, *Marriage Litigation in Medieval England* (Cambridge: Cambridge University Press, 1974); Richard M. Wunderli, *London Church Courts and Society on the Eve of the Reformation* (Cambridge, Mass.: Medieval Academy of America, 1981); Michael M. Sheehan, "Formation and Stability of Marriage in Fourteenth-Century England: Evidence of an Ely Register," in *Marriage, Family, and Law in Medieval Europe: Collected Studies*, ed. James K. Farge (Toronto: University of Toronto Press, 1996), 38–76. For a good summary of these issues, see Shannon McSheffrey, ed., *Love and Marriage in Late Medieval London* (Kalamazoo: Western Michigan University, for TEAMS, 1995), 1–36 and her *Marriage, Sex, and Civic Culture*.

70. Sheehan, "Formation and Stability of Marriage," 77.

71. McSheffrey, *Marriage, Sex, and Civic Culture*, 7–8.

72. Ibid., 8.

73. Sheehan, "The Formation and Stability of Marriage," 48.

74. McSheffrey, ed., *Love and Marriage*, 4.

75. Ibid., 41.

76. Ibid., 45.

77. McSheffrey, *Marriage, Sex, and Civic Culture*, 28.

78. Goldberg, *Women, Work and Life Cycle*, 236–37.

79. McSheffrey, *Marriage, Sex, and Civic Culture*, 32.

80. Shannon McSheffrey, "Place, Space, and Situation: Public and Private in the Making of Marriage in Late Medieval London," *Speculum* 79 (2004): 978–79.

81. Ibid., 981–85.

82. Ibid., 974–75.

83. Ibid., 976.

84. John Schofield, "Social Perception of Space in Medieval and Tudor London Houses," in *Meaningful Architecture: Social Interpretations of Buildings*, ed. Martin Locock (Aldershot: Ashgate, 1994), 188–206.

85. McSheffrey, *Marriage, Sex, and Civic Culture*, 45–46.

86. McSheffrey, ed., *Love and Marriage*, 57.

87. Albertus Magnus, *Book of Minerals*, trans. Dorothy Wyckoff (Oxford: Oxford University Press, 1967), 81; "North Midland Lapidary," in *English Medieaval Lapidaries*, ed. Joan Evans and Mary S. Serjeantson, EETS 190 (London: Oxford University Press, 1933), 53; "The Peterborough Lapidary," in *English Mediaeval Lapidaries*, 77; "Sloan Lapidary," *English Mediaeval Lapidaries*," 125.

88. McSheffrey, ed., *Love and Marriage*, 38–39.

89. WAC E2, 1510 [no folio numbers].

90. McSheffrey, ed., *Love and Marriage*, 68.

91. PRO Prob 11/19, fol. 70v.

92. McSheffrey, *Marriage, Sex, and Civic Culture*, 61.

93. Mirk, *Instructions for Parish Priests*, 7.

94. Jacques LeGoff, *The Birth of Purgatory*, trans. Arthur Goldhammer (Chicago: University of Chicago Press, 1984); Kathleen L. Wood-Legh, *Perpetual Chantries in Britain* (Cambridge: Cambridge University Press, 1965); Alan Kreider, *English Chantries: The Road to Dissolution* (Cambridge, Mass.: Harvard University Press, 1979).

95. Christopher Daniell, *Death and Burial in Medieval England, 1066–1550* (London: Routledge, 1997), 181.

96. Robert Dinn, "Death and Rebirth in Late Medieval Bury St. Edmunds," in *Death in Towns: Urban Responses to the Dying and the Dead, 1000–1600*, ed. Steven Bassett (London: Leicester University Press, 1992), 152; see also Miri Rubin, *Charity and Community in Medieval Cambridge* (Cambridge: Cambridge University Press, 1987), 250–64.

97. Harding, *Dead and the Living*, 208–9.

98. Ibid., 178.

99. Harding, "Burial Choice and Burial Location in Later Medieval London," in *Death in Towns*, 119–35; Robert Dinn, "'Monuments Answerable to Men's Worth': Burial Patterns, Social Status, and Gender in Late Medieval Bury St. Edmunds," *Journal of Ecclesiastical History* 46 (1995): 237–55.

100. Sharon T. Strocchia, "Funerals and the Politics of Gender in Early Renaissance Florence," in *Refiguring Woman: Perspectives on Gender and the Italian*

Renaissance, ed. Marilyn Migiel and Juliana Schiesari (Ithaca, N.Y.: Cornell University Press, 1991), 155–68.

101. Lucinda M. Becker, *Death and the Early Modern Woman* (Aldershot: Ashgate, 2003), 134–37.

102. WAC E1–3; Bodleian MS. Rawlinson D 786.

103. The records do not describe the range of clergy involved, special livery worn by mourners, involvement of the poor, or special prayers used to augment the liturgy. For a comparison of what a will can tell of funeral plans and what the churchwardens' accounts show, see the will of Bartelyn Stockwood and the accounts of her burial. In her will, she asks for an elaborate funeral. She asks to be buried in either the abbey or the parish church and specifies that "I will have on the day of my burial 8 priests and two clerks and the same day a trental of masses within the parish church . . . I will have a mass of our blessed lady by note in the said parish church with a great knell and also there peals with all the bells of the parish church . . . I will that all the priests of the city of London be at my burial . . . I will have 3s. 4d. given in alms to such poor people as shall be thought best by my executors . . . I will have at my burial 8 torches of the parish church bearing about the hearse besides the torches of the brotherhood . . . I will have a trental of masses done for my soul and my husband's soul in *Scala Coeli* in Westminster within 3 days next after my burial . . . I will have burning about my grave two tapers every day at the high mass during a month next after my departing . . . I will have if it may be performed the day of my burial, a peal with the bells of the abbey. . . . I will at my month's mind dirge and mass be performed by not less than 6 priests and 2 clerks and torches and tapers at the discretion of my executors . . . I will have done in the *Scala Coeli* 5 masses of the 5 wounds of our lord. . . . I will have mass of requiem and dirge by note in Little Marlow as shortly after my departing as may be conducted and on the same day of my mass and dirge to be given 7s. in bread and ale and cheese" (WAC Bracy, fols. 3–4v) The churchwardens' accounts show that she had knells and peals, 6 tapers, and 4 torches, and that the same torches would be used at a lady mass. She was buried in the parish church and there was both a month mind and year mind with peals, and 4 tapers and 4 torches. WAC E2, 1528 [no folio numbers]. The items for rituals performed in other locations would probably not appear in the churchwardens' accounts.

104. Westminster did not have the typical governmental structures of a medieval city. Throughout the Middle Ages, it was technically a manor and the Abbey its landlord. Rosser, *Medieval Westminster*, 226–50. For population see Rosser, 168–76. The chantry certificate lists 2,500 communicants for St. Margaret's, *London and Middlesex Chantry Certificates: 1548*, ed. C. J. Kitching, London Record Society 16 (1980), no. 139.

105. Clive Burgess, "London Parishes in Times of Change: St. Andrew Hubbard, Eastcheap, c. 1450–1570," *Journal of Ecclesiastical History* 53 (2002): 38.

106. For occupations of Westminster, see Rosser, *Medieval Westminster*, 119–65; 246.

107. Ibid., 221–24, 267–69.

108. I arrived at this figure by assuming that the 49–51 individuals listed on the two lay subsidy rolls for 1524 and 1525 represented two-thirds of the households.

Roger Schofield makes this assumption in his "Parliamentary Lay Taxation: 1485–1547" (Ph.D. dissertation, Cambridge University, 1963), 244–46.

109. Samantha Letters, *Online Gazetteer of Markets and Fairs in England Wales to 1516*, http://_www.history.ac.uk/cmh/gaz/gazweb2.html: [Lincolnshire] (Centre for Metropolitan History, Institute of Historical Research, 23 February 2005). Samantha Letters, *Online Gazetteer of Markets and Fairs in England and Wales to 1516*, http://www.history.ac.uk/_cmh/_gaz/_gazweb2.html: [county name] (Centre for Metropolitan History, Institute of Historical Research, 23 February 2005). See also Stewart Bennett and Nicholas Bennett, eds., *An Historical Atlas of Lincolnshire* (Hull: University of Hull Press, 1993), esp. 29–57. For more on fenland farming in the late Middle Ages and Early Modern period, see Joan Thirsk, *English Peasant Farming: The Agrarian History of Lincolnshire from Tudor to Recent Times* (London: Routledge and Kegan Paul, 1957), 6–49.

110. The wealthiest people on the Westminster 1524 lay subsidy were taxed on £100, while in Sutterton the wealthiest person was taxed on only £30. PRO E179/238/90 and 179/136/329.

111. WAC E1–E3; Bodleian MS. Rawlinson D 786. I have created prosopographical databases for each parish, where I have entered every action or entry with a person's name in a way that I can track years, last names, sex, cost of the action taken, and the type of action. All data for the funerals come from these databases.

112. I have not included the funerals of priests or children here. There are, however, 125 funerals for men who are probably or certainly priests, and 358 funerals for children. Only 20 of these children's funerals list the sex of the child. These statistics suggest that children are significantly underrepresented in the listings of burials.

113. Finlay has looked at burial figures for 8 London parishes for the period 1580–1640, and comes up with a ratio of 145–104 males for every 100 females, making women 41–48 percent of the population. Later periods allow him to extrapolate citywide figures. For 1664–99 there are 107 males for 100 females. Roger Finlay, *Population and Metropolis: The Demography of London 1580–1640* (Cambridge: Cambridge University Press, 1981), 140–42.

114. I have not included the funerals of children, which are routinely mentioned in this parish, or the funerals of priests.

115. There are 40 for women and 111 for men.

116. *Calendar of Inquisitions Post Mortem*, 19, 279.

117. Manuscript illustrations show women preparing the body; in other cultures, such as Judaism, women had this responsibility as well. Daniell, *Death and Burial in Medieval England*, 42–44.

118. WAM St. Mary's Guild Account, fol. 13. In 1506, 1507, and 1508, the guild paid 80d. for her yearly upkeep (fol. 6). In Bury St. Edmund's Alice Bumpsted left 2d. to each of "the two women that shall sew my winding sheet." Dinn, "Death and Rebirth," 155.

119. *Speculum Sacerdotale*, 234.

120. The parish paid for the dead woman's grave and a knell. *Lambeth Churchwardens' Accounts: 1504–1645 and Vestry Book: 1610*, ed. Charles Drew, Surrey Record Society 40 (London: Surrey Record Society, 1940), 33.

121. Dinn, "Death and Rebirth," 156; Judith Middleton-Stewart, *Inward Purity and Outward Splendour: Death and Remembrance in the Deanery of Dunwich, Suffolk, 1370–1547* (Woodbridge: Boydell, 2001), 116; Ralph A. Houlbrooke, *Death, Religion, and the Family in England, 1480–1750* (Oxford: Oxford University Press, 1998), 255–64.

122. WAC Wyks fols. 35–39; *Lincoln Wills*, vol. 1, 129–30.

123. The most commonly requested masses that testators could request were the Mass of the Holy Name of Jesus, Trental of St. Gregory, Mass of the Five Wounds, Mass of the *Scala Coeli*, and Mass of the Virgin Mary. See Middleton-Stewart, *Inward Purity and Outward Splendour*, 136; Daniell, *Death and Burial*, 60–64.

124. For chantries see Wood-Legh, *Perpetual Chantries*; Alan Kreider, *English Chantries*; Clive Burgess, "Strategies for Eternity: Perpetual Chantry Foundation in Late Medieval Bristol," in *Religious Belief and Ecclesiastical Careers in Late Medieval England*, ed. Christopher Harper-Bill (Woodbridge: Boydell, 1991), 1–32.

125. WAC E1, fols. 173, 330, 94.

126. Bodleian MS. Rawlinson D 786, fols. 2, 16v.

127. Of the 42 funerals for individuals described as either poor or paupers, 15 are women and 26 are men, but a third of women have nothing with their funeral while only 19 percent of men have nothing. Without additional information on these people, it is difficult to make sense of these findings, but we know that widowhood and poverty went together for many women and, without money or family, there would be little to put toward a funeral.

128. WAC Bracy, fol. 18v.

129. WAC, E2 1528 [no folio numbers].

130. Identifying married couples in Westminster is an imprecise process. Sutterton's accounts identify women who died as wives, which suggests that women identified by their first name are widows or single, but the accounts make no such designations for men. Similarly, the accounts for Westminster only occasionally identify a woman as married or name her husband. I have tentatively identified 150 couples where both husbands and wives had funerals in St. Margaret's parish church prior to 1536. Churchwardens' accounts do not consistently identify couples. In order to do so, I have also looked at wills and leases of property from the Abbey. This method is not helpful in all cases as most did not leave wills and most property in Westminster, while owned by the Abbey, was sublet directly from the Abbey. Many parishioners slip through the records. Even knowing the names of both husband and wife does not guarantee that both had funerals listed in the churchwardens' accounts. Some widows moved away, and second marriages changed their names. Identifying couples has been in some cases a process of educated guessing based on names, dates of death, and other parish activities.

131. Rosser, *Medieval Westminster*, 366–406; WAC Will Registers Wyks and Bracy, Churchwarden's Accounts, E1–3, WAM Lease Books 1–2.

132. WAC Bracy, fols. 2–2v.

133. WAC E2 1528 [no folio numbers].

134. Felicity Riddy, "Mother Knows Best: Reading Social Change in a Courtesy Text," *Speculum* 71, 1 (1996): 77.

135. Rosser, 400–401.

136. WAC E1, fol. 528.

137. WAM St. Mary's Guild Accounts, 10, 10v.

138. Richard Russell, who died in 1517, leaves a will, rents tenements from the Abbey. His son, William, becomes a gentlemen wax chandler. See WAC Wyks, fols. 249–51 for his will; WAM Lease Book 2, fol. 38 for his leases, and Rosser p. 397 for information on his son. Similarly Arthur Turfote's son Louis becomes a notary. See Rosser, *Medieval Westminster*, 403. William Caxton is also in this group by virtue of his funeral, but does not fit the profile of most others in this group. See WAC E1, fol. 283.

139. WAC Wyks, fol. 26, "pay my detts and bring my body in erth and doo for my soule as she may think to please god and profit my soule" There are similar instructions in John Wyks's will (Wyks, fols. 3–5) and Daniel Afforge's will (Wyks, fols. 10–11).

140. WAC E1, fol. 503.

141. WAC Wyks, fols. 227–29.

142. Bodleian MS. Rawlinson D 786.

143. My findings are quite similar to those of Christine Peters, but I have broken down the expenditures differently. She found that 83 percent of wives had funerals costing 2d. or more; I found 84 percent. Peters found that 58 percent of widows had funerals costing more than 2d. I found 61 percent. These minor differences are probably related to decisions on how to categorize some individual women or whether I thought some women had been counted twice. All in all our statistical analysis is in agreement, even if our interpretations are not. Peters, *Patterns of Piety*, 44–45.

144. "wax, of the churche, and other things at the buryalle of hur husband," *Kentish Visitations of Archbishop William Warham and His Deputies, 1511–1512*, ed. Kathleen Wood-Legh, Kent Records 24 (1984), 242.

145. For economic status of widows see Barbara Hanawalt, "The Widow's Mite: Provisions for Medieval London Widows," in *Upon My Husband's Death: Widows in the Literature and Histories of Medieval Europe*, ed. Louise Mirrer (Ann Arbor: University of Michigan Press, 1992), 21–46; Barbara Hanawalt, "Remarriage as an Option for Urban and Rural Widows in Late Medieval England," in *Wife and Widow in Medieval England*, ed. Sue Sharidan Walker (Ann Arbor: University of Michigan Press, 1993), 141–64.

146. Eamon Duffy, *Stripping of the Altars: Traditional Religion in England, 1400–1580* (New Haven, Conn.: Yale University Press, 1992), 362.

147. WAC Bracy, fol. 40v.

148. WAC E1, fol. 63; E2 1526, 1527 [no folio numbers]; E1 fol. 29; E2, 1524 [no folio numbers]; E1 fols. 304, 64, 393, 69, 93, E2, 1533 [no folio numbers]; E1, fol. 390.

149. WAC E1–3.

150. Strocchia, "Funerals and the Politics of Gender," 157.

151. Christopher Daniell, *Death and Burial in Medieval England, 1066–1550* (London: Routledge, 1997), 51. See also K. B. McFarlane, *Lancastrian Kings and Lollard Knights* (Oxford: Oxford University Press, 1972), 207–20; J. A. F. Thomson, "Knightly Piety and the Margins of Lollardy," in *Lollardy and the Gentry in the Later*

Middle Ages, ed. Margaret Aston and Colin Richmond (Stroud: Alan Sutton, 1997), 95–111.

Chapter 3. *"My Pew in the Middle Aisle": Women at Mass*

1. PRO STAC 2/28/54.

2. "Robert Stokes and all his ancestors . . . of long tyme have hadd and used a pewe or a sete for them and their wyfes and childre at all such tymes as they were disposed to serve God in the same church wøut interupcon of any man. . . ." Ibid.

3. "of late didd bestow ley ought dyvers great sumes of money uppon the buyldyng and reperacon of the same chapel to thentent she and hir childre mought have the more ease and commodytye to serve God w'tin the same." Ibid.

4. "dyv'rs oyr parishens as the seid Stookis have used for sitt or knele with'n for to her the service of God." Ibid.

5. "kepe the dore of the seid chapell which she had newly made always loked contrary to the custom & uses of the seid church. . . ." Ibid.

6. There are a number of possible explanations for this case. Bridget calls the chapel Stokes' Chapel, and her family's privilege with respect to the chapel might have been a sore point with the parish. Thus when her husband died, others in the parish used her new status as widow to bully her. She installed the lock anticipating such problems. The chantry priest might have been an innocent victim in this confrontation between Bridget and the parish. Conversely Bridget could also have been using her new status as widow to set up a mortuary chapel for her recently deceased husband and had not negotiated this with the churchwardens or the rest of the parish. John Carboit's petition says that the churchwardens had asked the defendants to reopen the chapel and thus in effect reclaiming it for the parish.

7. C. Pamela Graves, *The Form and Fabric of Belief: An Archaeology of Lay Experience of Religion in Medieval Norfolk and Devon*, British Series 311 (Oxford: British Archaeological Reports, 2000), 195–216, for sight lines to the high altar from various seating locations in the nave.

8. Shannon McSheffrey, "Place, Space and Situation: Public and Private in the Making of Marriage in Late Medieval London," *Speculum* 79 (2004): 979.

9. Roberta Gilchrist, *Gender and Material Culture: The Archaeology of Religious Women* (London: Routledge, 1994), 150.

10. Christopher Wordsworth and Henry Littlehales, *The Old Service-Books of the English Church* (London: Methuen, 1904), 15.

11. F.A. Gasquet, *Parish Life in Mediaeval England* (London: Methuen, 1906), 140–63; Eamon Duffy, *The Stripping of the Altars: Traditional Religion in England: 1400–1580* (New Haven, Conn.: Yale University Press, 1992), 123–26; Wordsworth and Littlehales, *Old Service-Books*, 21–22.

12. Go to chirche whanne þou may, / Loke þou spare for no reyn, / For ou farist e best at ilke day / Whanne ou has god y-seyn." "How the Good Wife Taught Her Daughter," in *The Babees Book*, ed. Frederick J. Furnivall, EETS 32 (1868), 36.

13. Katherine L. French, *The People of the Parish: Community Life in a Late*

Medieval English Diocese (Philadelphia: University of Pennsylvania Press, 2001), 154–62.

14. C. R. Cheney, "Rules for the Observance of Feast-Days, in Medieval England," *Bulletin for the Institute of Historical Research* 34, 90 (1961): 136, 137. His mandate also served further to associate women with these particular virgin martyrs. See also Barbara Harvey "Work and *Festa Ferianda* in Medieval England," *Journal of Ecclesiastical History* 23, 4 (October 1972): 291.

15. "But in the iiijth daye it is lawefull to men for to tikye and vse werkys of the erþe, but wymmen oweþ for to cese fro here werkys. And why? Rurale workis ben more nedeful þen other." *Speculum Sacerdotale*, ed. Edward Weatherly, EETS 200 (London: Oxford University Press, 1936), 128.

16. For a discussion of this value system see Barbara Hanawalt, *The Ties That Bound: Peasant Families in Medieval England* (New York: Oxford University Press, 1986), 141–55; Maryanne Kowaleski, "Women's Work in a Market Town: Exeter in the Late Fourteenth Century," in *Women and Work in Preindustrial Europe*, ed. Barbara Hanawalt (Bloomington: University of Indiana Press, 1986), 145–64.

17. "Þe halyday only ordeynet was, / To here goddess serues and þe mas, / And spene þat day in holynes, / And leue alle oþer bysynes / For a-pon þe werkeday, / Men be so bysy in vche way, / So that for here ocupacyone, / þey leue myche of here deuocyone." John Mirk, *Instructions for Parish Priests*, ed. Edward Peacock, EETS 31 (1868), 31.

18. Becky R. Lee, "Men's Recollections of a Women's Rite: Medieval English Men's Recollections Regarding the Rite of Purification of Women After Childbirth," *Gender and History* 14 (2002): 229–30.

19. "What the Wiseman Taught his Son," *The Babees Book*, 48–52; Sandy Bardsley, *Venomous Tongues: Speech and Gender in Late Medieval England* (Philadelphia: University of Pennsylvania Press, 2006), 49–51.

20. G. R. Owst, *Preaching in Medieval England* (New York: Russell and Russell, 1965), 173.

21. "Statutes of Exeter," *Councils and Synods*, vol. 2:2, ed. F. M. Powicke and C. R. Cheney (Oxford: Oxford University Press, 1964), 1007–8; see also Margaret Aston, "Segregation in Church," in *Women in the Church*, ed. W. J. Sheils and Diana Wood, Studies in Church History 27 (Oxford: Blackwell, 1990), 251.

22. Ibid., 254.

23. But ȝyt do wymmen gretter folye / Þat vse to stonde among þe clergye, / Oþer at matyns or at messe, / But ȝyt hyt were yn cas of stresse. For þer of may come temptacyun. / And dystourblyng of deuocyun. Robert Mannyng, *Handlyng Synne*, ed. Idelle Sullens (Binghamton: Center of Medieval and Renaissance Studies, State University of New York, 1983), 221.

24. "Visitation of Parishes by John Trefnant, Bishop of Hereford, 1397," typescript from original in Hereford Cathedral Archives MS 1779, transcribed by Christopher Whittick, no. 41.2.19, p. 137 (unpublished English translation by Christopher Whittick, no. 41.2.19, p. 68). Used with permission.

25. *Register of John Chandler, Dean of Salisbury, 1404–1417*, ed. T. C. B. Timmins, Wiltshire Record Society 39 (1983), no. 21, p. 12.

26. "Also, whan folke is at chirche, men and wommen schulle bere hem stille

and lowe and honestliche, and do honoure and reuerence to God and his halewen. For þe place is holy and ordeyned to bidde þer-ynne and not to iangle ne to iape." *The Book of Vices and Virtues*, ed. W. Nelson Francis, EETS 217 (Oxford: Oxford University Press, 1942), 237.

27. Þat whenne þey doth to chyrche fare, / Þenne bydde hem leue here mony wordes, / Here ydel speche, and nyce bordes, / And put a-way alle vanyte, / And say here *pater noster* & here *ave*. / No non in chyrche stonde schal, / Ney lene to pyler ny to wal, / But fayre on kneus þey schule hem sette, / Knelynge doun up on th flette. ^{Mirk,} *Instructions for Parish Priests*, 9.

28. G. R. Owst, *Literature and Pulpit*, 2nd ed. (Oxford: Blackwell, 1961), 390–402.

29. Françoise Piponnier and Perrine Mane, *Dress in the Middle Ages*, trans. Caroline Beamish (New Haven, Conn.: Yale University Press, 1997), 77.

30. "Seynt Poule techeþ how þe goode wommen schulle atire hem whan þei schulle go to chirche to bidde here bedes to God; he seiþ þei scholde have honest cloþinge and atire and not to moche, þat is to seie after þat þe womman is of state and as þe state askeþ. For þat þt is to moche too womman, nis not to moche to some oþere. For moche more bihoueþ to þe queen þan to a burgeies wife, or to a marchaundes or to a squyers or a-noþer symple lady, as a knyȝtes wif." *The Book of Vices and Virtues*, 239–40.

31. "Whanne þou sittist in þe chirche þi beedis þou / schalt bidde; / Make you no iangelynge To freende nor to / sibbe; / lauȝe þou to scorne nouþer oolde bodi ne / ȝonge, / But be of fair beerynge & of good tunge." "How the Good Wife Taught Her Daughter," 37.

32. PRO STAC 2/28/54. "your sayd oratrix of late didd bestow ley ought diverse great sumes of money upon the buyldyng and reperacon of the same chapel to thentent she and hir children mought have the more ease and commodytye to serve god wtin the same . . ."

33. "The Book of Nurture," in *The Babees Book*, 63.

34. WAC E2 ,1515 [no folio numbers].

35. Ibid., 1515, 1518 [no folio number].

36. Lawrence R. Poos, *A Rural Society After the Black Death: Essex, 1350–1525* (Cambridge: Cambridge University Press, 1991), 275.

37. Barbara Hanawalt and Ben R. McRee, "The Guilds of *Homo Prudens* in Late Medieval England," *Continuity and Change* 7, 2 (1992): 163–79.

38. J. Charles Cox, *Bench-Ends in English Churches* (London: Oxford University Press, 1916), 25.

39. Edwin Smith, Graham Hutton, and Olive Cook, *English Parish Churches* (New York: Thames and Hudson, 1976), 117–24; Beat A. Kümin, *The Shaping of a Community: The Rise and Reformation of the English Parish, c. 1400–1560* (Aldershot: Scolar, 1996), 125–47; French, *People of the Parish*, 144–54.

40. Graves, *The Form and Fabric of Belief*, 138.

41. BL Add. Ms. 40729 (Yeovil CWA for 1519, one year only).

42. Aston, "Segregation in Church," 238–42. There is some debate about when synagogues began to separate men and women during Jewish services. See Ross Shepard Kraemer, *Her Share of the Blessings: Women's Religion Among Pagans,*

Jews, and Christians in the Greco-Roman World (Oxford: Oxford University Press, 1992), 106.

43. The third-century work *Didascalia Apsotolorum* placed people at worship in a hierarchy, with women at the bottom. St. Chrysostom believed that separating men and women at worship was a new innovation because men's and women's morals had declined since the founding of the Church. Durandus in his thirteenth-century work *Rationale Divinorum Officiorum* believed men and women were separated because "the stronger saints should stand against the greater temptations of this world, and the weaker against the lesser." Aston, "Segregation in Church," 239–42.

44. Ibid., 238–42; Gilchrist, *Gender and Material Culture*, 133.

45. Aston, "Segregation in Church," 269–81; Gilchrist, *Gender and Material Culture*, 133–35.

46. Ibid.

47. I am drawing here on Henrietta Moore's distinction between the movement through space and its implications for cultural analysis and an analysis of spatial organization. H. L. Moore, *Space, Text, and Gender: An Anthropological Study of the Marakwet of Kenya* (Cambridge: Cambridge University Press, 1986), 79–90.

48. Barbara Hanawalt, "At the Margins of Women's Space in Medieval Europe," in *Of Good and Ill Repute: Gender and Social Control in Medieval England* (New York: Oxford University Press, 1998), 70–87.

49. Lincoln Record Office, *Calendar of Memoranda Book of Bishop John Dalderby of Lincoln*, vol. 3, 474. I am grateful to Sandy Bardsley for this reference. See also John Bossy, "The Mass as a Social Institution, 1200–1700," *Past and Present* 100 (1983): 56.

50. GL ms 9064/2, 163v. I am grateful to Shannon McSheffrey for this citation.

51. Ruth Mazo Karras, *Common Women: Prostitution and Sexuality in Medieval England* (New York: Oxford University Press, 1996), 95–101. On a day-to-day basis, so-called respectable women might in fact meet up with and interact with prostitutes. Some prostitutes provided women with sex education and information about prospective husbands. See Karras, 95–97.

52. Gervase Rosser, *Medieval Westminster, 1200–1540* (Oxford: Oxford University Press, 1989), 167–82.

53. Cox, *Bench-ends*; J. D. C. Smith, *Church Woodcarvings: A West Country Study* (New York: A.M. Kelley, 1969); Peter Poyntz Wright, *Rural Benchends of Somerset* (Amersham: Avebury, 1983).

54. J. C. D. Smith, *A Guide to Church Woodcarvings: Misericords and Bench-Ends* (Newton Abbot, Devon: David and Charles, 1974), 19.

55. Ibid.

56. Ibid., 12.

57. Ibid., 78–79.

58. Graves, *Form and Fabric of Belief*, 135–37.

59. Margaret Jennings, "Tutivillus: The Literary Career of the Recording Demon," *Studies in Philology, Texts and Studies* 74 (1977). See also Miriam Gill, "Preaching and Image: Sermons and Wall Paintings in Later Medieval England," in

Preacher, Sermons, and Audience in the Middle Ages, ed. Carolyn Muessig (Leiden: Brill, 2002), 171–72.

60. Miriam Gill, "Female Piety and Impiety: Selected Images of Women in Wall Paintings in England After 1300," in *Gender and Holiness: Men, Women, and Saints in Late Medieval Europe,* ed. Samantha J. E. Riches and Sarah Salih (London: Routledge, 2002), 108–10.

61. Bardsley, 50–58.

62. Gill, "Women in Wall Paintings," 109.

63. Ibid.

64. Ibid.

65. Rural parishes installed seats, but seem to have left the negotiation over who sat where to oral culture and local custom. The rural parish of Tintinhull, Somerset, built new seats in 1511 and 1512. To raise funds for this, they sold the old pews and held a Robin Hood ale. Seat sales, however, never appear as a part of the parish's income. SARS D/D/tin 4/1/1 fol. 95–96; see also French, *People of the Parish,* 162–63.

66. Winifred M. Bowman, "Order of Seating in Ashton Kirk," in *England in Ashton-Under-Lyne* (Cheshire: John Sherratt, 1960), 167–68; Aston, "Segregation in Church," 266.

67. Ibid., 167.

68. Ibid.

69. PRO STAC 2/12/224–26.

70. S. H. Rigby, *English Society in the Later Middle Ages: Class, Status, and Gender* (Basingstoke: Macmillan, 1995), 150–60.

71. Rosser, *Medieval Westminster,* 224.

72. Katherine French, "The Seat Under Our Lady: Gender and Seating in the Late Medieval English Parish Church," in *Women's Space: Parish, Place and Gender in the Middle Ages,* ed. Sarah Stanbury and Virginia Raguin (Albany: State University of New York Press, 2005), 152–55.

73. "Also it is aggreyd that all women that shall take any seate in the seid churche to pay for the same seate 6d. excepte in the mydle range & the north range be neth the font the which shall pay but 4d. & every woman to take her place ev'y day as they cumyth to church except such as hve ben mayo's wyfs." Charles Kerry, *A History of the Municipal Church of St. Lawrence, Reading,* (Reading: privately printed, 1883), 77.

74. "Ordinaunce"—"And ou' that it is ordered & enacted that all women of the said p'isshe whose husbands nowe be or heretofore have been bretherne of the Mass of Ihc, shall from hensforth sitt & have the hightest seats or pewes nexe unto the mayor's wifs seate towards the pulpit." Ibid., 78.

75. Andrew Brown, *Popular Piety in Late Medieval England: The Diocese of Salisbury, 1250–1550* (Oxford: Oxford University Press, 1995), 87.

76. Bowman, "Order of Seating in Ashton Kirk," 167–68.

77. *The Pre-Reformation Records of All Saints' Church, Bristol,* part 2, *The Churchwardens' Accounts,* ed. Clive Burgess, Bristol Records Society 53 (2000); "Churchwardens' Accounts for Sherbourne Minster," *Somerset and Dorset Notes and Queries,* 23: 209 (1941), 209–12; 23: 210 (1941), 229–35; 23: 211 (1941), 249–52; 23:

212 (1942), 269–72; 23: 213 (1942), 289–93; *Churchwardens' Accounts of Ashburton, 1479–1580,* ed. Alison Hanham, Devon and Cornwall Record Society, ns. 15 (1970). In Sherborne Minster, Dorset, women only purchased 40 percent of the seats, and in Ashburton, Devon they only purchased 11 percent of them.

78. Cox, *Bench-Ends,* 21.

79. *The Church Records of St. Andrew Hubbard, Eastcheap,* ed. Clive Burgess, London Record Society 34 (1999), 79.

80. GL ms 9065, fol. 79r. I am grateful to Shannon McSheffrey for this citation.

81. Bowman, "Order of Seating in Ashton Kirk," 167–68.

82. There are ninety-five women who change their pew, but because of the gaps in the records there is no record of their initial purchase of a pew. There are thirteen men in the same situation.

83. The churchwardens' accounts list 878 women as purchasing seats. An additional ninety-five change seats, but there is no listing of their initial purchase. This makes a total of 973 individual women purchasing seats in the nave from between 1460 and 1535. The accounts list 320 men purchasing seats for the same period with another nineteen who change their seats, but are not listed as ever initially purchasing one. (There are no accounts for 1462–63; 1466–67; 1472–73; 1476–76; 1486–87; 1492–93; 1506–7).

84. I arrived at this figure because I can either certainly or tentatively identify 158 couples who both bought seats.

85. Rosser, *Medieval Westminster,* 266.

86. WAC E1, fols. 161–62.

87. Specifically pews were built there in 1491, 1498, 1502–4, 1512. Ibid., fols. 291, 377, 453, 487, 514.

88. Ibid., fols. 431, 453–54, 487, 515.

89. Ibid., fol. 514; E2 1512, 1526 [no folio numbers].

90. WAC E1, fol. 369.

91. WAC Wyks, fol. 111.

92. Ibid., fol. 35.

93. WAC E1, fols. 111, 369–70, 417, 447, 514.

94. WAC Bracy, fol. 19v.

95. WAC E1, fols. 111, 308, 336, 370, 417, 447, 472, 508; E2 1514, 1515, 1525; E3, 1534 [no folio numbers].

96. In 1497 Thomas Bough, a gentleman and royal officer purchased a seat in the chapel. In 1509 his wife moved in with him. After Thomas Bough's death in 1515 (Margaret having died sometime around 1510), Anthony Legh, a member of the king's household, and his wife Elizabeth took over the seat. WAC E1, fols. 336, 565; E2, 1515 [no folio numbers].

97. This was also an issue for St. Martin-in-the-Fields. Julia F. Merritt, "The Social Context of the Parish Church in Early Modern Westminster," *Urban History Yearbook* 28 (1991), 25; Julia F. Merritt, *The Social World of Early Modern Westminster: Abbey, Court and Community, 1525–1640* (Manchester: Manchester University Press, 2005), 221–22.

98. Because there are ninety-five women and thirteen men for whom there is

no record of when they first purchase their pews, I have not included them in these calculations.

99. WAC E1, fol. 565; E2, 1517 [no folio numbers].

100. WAC E2, 1527, 1531 [no folio numbers].

101. WAC E3, 1534 [no folio numbers]. The records only say her grave was covered. She could have died in 1533 or 1534.

102. WAC E1, fol. 472 (Agnes Bird's seat purchase), fol. 461 (her death); E1, fol. 565 (Roberts Bettes wife's seat purchase), E2, 1510 (her death) [no folio numbers].

103. WAC E2, 1517 [no folio numbers].

104. There are fifteen women who clearly move when their husband's die, and another eleven who probably do, the uncertainty is based on the difficulty of linking women to men via last names and other evidence. WAC E1, fols. 158, 212.

105. Ibid., fol. 472.

106. Ibid., fol. 234.

107. Ibid., fols. 101, 202.

108. Ibid., fol. 360.

109. Ibid., fol. 472.

110. Ibid. (Agnes Stephenson's purchase), the accounts say that the previous occupant was Mistress Tebbe, wife of another gentleman and royal officer. E2, 1513 (Agnes's death), 1515 Ellen Attewell's purchase [no folio numbers]. The accounts for this year say that she purchased two seats, but it is likely that this is a late recording of an earlier purchase, given that Agnes Stephenson died in 1513, and Ellen purchased her seat.

111. Ellen's move left Agnes Stephenson's seat empty again, but we can trace it in the records because of its price of 40d. In 1515, there was only one 40d. seat sold, probably Agnes and Ellen's seat, and it was purchased by Mistress Green, wife of a master seaman. Unlike her predecessors in the seat, she is difficult to trace, largely because she has a common last name. Ibid., 1515 [no folio numbers].

112. While there is no information on Agnes's husband John, he was a man of some means as both he and Agnes were buried in graves in the church not the churchyard. Ibid., 1513, 1521 [no folio numbers]. Agnes got her seat from Mistress Tebbe, who was the wife of a royal officer, (Rosser, 402). Elizabeth Legh's second husband, Anthony, was also "of the king's house." WAC E2, 1515 [no folio numbers].

113. WAC E1, fol. 417.

114. Ibid., fols. 480–81.

115. Ibid., fols. 545, 569 et passim.

116. WAM St. Mary's Guild Accounts for 1518.

117. On the lay subsidy of 1524, Pomfrett was assessed at £100 of goods and Henbury was assessed at £13 6s. 8d. of land. PRO E179/238/98 fol. 1v.

118. Pomfrett is called a gentleman in his 1528 lease of four tenements with a garden on King Street. WAM Lease Book 2 fols. 245v-6.

119. He was churchwarden in 1516–18 and warden of the Assumption guild in 1522–24. WAC E2, 1516–18 [no folio numbers]; WAM Assumption Guild Accounts for 1522; WAM Lease Book 2, fols. 26, 40v, 219.

120. Rosser, *Medieval Westminster*, 127–28; WAC E1, fol. 471; WAM Lease Book 2, fol. 151v.

121. WAC E2, 1522, 1525 [no folio numbers].

122. WAC E1, fols. 471, 472. Joan's cost 40d. and John Henbury's wife's cost 28d. This difference in price does not necessarily mean, however, that the two women could not have been close together. E1 fols. 508, 565. Henbury's seat cost 32d. and Pomfrett's 36d.

123. WAC E2, 1515, 1517 [no folio numbers].

124. "toke up pavements & stones of walls & glass of windows & so utterly destroyed the same to thentent that the said abbot prior &convent shuld reentre unto the whole land and tent' letten to yo' sayd orator and yo' said orator being in danger as well of the seyd Pomfret . . ." PRO C1/517/57.

125. Henbury was able to secure representation by Thomas Cromwell; so despite Pomfrett's greater wealth, Henbury could still afford to take care of himself and his business. See also Rosser, *Medieval Westminster*, 127–28.

126. WAC E2 (1526–29) [no folio numbers]; E3 (1530–35) [no folio numbers]. WAM Lease Book 2, fols. 268v.

127. John Bossy, "The Mass as a Social Institution, 1200–1700," *Past and Present* 100 (1983): 27–61.

128. WAC E2, 1515 [no folio numbers].

129. WAC E1, fol. 111.

130. WAC E2, 1529 [no folio numbers].

131. *All Saints' Church, Bristol*, 3.

132. Ibid.

133. In 1449, Richard Ysgar died, and the next year his widow, Janet, purchased a seat. Ibid., 38; Katherine Hardware did the same thing in 1466, after her husband died (see pp. 44, 49).

134. *Churchwardens' Accounts of St. Edmunds and St. Thomas, Sarum: 1443–1702*, ed. Henry James Fowle Swayne, Wilts Record Society 1 (1896), 21.

135. *VCH-Wiltshire*, vol. 6 (London: Oxford University Press, 1962), 83–85; 151–53; Brown, 54–56.

136. *Churchwardens' Accounts of St. Edmunds, Sarum*. There are accounts from 1469 to 1541, with seven undated accounts and several gaps. Based on internal evidence, it is possible to date some of the undated accounts. I have dated the undated account from the 1490s (on pp. 34–36) to 1492–93; undated account on p. 62 to 1539–40; undated account on pp. 76–88 to before 1523; undated account on pp. 60–61 to 1531–32; undated account on p. 73 to between 1501 and 1509; undated accounts on pp. 70–71 to 1533–34.

137. Ibid., 64.

138. Ibid., 67, 35. The accounts say that Dimissa purchased a pew, but this must be a mistake. It should read that she changed her pew, as the accounts also say that William Greggrey's wife purchased Dimissa's old pew.

139. French, *People of the Parish*, 68–98, for a discussion of the relative power, status, and influence of churchwardens in different communities.

140. Kümin, *Shaping of a Community*, 77.

141. Assuming somewhat less social mobility in this parish than in Westmin-

ster, I have extended the range of years for matching parishioners on the lay subsidy and the churchwardens' accounts. PRO E179/96/140.

142. "wyth force and armyd that is to saye with sworde and uniklers daggers & other wepyns . . . toke out the said Margaret wyff to your said oratour of her said pue wher she was kneltng in the said churche and brought out in to an alye in the said churche agen her wyll and then and ther did her bete and ill tyntret [her]." PRO STAC 2/12/224.

143. PRO STAC2/3/163–68.

144. On the Sunday before Sent Edmond, after evyn songe, Augnes Ball com to me to my closet and bad me good evyn, an Clement Spycer with hyr. . . .And all that tyme Waryn Herman lenyd ovyr the parklos and lystynd what we seyd . . . " *The Paston Letters*, vol. 2, ed. James Gairdner, reprint (Gloucester: Sutton, 1983), 244; See also Colin Richmond, *The Paston Family in the Fifteenth Century: The First Phase* (Cambridge: Cambridge University Press, 1990), 8–9.

145. Ralph A. Houlbrooke, "Women's Social Life and Common Action in England from the Fifteenth Century to the Eve of the Civil War," *Continuity and Change* 1, 2 (1986): 171–89.

146. *Act Book of the Ecclesiastical Court of Whalley, 1510–1538*, ed. Alice M. Cooke, Chetham Society 44 (1901), 58.

147. Sarah Good, one of the first women accused of witchcraft in Salem, Massachusetts, stayed away from church for the same reason. See Carol Karlsen, *Devil in the Shape of a Woman: Witchcraft in Colonial New England* (New York: Norton, 1985), 149.

Chapter 4. Maidens' Lights and Wives' Stores: Women's Parish Groups

1. An earlier version was published as "Maidens' Lights and Wives' Stores: Women's Parish Guilds in Late Medieval England," *Sixteenth Century Journal* 29, 2 (1998): 399–425.

2. "fit and put the said ffronillet upon the Image of sent Margarat to garnysh the same Image . . . at ev'ry . . . ffest." PRO C1 1095/1. A frontlet is a decorative band worn around the head and covering the forehead.

3. "runnyng of blod & aȝens þe flyx of þe wombe." "The Peterborough Lapidary," in *English Mediaeval Lapidaries*, ed. Joan Evans and Mary S. Serjeantson, EETS 190 (1933), 108.

4. Some have disagreed with my use of the term "guild" for these permanent all-women's subparochial groups. See in particular Johanna Mattingly, "Stories in Glass—Reconstructing the St. Neot's Pre-Reformation Glazing Scheme," *Journal of the Royal Institution of Cornwall* n.s. 2, 3, parts 3 and 4 (2000): 9–55, esp. n. 116; Ken Farnhill, *Guilds and the Parish Community in Late Medieval East Anglia, c. 1470–1550* (York: York Medieval Press, 2001), 120 n. 130. While these groups do not seem to have the permanence of some groups generally agreed to be guilds, this could be related to their novelty. This begs the question of how long do they have to exist before they are granted some notion of permanence.

5. S. H. Rigby, *English Society in the Later Middle Ages: Class, Status, and Gender* (Basingstoke: Macmillan, 1995), 280.

6. Ralph A. Houlbrooke, "Women's Social Life and Common Action in England from the Fifteenth Century to the Eve of the Civil War," *Continuity and Change* 1 (1986): 171.

7. Ibid.

8. Katherine L. French, *The People of the Parish: Community Life in a Late Medieval English Diocese* (Philadelphia: University of Pennsylvania Press, 2001), 99–141.

9. SARS D/P/tin 4/1/1, fol. 26. Similarly, in Yatton, also in Somerset, Isabel Hurewych worked with William Durnebarne on the ale for 1453, Joan Milward and John Turban ran the ale together in 1485, and John Thurban and Johanna Hurdwych, a widow worked on one in 1498. D/P/yat 4/1/1 fols. 33, 172, 223.

10. WAC E2, 1514 [no folio numbers]

11. For example, the Somerset market-town parish of Bridgwater received most of its income from an annual door-to-door collection. Women are only individually listed when they are widows or servants. Three fifteenth-century collection reports survive, which list all the donors, where they lived, and the amounts they contributed. Two reports are dated, from 1445 and 1446, and one is undated but from about the same time. Individually listed women constitute 4.5 and 5 percent of the total number of donors for the collections of 1445 and 1446 respectively, a percentage that is equivalent of their financial contributions. The undated report, however, lists a greater number of women, they constitute 22 percent of all names on the list, but they provided only 11 percent of the income. Unlike the two dated collections, the undated one also includes servants as individual donors. Women servants outnumber male servants two to one, which accounts for some of the additional women on this report. The undated report lists 189 contributors; 25 are described as servants. There are 42 individually named women, of which 17 were servants. This leaves only 8 men identified as servants. In the two dated collections, servants were either excluded or gave as part of a household. This variation shows that collections could be tailored to meet a variety of needs. In some years poorer members were required to contribute, but in other years they did not. These collection reports also show how women's participation in parish finances was structured through their households. SARS D/P/bw #806, 807, 1649. See also *Bridgwater Borough Archives*, vol. 4, ed. Thomas Bruce Dilks, Somerset Record Society 60 (1948), 7–34.

12. For example, St. Margaret's, Westminster, owned several properties, known as Abingdon Rents. John Mason, a butcher, rented one of the tenements from 1498 to 1508 when he died. His wife stayed in the house until 1515, but her residency was not evident until his death. WAC E1, fols. 371, 372, 408, 419, 451 (John's rentals); fol. 442 (death); fols. 451, 482, 510, 555, 536 (widow's rentals).

13. Mattingly, "Stories in Glass," 22.

14. ERO D/P 11/5/1, fols. 9, 24v.

15. J. Charles Cox and W. H. St. John Hope, *Chronicle of the Collegiate Church of All Saints, Derby* (London: Bemrose, 1881), 49.

16. *The Church Book of St. Ewen's, Bristol: 1454–1485*, ed. Betty Masters and Elizabeth Ralph, Bristol and Gloucestershire Archaeological Society 6 (1967), 74–75.

17. Ibid., 40; 24, 29, 79; 30, 31, 86. Maud Core bought a seat in the nave. Her husband Robert was churchwarden on three occasions, and she had given the parish several gifts. Alice Griffith's husband was warden in 1466 (74). Johanna English's husband served in 1462 (50). Ellen Wyndric was possibly the wife of Wyndric Taylor, who served as warden in 1461 (67) or William Taylor, who served as churchwarden in 1460 (43). Whomever her husband, she bought a seat in the nave (36). Margaret Wolf organized a parish dance in 1467 (77), and her husband was probably Lawrence Wolf, who bought a seat the same year she did (25), and audited the parish accounts in 1454 (29). If Margaret's husband was John Wolf, he too was very prominent in the parish, serving as churchwarden on five occasions (32, 71, 86, 107, 125). Even though it is not always clear exactly who was the husband of these women, it is clear the women were from prominent families, and played a role in parish life.

18. Charles Kerry, *A History of the Municipal Church of St. Lawrence, Reading* (Reading: privately printed, 1883), 70

19. There is a huge literature on guilds. See, for example, Herbert Westlake, *The Parish Gilds of Mediaeval England* (London: SPCK, 1919); Barbara Hanawalt, "Keepers of the Lights: Parish Guilds in Medieval England," *Journal of Medieval and Renaissance Studies* 14, 1 (1984): 21–37; Barbara Hanawalt and Ben R. McRee, "The Guilds of *Homo Prudens* in Late Medieval England," *Continuity and Change* 7, 2 (1992): 163–79; Gervase Rosser, "Communities of the Parish and Guild in the Late Middle Ages," in *Parish, Church, and People*, ed. Susan Wright (London: Hutchinson, 1988), 29–55; Gervase Rosser, "Going to the Fraternity Feast: Commensality and Social Relations in Late Medieval England," *Journal of British Studies* 33 (1994): 430–46; Caroline M. Barron, "The Parish Fraternities of Medieval London," in *The Church in Pre-Reformation Society: Essays in Honour of F. R. H. Duboulay*, ed. Caroline M. Barron and Christopher Harper-Bill (Woodbridge: Boydell, 1985), 13–37; Joanna Mattingly, "The Medieval Parish Guilds of Cornwall," *Journal of the Royal Institution of Cornwall* 10 (1989): 290–329; David J. F. Crouch, *Piety, Fraternity, and Power: Religious Gilds in Late Medieval Yorkshire, 1389–1547* (York: York Medieval Press, 2000); Virginia Bainbridge, *Gilds in the Medieval Countryside: Social and Religious Change in Cambridgeshire, 1350–1558* (Woodbridge: Boydell Press, 1996); Farnhill, *Guilds and the Parish Community in Late Medieval East Anglia.*

20. Farnhill, *Guilds and the Parish Community*, 1–2.

21. Westlake has an index of the returns and the county of origin. Westlake, *Parish Gilds*. Toulmin Smith printed and translated many of them in *English Gilds: the Original Ordinances of More than 100 English Gilds*, ed. Toulmin Smith, EETS 40 (1870).

22. Ken Farnhill, "Guilds, Purgatory, and the Cult of the Saints: Westlake Reconsidered," in *Christianity and Community in the West: Essays for John Bossy*, ed. Simon Ditchfield (Aldershot: Ashgate, 2001), 59–71; Rosser, "Going to the Fraternity Feast," 430–46; Barron, "The Parish Fraternities of Medieval London," 13–37.

23. Rosser, "Communities of the Parish and Guild," 34. The parish could be

too large or too diverse, or it could be run by individuals or families that set a different agenda for parish administration.

24. Eamon Duffy, *Stripping of the Altars: Traditional Religion in England, 1400–1580* (New Haven, Conn.: Yale University Press, 1992), 141–54.

25. *"Croscombe Church-Wardens' Accounts,"* in *Church-Wardens' Accounts of Croscombe, Pilton, Yatton, Tintinhull, Morebath and St. Michael's Bath,* ed. Edmund Hobhouse, Somerset Record Society 4 (1890), 1–48. The originals are lost.

26. Hanawalt, "Keepers of the Light," 28.

27. SARS D/P/tin 4/1/1, fol. 4; *Somerset Medieval Wills,* vol.1, ed. F. W. Weaver, Somerset Record Society 16 (1901), 77. The originals are lost.

28. *The Churchwardens' Accounts of St. Michael's Church, Chagford: 1480–1600,* ed. Francis Mardon Osborne (Chagford: Devon: privately printed, 1979), 13.

29. Farnhill, "Westlake Reconsidered," 67; Farnhill, *Guilds and the Parish Community,* 34–40.

30. Farnhill, *Guilds and the Parish Community,* 36.

31. Hanawalt, "Keepers of the Light," 25.

32. Hanawalt, "Guilds of *Homo Prudens,*" 166. Single men, widowed women, not yet married, and never to marry women.

33. Farnhill, *Guilds and the Parish Community,* 49.

34. Ibid., 49.

35. WAM St. Mary's Guild Accounts for 1473, fol. 17.

36. Farnhill, *Guilds and the Parish Community,* 67–69.

37. Andrew Brown, *Popular Piety in Late Medieval England: The Diocese of Salisbury, 1250–1550* (Oxford: Oxford University Press, 1995), 145.

38. I am grateful to Ken Farnhill for explaining the intricacies of guild organization to me and for providing me with copies of relevant documents. NRO PD52/71, fol. 34v; PD52/233, fol. 24.

39. WAC E1, fol. 554.

40. WAC E2, 1515 [no folio numbers]; WAM St. Mary's Guild Accounts for 1515, fol. 10v.; 1516, fol. 10v., 1517, fol. 10v; 1518, fol. 10.

41. WAM St. Mary's Guild Accounts for 1515, fol. 12v.

42. Rosser, "Going to the Fraternity Feast," 430–446; Farnhill, "Westlake Reconsidered," 66.

43. WAM St. Mary Guild Accounts (1487), fol. 19. See also Gervase Rosser, *Medieval Westminster, 1200–1540* (Oxford: Oxford University Press, 1989), 29, and Rosser, "Going to the Fraternity Feast,"

44. WAM St. Mary Guild Accounts for 1487, fols. 16v-17v.

45. Ibid.,1515, fols. 18–18v.

46. Farnhill, "Westlake Reconsidered," 67.

47. Hanawalt, "Keepers of the Lights," 25–26; Hanawalt, "Guilds of *Homo Prudens,*" 167–68.

48. Charles Phythian-Adams, *Desolation of a City: Coventry and the Urban Crisis of the Late Middle Ages* (Cambridge: Cambridge University Press, 1979), 118–25.

49. John Bossy has argued that guilds fragmented late medieval religious life, and that fraternities or parish guilds and not the parish were the focus of religious

life. Guilds were exclusive by their very nature. John Bossy, *Christianity in the West: 1400–1700* (New York: Oxford University Press, 1985), 57–71.

50. SRO FC 185/E1/1, fols. 49, 72.

51. *The Register of John Chandler, Dean of Salisbury, 1404–17*, ed. T. C. B. Timmins, Wiltshire Record Society 39, 247 (1984), 90.

52. There are about 250 sets of churchwardens' accounts. At least 10 percent of them mention women's organizations, making them far more common than has been previously assumed. For a list of surviving churchwardens accounts see Ronald Hutton, *The Rise and Fall of Merry England: The Ritual Year, 1400–1700* (Oxford: Oxford University Press, 1994), 263–93, and Beat A. Kümin, *The Shaping of a Community: The Rise and Reformation of the English Parish, c. 1400–1560* (Brookfield, Vt.: Scolar Press, 1996), 265–69.

53. *Lincoln Wills*, vol. 2, ed. C. W. Foster, Lincoln Record Society 19 (1918), 15; LMA P92/SAV/24, fol. 6r. I want to thank Martha Carlin for giving me this reference. For Johanna Hodson's will see LMA DW/PA/7/1, fol. 22v.

54. Clive Burgess, "Pre-Reformation Churchwardens' Accounts and Parish Government: Lessons from London and Bristol," *English Historical Review* 117 (April, 2002): 306–32.

55. Christine Peters implies that widows with their greater legal status had no need for such women's groups, but I think this reflects a limited vision of the roles such groups played in parish society. Christine Peters, *Patterns of Piety: Women, Gender and Religion in Late Medieval and Reformation England* (Cambridge: Cambridge University Press, 2003), 28–33.

56. DHC PE/WM CW1/40, fols. 38, 50, 51 passim.

57. *St. Martin-in-the-Fields: The Accounts of the Churchwardens, 1525–1603*, ed. John V. Kitto (London: Simpkin, Marshall, Kent, Hamilton, 1901), 70. The originals are lost.

58. Mattingly, "The Medieval Parish Guilds of Cornwall," 321–22; Duffy, *Stripping of the Altars*, 150; Kümin, *Shaping of a Community*, 265–69.

59. "Women Churchwardens in Late Medieval England," in *The Parish in Late Medieval England: Proceedings of the 2002 Harlaxton Symposium*, ed. Clive Burgess and Eamon Duffy (Donington, Lincs.: Shaun Tyas/Paul Watkins), 301–24.

60. LMA P92/SAV/24, fol. 6r.

61. BL Add. MSS 6173; DRO, 1429A/PW2–4.

62. Mary Wack, "Women, Work, and Play in an English Medieval Town," in *Maids and Mistresses, Cousins and Queens: Women's Alliances in Early Modern England*, ed. Susan Frye and Karen Robertson (Oxford: Oxford University Press, 1999), 35–51.

63. *Churchwardens' Accounts of St. Edmund and St. Thomas, Sarum* (1443–1702), ed. Henry James Fowle Swayne, Wiltshire Record Society 1 (1896), 73, 76, 79, 83, 85, 365. A will from 1491 refers to the altar of the Virgin Mary as the Wives' Altar, showing an earlier existence than the wives' first recorded collection. PRO Prob 11/9 fols. 5r-5v. See also Audrey Douglas, "'Our Thanssyng Day': Parish Dance and Procession in Salisbury," in *English Parish Drama*, ed. Alexandra F. Johnston and Wim Hüsken (Amsterdam: Rodopi, 1996), 41–64; Audrey Douglas, "Salisbury Women in the Pre-Elizabethan Parish," in *Women, Marriage, and Family in Medie-*

val Christendom: Essays in Memory of Michael M. Sheehan, ed. Constance M. Rousseau and Joel T. Rosenthal (Kalamazoo, Mich.: Medieval Institute Publications, 1998), 111.

64. WAC E1, fols. 260, 286, 290, 310.

65. WAC E2, fol. 370, E2, [no folio numbers], see entries for years 1512, 1513, 1514, passim.

66. *Churchwardens' Accounts of Ashburton, 1479–1580*, ed. Alison Hanham, Devon and Cornwall Record Society n.s. 15 (1970) 15, 43–44.

67. DRO 1429A/PW1–4.

68. DRO 1429A/PW2, fols. early unnumbered folio, 83, 87.

69. *The Churchwardens' Accounts of St. Michael's Church, Chagford: 1480–1600* 13 (last mention of sisters), 21 (only brothers mentioned).

70. DRO, 2659A/PW1, fols. 1–4; 2260A/PW1, fols. 4–10.

71. Quoted in Sandy Bardsley, *Venomous Tongues: Speech and Gender in Late Medieval England* (Philadelphia: University of Pennsylvania Press, 2006), 1; see also "The Castle of Perseverance," in *The Macro Plays*, ed. Frederick J. Furnivall and Alfred W. Pollard, EETS 91 (1904), 156, lines 2649–52.

72. For, without any fayle, / I will not out of this towne. / But I have my gossips everichon / One foot further I will not gone; / They shall not drwone, by St. John, / and I may saver their Lyfe./ They loved me full well, by Christ; But though wilt let them in thy chist, / Else rowe forth, Noe, whether thou list, / And get thee a new wife. "Chester Noah Play," in ibid., lines 199–208.

73. "How sey yow, gossips is this wyne good? / That it is quod Elenore by the rood; / It cherisheth the hart and comfort the blood; / Such johnckettes among shal mak us lyv long." . . ."Thys is the thought that gossips tak, / Onse in the weke mery will thei mak, / And all small drynk thei will forsak; / But wyne off the best shall han no rest." "Wives at the Tavern," from *Songs and Carols*, ed. Thomas Wright (London: Percy Society, 1847), 93, 95.

74. Ech off them brought forth ther dysch; / Sum brought flesh and sume fysh. / Quod Margaret mek, now with a wysh, / "I wold Ane were here, she wold mak us chere. / . . . Wold God I had don aftur yowr counsell! / Fore my husbond is so fell/ He betyth me lyk the devill off hell; /and the more I cry the lesse mercy!"/ Alys with a lowd-voyce spak than / "I-wis she seid lytyll good he cane, / That betyth ore strykyths ony woman, / And specially his wyff; God gyve him short lyve!"/ Margaret mek seid, "So mot I thryffe, / I know no man that is alyffe, / That gyve me ij strokes, but he shal have fyffe; / I am not aferd, though I have no berd." Ibid., 93–94.

75. P. J. P. Goldberg, *Women, Work, and Life Cycle in a Medieval Economy: Women in York and Yorkshire, c. 1300–1520* (Oxford: Oxford University Press, 1992), 321.

76. Westlake, *Parish Gilds*, 61.

77. Hanawalt, "Keepers of the Lights," 26–27.

78. Ian J. Hart, "Religious Life in Essex, c. 1500–1570" (Ph.D. thesis, University of Warwick, 1992), chap. 1, 5.

79. Eamon Duffy, "Holy Maydens, Holy Wyfes: The Cult of Women Saints in

Fifteenth and Sixteenth Century England," in *Women in the Church*, ed. W. J. Sheils and Diana Wood, Studies in Church History 27 (Oxford: Blackwell, 1990), 175–96.

80. PRO Prob 11/9 fols. 5r–5v.

81. *The Church Book of St. Ewen's, Bristol: 1454–1485*, 94, 97–98.

82. Hutton, *Rise and Fall of Merry England*, 12–13.

83. *Churchwardens' Accounts of Ashburton*, 18, 49.

84. DRO 1429A/PW2, fols. 68, 74, 87, 91, 95, 108, 126.

85. WAC E1, fols. 256, 286, 335.

86. For example, WAC E2, 1519 [no folio numbers].

87. Ibid., 1523 [no folio numbers]. This is the only example I have found of a possible livery for a women's group.

88. "everyday or els every haly day as the wardeyns of the church see beste." WAC E1, fol. 386.

89. WAC E2, 1526 [no folio numbers].

90. Duffy, "Holy Maydens, Holy Wyfes," 175–96; W. W. Williamson, "Saints on Norfolk Rood-Screens and Pulpits," *Norfolk Archaeology* 31, part 3 (1956): 335–36.

91. Pamela Sheingorn, "The Holy Kinship: The Ascendancy and Materiality in Sacred Genealogy of the Fifteenth Century," *Thought: A Review of Culture and Ideas* 64 (1989), 267–69; Duffy, *Stripping of the Altars*, 181–83; Miriam C. Gill, "Late Medieval Wall Painting in England: Content and Context, c. 1300–1530" (Ph.D. thesis, Courtauld Institute of Art, University of London, 2002), 126–31.

92. Simon Cotton, "Medieval Roodscreens in Norfolk: Their Construction and Painting Dates," *Norfolk Archaeology* 40 (1987): 44–54; Williamson, "Saints on Norfolk Rood-Screens and Pulpits," 318, 332.

93. Carole Rawcliffe, "Women, Childbirth, and Religion in Later Medieval England," in *Women and Religion in Medieval England*, ed. Diana Wood (Oxford: Oxbow, 2003), 94.

94. Gill, "Late Medieval Wall Painting," 128 n. 198; Eamon Duffy offers the prominent Holditch family as another possibility. Eamon Duffy, "The Parish, Piety, and Patronage in Late Medieval East Anglia: The Evidence of Rood Screens," in *The Parish in English Life: 1400–1600*, ed. Katherine L. French, Gary G. Gibbs, and Beat A. Kümin (Manchester: Manchester University Press, 1997), 157.

95. Patricia Crawford, *Women and Religion in England: 1500–1720* (New York: Routledge, 1993), 24; Susan Karant-Nunn, "Continuity and Change: Some Effects of the Reformation on the Women of Zwickau," *Sixteenth Century Journal* 12 (1982): 28–30.

96. C. R. Cheney, "Rules for the Observance of Feast Days in Medieval England," *Bulletin of the Institute of Historical Research* 34, 90 (1961): 136, 137.

97. Karen A. Winstead, *Virgin Martyrs: Legends of Sainthood in Late Medieval England* (Ithaca, N.Y.: Cornell University Press, 1997); Kim M. Phillips, *Medieval Maidens: Young Women and Gender, 1270–1540* (Manchester: Manchester University Press, 2003), 77–83.

98. Duffy, "Holy Maydens, Holy Wyfes," 175–96; Winstead, *Virgin Martyrs*; Katherine Lewis, *The Cult of St. Katherine of Alexandria in Late Medieval England* (Woodbridge: Boydell, 2000).

99. Winstead, *Virgin Martyrs*.

100. Over fifty copies of *The South English Legendary* survive, particularly from the southwestern and northeastern parts of England. It is one of the most common medieval English manuscripts. The audience is somewhat of a mystery. There is evidence for well-to-do merchants owning it as well as clerics. Thomas Heffernan argues that clerics read it out loud to peasant audiences. Winstead describes the world of the *South English Legendary's* virgin martyrs as topsy-turvy, where "women were on top." Winstead, *Virgin Martyrs*, 71–73, 98–111; see also Manfred Görlach, *The Textural Tradition of the* South English Legendary (Leeds: University of Leeds Press, 1974). Thomas Heffernan, *Sacred Biography: Saints and Their Biographers in the Middle Ages* (New York: Oxford University Press, 1988), 261–65.

101. *The Book of the Knight of the Tower*, 113; Winstead, *Virgin Martyrs*, 117.

102. "What the Good Wife Taught Her Daughter," in *The Babees Book*, ed. F. J. Furnivall, EETS 32 (1868), 36–47; *The Book of the Knight of the Tower*, 152; Winstead, *Virgin Martyrs*, 117.

103. Lewis, *The Cult of St. Katherine*, 231.

104. Ibid., 111–74.

105. French, *The People of the Parish*, 196; Crouch, *Piety, Fraternity, and Power*, 99; Bainbridge, *Gilds in the Medieval Countryside*, 64. Popularity in this case refers to frequency of guild dedications and appearances of lights and images.

106. Lewis, *The Cult of St. Katherine*, 232.

107. "Wherfor a mayden most be of lytyll wordys, and loke þat scho speke by honeste and worschypto hur person; for hyt ys an old Englysch sawe: 'A mayde schuld be seen, but not herd.'" John Mirk, *Festial*, ed. Theodor Erbe, EETS 96 (1905), 229–30.

108. *Middle English Sermons*, 143.

109. Duffy, *Stripping of the Altars*, 173–83.

110. Mirk, *Festial*, 6.

111. Winstead, *Virgin Martyrs*, 112; see also the *Festial*, 200–201.

112. Winstead, *Virgin Martyrs*, 112; see also the *Speculum Sacerdotale*, 243–44.

113. Winstead, *Virgin Martyrs*, 113, see also n. 4. This new presentation coincided with other cultural initiatives to develop women's modest demeanor. Riddy, "'Mother Knows Best,'" 66–86.

114. Winstead, *Virgin Martyrs*, 132.

115. Ibid., 121.

116. But when Margret was borne, þe fadyr sende hor ynto þe contrey to a nors. Soo whyl þat scho was long þer among oþer maydyns, scho herde speke of God and of oure Lorde Ihesu Crist, how he boȝt mankynd wyth his deth out of thraldom of þe fende, and how he louyd specialy all þat woldon leven in chastite, and scruyn hym yn sympulnes and yn poverte. Then Margret herde of ys, scho toke such a loue to Ihesu Cryst, at scho mad a vow yn her hert, at scho wold neuer haue part of a manys body, but lyf yn her maydenhed al her lyfe-dayes aftyr. Mirk, *Festial*, 200.

117. Mirk, *Festial*, 177.

118. *Lincoln Wills*, vol. 2, 115, vol. 3, 183.

119. Barbara Hanawalt, *The Ties That Bound: Peasant Families in Medieval En-*

gland (New York: Oxford University Press, 1986), 188–204; Goldberg, *Women, Work and Life Cycle.*

120. "Church-Wardens' Accounts of Croscombe," 8; BL Add. Mss 32244, fol. 7v.

121. Sharon Farmer, "Down, Out, and Female in Thirteenth Century Paris," *American Historical Review* 103 (1998): 345–72.

122. For more on expectations for maidens see Phillips, *Medieval Maidens.* She argues that parents tempered their desires for submissive daughters by giving important roles in family, and local life. Phillips describes this as "active docility" (13).

123. "So a pon *ys ye* yong men & maydyns of *ys* p'rysse dru themselffe to gethers & wt there geftis & p'vysyon the bofth *yn* a nother challis wt out an chargis of *ye* p'rysse." *Accounts of the Wardens of the Parish of Morebath, Devon: 1520–1573,* ed. Erskine Binney, *Devon Notes and Queries* 2, 3 (1904), 64.

124. Kerry, *A History of St. Lawrence, Reading,* 228.

125. *The Church Book of St. Ewen's,* 68.

126. "to helppe to pay for *ye* gyltyng of our Lady as *ye* maydyns be contendyd wt." *Accounts of the Wardens of Morebath,* 38.

127. "received from Symon Smytte's wyffe and Symken Barber's Wyffe of money by them gadered with [the] virgens upon May day—7s. 7½d." WAC E1, fol. 361.

128. Ibid., fol. 370.

129. *Church Book of St. Ewen's,* 68, 77, 94, 110, 129, 169.

130. Ibid., 68.

131. Ibid., 105, 110.

132. Ibid., 169.

133. Judith Bennett, "Ventriloquisms: When Maidens Speak in English Songs, c. 1300–1550," in *Medieval Woman's Song: Cross Cultural Approaches,* ed. Anne L. Klinck and Ann Marie Rasmussen (Philadelphia: University of Pennsylvania Press, 2002), 187–203.

134. Ibid., 195.

135. Maryanne Kowaleski, "Singlewomen in Medieval and Early Modern Europe: The Demographic Perspective," in *Singlewomen in the European Past, 1250–1800,* ed. Judith Bennett and Amy Froide (Philadelphia: University of Pennsylvania Press, 1998), 38–81.

136. This parish was located in the eastern part of town, not far from the market, and across town from most of the college halls. Cambridge was not only a university town, it was the center of trade for the county and for northern East Anglia. Miri Rubin, *Charity and Community in Medieval Cambridge* (Cambridge: Cambridge University Press, 1987), 33–53.

137. Both guilds have guild certificates from the guild inquiry. Westlake, *The Parish Gilds of Mediaeval England,* 131, 139; Bainbridge, *Gilds in the Medieval Countryside,* 152.

138. Each year the accounts record the elections of the new wardens. The wives of the parish ran Our Lady's light. *Churchwardens' Accounts of St. Mary the*

Great, Cambridge from 1504–1635, ed. J. E. Foster, Cambridge Antiquarian Society 35 (1905).

139. CRO P22/5/1, fol. 75. "Itm rec' of Amy (Anne) Malte money to hir deli-v'red atte foote of the compte in year past—8s. 4d."

140. Ibid., fol. 75.

141. Ibid., fols. 89v, 91.

142. Hanawalt shows that in town parish guilds membership was more exclusive than in rural parish guilds. Hanawalt, "Keepers of the Lights."

143. See, for example, Alice Eyre's will in *The Courts of the Archdeaconry of Buckingham, 1483–1523*, ed. E. M. Elvey, Buckinghamshire Record Society 19 (1975), 412; or Laurence Sowter's will in *Lincoln Wills*, vol. 2, ed. C. W. Foster, Lincolnshire Record Society 10 (1918), 115.

144. LMA DW/PA/7/1 fol. 79; DW/PA/7/2 fols. 1v, 32v, 42, 135, 140, 162v, 172v, DW/PA/7/3 fols. 87, 207-v.; DW/PA/7/4 fols. 34, 55v-56, 80–81v., 89–91.

145. LMA DW/PA/7/4, fol. 117.

146. "Church-Wardens' Accounts of Croscombe," 19, 20.

147. *Somerset Medieval Wills*, vol. 1, ed. F. W. Weaver, Somerset Record Society 16 (1901), 346–48; ibid., vol. 2, ed. F. W. Weaver, Somerset Record Society 19 (1903), 271–72.

148. WAC E1, fol. 370; "Churchwardens' Accounts of St. Thomas, Sarum," 273–75; DRO 1718 ADD/PW3.

149. DRO 2260 A/PW1, fols. 4–9; 1429A/PW2, fol. 1.

150. DRO 1429A/PW2, fols. 63k, 63, 68, 74 passim.

151. DHC PE/WM CW1/40, fol. 22.

152. Ibid., fols. 59–62.

153. BL Add. MSS 6173.

154. *Accounts of the Wardens of Morebath*, 101, 113, 118.

155. WAC E3, 1535–1538 [no folio numbers].

156. *St. Martin-in-the-Fields*, 70

157. Most of Devon's wills were destroyed in World War II.

158. DRO 1429A/PW2; BL Add. Mss. 32244; Eamon Duffy, *The Voices of Morebath: Reformation and Rebellion in an English Village* (New Haven, Conn.: Yale University Press, 2001), 24–32.

159. "Church-Wardens' Accounts for Croscombe," 1–48. The editor did not include names of the guild wardens in the accounts after 1500; so it is not possible to compare this parish with the lay subsidy, and the originals are lost. For Branch family members see "Church-Wardens' Accounts for Croscombe," 19, 26.

160. Peters claims that the position of the female wardens in Horley depended on their husbands serving as warden in the St. Nicholas guild, but his would seem to be incorrect. Peters, *Patterns of Piety*, 36.

161. CRO P22/5/1.

162. Bainbridge, *Gilds in the Medieval Countryside*, 48.

163. Judy Ann Ford, "The Community of the Parish in Late Medieval Kent" (Ph. D. dissertation, Fordham University, 1994), 107–20.

164. PRO E179/184/168, fol. 3

165. BL Add. MSS 6173, fols. 3b, 6b, 7, 7b, 10.

166. Large and prestigious guilds did attract membership from outside the parish. Phythian-Adams, *Desolation of a City*, 139–40; Hanawalt and McRee, "The Guilds of *Homo Prudens*," 166. One man missing from the subsidy was John Peers, whose wife served as a guild warden in 1524, the year of the subsidy he left a will. He names his wife, Joan, and leaves her 20 marks. He also leaves to two older children £6 13s. 4d. each. Poverty was not what kept him off the subsidy. LMA DW/PA/ 7/3 fols. 80v–81r.

167. PRO E179/97/188, fol. 4.

168. PRO E179/96/150.

169. This would fit in with the findings of those who have argued that the gentry were retreating to their manor houses and private chapels, and leaving parish maintenance and administration to the non-elites. See Kümin, *Shaping of a Community*, 32–40.

170. PRO E179/81/144. This roll is very mutilated and between 40 and 50 names are unreadable.

171. CRO P22/5/1, fol. 46v.

172. Ibid., fols. 43v, 57r, 75r, 94v.

173. Ibid., fols. 65v, 57r.

174. *Cambridge Borough Documents*, vol. 1, ed. William Palmer (Cambridge: Bowes and Bowes, 1931), 120.

175. PRO E179/81/144; *Cambridge Borough Documents*, vol. 1, 120.

176. "Church-wardens' Accounts for Croscombe," 12.

177. *Accounts of the Wardens of Morebath*, 22, 160, 94, 105, 29.

178. There do not seem to be any all-women's confraternities in Italy, and women's activities in mixed-sex confraternities were systematically restricted over the course of the fifteenth century. James R. Banker, *Death in the Community: Memorialization and Confraternities in an Italian Commune in the Late Middle Ages* (Athens: University of Georgia Press, 1988), 68–71, 149; Giovanna Casegrande, "Women in Confraternities Between the Middle Ages and the Modern Age: Research in Umbria," *Confraternities: The Newsletter of the Society for Confraternity Studies* 5 (1994): 8–9; Nicholas Terpstra, *Lay Confraternities and Civic Religion in Renaissance Bologna* (Cambridge: Cambridge University Press, 1995), 116–31.

Chapter 5. "To Save Them from Binding on Hock Tuesday": The Rise of a Women's Holiday

1. An earlier version of this chapter was published as "'To Free Them from Binding': Women in the Late Medieval English Parish," *Journal of Interdisciplinary History* 27, 3 (1997): 387–412.

2. WAC E1, fol. 335.

3. A few communities appear to have switched the days around, with the women doing the capturing on Tuesday, while other communities dropped the men's portion of the events altogether. "Churchwardens' Accounts of St. Margaret's, Southwark," ed. J. Payne Collier, *British Magazine* 32 (Nov./Dec. 1847): 493;

Churchwardens' Accounts of St. Mary the Great Cambridge, 1504–1635, ed. J. E. Foster, Cambridge Antiquarian Society 35 (1905), 34, 35, et passim. See E. K. Chambers, *The Mediaeval Stage*, vol. 1 (Oxford: Oxford University Press, 1903), 155 n. 1; Rev. Denne, "Memoir on Hockday," *Archaeologia* 7 (1785): 244–68; Charles Kerry, *A History of the Municipal Church of St. Lawrence, Reading* (Reading: privately printed, 1883), 239; W. Carew Hazlitt, *Faiths and Folklore of the British Isles*, vol. 1 (reprint New York: Benjamin Bloom, 1965), 317; F. A. Gasquet, *Parish Life in Mediaeval England* (London: Methuen, 1906), 242–43; J. Charles Cox, *Churchwardens' Accounts from the Fourteenth Century to the Close of the Seventeenth Century* (London: Methuen, 1913), 261; *REED-Coventry*, ed. R. W. Ingram (Toronto: University of Toronto Press, 1981), lxiii.

4. Gervase Rosser, *Medieval Westminster: 1200–1540* (Oxford: Oxford University Press, 1989), appendix 8, "List of Office Holders," 836–406.

5. WAC E1, fol. 361.

6. Bough and Morland, both gentlemen, lent the parish money on at least one occasion. Bough was also a churchwarden in 1474–1476 and again in 1484–1487. WAC, E1, fols. 361, 380, 421; Rosser, *Medieval Westminster*, 371, 390.

7. Ibid., 396.

8. WAC E1, 361.

9. WAM Lease Book I, fols. 86v, 89v–90, 130, 131v.

10. Ibid., fols. 23v–24.

11. WAC E1, fol. 380.

12. Mistress Hachet's husband or father was warden from 1480 to 1482. WAC E1, fol. 171; Rosser, *Medieval Westminster*, 380. Walter Gardener was warden from 1498 to 1500. E1 fol. 351; Rosser, *Medieval Westminster*, 378.

13. WAC E1, 446.

14. Ibid., fol. 361.

15. Barbara Hanawalt, *The Ties That Bound: Peasant Families in Medieval England* (New York: Oxford University Press, 1986), 188–267; George C. Homans, *English Villagers of the Thirteenth Century* (Cambridge, Mass.: Harvard University Press, 1941), 353–401; Cox, *Churchwardens' Accounts*, 261; Gasquet, *Parish Life*, 241–44; Ronald Hutton, *The Rise and Fall of Merry England: The Ritual Year, 1400–1700* (Oxford: Oxford University Press, 1994), 59.

16. C. R. Cheney, "Rules for the Observance of Feast Days in Medieval England," *Bulletin for the Institute of Historical Research* 34, 90 (November, 1961): 117–47. Hocktide does not appear in any of the episcopal lists of feast days.

17. *Sir Gawain and the Green Knight*, ed. and trans. Brian Stone, 2nd ed. (London: Penguin, 1974) fit III: 48–52; the wardrobe account for Edward I states "to seven ladies of the Queen's bedchamber who took the king in bed on the morrow of Easter and made him fine himself." Chambers, *The Mediaeval Stage*, vol. 1, 156.

18. Lawrence M. Clopper, *Drama, Play, and Game: English Festive Culture in the Medieval and Early Modern Period* (Chicago: University of Chicago Press, 2001), 162–63.

19. Cox, *Churchwardens' Accounts*, 65, 261; Gasquet, *Parish Life*, 242; Kerry, *A History of St. Lawrence, Reading*, 239.

20. Chambers, *The Mediaeval Stage*, vol. 1, 158.

21. Kerry, *A History of the St. Lawrence Reading*, 239.

22. Hutton, *Rise and Fall of Merry England*, 59–60; Andrew Brown, *Popular Piety in Late Medieval England: The Diocese of Salisbury, 1250–1550* (Oxford: Oxford University Press, 1995), 84.

23. Peter Burke, *Popular Culture in Early Modern Europe* (New York: Harper Torchbooks, 1978), 192–94; Sally-Beth MacLean, "Hocktide: A Reassessment of a Popular Pre-Reformation Festival," in *Festive Drama*, ed. Meg Twycross (Woodbridge: D.S. Brewer, 1996), 233–41.

24. Natalie Zemon Davis, "Women on Top," in *Society and Culture in Early Modern France* (Stanford, Calif.: Stanford University Press, 1965), 143–47.

25. Ibid., 150.

26. Ibid., "The Reasons of Misrule,"103, 109.

27. Burke, *Popular Culture*, 200.

28. Chris Humphrey, *The Politics of Carnival: Festive Misrule in Medieval England* (Manchester: Manchester University Press, 2001), 38–62.

29. Pamela Allen Brown, *Better a Shrew Than a Sheep: Women, Drama, and the Culture of Jest in Early Modern England* (Ithaca, N.Y.: Cornell University Press, 2003), 3.

30. Ibid., 9.

31. MacLean, "Hocktide," 239.

32. Quoted in Chambers, *The Mediaeval Stage*, vol. 1, 155 n. 1.

33. In German the word for marriage is *hochzeit*, which might be relevant, although the *OED* claims this is not the case. It is also possible that Hocktide stems from misunderstanding the Latin for *hoc tempus*, "this time," much like St. Sunday was a misunderstanding of "Holy Sunday." See MacLean, "Hocktide," 234.

34. Chambers, *The Mediaeval Stage*, vol. 1, 156.

35. *Calendar of Letter-Books of the City of London at the Guildhall: Letter-Book I (c. 1400–1422)*, ed. Reginald R. Sharpe (London: Corporation of London, 1909), 48, 72, 85, 124, 161, 194, 211.

36. Ibid., 72.

37. *REED-Herefordshire and Worcestershire*, ed. David N. Klausner (Toronto: University of Toronto Press, 1990), 349–50, 553–54.

38. Ibid., 349–50, 553–54.

39. Ibid., 553–54.

40. Quoted in Chambers, *The Mediaeval Stage*, vol. 1, 155 n. 1, "illa die vulgariter dicta Hox Tuisday ludunt in villis trahendo cordas partialiter cum aliis iocis."

41. *REED-Oxford*, vol. 1, ed. John R. Elliott, Jr. and Alan H. Nelson, Alexandra F. Johnston, and Diana Wyatt (Toronto: University of Toronto Press; London: British Library, 2004), 55.

42. See Hutton, *Rise and Fall of Merry England*, 60, nn. 55–57 and 87, n. 94 for his list of pre-Reformation parishes that celebrate Hocktide.

43. The accounts says that the men hid under a place called Castle Hill and it fell on them. Chambers, *The Mediaeval Stage*, vol. 1, 156.

44. It is quite celebrated among scholars of medieval and Early Modern drama. See Chambers, *Mediaeval Stage*, vol. 1, 154–56; *REED-Coventry*, xx. Charles Phythian-Adams studied Coventry and its civic rituals in his article "Ceremony and

the Citizen: The Communal Year at Coventry 1450–1550," in *Crisis and Order in English Towns: 1500–1700*, ed. Peter Clark and Paul Slack (London: Routledge and Kegan Paul,1972), 57–85. He explains that the prominent role of women in the Hocktide reveals a way of temporarily including them in the city's events. Ordinarily the women of Coventry, even the mayor's wife, were excluded from civic processions and ceremony. Civic ceremony served to create and solidify "the welth & worship of the hole body" (58). The "whole body," however, only referred to journeymen and their masters, not laborers, servants and women. Hocktide momentarily reversed this situation and provided an outlet for tension that built up from such a restrictive social and communal structure. He writes, "the Hock Tuesday play used the anonymity of the generalized division of the sexes to reverse temporarily the inequalities existing between married men and women through the medium of conflict" (66). Other towns celebrating this holiday include Henley on Thames, Oxfordshire, and Wallingford, Berkshire.

45. *REED-Coventry*, xx, 7. Many of the original documents for Coventry are now lost, but were partially copied in the early nineteenth century by Thomas Sharp. Chambers remarks that the *Annals* were notoriously inaccurate (*Mediaeval Stage*, vol. 1, 155).

46. "St. Margaret's, Southwark," 493, 495; *The Churchwardens' Accounts of the Parish of All Hallows, London Wall, in the City of London*, ed. Charles Welch (London: privately printed, 1912), 4, 7, 20, 23, et passim. Hutton erroneously attributes the first parish Hocktide celebration to 1468/1470 in the parish of St. Mary the Great in Cambridge (60).

47. Charles Drew, *Early Parochial Organization, in England: The Origins of the Office of Churchwarden*, St. Anthony's Hall Publications 7 (York: Borthwick Institute of Historical Research, 1954), 14–16; Hutton, *Rise and Fall of Merry England*, 49–68.

48. WAC E1, fols. 260, 286, 290.

49. Hocktide was already part of the yearly calendar by the time that the accounts start surviving for the Canterbury parishes of St. Andrew's and St. Dunstan's in 1485, St. Mary, Lambeth, in 1504, St. Giles, Reading, in 1518, St. Martin-in-the-Fields, Westminster, in 1525, and Boxford, Suffolk, in 1530.

50. "receyved of diverse wiffes and maydens to save them from byndyng in hok Tuysday in alle this yere—5s." *Churchwardens' Accounts of St. Edmunds and St. Thomas, Sarum: 1443–1702*, ed. Henry James Fowle Swayne, Wilts Record Society 1 (1896), 50.

51. "devocyon' off the pepull apon hoke tewsday" *St. Edmund's, Salisbury*, 66, 70, 71.

52. "for iij ribbes of bieff to the wyven on hokmonday & for ale & bred for them that gaderyd." GH ms 1239/1 part 1 (St. Mary at Hill CWA), fol. 159.

53. Ibid., fols. 164, 179.

54. "mete and drynke at Hocktyde." KBA KG2/2/1(Kingston-Upon-Thames CWA), fol. 24.

55. *St. Edmund's and St. Thomas', Sarum*, 57.

56. *The Churchwardens' Account Book for the Parish of St. Giles, Reading*, part 1 (1518–1546), ed. W. L. Nash (Reading: privately printed, 1881), 40, 46, 49.

57. MacLean, "Hocktide," 236.

58. Gervase Rosser, "Going to the Fraternity Feast: Commensality and Social Relations in Late Medieval England," *Journal of British Studies* 33, 4 (October 1994): 431.

59. Ibid., 432–33.

60. Ralph A. Houlbrooke, "Women's Social Life and Common Action in England from the Fifteenth Century to the Eve of the Civil War," *Continuity and Change* 1 (1986): 171–75; James C. Scott, *Domination and the Arts of Resistance: Hidden Transcripts* (New Haven, Conn.: Yale University Press, 1990), 65–66.

61. Although I am not trying to suggest a situation that simply places men and women in direct opposition to each other, the lack of a male dinner and the accepted male dominance of parish administrations does imply a certain wariness on the part of the male establishment. It is important, however, to remember that the parish was a unit comprised of men and women, and that while there were times when men and women were separated both physically (church seating), and emotionally (churching) they also shared common goals for the community.

62. *The Early Churchwardens' Accounts of Bishops Stortford, 1431–1558*, ed. Stephen G. Doree, Hertfordshire Record Society 10 (1994), 23.

63. Ibid., 165.

64. Ibid., 171, 177.

65. Ibid., 189, 195.

66. SARS D/P/yat 4/1/1, fol. 66 and possibly 33.

67. Katherine L. French, *The People of the Parish: Community Life in a Medieval English Diocese* (Philadelphia: University of Pennsylvania Press, 2001), 136.

68. SARS D/P/yat 4/1/1, fol. 33, 66, 223, 4/1/2 fol. 23.

69. Some American churches follow similar practices today at their own fairs, although the motif is often a western or cops and robbers one. At the church I attended as a child, the annual fair included a "jail" with a "sheriff" who could be hired to "arrest" anyone. To be released required payment of a "fine." The vicar and parents were favorite targets for children to have "arrested." In this case, the activities outline divisions by age and authority rather than gender. In other respects, Hocktide is similar to Sadie Hawkins day (29 February), when women can ask a men out on a date, a theme often drawn on for high school dances in the late twentieth century. The origin of this day is from Al Capp's comic strip *Li'l Abner*.

70. French, *People of the Parish*, 135–36.

71. Ibid., 99–141.

72. Chambers, *Mediaeval Stage*, vol. 1, 172–75.

73. Hutton, *Rise and Fall of Merry England*, 9, 30–31.

74. French, *People of the Parish*, 130–32.

75. Many antiquarians conflate Hocktide with Hoggling or Hognels, because they sound similar. More recent research has suggested this was not the case. James Stokes, "The Hoglers: Evidence of the Entertainment Tradition in Eleven Somerset Parishes," *Notes and Queries for Somerset and Dorset* 32 (March, 1990): 807–16; Hutton, *Rise and Fall of Merry England*, 12–13; 16–17; 50; 75; 87–89. The seventeenth-century depositions cited by Stokes suggest that some of the seventeenth-century communities that revived Hocktide conflated the two holidays as well. In one parish

men's "hoggling" took place at Christmas and the women's "hoggling" took place at Easter (808).

76. French, *People of the Parish*, 116–27.

77. *Lambeth Churchwardens' Accounts, 1504–1645 and Vestry Book, 1610*, ed. Charles Drew, Surrey Record Society 40 (1940): 1514 the women collected 9s. 7d., the men 3s. 4d. (14); 1515 the women collected 10s. 1d., the men 5s. 7d. (14); 1516 the women collected 6s. 4d., the men 5s. (18). For Croscombe, see French, *People of the Parish*, 117–36.

78. *St. Giles, Reading*, 3–4.

79. Ibid., 12, 32, 39, et passim.

80. *The Churchwardens' Accounts of St. Michael's Church, Oxford*, ed. H. E. Salter, Oxfordshire Archaeological Society 78 (1933): 50, 61.

81. Ibid., 61–102.

82. In Henley on Thames, the King Play was older and apparently longer-lasting than the Hocktide observations. *Henley Borough Records: Assembly Books 1–4: 1395–1543*, ed. P.M. Briers, Oxfordshire Record Society 41 (1960), 58, 125, 147, 189, 198, 204.

83. KBA KG2/2/1, fol. 64.

84. Alexandra F. Johnston and Sally-Beth MacLean, "Reformation and Resistance in Thames/Severn Parishes: The Dramatic Witness," in *The Parish in English Life: 1400–1600*, ed. Katherine L. French, Gary G. Gibbs, and Beat A. Kümin (Manchester: Manchester University Press, 1997), 178–200.

85. Ibid., 182.

86. *Boxford Churchwardens' Accounts: 1530–1561*, ed. Peter Northeast, Suffolk Record Society 23 (1982), xiii.

87. *REED-Cambridge*, vol. 1, ed. Alan H. Nelson (Toronto: University of Toronto Press, 1989), 91.

88. *St. Mary the Great*, 34.

89. Ibid., 82.

90. DRO DD70914 & DD70915.

91. *St. Edmund's, Salisbury*, 79; *St. Thomas', Salisbury*, 274–75.

92. Ibid., 365, 47.

93. WAC E1, fol. 574.

94. "receved of the wymen of Duram rents (in the Strand near Durham St.) the nether parte of the clothe for the said auter being of satten. . . . which was bought wt the money that was gathered amongst the women in Duram Rent on Hoke Monday; receved of the gyft of W. Hebyltwayte two curtaynes of sarcenet colored lyke, being bought wt parte of the said money gathered on hokmonday." *St. Martin-in-the Fields: The Accounts of the Churchwardens; 1525–1603*, ed. trans. John V. Kitto (London: Simpkin, Marshall, Kent, Hamilton, and Co., 1901), 31 (originals destroyed in World War II).

95. Eamon Duffy, *The Stripping of the Altars: Traditional Religion in England, 1400–1580* (New Haven, Conn.: Yale University Press, 1992), 149.

96. GH ms 1239/1 part 2, fol. 488.

97. "Churchwardens' Accounts of St. Andrew's and St. Michael's, Lewes from 1522–1601," ed. Michael Whitley, *Sussex Archaeological Collections* 45 (1902), 47.

98. *All Hallow's, London*, 4, 20, 23, 24, 55.

99. The parish "receyved in gaderyng of almes of dyvers people toward the chirch werks by the chirch wardeyns and their wifs at Witsontyde last past—21s. 4d." Ibid., 24.

100. Ibid., 56, 59.

101. The women of St. Edmund's, Salisbury, held similar collection activities outside of their Hocktide festivities. *St. Edmund's, Salisbury*, 48.

102. *Lambeth Churchwardens' Accounts*, 21, 25, 29, 30, 35 41.

103. *Kentish Visitations of Archbishop William Warham and His Deputies, 1511–1512*, ed. Kathleen Wood-Legh, Kent Records 24 (1984), 101.

104. Burke, *Popular Culture*, 207.

105. "St. Margaret's, Southwark," 489. GH ms 1239/1 part 2, fols. 524, 545b, 559.

106. The form of the accounts until Mary's reign make it impossible to tell if the parish celebrated Hocktide during the Henrecian and Edwardian reforms. *Lambeth Churchwardens' Accounts*, 69–70.

107. Some parishes attempted conscious revivals in the 1660s. David Cressy, *Bonfires and Bells: National Memory and the Protestant Calendar in Elizabethan and Stuart England* (Berkeley: University of California, 1989), 19–20; Hutton, *Rise and Fall of Merry England*, 87.

108. *REED-Oxford*, vol. 1.

109. *REED-Coventry*, xx.

110. "And for becauz the matter mencioneth how valiantly our English women for loove of their cuntree behaved themselves: expressed in actionz & rymez after their maner, they thought it moought moove sum myrth to her Maiestie." Ibid., 273.

111. Martin Ingram, *Church Courts, Sex and Marriage in England, 1570–1640* (Cambridge: Cambridge University Press, 1987), 251.

Chapter 6. A Cross Out of Bread Crumbs: Women's Piety and Impiety

1. W. A. Pantin, "Instructions for a Devout and Literate Layman," in *Medieval Learning and Literature: Essays Presented to Richard William Hunt*, ed. J. J. G. Alexander and M. T. Gibson (Oxford: Oxford University Press, 1979), 398–422. Pantin argues that he was probably a London merchant.

2. Ibid., 400, for Latin see 421.

3. Ibid.

4. Ibid., 408. Pantin, who edited the text, comments that the woman's silence might be a sign or her willingness to put up with her husband's religious eccentricities.

5. Felicity Riddy, "Looking Closely: Authority and Intimacy in the Late Medieval Home," in *Gendering the Master Narrative: Women and Power in the Middle Ages*, ed. Mary C. Erler and Maryanne Kowaleski (Ithaca, N.Y.: Cornell University Press, 2003), 220.

6. Felicity Riddy, "Mother Knows Best: Reading Social Change in a Courtesy Text," *Speculum*, 71 (1996): 66–86: Karen Winstead, *The Virgin Martyrs: Legends of Sainthood in Late Medieval England* (Ithaca, N.Y.: Cornell University Press, 1997), 112–46.

7. Riddy, "Mother Knows Best," 67.

8. H. Leith Spencer, *English Preaching in the Late Middle Ages* (Oxford: Oxford University Press, 1993), 58–60, 166–74.

9. Sermon writers borrowed heavily from each other. Thirteenth-century mendicant sermon collections such as the *Speculum Laicorum*, Jacobus de Voragine's *The Golden Legend*, and John Bromyard's, fourteenth-century *Summa Predicantium* supplied later generations of sermon writers with *exempla*, saints' lives, and moral exhortations. G. R. Owst, *Literature and Pulpit*, 2nd ed. (Oxford: Basil Blackwell, 1961), 181; G. R. Owst, *Preaching in Medieval England* (Cambridge: Cambridge University Press, 1922); Spencer, *English Preaching*; R. N. Swanson, *Religion and Devotion in Europe, c. 1215–1515* (Cambridge: Cambridge University Press, 1995), 64–71.

10. Swanson, *Religion and Devotion*, 63; see also Spencer, *English Preaching*, 163–88, for a discussion of the concern over preaching doctrine. At the beginning of the fifteenth century, the Archbishop of Canterbury, Thomas Arundel, published his *Provincial Constitutions*, which limited the content of what could be preached to the laity and required all preachers to be licensed by the bishop. Only the beneficed clergy could preach on scripture, the unbeneficed were confined to the topics outlined in Pecham's *Ignorantia Sacerdotum*.

11. Spencer argues that the audience for sermons was mixed, and that preachers focused on those whose faith was "lukewarm" and guilty of sins such as uncharity and inconstancy. They did not preach to those lost and unredeemable. *English Preaching*, 64–65.

12. Leo Carruthers, "'No Womman of No Clerk is Preysed': Attitudes to Women in Medieval English Religious Literature," in *A Wyf Ther Was: Essays in Honour of Paule Mertens-Fonck*, ed. Juliette Dor (Liège: Université de Liège, 1992), 49–60.

13. Quoted in Ruth Mazo Karras, *Common Women: Prostitutions and Sexuality in Medieval England* (Oxford: Oxford University Press, 1996), 105.

14. Nerit Ben-Aryeh Debby argues a similar point in her article, "The Preacher as Woman's Mentor," in *Preacher, Sermon, and Audience in the Middle Ages*, ed. Carolyn Muessig (Leiden: Brill, 2002), 229–54.

15. Riddy, "Looking Closel," 212–28.

16. Winstead, 112–46.

17. Anna Dronzek, "Gendered Theories of Education in Fifteenth-Century Conduct Books," in *Medieval Conduct*, ed. Kathleen Ashley and Robert L. A. Clark (Minneapolis: University of Minnesota Press, 2001), 143.

18. Ibid., 142.

19. Sandy Bardsley, *Venomous Tongues: Speech and Gender in Late Medieval England* (Philadelphia: University of Pennsylvania Press, 2006).

20. Sarah Salih, "At Home; Out of the House," in *Cambridge Companion to Medieval Women's Writing*, ed. Carolyn Dinshaw and David Wallace (Cambridge: Cambridge University Press, 2003), 132–33.

21. "How the Good Wife Taught Her Daughter," in *The Babees Book*, ed. Frederick J. Furnivall, EETS 32 (1868), 37–39.

22. For more on the relationship between women's speech and sin see Bardsley, *Venomous Tongues*.

23. Ibid., 26–44.

24. "What the Wise Man Taught His Son," in *The Babees Book*, 49–50.

25. Miri Rubin, *Charity and Community in Medieval Cambridge* (Cambridge: Cambridge University Press, 1987), 291–99.

26. Patricia Cullum, "'And Her Name Was Charite': Charitable Giving by and for Women in Late Medieval Yorkshire," in *Women in Medieval English Society*, ed. P. J. P. Goldberg (Stroud: Sutton Publishing, 1997), 182–211.

27. Ibid., 203.

28. Sharon Farmer, "The Leper in the Master Bedroom: Thinking Through a Thirteenth-Century *Exemplum*," in *Framing the Family: Narrative and Representation in the Medieval and Early Modern Periods*, ed. Rosalynn Voaden and Diane Wolfthal (Tempe: Arizona Center for Medieval and Renaissance Studies, 2005), 79.

29. *Middle English Sermons*, ed. Wooburn O. Ross, EETS 209 (1940), 186.

30. "Come O blessed of my Father, inherit the kingdom prepared for you from the foundation of the world; for I was hungry and you gave me food, I was thirsty and you gave me drink, I was a stranger and you welcomed me, I was naked and you clothed me, I was sick and you visited me, I was in prison and you came to me." Burial of the dead comes from the book of Tobit 1: 16–17: "And in the time of Enemessar I gave many alms to my brethren and gave my bread to the hungry, and my clothes to the naked: and if I saw any of my nation dead, or cast about the walls of Nineveh, I buried him."

31. *The Lay Folks Catechism* taught that the clergy must instruct the laity regularly on the seven works of mercy. *Lay Folks Catechism*, ed. T. F. Simmons and H. E. Nolloth, EETS 118 (1901), 70.

32. John Mirk, *Festial*, ed. Theodor Erbe, EETS 96 (1905), 221–35.

33. Ibid., 231.

34. Ibid., 230–32; Mirk's discussion of Mary and Martha on the feast of the Assumption followed a long tradition of sermon construction. Bernard of Clairvaux preached on this subject in his Feast of the Assumption sermon. See Giles Constable, "The Interpretation of Mary and Martha," in *Three Studies in Medieval Religious and Social Thought* (Cambridge: Cambridge University Press, 1995), 66 n. 232.

35. "By þes too sustyrs holy chyrch undyrstondyth too maner of lyuyng of man, þat on ys actyf, þat oþer ys contemplatyf. Actyf yn besynes of þe world þe whech may not be wythout trowbull and gret bysynes. But hit schall be done only for God sake, and forto haue wherwyth a mon may receyue pore, and ȝeve þat hom nedyth mete and dryng, and cloþyng, and herbar and helpe þe seke, and vysed hom þat be in prison, and bury þe dede. Þys ys understond by Martha." Mirk, *Festial*, 230–31.

36. See Constable, "The Interpretation of Mary and Martha," 1–141, for a full discussion of the changing interpretations and attitudes toward these two women. The increasing value of Martha was part of the change in medieval Christianity that

developed in the twelfth century, as theologians began to grapple with the issue of how those outside of the monastery were to be saved.

37. Maiju Lehmijoki-Gardner, *Worldly Saints: Social Interaction of Dominican Penitent Women in Italy, 1200–1500* (Helsinki: Suomen Historiallinen Seura, 1999), 94.

38. Ibid., 92–123.

39. Judy Ann Ford, *John Mirk's* Festial: *Orthodoxy, Lollardy, and the Common People in Fourteenth-Century England* (Cambridge: D.S. Brewer, 2006).

40. Mirk, *Festial*, 232.

41. Ibid., 231.

42. Constable, "The Interpretation of Mary and Martha," 5, 107.

43. *The Book of the Knight of the Tower*, trans. William Caxton, ed. M.Y. Offord, EETS supp. ser. 2 (1971), 134.

44. Riddy, "Mother Knows Best," 67–68.

45. Þey seruyn of thre thynggys. For þey been ordeynyd to steryn manys mende to thynkyn of Cristys incarnacioun and of his passioun and of holye seyntys lyuys. Alos þey been ordeynyd to steryn mannys affeccioun and his herte to deuocioun, for often man is more steryd be syghte þan by heryng or redyngge. Also þey been ordeynyd to been a tokene and a book to þe lewyd peple, þat þey moun redyn in ymagerye and peynture þat clerkys redyn in boke. . . . *Dives and Pauper*, vol. 1, part 1, ed. Priscilla Heath Barnum, EETS 275 (1976), 82.

46. These paintings were not frescos, which are paint applied to wet plaster. In the case of English wall paintings, the artists typically employed the technique called secco, pigment applied to dry plaster. The paint did not become part of the plaster as in frescos. The two most common textual sources for church images were the *Golden Legend* and the *Speculum Historiale* by Vincent de Beauvais. Both were educated clerics concerned about the quality and orthodoxy of pastoral care. Marian C. Gill, "Late Medieval Wall Painting in England: Content and Context, 1350–1530" (Ph.D. thesis, Courtauld Institute of Art, University of London, 2002), 223.

47. E. W. Tristram, *English Wall Paintings in the Fourteenth Century* (London: Routledge and Kegan Paul, 1955), 4; E. Clive Rouse, *Medieval Wall Paintings* (Princes Risborough, Bucks.: Shire Publications, 1991), 25–30. Tristram argues that large murals disappears, but Gill has found that several churches, such as the guild chapel in Stratford-upon-Avon and Astbury in Cheshire, had large murals painted after rebuilding their church in perpendicular gothic. Gill, "Late Medieval Wall Painting," 121.

48. Heather Swanson, *Medieval Artisans: An Urban Class in Late Medieval England* (Oxford: Basil Blackwell, 1989), 92–94. Organization of the trade combined with relatively large amounts of surviving glass makes it possible to identify schools or workshops of glaziers. Christopher Woodforde, *Stained Glass in Somerset 1250–1830* (London: Oxford University Press, 1946); Christopher Woodforde, *The Norwich School of Glass Painting in the Fifteenth Century* (London: Oxford University Press, 1950).

49. Richard Marks explains that while yeoman farmers could often afford monumental brasses, which might only cost £2, windows such as the seven sacraments at Lydd, Kent, cost £10. Richard Marks, *Stained Glass in England During the*

Middle Ages (Toronto: University of Toronto Press, 1993), 6; Swanson, *Medieval Artisans*, 93–94.

50. Marks, *Stained Glass,* 67–91; C. David Benson, *"Piers Plowman* and Parish Wall Paintings," *Yearbook of Langland Studies* 11 (1998): 5 n. 11; see also Rouse, *Medieval Wall Paintings,* 35 for a slightly different list of categories.

51. Rouse, *Medieval Wall Paintings,* 30.

52. He is the most commonly depicted saint in the surviving wall paintings.

53. SARS D/P/yat 4/1/1, fol. 80.

54. Ibid., fols. 80–82, 86, 88.

55. *The Pre-Reformation Record of All Saints', Bristol,* part 1, ed. Clive Burgess, Bristol Record Society's Publications 46 (1995), 14.

56. David Park, "Wall Paintings," in *The Art of Chivalry: Art in Plantagenet England, 1200–1400,* ed. J. Alexander and Paul Binski (London: Royal Academy of Arts in Association with Weidenfeld and Nicolson, 1987), 129.

57. Gill, "Late Medieval Wall Painting in England," 522–25.

58. Women: Booke, Norfolk (destroyed); Dalham, Suffolk; Edingthorpe, Norfolk, Hardwick, Cambridgeshire; Hoxne, Suffolk; Irthlingborough, Northants. (destroyed); Lathbury, Buckinghamshire (destroyed and uncertain); Potter Heigham, Norfolk; Ringshall, Suffolk; Toddington, Bedfordshire. Men: Arundel, Sussex (angels); Baulking, Berkshire; Catfield, Norfolk (uncertain); Kimpton, Bedfordshire (destroyed); Kingston, Cambridgeshire; Linkinhorne, Cornwall; Netherbury, Dorset (destroyed); Oddington, Gloucestershire; Pickering, North Yorkshire; Quatt, Shropshire (destroyed). Both are: Barnby, Suffolk (uncertain); Ruislip, Middlesex (uncertain); Trotton, Sussex; Wickhampton, Norfolk; Moulton, St. Mary, Norfolk; and Ruabon, Clwyd, Wales. See also Gill, "Preaching and Image," 175.

59. I am working here from the same assumption as David Benson, which he lays out in *"Piers Plowman* and Parish Wall Paintings," 5. "Every image now extant represents many that were present in the Middle Ages. If several survive today, we can be reasonably confident that many more existed in the Middle Ages."

60. The painting's location could also encourage women to pay particular attention to these images. Without knowledge of specific seating plans, however, this is much harder to demonstrate. Paintings located on the north wall might address women, because in many churches women sat on the north side of the nave. Of the 35 known locations for works of mercy paintings, 18 (51 percent) were on north walls; of these, four show women, eight depict men, and six are now destroyed and are unknown. At the same time, murals on the south wall would be more visible to women sitting across from them. Gill, "Late Medieval Wall Painting in England," 522–25; Gill argues that the painting "warning to gossips" is often positioned in the back of the church, where those less interested in the service probably sat. Mariam Gill, "Female Piety and Impiety: Selected Images of Women in Wall Paintings in England After 1300," in *Gender and Holiness: Men, Women, and Saints in Late Medieval Europe,* ed. Samantha J. E. Riches and Sarah Salih (London: Routledge, 2002), 109.

61. Ibid. *Literature and Pulpit,* 2nd ed. (Oxford: Blackwell, 1961), 112.

62. Kim M. Phillips, "Maidenhood as the Perfect Age of Women's Life," in

Young Medieval Woman, ed. Katherine J. Lewis, Noel James Menuge, and Kim M. Phillips (New York: St. Martin's Press, 1999), 1–24.

63. Gill, "Female Piety and Impiety," 112.

64. Phillips, "Maidenhood," 2–3.

65. Shannon McSheffrey, "Place, Space and Situation: Public and Private in the Making of Marriage in Late Medieval London," *Speculum* 79 (2004): 979.

66. Gill, "Late Medieval Wall Painting in England," 94–112; Gill, "Female Piety and Impiety," 102.

67. Aqweynte þee not with eche man þat gooþ bi / þe stete; / Þouȝ ony man speke to þee, Swiftli þou him grete; / Lete him go bi þe wey: bi him þat þou ne / stoned. "How the Good Wife Taught Her Daughter," 40.

68. Go not to þe wrastelinge, ne to schotynge at/ cok, / As it were a strumpet or a gigggelot [sic]: / wone at hom, douȝtir, and loue þi werk myche." Ibid., 40.

69. The same artist or workshop produced the two Norfolk paintings in Wickhampton and Moulton St. Mary, and possibly the one in Hoxne, Suffolk. They share details of composition and framing, although the extensive damage to the paintings at Hoxne and Moulton St. Mary make them difficult to see. Gill, "Female Piety and Impiety," 103.

70. This may also be the case at Moulton St. Mary, although the damage makes it difficult to see. There are only two figures standing over the coffin, one a priest. The figure attending the priest does not have the same shaped head covering as the women performing other works, suggesting that it is also a man.

71. See Miriam Gill's database: http://www.le.ac.uk/arthistory/seedcorn/contents.html.

72. Gill, "Female Piety and Impiety," 113–14.

73. http://www.le.ac.uk/ha/seedcorn/contents.html

74. She is Rose the Regrater in *Piers Plowman*, there is an alewife in one of the Chester Mystery plays, and she is the main character in the misogynistic poem "The Tunning of Elynour Rummyng." For a discussion of this image see Judith Bennett, "Misogyny, Popular Culture, Women's Work," *History Workshop* 31 (1991): 166–88; Ralph Hanna, "Brewing Trouble: On Literature and History—and Alewives," in *Bodies and Disciplines: Intersections of Literature and History in Fifteenth-Century England*, ed. Barbara A. Hanawalt and David Wallace (Minneapolis: University of Minnesota Press, 1996), 1–18.

75. Gill, "Late Medieval Wall Painting in England," 419–22. St. Edmund's wall painting has been much restored, while that at Holy Trinity, Coventry is quite disfigured. She is also possibly present in the doom at Brooke, Norfolk. J. E. Ashby, "English Medieval Murals of the Doom. A Descriptive Catalogue and Introduction" (M. Phil. thesis, University of York, 1980), 213–15. See also http://www.le.ac.uk/ha/seedcorn/contents.html

76. Marks, *Stained Glass*, 80.

77. Woodforde, *The Norwich School*, 195–96.

78. *William Langland's Piers the Plowman, the C Version*, trans. George Economou (Philadelphia: University of Pennsylvania Press, 1996), passus 8, 70.

79. Benson, "*Piers Plowman* and Parish Wall Paintings," 1–11.

80. This was also a concern for Jacques de Vitry in his *Sermones Vulgares*. See Farmer, "Leper in the Master Bedroom," 94–99.

81. Kay E. Lacey, "Women and Work in Fourteenth and Fifteenth Century London," in *Women and Work in Pre-Industrial England*, ed. Lindsey Charles and Lorna Duffin (London: Croom Helm, 1985), 24–82; Kowaleski, "Women's Work in a Market Town: Exeter in the Late Fourteenth Century," in *Women and Work in Preindustrial Europe*, ed. Barbara Hanawalt (Bloomington: Indiana University Press, 1986), 145–64; Judith Bennett, "The Village Ale-Wife: Women and Brewing in Fourteenth-Century England," in *Women and Work in Preindustrial Europe*, 20–36; Barbara Hanawalt, *The Ties That Bound: Peasant Families in Medieval England* (New York: Oxford University Press, 1986); P. J. P. Goldberg, *Women, Work, and Life Cycle in a Medieval Economy: Women in York and Yorkshire, c. 1300–1520* (Oxford: Oxford University Press, 1992); Judith M. Bennett, *Ale, Beer and Brewsters in England: Women's Work in a Changing World, 1300–1600* (Oxford: Oxford University Press, 1996); Marjorie Keniston McIntosh, *Working Women in English Society, 1300–1620* (Cambridge: Cambridge University Press, 2005).

82. Ruth Mazo Karras, "Gendered Sin and Misogyny in John of Bromyard's *Summa Predicantium*," *Traditio* 47 (1992): 242–44.

83. Ibid.

84. Ibid., 237.

85. Alan Caiger-Smith, *English Medieval Mural Paintings* (Oxford: Oxford University Press, 1963), 54–55.

86. Arundel, Sussex; Brooke, Norfolk (destroyed); Catfield, Norfolk; Dalham, Suffolk; Hardwick, Cambridgeshire; Hoxne, Suffolk; Hunworth, Norfolk (destroyed); Ingatestone, Essex (destroyed, uncertain); Kentford, Suffolk; Kidlington, Oxfordshire (destroyed); Kingson, Cambridgeshire; Langar, Clwyd; Milcombe, Oxfordshire (destroyed); Milton Abbas, Dorset (destroyed); Netherbury, Dorset (destroyed); Oddington, Gloucestershire; Quatt, Shropshire (destroyed); Ruabon, Clwyd (uncertain); Ruislip, Middlesex; Trotton, Sussex. Gill, "Late Medieval Wall Painting," 517–25.

87. Woodforde, *Stained Glass in Somerset*, 170–71.

88. This is in variance with the more learned discourse that associated women with lust quite often. See Karras, *Common Women*, 107. To be sure, wall paintings of the sin of lust frequently have both a man and a woman, but this does not focus them on women particularly.

89. http://www.le.ac.uk/ha/seedcorn/contents.html; Gill, "Late Medieval Wall Painting in England," 419.

90. http://www.le.ac.uk/ha/seedcorn/contents.html

91. *The Book of the Knight of the Tower*, 74.

92. *Middle English Sermons*, 156.

93. "For þe shame of þe world more þan for þe awe of god she forȝave hure þe tresspasse, for she wold not þat worthy Estur day be withowte her ryghtynges." Ibid., 40.

94. Mirk, *Festial*, 279–80.

95. "In al the parisshe wif ne was ther noon / That to the offtynge before hire sholde goon; / And if ther dide, certeyn so wroth was she / That she was out of alle

charitee. / Hir coverchiefs ful fine weren of ground; / I dorste swere they weyeden ten pound / That on a Sonday weren upon hir heed. Hir hosen weren of fyn scarlet reed, Ful streite yteyd, and shoes ful moyste and newe." Geoffrey Chaucer, "General Prologue," *The Riverside Chaucer*, ed. Larry D. Benson (Boston: Houghton Mifflin, 1987), lines 450–57; 30.

96. Originally from the *Golden Legend*. See Jacobus de Voragine, *The Golden Legend*, vol. 2, trans. William Granger Ryan (Princeton, N.J.: Princeton University Press, 1993), 155.

97. Mirk, *Festial*, 247–48.

98. Ibid., 248.

99. "Blessyd maydyn, oft I haue prayed þe for delyuerance of my sonne, and am not holpen. Wherfore, so as ȝe wyll not helpe me to haue my son, I wyll take youris ynstyd of myn, tyll ȝe send myn home,' and toke þe ymage þat was on oure lady kne, and bare hit home, and lappyt hit yn whitte cloþes, and clene lokket hyt vp yn hur cofur. They, yn þe nyght aftyr, oure lady aperet to hur sonne yn þe prison, and vndyd his bondes, and openet all þe dyrres, and sayde to hym: 'Go hom to þi modyr, and say I pray hur, as I send to hir hor sonne hole and sownde, so bring scho my sonne aȝeyne to me without harme,'" Ibid., 248.

100. "was soo deuot yn oure lady seruyce, þat scho ȝaf for hor loue all þe cloþys þat scho had, saue þe febullyst þat sche ȝod yn herselfe." Ibid., 60–61.

101. "Hit fell so þat on Condylmasse-day, scho wold haue goon to chyrche. But for scho was not honest arayede, scho dyrst not for schame; for scho had not honest cloþes, as scho was wont to have. Then when othyr men went to þe chyrch, scho was wondyr sory; for scho schuld be without masse þat holy fest." Ibid., 60–61.

102. "Seynt Poule techeþ how þe goode wommen schulle atire hem whan þei schulle go to chirche to bidde here bedes to God; he seiþ þei scholde have honest cloþinge and atire and not to moche, þat is to seie after þat þe womman is of state and as þe state askeþ. For þat þt is to moche too womman, nis not to moche to some oþere. For moche more bihoueþ to þe queen þan to a burgeies wife, or to a marchaundes or to a squyers or a-noþer symple lady, as a knyȝtes wif." *The Book of Vices and Virtues*, ed. W. Nelson Francis, EETS 217 (1942), 239–40.

103. Frances Elizabeth Baldwin, *Sumptuary Legislation and Personal Regulation in England* (Baltimore: Johns Hopkins University Press, 1926), 45–72; Alan Hunt, *Governance of the Consuming Passions: A Brief History of Sumptuary Law* (New York: St. Martin's Press, 1996).

104. Gail McMurray Gibson, "Blessing from Sun and Moon: Churching as Women's Theater," in *Bodies and Disciplines: Intersections of Literature and History in Fifteenth-Century England*, ed. Barbara A. Hanawalt and David Wallace (Minneapolis: University of Minnesota Press, 1996), 139–43; Eamon Duffy, *The Stripping of the Altars: Traditional Religion in England, 1400–1580* (New Haven, Conn.: Yale University Press, 1992), 15–17.

105. Ford, *John Mirk's Festial*, 32–33.

106. Peter Biller, "Marriage Patterns and Women's Lives: A Sketch of a Pastoral Geography," in *Women in Medieval English Society*, ed. P. J. P. Goldberg (Stroud: Sutton, 1997), 60–107.

107. "Hyt were fulle harde þat penaunce to do / That þe lawes ordeyneth to, /

Therefore by gode dyscrecyone,' Þow moste in confessyone, / Ioyne penaunce both hared & lyȝte, / As þou here aftere lerne myȝte. But sykerly penaunce wyþowte schryfte / Helpeþ luytel þþe sowle ryte"; John Mirk, *Instructions for Parish Priests*, ed. E. Peacock, EETS 31 (1868), 25.

108. "But when a wommon cometh to þe, / Loke hyre face þat þou ne se, / But teche hyre to knele downe þe by, / And sum what þy face from hyre ou wry, / Stylle as stone þer þow sytte, / And kepe þe welle þat þou ne spytte. / Koghe þow not þenne þy þonkes, / Ny wrynge þou not with þy schonkes, / Lest heo suppose þow make þat fare / For wiatynge þat þou herest þare, / But syt þou style as any mayde / Tyle þat heo have alle I-sayed, / And when heo stynteþ & seyþ no more, / ȝef þour syst heo nedeth lore / Þenne spek to hyre on þys wyse, / And say, "take þe gode a-vyse, / And what maner þynge þou art gulty of, / Telle me boldely & make no scoff." Ibid., 27–28.

109. Biller, 65–66; BL Sloane Ms. 1584.

110. BL Sloane Ms. 1584, fol. 9b.

111. Ibid., fol. 8.

112. Ibid., fol. 9b, 8.

113. Ibid., fol. 8.

114. Swanson, *Church and Society*, 165. A few visitation reports from medieval England do exist, see, for example, "Visitation Returns of Hereford in 1397," ed. Arthur T. Bannister, *English Historical Review* 44 (1929): 92–101; 45 (1930): 444–63; *The Courts of the Archdeaconry of Buckingham, 1483–1523*, ed. E. M. Elvey, Buckingham Record Society 19 (1975); *Kentish Visitations of Archbishop William Warham and His Deputies, 1511–1512*, ed. Kathleen Wood-Legh, Kent Records 24 (1984); *Visitations in the Diocese of Lincoln: 1517–1531*, vols. 1–3, Lincoln Record Society 33, 35, 37 (1936, 1938, 1940); *The Register of John Chandler, Dean of Salisbury, 1404–1417*, ed. T. C. B. Timmins, Wiltshire Record Society, 39 (1983). The Council of Trent required regular visitations to investigate and correct the local clergy and educate the superstitious population about Rome's new religious policies. As a result, visitation records become more common, allowing scholars to compare the effectiveness of religious reformers from region to region and over time. Scholars' primary concern is the effect of clerical mandates on the lay population and its practice of religion. See, for example, Robert Sauzet, *Les visites pastorales dans le diocèse de Chartres pendant la première moitié du XVIIe siècle* (Rome: Edizioni di Storia e Letteratura, 1975); Keith P. Luria, *Territories of Grace: Cultural Changes in the Seventeenth-Century Diocese of Grenoble* (Berkeley: University of California Press, 1991); Allyson M. Poska, *Regulating the People: The Catholic Reformation in Seventeenth-Century Spain* (Leiden: Brill, 1998).

115. Dorothy Owen, *Church and Society in Medieval Lincolnshire* (Lincoln: Lincolnshire Local History Society, 1971), 35; Robert Brentano, *Two Churches: England and Italy in the Thirteenth Century* (Berkeley: University of California Press, 1988), 66–69.

116. Marjorie Keniston McIntosh, *Controlling Misbehavior in England, 1370–1600* (Cambridge: Cambridge University Press, 1998).

117. *Kent Visitations*, xxi–xxii. Only a tenth of complaints were referred to the bishop.

118. In Kent, 16 of 260 parishes, 6 percent, had no complaints or citations. In Lincoln, 201 of 1,143 parishes and chapels, 18 percent, reported all was well.

119. Ibid., vol. 1, xxiv.

120. Ibid.

121. Ibid.

122. Ibid., 23.

123. "the parson dealithe not fairly with the vestments whan he puttith them on hym." *Kentish Visitations*, 224.

124. The full numbers and percentages are as follows:

	Hereford, 1397	Wiltshire, 1405	Lincoln, 1815–19
Single men	310 (63)	32 (46)	61 (52)
Married men	169 (34)	27 (39)	30 (25)
Unknown	16 (3)	10 (14)	27 (23)
Total lay men	495	69	118
Single women	403 (68)	49 (51)	75 (56)
Married women	151 (26)	44 (45)	43 (32)
Unknown	38 (6)	4 (4)	15 (11)
Total lay women	592	97	133

125. For these and all other Hereford statistics see "Visitation of Parishes by John Trefnant, Bishop of Hereford, 1397," typescript from original in Hereford Cathedral Archives MS 1779, transcribed by Christopher Whittick, unpublished English translation also by Christopher Whittick, used with permission.

126. See also Karen Jones, *Gender and Petty Crime in Late Medieval England: the Local Courts in Kent, 1460–1660* (Woodbridge: Boydell, 2006), 156–71.

127. *Register of John Chandler*, 1–50.

128. *Lincoln Visitations*, 1, 69; for appearance of maidens see *Lincoln Wills*, vol. 3, ed. C. W. Foster, Lincoln Record Society 24 (1930), 28.

129. Karen Jones found similar behavior in Kent; see her *Gender and Petty Crime*, 179–85.

130. "Visitation of Parishes by John Trefnant, Bishop of Hereford, 1397," 1.3.10; 10.2.5; 10.3.4; 44.1.9. For women cited alone see 1.3.9 and 1.3.10.

131. *Visitations in the Diocese of Lincoln*, vol. 1.

132. *Kentish Visitations*, 57, 73, 74.

133. *Lincoln Visitations*, 1, 113; *Kentish Visitations*, 74.

134. *Lincoln Visitations*, 1, 138.

135. Beat Kümin, "Sacred Church and Worldly Tavern: Reassessing an Early Modern Divide," in *Sacred Space in Early Modern Europe*, ed. Will Coster and Andrew Spicer (Cambridge: Cambridge University Press, 2005), 17–38.

136. *Kent Visitations*, 73, 118.

137. Bardsley, *Venomous Tongues*, 26–44.

138. Ibid., 67–89.

139. *Visitations in the Diocese of Lincoln: 1517–1531*, vol. 1, 44, 60, 71, 96, 97, 107, 113.

140. *Kent Visitations*, 203–4.

Epilogue: Women and the Reformation

1. "a greate number of wemen which were among other the chief doers of the said unlawfull assemble and also diverse of thaier husbands," who denied that "there were any men disguised or appareled in wemens appareill amonge them" and that "they were comaunded procured conceilled or abetted by thaier husbondes or by any other men," quoted in Christine Peters, *Patterns of Piety: Women, Gender and Religion in Late Medieval and Reformation England* (Cambridge: Cambridge University Press, 2003), 156.

2. Ralph A. Houlebrooke, "Women's Social Life and Common Action in England from the Fifteenth Century to the Eve of the Civil War," *Continuity and Change* 1 (1986): 171–89.

3. Eamon Duffy, *The Stripping of the Altars: Traditional Religion in England, 1400–1580* (New Haven, Conn.: Yale University Press, 1992), 385, points out the danger in criticizing the king for his changes.

4. Peters, *Patterns of Piety*, 154–69.

5. Ibid., 158.

6. Ibid., 155.

7. Ronald Hutton, "The Local Impact of the Tudor Reformations," in *The English Reformation Revised*, ed. Christopher Haigh (Cambridge: Cambridge University Press, 1987), 116.

8. *The Church Book of St. Ewen's : 1454–1485*, ed. Betty Masters and Elizabeth Ralph, Bristol and Gloucestershire Archaeological Society 6 (1967), 170, 182.

9. ERO D/P/27/5/1, fol. 43.

10. Sara Mendelson and Patricia Crawford, *Women in Early Modern England, 1550–1720* (Oxford: Oxford University Press, 1998), 226.

11. WCA E3, 1536 [no folio numbers].

12. *Acounts of the Wardens of the Parish of Morebath, Devon: 1520–1573*, ed. Erskine Binney, *Devon Notes and Queries* 2, 3 (1904), 113.

13. Women's collective activities reappeared only once in 1564, but they were called the Maiden's guild and did not have the same kind of membership. *The Churchwardens' Accounts of St. Michael's Church, Chagford: 1480–1600*, ed. Francis Mardon Osborne (Chagford: Devon: privately printed, 1979), 203.

14. Katherine L. French, *The People of the Parish: Community Life in a Medieval English Diocese* (Philadelphia: University of Pennsylvania Press, 2001), 168.

15. Peters, *Patterns of Piety*, 171–74.

16. Duffy, *Stripping of the Altars*, 427.

17. David Cressy, "Purifications, Thanksgiving and the Churching of Women in Post-Reformation England," *Past and Present* 141 (1993): 106–46.

18. See Eric Josef Carlson, *Marriage and the English Reformation* (Oxford: Blackwell, 1994).

19. Diana O'Hara, "The Language of Tokens and the Making of Marriage," *Rural History* 3 (1992): 1–40.

20. For more on women churchwardens see Katherine L. French, "Women Churchwardens in Late Medieval England," in *The Parish in Late Medieval England:*

Proceedings of the 2002 Harlaxton Symposium, ed. Clive Burgess and Eamon Duffy (Donington, Lincs.: Shaun Tyas/Paul Watkins, 2006), 302–21.

21. *Accounts of Morebath*, 111, 114.

22. Ibid., 146.

23. SARS DD/WO 49/1, fol. 80.

24. SARS DD/CT 77, fol. 63.

25. PRO E179/170/194.

26. No churchwardens' accounts survive for this parish, but Elizabeth is listed as churchwarden in the Chantry Survey that preceded Edward VI's confiscation of guild and parish goods and property. "Inventories of the Goods and Ornaments of the Churches of the County of Surrey in the Reign of Edward VI," *Surrey Archaeological Collections* 4 (1899), 181–82.

27. *VCH-Surrey*, III, ed. H. E. Malden (London: Institute for Historical Study, 1967), 197.

28. SARS DD/CT 77 fols. 63, 68; D/P/tin, 4/1/1 fol. 148; *Accounts of the Wardens of Morebath*, 161.

29. Eamon Duffy, *Voices of Morebath: Reformation and Rebellion in an English Village* (New Haven, Conn.: Yale University Press, 2001), 111–51, esp. 124–25.

30. *Accounts of Morebath*, 160; see also Duffy, *Voices of Morebath*, 124.

31. *Accounts of Morebath*, 2, 77.

32. Duffy reads her and her husband's behavior against their relative poverty, but certainly her later behavior, while still probably informed by poverty, could also have assumed a religious dimension. With the abolition of stocks and the dismantling of side altars dedicated to saints, she might have believed that mandatory parish involvement was going to cost her less. See *Voices of Morebath*, 35, 124–25.

33. Lyndal Roper, *The Holy Household: Women and Morals in Reformation Augsburg* (Oxford: Oxford University Press, 1989).

Bibliography

Unpublished Primary Sources

British Library
  Add. Ms. 40729—CWA Yeovil, Somerset (1519 only)
  Add Ms. 6173—CWA Horley, Surrey
  Add. Ms. 32244—CWA Stratton, Cornwall
  Edgerton Ms. 1912—CWA St. Mary's Dover, Kent
  Sloane, Ms. 1584—John Gybson's Confessor's Manual
  Add Ms. 24202—Lollard Treatise against Saints
Bodleian, Duke Humphrey Library
  Rawlinson D 786—CWA Sutterton, Lincolnshire
Cambridgeshire Record Office-Cambridge
  P11/5/2—CWA Bassingbourn
  P22/5/1—CWA Holy Trinity
Devon Record Office-Exeter
  2659A/PW1—CWA Broadhempston
  1429A/PW2–4—CWA Chagford
  DD61218-DD61325—CWA Dartmouth
  DD7091-DD709—CWA Exeter-St Mary Steps
  PW 1–2—CWA Exeter-St. Petrock
  482APW1–18—CWA Tavistock
  2260A/PW1—CWA Woodland
Dorset Record Office-Dorchester
  PE/WM/CW—CWA Wimborne Minster
Essex Record Office-Chelmsford
  D/P 11/5/1—CWA Great Dunmow
  D/DBy Q18—CWA Saffron Walden
Hereford Cathedral Archives
  "Visitation of Parishes by John Trefnant, Bishop of Hereford, 1397," tran-
    scription and translation by Christopher Whittick.
Kingston Borough Library
  KG2/2/1—CWA Kingston-Upon-Thames
Lincoln Record Office
  Calendar of Memoranda Book of Bishop John Dalderby of Lincoln, vol. 3.
London Guildhall Library
  1239/1 parts 1 and 2—CWA St. Mary at Hill
  1454/1–12—CWA St. Botolph Aldersgate

1279/1—CWA St. Andrew Hubbard
9064/2—Act Book of the Commissary Court of the Diocese of London,
    1487–97
London Metropolitan Archives
    SP92/SAV/24—Inventory, Southwark, St. Olave,
    DL/C/205—Consistory Court of the Diocese of London Deposition Book,
        1467–76.
    DW/PA/7/1—Archdeanery of Surrey Wills
National Archive: Public Record Office-London
    C1—Early Chancery Documents
    STAC 1 and STAC 2—Early Proceedings for the Court of Star Chamber
    E179—Lay Subsidies
    E117—Chantry Certificates
    Prob 11—Prerogative Court of Canterbury Will Registers
Norfolk Record Office-Norfolk
    PD52/71—CWA Swaffham
    PD52/233—GA St. John's, Swaffham
Somerset Archive and Record Service-Taunton
    D/P/ba. mi. 4/1/1–6—CWA Bath
    D/P/ban 4/1/1—CWA Banwell
    D/P/bw—CWA Bridgwater
    D/P/gla.j. 4/1/1–11—CWA Glastonbury
    DD/WO 49/1—CWA Nettlecombe
    D/P/pilt 4/1/1–2—CWA Pilton
    D/P/stogs 4/1/1—CWA Stogursey
    D/P/tin 4/1/1–2—CWA Tintinhull
    DD/CT 77—CWA Trull
    D/P/yat 4/1/1–3—CWA Yatton
    D/P/yeo. j. 4/1/6; T/PH/bm 31 s/1800—CWA Yeovil
Suffolk Record Office-Ipswich
    FC 89/A2/1—CWA Brundish
    FC112/E1/1—CWA Dennington
    FC 185/E1/1—CWA Walbersick
Surrey History Centre
    Sher/10/1—CWA Shere
Westminster Abbey Muniments
    Assumption Guild Accounts
    St. Mary Rounceval Guild Accounts
    Abbey Lease Books I and II
Westminster Archive Centre
    CWA St. Margaret's Westminster, E1 and E2
    Peculiar Court of Westminster Wills, Registers-Bracy and Wyks

Printed Primary Sources

"Accounts of the Churchwardens of St. Dunstan's, Canterbury." Ed. J. M. Cowper. *Archaeologia Cantiana: Transactions of the Kent Archaeological Society* 17 (1887): 289–321.

Accounts of the Churchwardens of St. Martin's, Leicester: 1489–1844. Ed. Thomas North. Leicester: Samuel Clarke, 1884.

Accounts of the Wardens of the Parish of Morebath, Devon: 1520–1573. Ed. Erskine Binney. *Devon Notes and Queries* 2, 3 (1904).

Act Book of the Ecclesiastical Court of Whalley, 1510–1538. Ed. Alice M. Cooke. Chetham Society 44. 1901.

Ancient Deeds Belonging to the Corporation of Bath. Ed. C. W. Shickle. Bath: Bath Record Society, 1921.

Anglo Saxon Wills. Ed. Dorothy Whitelock. Cambridge: Cambridge University Press, 1930.

The Babees Book. Ed. F. J. Furnivall. EETS 32. 1868.

Bede. *Ecclesiastical History of the English People.* Trans. Leo Sherley-Price. Harmondsworth: Penguin, 1990.

The Black Death. Ed. Rosemary Horrox. Manchester: Manchester University Press, 1994.

The Book of the Knight of La Tour-Laundry. Ed. Thomas Wright. EETS 33. 1868.

The Book of the Knight of the Tower. Trans. William Caxton. Ed. M. Y. Offord. EETS supp. ser. 2. 1971.

The Book of Vices and Virtues. Ed. W. Nelson Francis. EETS 217. 1942.

Boxford Churchwardens' Accounts: 1530–1561. Ed. Peter Northeast. Suffolk Record Society 23. 1982.

Bridgwater Borough Archives: 1200–1468. Vols. 1–4. Ed. Thomas Bruce Dilks. Somerset Record Society 48, 53, 58, 60. 1933, 1938, 1945, 1948.

Bridgwater Borough Archives: 1468–1485. Vol. 5. Ed. R. W. Dunning and T. D. Tremlett. Somerset Record Society 70. 1971.

Cambridge Borough Documents. Vol. 1. Ed. William Palmer. Cambridge: Bowes and Bowes, 1931.

Cambridge Gild Records. Ed. Mary Bateson. Cambridge Antiquarian Society 39. 1903.

Calendar of Inquisitions Post Mortem. Vol. 6 (Edward II). London: HMSO, 1910.

Calendar of Inquisitions Post Mortem. Vol. 19 (7–14 Henry IV). Ed. J. L. Kirby. London: HMSO, 1992.

Calendar of Inquisitions Post Mortem. Vol. 22, 1–5 Henry VI (1422–1427). Ed. Kate Parkin. London: Boydell Press and National Archives: Public Record Office, 2003.

Calendar of Inquisitions Post Mortem. Vol. 2, *Henry VII.* London: HMSO, 1915.

Calendar of Letter Books of the City of London at the Guildhall: Letter-Book I (c. 1400–1422). Ed. Reginald R. Sharpe. London: Corporation of London, 1909.

Chaucer, Geoffrey. *The Riverside Chaucer.* Ed. Larry D. Benson. Boston: Houghton Mifflin, 1987.

The Church Book of St. Ewen's, Bristol: 1454–1485. Ed. Betty R. Masters and Elizabeth Ralph. Bristol and Gloucestershire Archaeological Society 6. 1967.

The Church Records of St. Andrew Hubbard, Eastcheap, c. 1450–c. 1570. Ed. Clive Burgess. London Record Society 34. 1999.

Churchwarden Account Book for the Parish of St. Giles, Reading. Part 1 (1518–1546). Ed. W. L. Nash. Reading: privately printed, 1881.

"Churchwardens' Account Book of Rotherfield." Ed. Canon Goodwyn. *Sussex Archaeological Collections* 41 (1898): 25–48.

Church-Wardens' Accounts for Croscombe, Pilton, Yatton, Tintinhull, Morebath and St. Michael's Bath: Ranging from 1349–1560. Ed. Edmund Hobhouse. Somerset Record Society 4. 1890.

"Churchwardens' Accounts for Sherbourne Minster." *Somerset and Dorset Notes and Queries* Vol. 23: 209 (1941), 209–12; Vol. 23: 210 (1941), 229–35; Vol. 23: 211 (1941), 249–52; Vol. 23: 212 (1942), 269–72; Vol. 23: 213 (1942), 289–93.

"Churchwardens' Accounts for St. John's Glastonbury." Ed. F. W. Weaver and C. H. Mayo. *Somerset and Dorset Notes and Queries* Vol. 4 (1895): 89–96, 137–44, 185–92, 235–40, 281–88, 329–36, 379–84.

Churchwardens' Accounts of Ashburton, 1479–1580. Ed. Alison Hanham. Devon and Cornwall Record Society n.s. 15. 1970.

Churchwardens' Accounts of the Church and Parish of St. Michael Without the North Gate, Bath: 1349–1575. Ed. C. B. Pearson. Somerset Archaeological and Natural History Society 23. 1877.

"Churchwardens' Accounts of the Parish of St. Andrew, Canterbury." Ed. Charles Cotton. *Archaeologia Cantiana: Transactions of the Kent Archaeological Society* 32 (1917): 181–246; 33 (1920): 1–46.

The Churchwarden's Accounts of Prescot, Lancashire: 1523–1607. Ed. F. A. Bailey. Lancashire and Cheshire Record Society 106. 1953.

"Churchwardens' Accounts of St. Andrews and St. Michael's, Lewes from 1522–1601." Ed. Michael Whitley. *Sussex Archaeological Collections* 45 (1902): 40–61.

Churchwardens' Accounts of St. Edmund and St. Thomas, Sarum: 1443–1702. Ed. Henry James Fowle Swayne. Wiltshire Record Society 1. 1896.

Churchwardens' Accounts of the Parish of All Hallows, London Wall, in the City of London. Ed. Charles Welch. London: privately printed, 1912.

"Churchwardens' Accounts of St. Margaret's, Southwark." Ed. J. Payne Collier. *British Magazine* 32 (November 1847): 481–96; (December 1847): 638–51.

Churchwardens' Accounts of St. Mary the Great, Cambridge from 1504–1635. Ed. J. E. Foster. Cambridge Antiquarian Society 35. 1905.

The Churchwardens' Accounts of St. Michael's Church, Chagford: 1480–1600. Ed. Francis Mardon Osborne. Chagford, Devon: privately printed, 1979.

Churchwardens' Accounts of St. Michael's Church, Oxford. Ed. H. E. Salter. Oxfordshire Archaeological Society 78. 1933.

Corpus Juris Civilis II: Codex Iustianus. Ed. Paulus Krueger. Berlin: Weidmannsche, 1954.

Councils and Synods. Vol. 2, parts 1 and 2, ed. F. M. Powicke and C. R. Cheney. Oxford: Oxford University Press, 1964.

The Courts of the Archdeaconry of Buckingham: 1483–1523. Ed. E. M. Elvey. Buckingham Record Society 19. 1975.

Dives and Pauper. Vol. 1, parts 1 and 2. Ed. Priscilla Heath Barnum. EETS 275, 280. 1976, 1980.

The Early Churchwardens' Accounts of Bishops Stortford. Ed. Stephen G. Doree. Hertfordshire Record Society 10. 1994.

English Gilds: The Original Ordinances of More Than 100 English Gilds. Ed. Toulmin Smith. EETS 40. 1870.

English Medieaval Lapidaries. Ed. Joan Evans and Mary S. Serjeantson. EETS 190. 1933.

Forunatus, Venantius. "The Life of Holy Radegund." In *Sainted Women of the Dark Ages,* ed. and trans. Jo Ann McNamara and John E. Halborg with Gordon Whatley. Durham, N.C.: Duke University Press, 1992. 65–70.

"Gaton: Inventories of the Goods and Ornaments of the Churches of the County of Surrey in the Reign of Edward VI." *Surrey Archaeological Collections* 4 (1899): 181–82.

Henley Borough Records: Assembly Books 104: 1395–1543. Ed. P. M. Briers. Oxford Record Society 41. 1960.

Index of the Probate Records of the Consistory Court of Ely: 1449–1858. Part 2 (F-P). Comp. Clifford and Dorothea Thurley, ed. Elisabeth Leedham-Green and Rosemary Rudd. British Record Society 106. 1994.

Kentish Visitations of Archbishop William Warham and His Deputies, 1511–1512. Ed. Kathleen L. Wood-Legh. Kent Records 24. 1984.

Lambeth Churchwardens' Accounts, 1504–1645 and Vestry Book: 1610. Part 1. Ed. Charles Drew. Surrey Record Society 40. 1940.

Langland, William. *Piers the Plowman, the C Version.* Trans. George Economou. Philadelphia: University of Pennsylvania Press, 1996.

Lay Folk's Catechism. Ed. T. F. Simmons and H. E. Nolloth. EETS 118. 1901.

The Lay Folk's Mass Book. Ed. T. F. Simmons. EETS 71. 1879.

Lincoln Wills: 1427–1532. Vols. 1–3. Ed. C. W. Foster. Lincoln Record Society 5, 10, 24, 1914, 1918, 1930.

Lincoln Wills. Vol. 4. Ed. David Hickman. Lincoln Record Society 89. 2001.

London and Middlesex Chantry Certificates: 1548. Ed. C. J. Kitching. London Record Society 16. 1980.

The Macro Plays. Ed. Frederick J. Furnivall. EETS 91. 1904.

Magnus, Albertus. *Book of Minerals.* Trans. Dorothy Wyckoff. Oxford: Oxford University Press, 1967.

Mannyng, Robert. *Handlyng Synne.* Ed. Idelle Sullens. Binghamton: Center of Medieval and Renaissance Studies, State University of New York, 1983.

The Medieval Records of a London City Church (St. Mary at Hill): 1420–1559. Ed. Henry Littlehales. EETS 125. 1904.

Middle English Sermons. Ed. Woodburn Ross. EETS 209. 1940.

Mirk, John. *Festial.* Ed. Theodor Erbe. EETS 96. 1905.

———. *Instructions for Parish Priests.* Ed. Edward Peacock. EETS 31. 1868.

"Order of Seating in Ashton Kirk." Ed. Winifred M. Bowman. In *England in Ashton-Under-Lyne.* Cheshire: John Sherratt, 1960. 167–68.

Pantin, W. A., ed. "Instructions for a Devout and Literate Layman." In *Medieval Learning and Literature: Essays Presented to Richard William Hunt*, ed. J. J. G. Alexander and M. T. Gibson. Oxford: Oxford University Press, 1979. 398–422.

The Paston Letters. Ed. James Gairdner. Reprint Gloucester: Sutton, 1986.

The Peasants' Revole of 1381. 2nd ed. Ed. Barrie Dobson. Houndsmill: Macmillan, 1983.

The Pre-Reformation Record of All Saints', Bristol. Parts 1 and 2. Ed. Clive Burgess. Bristol Record Society's Publications 46 and 53. 1995 and 2000.

REED-Cambridge. 2 vols. Ed. Alan H. Nelson. Toronto: University of Toronto Press, 1989.

REED-Coventry. Ed. R. W. Ingram. Toronto: University of Toronto Press, 1981.

REED-Herefordshire and Worcestershire. Ed. David N. Klausner. Toronto: University of Toronto Press, 1990.

REED-Oxford. 2 vols. Ed. John R. Elliott, Jr. and Alan H. Nelson, Alexandra F. Johnston, and Diana Wyatt. Toronto: University of Toronto Press: London: British Library, 2004.

The Register of John Chandler Dean of Salisbury, 1404–1407. Ed. T. C. B. Timmins, Wiltshire Record Society 39. 1984.

"Reports and Expenses in the Building of Bodmin Church: 1469–1472." Ed. John James Wilkinson. *Camden Miscellany VII*. Camden Society o.s. 14. 1874. iii–49.

St. Martin-in-the-Fields: The Accounts of the Churchwardens, 1525–1603. Ed. John V. Kitto. London: Simpkin, Marshall, Kent, Hamilton, 1901.

The Sarum Missal. Ed. J. Wickam Legg. Oxford: Oxford University Press, 1916.

The Sarum Missal in English. Part 1. Trans. Frederick E. Warren. London: Alexander Moring, 1911.

Sir Gawain and the Green Knight. 2nd ed. Ed. and trans. Brian Stone. London: Penguin, 1974.

Somerset Medieval Wills: 1383–1500. Vols. 1–3. Ed. F. W. Weaver. Somerset Record Society 16, 19, 21. 1901, 1903, 1905.

Speculum Sacerdotale. Ed. Edward Weatherly. EETS 200. 1936.

The Transcript of the Churchwardens' Accounts of the Parish of Tilney, All Saints, Norfolk: 1443–1589. Ed. A. D. Stallard. London: Mitchell, Hughes and Clarke, 1922.

"Visitation Returns of Hereford in 1397." Ed. Arthur T. Bannister. *English Historical Review* 44 (1929): 92–101; 45 (1930): 444–63.

Visitations in the Diocese of Lincoln: 1517–1531. Ed. A. Hamilton Thompson. Lincoln Record Society 33, 35. 1940–41.

Voragine, Jacobus de. *The Golden Legend: Readings of the Saints*. Vols. 1 and 2. Ed. William Granger Ryan. Princeton, N.J.: Princeton University Press, 1993.

"Wives at the Tavern." In *Songs and Carols*. Ed. Thomas Wright. London: Percy Society, 1847. 91–95.

Secondary Works

Aers, David. "Altars of Power: Reflections on Eamon Duffy's *The Stripping of the Altars*." *Literature and History* 3 (1994): 90–105.

Aers, David and Lynn Staley. *The Powers of the Holy: Religion, Politics, and Gender in Late Medieval English Culture*. University Park: Pennsylvania State University Press, 1996.

Armstrong, C. A. J. "The Piety of Cicely, Duchess of York. In *England, France and Burgundy in the Fifteenth Century*. London: Hambledon Press, 1983. 135–56.

Ashby, J. E. "English Medieval Murals of the Doom. A Descriptive Catalogue and Introduction." M. Phil. thesis, University of York, 1980.

Aston, Margaret. "Lollard Women Priests?" In *Lollards and Reformers: Images and Literacy in Late Medieval Religion*. London: Hambledon, 1983. 49–70.

———. "Segregation in Church." In *Women in the Church*, ed. W. J. Sheils and Diana Wood. Studies in Church History 27. Oxford: Blackwell, 1990. 237–94.

Baily, Mark. "Rural Society." In *Fifteenth-Century Attitudes: Perceptions of Society in Late Medieval England*, ed. Rosemary Horrox. Cambridge: Cambridge University Press, 1994. 105–68.

Bainbridge, Virginia. *Gilds in the Medieval Countryside: Social and Religious Change in Cambridgeshire, 1350–1558*. Woodbridge: Boydell, 1996.

Baker, Nigel and Richard Holt. "The Origin of Urban Parish Boundaries." In *The Church in the Medieval Town*, ed. T. R. Slater and Gervase Rosser. Aldershot: Ashgate, 1998. 209–35.

Baldwin, Frances Elizabeth. *Sumptuary Legislation and Personal Regulation in England*. Baltimore: Johns Hopkins University Press, 1926.

Banker, James R. *Death in the Community: Memorialization and Confraternities in an Italian Commune in the Late Middle Ages*. Athens: University of Georgia Press, 1998.

Bardsley, Sandy. *Venomous Tongues: Speech and Gender in Late Medieval England*. Philadelphia: University of Pennsylvania Press, 2006.

Barron, Caroline M. "'The Golden Age' of Women in Medieval London." *Reading Medieval Studies* 15 (1989): 35–58.

———. "Johanna Hill (d. 1441) and Johanna Sturdy (d. 1460), Bell Founders." In *Medieval London Widows: 1300–1500*, ed. Caroline M. Barron and Anne F. Sutton. London: Hambleton Press, 1994. 99–111.

———. "The Parish Fraternities of Medieval London." In *The Church in Pre-Reformation Society: Essays in Honour of F. R. H. Duboulay*, ed. Caroline M. Barron and Christopher Harper-Bill. Woodbridge, Suffolk: Boydell, 1985. 13–37.

Becker, Lucinda M. *Death and the Early Modern Woman*. Aldershot: Ashgate, 2003.

Bedell, John. "Memory and Proof of Age in England." *Past and Present* 162 (1999): 3–27.

Bell, Susan Groag. "Medieval Women Book Owners: Arbiters of Lay Piety and Ambassadors of Culture." *Signs* 7 (1981–82): 742–68.

Benadusi, Giovanna. "Investing the Riches of the Poor: Servant Women and Their Last Wills." *American Historical Review* 109 (2004): 805–26.

Ben-Aryeh Debby, Nerit. "The Preacher as Woman's Mentor." In *Preacher, Sermon, and Audience in the Middle Ages*, ed. Carolyn Muessig. Leiden: Brill, 2002. 229–54.

Bennett, Judith M. *Ale, Beer and Brewsters in England: Women's Work in a Changing World, 1300–1600*. Oxford: Oxford University Press, 1996.

————. "Confronting Continuity." *Journal of Women's History* 9 (1997): 73–94.

————. "Medieval Women, Modern Women: Across the Great Divide." In *Culture and History, 1350–1600*, ed. David Aers. Detroit: Wayne State University Press, 1992. 147–75.

————. "Misogyny, Popular Culture, Women's Work." *History Workshop* 31 (1991): 166–88.

————. "Ventriloquisms: When Maidens Speak in English Songs, c. 1300–1550." In *Medieval Woman's Song: Cros- Cultural Approaches*, ed. Anne L. Klinck and Anne Marie Rasmussen. Philadelphia: University of Pennsylvania Press, 2002. 187–203.

————. "The Village Ale-Wife: Women and Brewing in Fourteenth-Century England." In *Women and Work in Preindustrial Europe*, ed. Barbara A. Hanawalt. Bloomington: Indiana University Press. 1986. 20–36.

Bennett, Stewart and Nicholas Bennett, eds. *An Historical Atlas of Lincolnshire*. Hull: University of Hull Press, 1993.

Benson, David. "*Piers Plowman* and Parish Wall Paintings." *Yearbook of Langland Studies* 11 (1998): 1–38.

Beresford, Maurice and H. P. R. Finberg. *English Medieval Boroughs: A Hand-List*. Totowa, N.J.: Rowman and Littlefield, 1973.

Biller, Peter. "The Common Women in the Western Church in the Thirteenth and Fourteenth Centuries." In *Women in the Church*, ed. W. J. Sheils and Diana Wood. Studies in Church History 27. Oxford: Blackwell, 1990. 127–57.

————. "Marriage Patterns and Women's Lives: A Sketch of a Pastoral Geography." In *Women in Medieval English Society*, ed. P. J. P. Goldberg. Stroud: Sutton, 1997. 60–107.

Blamires, Alcuin. "Beneath the Pulpit." In *Cambridge Companion to Medieval Women's Writing*, ed. Carolyn Dinshaw and David Wallace. Cambridge: Cambridge University Press, 2003. 141–60.

Bolton, James. *The Medieval English Economy: 1150–1500*. London: Dent, 1980.

————. " 'The World Upside Down': Plague as an Agent of Economic and Social change." In *The Black Death in England*, ed. Mark Ormrod and Phillip Lindley. Stamford, Lincs.: Paul Watkins, 1996. 17–78.

Bossy, John. *Christianity in the West: 1400–1700*. New York: Oxford University Press, 1985.

————. "The Mass as a Social Institution, 1200–1700." *Past and Present* 100 (1983): 27–61.

Brentano, Robert. *Two Churches: England and Italy in the Thirteenth Century*. Berkeley: University of California Press, 1988.

Britnell, Richard. "The Feudal Reaction After the Black Death in the Palatinate of Durham." *Past and Present* 128 (1990): 28–47.

Brown, Andrew. *Popular Piety in Late Medieval England: The Diocese of Salisbury, 1250–1550*. Oxford: Oxford University Press, 1995.

Brown, Pamela Allen. *Better a Shrew Than a Sheep: Women, Drama, and the Culture of Jest in Early Modern England*. Ithaca, N.Y.: Cornell University Press, 2003.

Brusco, Elizabeth E. *The Reformation of Machismo: Evangelical Conversion and Gender in Colombia*. Austin: University of Texas Press, 1995.

Burdick, John R. *Looking for God in Brazil*. Berkeley: University of California Press, 1993.

Burgess, Clive. "The Benefactions of Mortality: The Lay Response in the Medieval Urban Parish." In *Studies in Clergy and Ministry in Medieval England: Purvis Seminar Series*, ed. David M. Smith. York: Borthwick Institute of Historical Research, 1991. 65–87.

———. "'By Quick and by Dead': Wills and Pious Provision in Late Medieval Bristol." *English Historical Review* 142 (1982): 837–58.

———. "'A Fond Thing Vainly Invented': An Essay on Purgatory and Pious Motive in Late Medieval England." In *Parish, Church and People: Local Studies in Lay Religion, 1350–1750*, ed. S. J. Wright. London: Hutchinson, 1988. 56–84.

———. "Late Medieval Wills and Pious Conventions: Testamentary Evidence Reconsidered." In *Profit, Piety and the Professions in Later Medieval England*, ed. Michael Hicks. Gloucester: Alan Sutton, 1990. 14–33.

———. "London Parishes in Times of Change: St. Andrew Hubbard, Eastcheap, c. 1450–1570." *Journal of Ecclesiastical History* 53 (2002): 38–64.

———. "Pre-Reformation Churchwardens' Accounts and Parish Government: Lessons from London and Bristol." *English Historical Review* 117 (2002): 306–32.

———. "Shaping the Parish: St. Mary at Hill, London, in the Fifteenth Century." In *The Cloister and the World: Essays in Medieval History in Honour of Barbara Harvey*, ed. John Blair and Brian Golding. Oxford: Oxford University Press, 1996. 246–86.

———. "Strategies for Eternity: Perpetual Chantry Foundation in Late Medieval Bristol." In *Religious Belief and Ecclesiastical Careers in Late Medieval England*, ed. Christopher Harper-Bill. Woodbridge: Boydell, 1991. 1–32.

Burgess, Clive and Beat A. Kümin. "Penitential Bequests and Parish Regimes in Late Medieval England." *Journal of Ecclesiastical History* 44 (1993): 610–30.

Burke, Peter. *Popular Culture in Early Modern Europe*. New York: Harper Torchbooks, 1978.

Bynum, Carolyn Walker. *Holy Feast and Holy Fast: The Religious Significance of Food to Medieval Women*. Berkeley: University of California Press, 1987.

———. *Jesus as Mother: Studies in the Spirituality of the High Middle Ages*. Berkeley: University of California Press, 1982.

Caiger-Smith, Alan. *English Medieval Mural Paintings*. Oxford: Oxford University Press, 1963.

Campbell, B. M. S. "Population Pressure, Inheritance and the Land Market in a Fourteenth-Century Peasant Community." In *Land, Kinship, and Life-Cycle*, ed. Richard M. Smith. Cambridge: Cambridge University Press, 1984. 87–134.

Carlson, Eric Josef. *Marriage and the English Reformation*. Oxford: Blackwell, 1994.

Carpenter, Christine. "Religion of the Gentry of Fifteenth-Century England." In *England in the Fifteenth Century: Proceedings of the 1986 Harlaxton Symposium*, ed. Daniel Williams. Woodbridge: Boydell, 1987. 53–74.

Carruthers, Leo. "'No Womman of No Clerk is Preysed': Attitudes to Women in Medieval English Religious Literature." In *A Wyf Ther Was: Essays in Honour of Paule Mertens-Fonck*, ed. Juliette Dor. Liège: Université de Liège, 1992. 49–60.

Casegrande, Giovanna. "Women in Confraternities Between the Middle Ages and the Modern Ages: Research in Umbria." *Confraternities: The Newsletter of the Society for Confraternity Studies* 5 (1994): 3–13.

Catalogue of English Ecclesiastical Embroideries of the Thirteenth and Fourteenth Centuries. London: Victoria and Albert Museum Department of Textiles, 1930.

Cavassa, Silvano. "Double Death: Resurrection and Baptism in a Seventeenth-Century Rite." Trans. Mary M. Gallucci. In *History from Crime*, ed. Edward Muir and Guido Ruggiero. Baltimore: Johns Hopkins University Press, 1994. 1–31.

Chambers, E. K. *The Medieval Stage.* 2 vols. Oxford: Oxford University Press, 1903.

Cheney, C. R. *English Synodalia of the Thirteenth Century.* Oxford: Oxford University Press, 1941.

———. *From Becket to Langton.* Manchester: Manchester University Press, 1956.

———. "Rules for the Observance of Feast Days in Medieval England." *Bulletin for the Institute of Historical Research* 34, 90 (1961): 117–47.

Chong, Kelly H. "Agony in Prosperity: Conversion and the Negotiation of Patriarchy Among South Korean Evangelical Women." *Harvard Divinity Bulletin* 32 (2004): 11–15.

Cipolla, Carlo M. *Before the Industrial Revolution: European Society and Economy, 1000–1700.* 2nd ed. New York: Norton, 1980.

Clopper, Lawrence M. *Drama, Play, and Game: English Festive Culture in the Medieval and Early Modern Period.* Chicago: University of Chicago Press, 2001.

Cohn, Samuel. "The Black Death: End of a Paradigm." *American Historical Review* 107 (2002): 703–38.

———. *The Cult of Remembrance and the Black Death: Six Renaissance Cities in Central Italy.* Baltimore: Johns Hopkins University Press, 1992.

Constable, Giles. "The Interpretation of Mary and Martha." In *Three Studies in Medieval Religious and Social Thought.* Cambridge: Cambridge University Press, 1995. 1–142.

Coster, William. "Community, Piety, and Family in Yorkshire Wills Between the Reformation and the Restoration." In *Life and Thought in the Northern Church, c. 1100–1700: Essays in Honour of Claire Cross*, ed. Diana Wood. Woodbridge: Boydell, 1999. 511–31.

———. "Purity, Profanity, and Puritanism: The Churching of Women, 1500–1700." In *Women in the Church*, ed. W. J. Sheils and Diana Wood. Oxford: Blackwell for the Ecclesiastical History Society, 1990. 377–87.

Cotton, Simon. "Medieval Roodscreens in Norfolk: Their Construction and Painting Dates. *Norfolk Archaeology* 40 (1987): 44–54.

Cox, J. Charles. *Bench-Ends in English Churches.* Oxford: Oxford University Press, 1916.

———. *Churchwardens' Accounts: From the Fourteenth Century to the Close of the Seventeenth Century.* London: Methuen, 1913.

Cox, J. Charles and W. H. St. John Hope. *Chronicle of the Collegiate Church of All Saints, Derby.* London: Bemrose and Sons, 1881.

Crawford, Patricia. *Women and Religion in England: 1500–1720.* New York: Routledge, 1993.

Cressy, David. *Bonfires and Bells: National Memory and the Protestant Calendar in Elizabethan and Stuart England*. Berkeley: University of California Press, 1989.
———. "Purifications, Thanksgiving and the Churching of Women in Post-Reformation England." *Past and Present* 141 (1993): 106–46.
Crouch, David J. F. *Piety, Fraternity, and Power: Religious Gilds in Late Medieval Yorkshire*. York: York Medieval Press, 2000.
Cullum, Patricia. "'And Her Name Was Charite': Charitable Giving by and for Women in Late Medieval Yorkshire." In *Women in Medieval English Society*, ed. P. J. P. Goldberg. Stroud: Sutton, 1997. 182–210.
Dale, Marian K. "The London Silkwomen of the Fifteenth Century." *Economic History Review* 4, 3 (1933): 324–35.
Daniell, Christopher. *Death and Burial in Medieval England, 1066–1550*. London: Routledge, 1997.
Davies, R. A. "The Effects of the Black Death on the Parish Priests of the Medieval Diocese of Coventry and Litchfield." *Historical Research* 62 (1989): 85–90.
Davis, Natalie Zemon. *Society and Culture in Early Modern France*. Stanford, Calif.: Stanford University Press, 1965.
Denne, Reverend. "Memoir on Hockday." *Archaeologia* 7 (1785): 244–68.
Dinn, Robert. "Death and Rebirth in Late Medieval Bury St. Edmunds." In *Death in Towns: Urban Responses to the Dying and the Dead, 1000–1600*, ed. Steven Bassett. London: Leicester University Press, 1992. 151–69.
———. "'Monuments Answerable to Men's Worth': Burial Patterns, Social Status, and Gender in Late Medieval Bury St. Edmunds." *Journal of Ecclesiastical History* 46 (1995): 237–55.
Dohar, William J. *The Black Death and Pastoral Leadership: The Diocese of Hereford in the Fourteenth Century*. Philadelphia: University of Pennsylvania Press, 1995.
Douglas, Audrey. "'Our Thanssyng Day': Parish Dance and Procession in Salisbury." In *English Parish Drama*, ed. Alexandra F. Johnston and Wim Hüsken. Amsterdam: Rodopi, 1996. 41–64.
———. "Salisbury Women and the Pre-Elizabethan Parish." In *Women, Marriage, and Family in Medieval Christendom: Essays in Memory of Michael M. Sheehan*, ed. Constance M. Rousseau and Joel T. Rosenthal. Kalamazoo, Mich.: Medieval Institute Publications, 1998. 79–117.
Drew, Charles. *Early Parochial Organisation in England: The Origin of the Office of Churchwarden*. St. Anthony's Hall Publications 7. York: Borthwick Institute of Historical Research, 1954.
Dronzek, Anna. "Gendered Theories of Education in Fifteenth-Century Conduct Books." In *Medieval Conduct*, ed. Kathleen Ashley and Robert L. A. Clark. Minneapolis: University of Minnesota Press, 2001. 135–39.
Duffy, Eamon. "Holy Maydens, Holy Wyfes: The Cult of Women Saints in Fifteenth and Sixteenth Century England." In *Women in the Church*, ed. W. J. Sheils and Diana Wood. Studies in Church History 27. Oxford: Blackwell, 1990. 175–96.
———. "The Parish, Piety, and Patronage in Late Medieval East Anglia: The Evidence of Rood-Screens." In *The Parish in English Life: 1400–1600*, ed. Kather-

ine L. French, Gary G. Gibbs, and Beat A. Kümin. Manchester: Manchester University Press, 1997. 133–62.

———. *The Stripping of the Altars: Traditional Religion in England, 1400–1580*. New Haven, Conn.: Yale University Press, 1992.

———. *The Voices of Morebath: Reformation and Rebellion in an English Village*. New Haven, Conn.: Yale University Press. 2001.

———. "Religious Belief." In *A Social History of England: 1200–1500*, ed. Rosemary Horrox and W. Mark Ormord. Cambridge: Cambridge University Press, 2005. 293–339.

Dyer, Christopher. *An Age of Transition: Economy and Society in England in the Later Middle Ages*. Oxford: Oxford University Press, 2005.

———. "The English Medieval Village Community and Its Decline." *Journal of British Studies* 33 (1994): 419–24.

———. "The Social and Economic Background to the Rural Revolt of 1381." In *The English Rising of 1381*, ed. Rodney H. Hilton and T. H. Aston. Cambridge: Cambridge University Press, 1984. 9–42.

———. *Standards of Living in the Later Middle Ages: Social Change in England, c. 1200–1520*. Cambridge: Cambridge University Press, 1989.

———. "Work Ethics in the Fourteenth Century." In *The Problem of Labour in Fourteenth-Century England*, ed. James Bothwell, P. J. P. Goldberg, and W. M. Ormrod. York: York Medieval Press, 2000. 21–42.

Egan, Geoff and Frances Pritchard. *Medieval Excavations in London*. Vol. 3, *Dress Accessories, 1150–1450*. Woodbridge: Boydell, 2002.

Farmer, Sharon. "Down, Out, and Female in Thirteenth Century Paris." *American Historical Review* 103 (1998): 345–72.

———. "The Leper in the Master Bedroom: Thinking Through a Thirteenth-Century *Exemplum*." In *Framing the Family: Narrative and Representation in the Medieval and Early Modern Periods*, ed. Rosalynn Voaden and Diane Wolfthal. Tempe: Arizona Center for Medieval and Renaissance Studies, 2005. 79–100.

Farnhill, Ken. *Guilds and the Parish of Community in Late Medieval East Anglia, c. 1470–1550*. York: York Medieval Press. 2001.

———. "Guilds, Purgatory, and the Cult of the Saints: Westlake Reconsidered." In *Christianity and Community in the West: Essays for John Bossy*, ed. Simon Ditchfield. Aldershot: Ashgate, 2001. 59–71.

Federico, Sylvia. "The Imaginary Society: Women in 1381." *Journal of British Studies* 40 (2001): 159–83.

Finlay, Roger. *Population and Metropolis: The Demography of London, 1580–1640*. Cambridge: Cambridge University Press, 1981.

Ford, Judy Ann. "The Community of the Parish in Late Medieval Kent." Ph.D. dissertation, Fordham University, 1994.

———. *John Mirk's Festial: Orthodoxy, Lollardy and the Common People in Fourteenth-Century England*. Cambridge: D.S. Brewer, 2006.

French, Katherine L. "'I Leave My Best Gown as a Vestment': Women's Spiritual Interests in the Late Medieval English Parish." *Magistra* 4 (1998): 57–77.

———. "Maidens' Lights and Wives' Stores: Women's Parish Guilds in Late Medieval England." *Sixteenth Century Journal* 29, 2 (1998): 399–425.

———. "Parochial Fund-Raising in Late Medieval Somerset." In *The Parish in English Life: 1400–1600*, ed. Katherine L. French, Gary G. Gibbs, and Beat A. Kümin. Manchester: Manchester University Press, 1997. 115–32.

———. *The People of the Parish: Community Life in a Medieval English Diocese.* Philadelphia: University of Pennsylvania Press, 2001.

———. "'The Seat Under Our Lady': Gender and Seating in the Late Medieval English Parish Church," In *Women's Space: Parish, Place, and Gender in the Middle Ages*, ed. Sarah Stanbury and Virginia Raguin. Albany: State University of New York Press, 2005. 141–60.

———. "'To Free Them from Binding': Women in the Late Medieval English Parish." *Journal of Interdisciplinary History* 27, 3 (1997): 387–412.

———. "Women Churchwardens in Late Medieval England." In *The Parish in Late Medieval England: Proceedings of the 2002 Harlaxton Symposium*, ed. Clive Burgess and Eamon Duffy. Donington, Lincs.: Shaun Tyas/Paul Watkins, 2006. 302–21.

Gasquet, F. A. *Parish Life in Mediaeval England.* London: Methuen, 1906.

Gibbs, Marion and Jane Lang. *Bishops and Reform 1215–1275: With Special References to the Lateran Council of 1215.* Oxford: Oxford University Press, 1932.

Gibson, Gail McMurray. "Blessing from Sun and Moon: Churching as Women's Theater." In *Bodies and Disciplines: Intersections of Literature and History in Fifteenth-Century England*, ed. Barbara A. Hanawalt and David Wallace. Minneapolis: University of Minnesota Press, 1996. 139–54.

———. *Theater of Devotion: East Anglian Drama and Society in the Late Middle Ages.* Chicago: University of Chicago Press, 1989.

Gilchrist, Roberta. *Gender and Material Culture: The Archaeology of Religious Women.* London: Routledge, 1994.

Gill, Marian C. "Database of Wall Paintings of the Seven Deadly Sins and Seven Works of Mercy." http://www.le.ac.uk/arthistory/seedcorn/contents.html

———. "Female Piety and Impiety: Selected Images of Women in Wall Paintings in England After 1300." In *Gender and Holiness: Men, Women, and Saints in Late Medieval Europe*, ed. Samantha J. E. Riches and Sarah Salih. London: Routledge, 2002. 101–20.

———. "Late Medieval Wall Painting in England: Content and Context, 1350–1530." Ph.D. thesis, Courtauld Institute of Art, University of London, 2002.

———. "Preaching and Image: Sermons and Wall Painting in Later Medieval England." In *Preacher, Sermon, and Audience in the Middle Ages*, ed. Carolyn Muessig. Leiden: Brill, 2002. 155–80.

Given-Wilson, Chris. "The Problem of Labour in the Context of English Government, c. 1350–1450." In *The Problem of Labour in Fourteenth-Century England*, ed. James Bothwell, P. J. P. Goldberg, and W. M. Ormrod. York: York Medieval Press, 2000. 85–100.

Goldberg, P. J. P. "'For Better or Worse': Marriage and Economic Opportunity for Women in Town and Country." In *Women in Medieval English Society*, ed. P. J. P. Goldberg. Stroud: Sutton, 1997. 108–25.

———. "Women." In *Fifteenth-Century Attitudes: Perceptions of Society in Late*

Medieval England, ed. Rosemary Horrox. Cambridge: Cambridge University Press. 1994. 112–31.

———. *Women in England, c. 1275–1525: Documentary Sources*. Manchester: Manchester University Press, 1995.

———. *Women, Work and Life Cycle in a Medieval Economy: Women in York and Yorkshire, c. 1300–1520*. Oxford: Oxford University Press, 1992.

Görlach, Manfred. *The Textual Tradition of the* South English Legendary. Leeds: University of Leeds Press, 1974.

Gottfried, Robert. *Bury St. Edmunds and the Urban Crisis: 1290–1539*. Princeton, N.J.: Princeton University Press. 1982.

Graves, Pamela C. *The Form and Fabric of Belief: An Archaeology of Lay Experience of Religion in Medieval Norfolk and Devon*. British Series 311. Oxford: Oxford Archaeological Reports, 2000.

———. "Social Space in the English Medieval Parish Church." *Economy and Society* 18, 3 (1989): 297–322.

Grundmann, Herbert. *Religious Movements in the Middle Ages*. Trans. Steven Rowan. Notre Dame, Ind.: University of Notre Dame Press, 1995.

Gurevich, Aaron J. "Medieval Attitudes To Wealth and Labour." In *Categories of Medieval Culture*. Trans. G. L. Campbell. London: Routledge and Kegan Paul, 1985. 211–85.

Halpin, Patricia A. "The Religious Experience of Women in Anglo-Saxon England." Ph.D. dissertation, Boston College, 2000.

Hanna, Ralph. "Brewing Trouble: On Literature and History—and Alewives." In *Bodies and Disciplines: Intersections of Literature and History in Fifteenth-Century England*, ed. Barbara A. Hanawalt and David Wallace. Minneapolis: University of Minnesota Press, 1996. 1–18.

Hanawalt, Barbara A. *Of Good and Ill Repute: Gender and Social Control in Medieval England*. New York: Oxford University Press, 1998. 104–23.

———, ed. *Growing Up in Medieval London: The Experience of Childhood in History*. New York: Oxford University Press, 1993.

———. "Keepers of the Lights: Late Medieval English Parish Gilds." *Journal of Medieval and Renaissance Studies* 14, 1 (1984): 21–37.

———. "Peasant Women's Contributions to the Home Economy in Late Medieval England." In *Women and Work in Preindustrial Europe*, ed. Barbara Hanawalt. Bloomington: University of Indiana Press, 1986. 3–19.

———. "Remarriage as an Option for Urban and Rural Widows in late Medieval England." In *Wife and Widow in Medieval England*, ed. Sue Sheridan Walker. Ann Arbor: University of Michigan Press, 1993. 141–64.

———. *The Ties That Bound: Peasant Families in Medieval England*. New York: Oxford University Press, 1986.

———. "The Widow's Mite: Provisions for Medieval London Widows." In *Upon My Husband's Death: Widows in the Literature and Histories of Medieval Europe*, ed. Louise Mirrer. Ann Arbor: University of Michigan Press, 1992. 21–46.

Hanawalt, Barbara A. and Ben R. McRee. "The Guilds of *Homo Prudens* in Late Medieval England." *Continuity and Change* 7, 2 (1992): 163–79.

Harding, Vanessa. "Burial Choice and Burial Location in Later Medieval London."

In *Death and Towns: Urban Responses to the Dying and the Dead, 100–1600*, ed. Steven Bassett. Leicester: Leicester University Press, 1992. 119–35.

———. *The Dead and the Living in Paris and London, 1500–1670*. Cambridge: Cambridge University Press, 2002.

Harper-Bill, Christopher. "The English Church and English Religion After the Black Death." In *The Black Death in England*, ed. Mark Ormrod and Phillip Lindley. Stamford, Lincs.: Paul Watkins, 1997. 79–124.

Hart, Ian J. "Religious Life in Essex, c. 1500–1570." Ph.D. dissertation, University of Warwick, 1992.

Harvey, Barbara. *Living and Dying in Medieval England, 1100–1540: The Monastic Experience*. Oxford: Oxford University Press, 1993.

———. "Work and *Festa Ferianda* in Medieval England." *Journal of Ecclesiastical History* 23, 4 (1972): 289–308.

Hatcher, John. "England in the Aftermath of the Black Death." *Past and Present* 144 (1994): 3–35.

———. "Mortality in the Fifteenth Century: Some New Evidence." *Economic History Review* 2nd ser. 39 (1986): 19–38.

———. *Plague, Population and the English Economy, 1348–1530*. London: Macmillan, 1977.

Hazlitt, W. Carew. *Faiths and Folklore of the British Isles*. 2 vols. Reprint. New York: Benjamin Bloom, 1965.

Heffernan, Thomas. *Sacred Biography: Saints and Their Biographers in the Middle Ages*. New York: Oxford University Press, 1988.

Helmholtz, Richard. *Marriage Litigation in Medieval England*. Cambridge: Cambridge University Press, 1974.

Herlihy, David. *Opera Muliebria: Women and Work in Medieval Society*. New York: McGraw-Hill, 1990.

Hicks, Michael. "The Piety of Margaret, Lady Hungerford (d. 1487)." *Journal of Ecclesiastical History* 38 (1987): 19–38.

Hindle, Steve. "The Shaming of Margaret Knowsley: Gossip, Gender and the Experience of Authority in Early Modern England." *Continuity and Change* 9 (1994): 391–419.

Homans, George C. *English Villagers of the Thirteenth Century*. Cambridge, Mass.: Harvard University Press, 1941.

Houlebrooke, Ralph A. *Death, Religion, and the Family in England, 1480–1750*. Oxford: Oxford University Press, 1998.

———. "Women's Social Life and Common Action in England from the Fifteenth Century to the Eve of the Civil War." *Continuity and Change* 1 (1986): 171–89.

Howell, Martha C. "Fixing Movables: Gifts by Testament in Late Medieval Douai." *Past and Present* 150 (1996): 3–45.

———. *The Marriage Exchange: Property, Social Place, and Gender in Cities of the Low Countries, 1300–1550*. Chicago: University of Chicago Press, 1998.

Hudson, Anne. *The Premature Reformations: Wycliffite Texts and Lollard History*. Oxford: Oxford University Press, 1988.

Humphrey, Chris. *The Politics of Carnival: Festive Misrule in Medieval England*. Manchester: Manchester University Press, 2001.

Hunt. Alan. *Governance of the Consuming Passions: A Brief History of Sumptuary Legislation.* New York: St. Martin's Press, 1996.

Hutton, Ronald. "The Local Impact of the Tudor Reformations." In *The English Reformation Revised.* Ed. Christopher Haigh. Cambridge: Cambridge University Press, 1987. 114–38.

———. *The Rise and Fall of Merry England: The Ritual Year, 1400–1700.* Oxford: Oxford University Press, 1994.

Ingram, Martin. *Church Courts, Sex and Marriage in England, 1570–1640.* Cambridge: Cambridge University Press, 1987.

James, Mervyn. "Ritual, Drama and the Social Body in the Late Medieval English Town." *Past and Present* 98 (1983): 3–29.

Jennings, Margaret. "Tutivillus: The Literary Career of the Recording Demon." *Studies in Philology, Texts, and Studies* 74. 1977.

Johnston, Alexandra. "Parish Entertainments in Berkshire." In *Pathways to Medieval Peasants*, ed. J. A. Raftis. Papers in Medieval Studies 2. Toronto: Pontifical Institute of Medieval Studies, 1981. 335–38.

Johnston, Alexandra and Sally-Beth MacLean, "Reformation and Resistance in Thames/Severn Parishes: The Dramatic Witness." In *The Parish in English Life: 1400–1600*, ed. Katherine L. French, Gary G. Gibbs, and Beat A. Kümin. Manchester: Manchester University Press, 1997. 178–200.

Jones, Karen. *Gender and Petty Crime in Late Medieval England: the Local Courts in Kent, 1460–1660.* Woodbridge: Boydell, 2006.

Jones, Michael and Malcolm G. Underwood. *The King's Mother: Lady Margaret Beaufort, Countess of Richmond and Derby.* Cambridge: Cambridge University Press, 1992.

Jordan, William C. *The Great Famine: Northern Europe in the Early Fourteenth Century.* Princeton, N.J.: Princeton University Press, 1996.

Kamerick, Kathleen. *Popular Piety and Art in the Late Middle Ages: Worship and Idolatry in England, 1350–1500.* New York: Palgrave, 2002.

Karant-Nunn, Susan. "Continuity and Change: Some Effects of the Reformation on the Women of Zwickau." *Sixteenth Century Journal* 12 (1982): 17–42.

———. *Reformation of Ritual: An Interpretation of Early Modern Germany.* London: Routledge, 1997.

Karlsen, Carol. *Devil in the Shape of a Woman: Witchcraft in Colonial New England.* New York: Norton, 1985.

Karras, Ruth Mazo. *Common Women: Prostitution and Sexuality in Medieval England.* New York: Oxford University Press, 1996.

———. "Gendered Sin and Misogyny in John of Bromyard's *Summa Predicantium.*" *Traditio* 47 (1992): 233–57.

Keene, Derek. "Issues of Water in Medieval London c. 1300." *Urban History* 28 (2001): 161–79.

Kendrick, A. F. *English Embroidery.* London: George Newnes, 1905.

———. *English Needle Work.* London: A & C. Black, 1933.

Kermode, Jennifer. "Obvious Observations on the Formation of Oligarchies in Late Medieval English Towns." In *Towns and Townspeople in the Fifteenth Century*, ed. J. A. F. Thomson. Gloucester: Sutton, 1988. 87–106.

Kerry, Charles. *A History of the Municipal Church of St. Lawrence, Reading*. Reading: privately printed, 1883.

Kieckhefer, Richard. *Unquiet Souls: Fourteenth-Century Saints and Their Religious Milieu*. Chicago: University of Chicago Press, 1984.

Kowaleski, Maryanne. "Introduction to 'Vill, Gild, and Gentry': Forces of Community in Later Medieval England." *Journal of British Studies* 33 (1994): 337–39.

———. "Singlewomen in Medieval and Early Modern Europe: The Demographic Perspective." In *Singlewomen in the European Past, 1250–1800*, ed. Judith M. Bennett and Amy M. Froide. Philadelphia: University of Pennsylvania Press, 1999. 38–81.

———. "Women's Work in a Market Town: Exeter in the Late Fourteenth Century." In *Women and Work in Preindustrial Europe*, ed. Barbara A. Hanawalt. Bloomington: Indiana University Press. 1986. 145–64.

Knowles, David. *The Religious Orders in England*. Vol. 2, *The End of the Middle Ages*. Cambridge: Cambridge University Press, 1955.

Kraemer, Ross Shepard. *Her Share of the Blessings: Women's Religion Among Pagans, Jews and Christians in the Greco-Roman World*. Oxford: Oxford University Press, 1992.

Kreider, Alan. *English Chantries: The Road to Dissolution*. Cambridge, Mass.: Harvard University Press, 1979.

Krug, Rebecca. *Reading Families: Women's Literate Practice in Late Medieval England*. Ithaca, N.Y.: Cornell University Press, 2002.

Kümin, Beat A. "Parishioners in Court: Litigation and the Local Community, 1350–1650." In *Belief and Practice in Reformation England: A Tribute to Patrick Collinson from His Students*, ed. Susan Wabuda and Caroline Litzenberger. Aldershot: Ashgate, 1998. 20–39.

———. "Sacred Church and Worldly Tavern: Reassessing an Early Modern Divide." In *Sacred Space in Early Modern Europe*, ed. Will Coster and Andrew Spicer. Cambridge: Cambridge University Press, 2005. 17–38.

———. *The Shaping of a Community: The Rise and Reformation of the English Parish, c. 1400–1560*. Brookfield, Vt.: Scolar Press, 1996.

Lacey, Kay E. "Women and Work in Fourteenth and Fifteenth Century London." In *Women and Work in Pre-Industrial England*, ed. Lindsey Charles and Lorna Duffin. London: Croom Helm, 1985. 24–82.

Lee, Becky R. "Men's Recollections of a Women's Rite: Medieval English Men's Recollections Regarding the Rite of Purification of Women After Childbirth." *Gender and History* 14 (2002): 224–41.

———. "'Women ben purifyid of her childeryn': The Purification of Women After Childbirth in Medieval England." Ph.D. dissertation. University of Toronto, 1998.

LeGoff, Jacques. *The Birth of Purgatory*. Chicago: University of Chicago Press, 1981.

———. "Merchants' Time and Church Time in the Middle Ages." In *Time, Work, and Culture in the Middle Ages*. Trans. Arthur Goldhammer. Chicago: University of Chicago Press, 1980. 29–42.

———. "Labor, Techniques, and Craftsmen in the Value Systems of the Early Middle Ages." In *Time, Work, and Culture in the Middle Ages*. 71–86.

Lehmijoki-Gardner, Maiju. *Worldly Saints: Social Interaction of Dominican Penitent Women in Italy, 1200–1500.* Helsinki: Soumen Historiallinen Seura, 1999.

Letters, Samatha. *Online Gazetteer of markets and Fairs in England and Wales to 1516.* http://_www.history.ac.uk/cmh/gaz/gazweb2.html

Lewis, Katherine. *The Cult of St. Katherine of Alexandria in Late Medieval England.* Woodbridge: Boydell, 2000.

Lindenbaum, Sheila. "London Texts and Literate Practice." In *The Cambridge History of Medieval English Literature,* ed. David Wallace. Cambridge: Cambridge University Press, 1999. 284–309.

Litzenberger, Caroline. *The English Reformation and the Laity.* Cambridge: Cambridge University Press, 1997.

———. "St. Michael's Gloucester, 1540–80: The Cost of Conformity in Sixteenth Century England." In *The Parish in English Life: 1400–1600,* ed. Katherine L. French, Gary G. Gibbs, and Beat A. Kümin. Manchester: Manchester University Press, 1997. 230–49.

Luria, Keith P. *Territories of Grace: Cultural Changes in the Seventeenth-Century Diocese of Grenoble.* Berkeley: University of California Press, 1991.

Macfarlane, Alan. *Marriage and Love in England: Modes of Reproduction, 1300–1850.* Oxford: Blackwell, 1986.

MacLean, Sally-Beth. "Hocktide: A Reassessment of a Popular Pre-Reformation Festival." In *Festive Drama,* ed. Meg Twycross. Woodbridge: D.S. Brewer, 1996. 233–41.

Marks, Richard. *Stained Glass in England During the Middle Ages.* Toronto: University of Toronto Press, 1993.

Mattingly, Joanna. "The Medieval Parish Guilds of Cornwall." *Journal of the Royal Institution of Cornwall* 10, 3 (1989): 290–329.

———. "Stories in Glass: Reconstructing the St. Neot's Pre-Reformation Glazing Scheme." *Journal of the Royal Institution of Cornwall* n.s. 2, 3, parts 3, 4 (2000): 9–55.

McFarlane, K. B. *Lancastrian Kings and Lollard Knights.* Oxford: Oxford University Press, 1972.

McIntosh, Marjorie Keniston. *Controlling Misbehavior in England, 1370–1600.* Cambridge: Cambridge University Press, 1998.

———. *Working Women in English Society, 1300–1620.* Cambridge: Cambridge University Press, 2005.

McSheffrey, Shannon. *Gender and Heresy: Women and Men in Lollard Communities, 1420–1530.* Philadelphia: University of Pennsylvania Press, 1995.

———. "Heresy, Orthodoxy and English Vernacular Religion, 1450–1525." *Past and Present* 186 (2005): 47–80.

———, ed. *Love and Marriage in Late Medieval London.* Kalamazoo: Western Michigan University, for TEAMS, 1995.

———. *Marriage, Sex, and Civic Culture in Late Medieval London.* Philadelphia: University of Pennsylvania Press, 2006.

———. "Place, Space, and Situation: Public and Private in the Making of Marriage in Late Medieval London." *Speculum* 79 (2004): 960–90.

Meale, Carol M. "'alle the bokes that I haue of latyn, englisch, and frensch': Laywomen and Their Books in Late Medieval England." In *Women and Literature in Britain: 1150–1500*, ed. Carol M. Meale. Cambridge: Cambridge University Press, 1993. 128–58.

Mendelson, Sara and Patricia Crawford. *Women in Early Modern England, 1550–1720*. Oxford: Oxford University Press, 1998.

Merritt, Julia F. "The Social Context of the Parish Church in Early Modern Westminster." *Urban History Yearbook* 28 (1991): 20–29.

———. *The Social World of Early Modern Westminster: Abbey, Court and Community, 1525–1640*. Manchester: Manchester University Press, 2005.

Middleton-Stewart, Judith. *Inward Purity and Outward Splendour: Death and Remembrance in the Deanery of Dunwich, Suffolk, 1370–1547*. Woodbridge: Boydell, 2001.

Moore, H. L. *Space, Text and Gender: An Anthropological Study of the Marakwet of Kenya*. Cambridge: Cambridge University Press, 1986.

Muir, Edward. *Ritual in Early Modern Europe*. Cambridge: Cambridge University Press, 1997.

O'Hara, Diana. *Courtship and Constraint: Rethinking the Making of Modern Marriage in Tudor England*. Manchester: Manchester University Press, 2000.

———. "The Language of Tokens and the Making of Marriage." *Rural History* 3 (1992): 1–40.

Orme, Nicholas. *Medieval Children*. New Haven, Conn.: Yale University Press, 2001.

Ormrod, Mark. "The Politics of Pestilence: Government in England After the Black Death." In *The Black Death in England*, ed. Mark Ormrod and Phillip Lindley. Stamford, Lincs: Paul Watkins, 1997. 147–77.

Ovitt, George, Jr. *The Restoration of Perfection: Labor and Technology in Medieval Culture*. New Brunswick, N.J.: Rutgers University Press, 1987.

Owen, Dorothy. *Church and Society in Medieval Lincolnshire*. Lincoln: Lincolnshire Local History Society, 1971.

Owst, G. R. *Preaching in Medieval England*. Cambridge: Cambridge University Press, 1922.

———. *Literature and Pulpit*. 2nd ed. Oxford: Blackwell, 1961.

Pantin, W. A. *The English Church in the Fourteenth Century*. Medieval Academy Reprints for Teaching. Toronto: University of Toronto Press, 1980.

Park, David. "Wall Paintings." In *The Age of Chivalry: Art in Plantagenet England, 1200–1400*, ed. J. J. G. Alexander and Paul Binski. London: Royal Academy of Arts in Association with Weidenfeld and Nicholson, 1987. 125–30.

Pendrill, Charles. *Old Parish Life in London*. Oxford: Oxford University Press, 1937.

Peters, Christine. *Patterns of Piety: Women, Gender and Religion in Late Medieval and Reformation England*. Cambridge: Cambridge University Press, 2003.

Petroff, Elizabeth Alvilda. *Body and Soul: Essays on Medieval Women and Mysticism*. Oxford: Oxford University Press, 1994.

Phillips, Kim M. "Maidenhood as the Perfect Age of Women's Life." In *Young Medieval Women*, ed. Katherine J. Lewis, Noel James Menuge, and Kim M. Phillips. New York: St. Martin's Press, 1999. 1–24.

———. *Medieval Maidens: Young Women and Gender, 1270–1540*. Manchester: Manchester University Press, 2003.

Phythian-Adams, Charles. "Ceremony and the Citizen: The Communal Year at Coventry: 1450- 1550." In *Crisis and Order in English Towns: Essays in Urban History, 1500–1700*, ed. Peter Clark and Paul Slack. London: Routledge and Kegan Paul, 1972. 57–85.

———. *Desolation of a City: Coventry and the Urban Crisis of the Late Middle Ages.* Cambridge: Cambridge University Press, 1979.

———. *Local History and Folklore: A New Framework.* London: Bedford Square Press for the Standing Conference for Local History, 1975.

Piponnier, Françoise and Perrine Manne. *Dress in the Middle Ages.* Trans. Caroline Beamish. New Haven, Conn.: Yale University Press, 1997.

Platt, Colin. *King Death.* Toronto: University of Toronto Press, 1996.

———. *The Parish Churches of Medieval England.* London: Secker and Warburg, 1981.

Pollock, Frederick and Frederic W. Maitland. *The History of English Law Before the Time of Edward I.* Vol. 1. 2nd ed. Cambridge: Cambridge University Press, 1968.

Poos, L. R. *A Rural Society After the Black Death: Essex, 1350–1525.* Cambridge: Cambridge University Press, 1991.

———. "Social Context of Statute of Labourers Enforcement." *Law and History Review* 1 (1983): 27–52.

Poska, Allyson M. *Regulating the People: The Catholic Reformation in Seventeenth-Century Spain.* Leiden: Brill, 1998.

Powell, Susan. "What Caxton Did to the *Festial*: The *Festial* From Manuscript to Printed Edition." *Journal of the Early Book Society* 1 (1997): 48–77.

Poyntz Wright, Peter. *Rural Benchends of Somerset.* Amersham, Somerset: Avebury, 1983.

Rawcliffe, Carole. "Women, Childbirth and Religion in Later Medieval England." In *Women and Religion in Medieval England*, ed. Diana Wood. Oxford: Oxbow, 2003. 91–117.

Reiss, Pallas Athena. "The Sunday Christ." Ph.D. dissertation, University of Chicago, 1995.

Renevey, Denis. "Household Chores in *The Doctrine of the Hert*." In *The Medieval Household in Christian Europe, c. 850–c. 1550*, ed. Cordelia Beattie, Anna Maslakovic, and Sarah Rees Jones. Turnhout: Brepols, 2003. 167–86.

Reynolds, Susan. *An Introduction to the History of English Medieval Towns.* Oxford: Oxford University Press, 1977.

———. *Kingdoms and Communities in Western Europe: 900–1300.* Oxford: Clarendon Press, 1984.

Richmond, Colin. "Halesworth Church, Suffolk, and Its Fifteenth-Century Benefactors." In *Recognitions: Essays Presented to Edmund Fryde*, ed. Colin Richmond and Isobel Harvey. Aberystwyth: National Library of Wales, 1996. 243–66.

———. *The Paston Family in the Fifteenth Century: The First Phase.* Cambridge: Cambridge University Press, 1990.

———. "Religion and the Fifteenth-Century Gentleman." In *The Church, Politics and Patronage*, ed. R. B. Dobson. Gloucester: Sutton, 1984. 193–208.

Riddy, Felicity. "Looking Closely: Authority and Intimacy in the Late Medieval Home." In *Gendering the Master Narrative: Women and Power in the Middle Ages*, ed. Mary C. Erler and Maryanne Kowaleski. Ithaca, N.Y.: Cornell University Press, 2003. 212–28.

———. "'Mother Knows Best': Reading Social Change in a Courtesy Text." *Speculum* 71: 1 (1996): 66–86.

———. "'Women Talking About Things of God': A Late Medieval Sub-Culture." In *Women and Literature in Britain: 1150–1500*, ed. Carol M. Meale. Cambridge: Cambridge University Press, 1993. 104–27.

Riesebrodt, Martin and Kelly H. Chong, "Fundamentalisms and Patriarchal Gender Politics." *Journal of Women's History* 10 (1999): 55–77.

Rigby, S. H. *English Society in the Later Middle Ages: Class, Status, and Gender*. Basingstoke: Macmillan, 1995.

———. *Medieval Grimsby: Growth and Decline*. Hull: University of Hull Press, 1993.

———. "Urban Oligarchy in Late Medieval England." In *Towns and Towns People in the Fifteenth Century*, ed. J. A. F. Thomson. Gloucester: Sutton, 1988. 62–86.

Roper, Lyndal. *The Holy Household: Women and Morals in Reformation Augsburg*. Oxford: Oxford University Press, 1989.

Rosenthal, Joel T. *Telling Tales: Sources and Narration in Late Medieval England*. University Park: Pennsylvania State Press, 2003.

Rosser, Gervase. "Communities of Parish and Guild." In *Parish, Church and People: Local Studies in Lay Religion, 1350–1750*, ed. S. J. Wright. London: Hutchinson, 1988. 29–55.

———. "Going to the Fraternity Feast: Commensality and Social Relations in Late Medieval England." *Journal of British Studies* 33, 4 (1994): 430–46.

———. *Medieval Westminster, 1200–1540*. Oxford: Oxford University Press, 1989.

———. "Parochial Conformity and Voluntary Religion in Late-Medieval England." *Transactions of the Royal Historical Society* 6th ser. 1 (1991): 173–89.

Rouse, E. Clive. *Medieval Wall Paintings*. Princes Risborough, Bucks.: Shire Publications, 1991.

Rubin, Miri. *Charity and Community in Medieval Cambridge*. Cambridge: Cambridge University Press, 1987.

———. *Corpus Christi: The Eucharist in Late Medieval Culture*. Cambridge: Cambridge University Press, 1991.

Salih, Sarah. "At Home; Out of the House." In *Cambridge Companion to Medieval Women's Writing*, ed. Carolyn Dynshaw and David Wallace. Cambridge: Cambridge University Press, 2003. 124–40.

Sauzet, Robert. *Les visites pastorals dans le diocese de Chartres pendant la première moitié du XVIIe siècle*. Rome: Storia e Letterature, 1975.

Scarisbrick, J. J. *The Reformation and the English People*. Oxford: Blackwell, 1984.

Schofield, John. "Social Perception of Space in Medieval and Tudor London Houses." In *Meaningful Architecture: Social Interpretations of Buildings*, ed. Martin Locock. Aldershot: Ashgate, 188–206.

Schofield, Phillip. *Peasant and Community in Medieval England*. Houndsmills: Palgrave/Macmillan, 2003.

Schofield, Roger. "The Geographic Distribution of Wealth, 1344–1649." *Economic History Review* 2nd ser. 18 (1965): 483–510.

———."Parliamentary Lay Taxation: 1485–1547." Ph.D. dissertation, Cambridge University, 1963.

Scott, James C. *Domination and the Arts of Resistance: Hidden Transcripts.* New Haven, Conn.: Yale University Press, 1990.

Shaw, David Gary. *The Creation of a Community: The City of Wells in the Middle Ages.* Oxford: Oxford University Press, 1993.

Sheehan, Michael M. "Formation and Stability of Marriage in Fourteenth-Century England: Evidence of an Ely Register." In *Marriage, Family and Law in Medieval Europe: Collected Studies*, ed. James K. Farge. Toronto: University of Toronto Press, 1996.

Sheingorn, Pamela. *The Easter Sepulchre in England.* Kalamazoo, Mich.: Medieval Institute Publications, 1987.

———. "The Holy Kinship: The Ascendance and Materiality in Sacred Genealogy of the Fifteenth Century." *Thought: A Review of Culture and Ideas* 64 (1989): 268–86.

Smith, Edwin, Graham Hutton, and Olive Cook. *English Parish Churches.* London: Thames and Hudson, 1976.

Smith, J. C. D. *Church Woodcarvings: A West Country Study.* New York: Augustus M. Kelley, 1969.

———. *A Guide to Church Wood Carvings: Misericords and Bench-Ends.* Newton Abbot, Devon: David and Charles, 1974.

Spencer, H. Leith. *English Preaching in the Late Middle Ages.* Oxford: Oxford University Press, 1993.

Sponsler, Claire. "Narrating the Social Order: Medieval Clothing Laws." *Clio* 23 (1992): 265–83.

Staniland, Kay. *Embroiderers.* Toronto: University of Toronto Press, 1991.

———. "Royal Entry into the World." In *England in the Fifteenth Century: Proceedings of the 1986 Harlaxton Symposium*, ed. Daniel Williams. Woodbridge: Boydell, 1987. 297–313.

Stokes, James. "The Hoglers: Evidence of the Entertainment Tradition in Eleven Somerset Parishes." *Notes and Queries for Somerset and Dorset* 32 (1990): 807–16.

Stone, Lawrence. *The Family, Sex and Marriage in England, 1500–1800.* New York: Harper Torchbooks, 1979.

Strocchia, Sharon T. "Funerals and the Politics of Gender in Early Renaissance Florence." In *Reconfiguring Women: Perspectives on Gender and the Italian Renaissance.* Ithaca, N.Y.: Cornell University Press, 1991. 155–68.

Sutcliffe, Sebastian. "The Cult of St. Sitha in England: An Introduction." *Nottingham Medieval Studies* 37 (1993): 83–89.

Sutton, Anne F. "Alice Claver, Silkwoman (d. 1489)." In *Medieval London Widows: 1300–1500*, ed. Caroline M. Barron and Anne F. Sutton. London: Hambleton Press, 1994. 129–42.

Swanson, Heather. *Medieval Artisans: An Urban Class in Late Medieval England.* Oxford: Blackwell, 1989.

Swanson, R. N. *Church and Society in Late Medieval England*. Oxford: Blackwell, 1989.

———. *Religion and Devotion in Europe, c. 1215-c. 1515*. Cambridge: Cambridge University Press, 1995.

Terpstra, Nicholas. *Lay Confraternities and Civic Religion in Renaissance Bologna*. Cambridge: Cambridge University Press, 1995.

Thirsk, Joan. *English Peasant Farming: The Agrarian History of Lincolnshire from Tudor to Recent Times*. London: Routledge and Kegan Paul, 1957.

Thomas, Keith. *Religion and the Decline of Magic*. New York: Scribner's, 1971.

Thomson, J. A. F. "Knightly Piety and the Margins of Lollardy." In *Lollardy and the Gentry in the Later Middle Ages*, ed. Margaret Aston and Colin Richmond. Stroud: Alan Sutton, 1997. 95–111.

Tristram, E. W. *English Wall Paintings in the Fourteenth Century*. London: Routledge and Kegan Paul, 1955.

Tudor-Craig, Pamela. "Painting in Medieval England: The Wall-to-Wall Message." In *The Age of Chivalry: Art and Society in Late Medieval England*, ed. Nigel Saul. London: Brockhampton Press, 1995. 106–19.

Twigg, Graham. *The Black Death: A Biological Reappraisal*. New York: Schocken Books, 1985.

Vauchez, André. "The Pastoral Transformation of the Thirteenth Century." In *The Laity in the Middle Ages: Religious Beliefs and Devotional Practice*, ed. Daniel E. Bornstein. Translated by Margery J. Schneider. Notre Dame, Ind.: University of Notre Dame Press, 1993. 95–106.

Victoria County History: Cambridge. Vol. 3. Ed. J. P. Croach. London: University of London, Institute of Historical Research, 1959.

Victoria County History: Surrey. Vol. 3. Ed. H. E. Malden. London: University of London, Institute of Historical Research, 1967.

Victoria County History: Wiltshire. Vol. 6. London: Oxford University Press, Institute of Historical Research, 1962.

Wack, Mary. "Women, Work, and Play in an English Medieval Town." In *Maids and Mistresses, Cousins and Queens: Women's Alliances in Early Modern England*, eds. Susan Frye and Karen Robertson. Oxford: Oxford University Press, 1999. 33–51.

Walker, Sue Sheridan. "Proof of Age of Feudal Heirs in Medieval England." *Medieval Studies* 35 (1973): 306–23.

Ward, Jennifer. *English Noble Women in the Later Middle Ages*. London: Longman, 1992.

———. "Townswomen and Their Households." In *Daily Life in the Middle Ages*, ed. Richard Britnell. Thrupp, Gloucestershire: Sutton, 1998. 27–42.

Webb, Diana. *Pilgrimage in Medieval England*. London: Hambledon Press, 2000.

Wenzel, Sigfried. *The Sin of Sloth: Acedia in Medieval Thought and Literature*. Chapel Hill: University of North Carolina Press, 1960.

Westlake. Herbert F. *The Parish Gilds of Mediaeval England*. London: SPCK, 1919.

Whiting, Robert. *Blind Devotion of the People: Popular Religion and the English Reformation*. Cambridge: Cambridge University Press, 1989.

———. *Local Responses to the English Reformation*. London: St. Martin's Press, 1998.

Williamson, W. W. "Saints on Norfolk Rood-Screens and Pulpits." *Norfolk Archae-ology* 31, part 3 (1956): 299–346.

Wilson, Adrian. "The Ceremony of Childbirth and Its Interpretation." In *Women and Mothers in Pre-Industrial England: Essays in Memory of Dorothy McLaren*, ed. Valerie Fields. London: Routledge, 1990. 68–107.

Winstead, Karen A. *The Virgin Martyrs: Legends of Sainthood in Late Medieval England*. Ithaca, N.Y.: Cornell University Press, 1997.

Winston-Allen, Anne. *Stories of the Rose: Making of the Rosary in the Middle Ages*. University Park: Pennsylvania State University Press, 1998.

Wood, Robert. "Poor Widows, c. 1393–1415." In *Medieval London Widows: 1300–1500*, ed. Caroline M. Barron and Anne F. Sutton. London: Hambleton Press, 1994. 55–69.

Wood-Legh, Kathleen L. *Perpetual Chantries in Britain*. Cambridge: Cambridge University Press, 1965.

Woodcock, Brian. *Medieval Ecclesiastical Courts*. London: Oxford University Press, 1952.

Woodforde, Christopher. *The Norwich School of Glass Painting in the Fifteenth Century*. London: Oxford University Press, 1950.

———. *Stained Glass in Somerset: 1250–1830*. London: Oxford University Press, 1946.

Wordsworth, Christopher and Henry Littlehales. *The Old Service-Books of the English Church*. London: Methuen, 1904.

Wunderli, Richard M. *London Church Courts on the Eve of the Reformation*. Cambridge, Mass.: Medieval Academy of America, 1981.

Index

Acknowledgments

Throughout the years of working on this book, many people and institutions have been generous of their time and money, and it is now my pleasure to acknowledge them. Initial funding for archival work was provided by William Vasse, retired provost of SUNY-New Paltz. Further archival work was funded by a Bernadotte E. Schmitt grant from the American Historical Association and several Research and Creative Projects Awards from the New Paltz Foundation. The dean of Liberal Arts and Sciences, several Term Faculty Development Awards from the New York State United University Professors Joint Labor Management Committee, and the Department of History provided travel money. The dean of Liberal Arts and Sciences also provided funding for the images and maps. In 1997–98, I spent a year at the Harvard Divinity School as a research associate and visiting lecturer in the Women and Religion Program. In particular I would like to thank Clarissa Atkinson, Deborah Valenze, Carol Karlsen, Rebecca Krawiec, Susan Shapirio, Amina Wadud and the students in my graduate seminar, especially Nancy McLoughlin. Their insightful comments, delicious dinners, and emotional and intellectual support in the early stages of this project pushed me to think about it in much broader and more interesting ways and gave life to the idea of an intellectual community. A National Endowment for the Humanities Full-Year Fellowship for College Professors in 2003–4 provided funding for a sabbatical, which I took at the Institute for Advanced Study in Princeton. Giles Constable and Caroline Bynum fostered a congenial and stimulating environment for writing and discussion, and Robin Fleming and Chris Kraus kept me company first in the dinning hall and then in the gym.

I would also like to thank Christopher Whittick for giving me access and permission to use his transcript of "Visitation of Parishes by John Trefnant, Bishop of Hereford, 1397." Ken Farnhill, Shannon McSheffrey, Sandy Bardsley, Martha Carlin, and Frank Henderson provided material from their unpublished work and Ian Hart, Becky Lee, and Miriam Gill generously gave me copies of their unpublished dissertations. Beat Kümin, Clive

Burgess, Marc Forrest, and Peter Marshall were and are kind, interested, and sympathetic friends, who advised me on archives and pubs and provided venues for me to present my work in England. Numerous archives, especially the Westminster Abbey Muniment Room, the Westminster Archive Centre, the Somerset Archive and Record Services, and the Devon Record Office, gave me access to their collections. Also, over the many years of this project Barbara Hanawalt has remained encouraging and interested. Her own work has been a model and an inspiration.

SUNY New Paltz, especially the Department of History, has been a supportive and collegial place to work. I am also appreciative of the efforts of the staff at the Sojourner Truth Library, especially the interlibrary loan office, which tracked down many a hard-to-find book. Kathy Dowley, Nancy Johnson, and Maureen Morrow provided much needed distraction, support, and sushi along the way. While working on her undergraduate honors thesis, Chloe Torres created my first database for the Westminster funerals. Her initial findings allowed me to refine my methods and data collecting. Christianna Thomas worked with the visitation records for her honors thesis and convinced me that I should take a more serious look at them.

Judith Bennett, Ruth Karras, and the anonymous reader at the press provided guidance and advice on improving the manuscript, and Jerry Singerman has remained a patient and supportive editor as has Alison Anderson. David Benson, Lydia Murdoch, and Sandy Bardsley gave generously of their own photographs, Stephen Hanna is the cartographer extraordinaire, and Susan DeMaio provided much needed technical help with the images.

My family, especially my parents David and Louise, have always been interested and supportive of my work, even when I canceled visits to meet deadlines. Allyson Poska, Shannon McSheffrey, Robin Fleming, Sandy Bardsley, Gary Gibbs, and Gareth Bestor have talked endlessly and patiently with me about this project. Sandy pointed me to wall paintings as a valuable source and Shannon navigated flawlessly as we drove around Norfolk in search of them. Allyson, Robin, and Shannon all read and commented extensively on the manuscript as it was in its final stages. Finally, when I needed her the most, Allyson read portions of the manuscript yet again, and talked me through my doubts and frustrations. Without her friendship, help, and advice this book would never have seen the light of day.

Earlier versions of parts of this book have appeared previously as articles. A portion of Chapter 1 first appeared as "'I Leave My Best Gown as a Vestment': Women's Spiritual Interests in the Late Medieval English Parish," *Magistra* 4, 1 (1998): 57–77, reprinted by permission of the editors. An earlier version of Chapter 5 appeared as "'To Free Them from Binding': Women in the Late Medieval English Parish," *Journal of Interdisciplinary History* 28 (1997): 387–412, copyright © 1997 Massachusetts Institute of Technology and *Journal of Interdisciplinary History*, Inc., used by permission of *Journal of Interdisciplinary History* and MIT Press. Portions of Chapter 4 appeared as "Maidens' Lights and Wives' Stores: Women's Parish Guilds in Late Medieval England," *Sixteenth Century Journal* 29, 2 (1998): 399–425, reprinted by permission of *Sixteenth Century Journal*.